THE PARENTING QUIZ

1 Your baby won't stop crying. The first thing to try is:

a) send it back to the hospital for a refund.

b) offer it a Kit Kat.

c) look for hairline cracks on the ceiling and check the electricals.

d) wear one of those deerhuntin' hats with furry flaps you can tie over your ears.

lower in case of ≥NOISE≥

2 A robe is:

a) only to be worn over jammies.

b) attractive all-day before-five wear.

c) too much trouble if you have to do up the cord.

3 Sleep deprivation can lead to you losing your:

a) vocabulary.

b) mind.

a) short-term memory (the **a** again is a joke).

d) "What?"

4 You'll only have time to wear one article of clothing a day. To make it count as a whole outfit, you choose:

...auty regime now consists of:

a) cleanse, exfoliate, moisturize, pluck, wax, joosh, phoof, style, curl, apply lipstick, mascara, blusher, eyeshadow blends, contouring cream and nail polish.

b) quickly brushing all the hairs on your body in the same direction.

c) checking whether face washer has baby poop on it. If not, wave near face and fall unconscious on bathroom floor.

6 (Men may skip this one.) A week after giving birth, your breasts leak visibly at the supermarket and milk drips onto the counter. You look at the horrified checkout-operator and say:

a) "Care for a squirt?"

b) "That reminds me, do you sell guinea-pig food?"

c) "Excuse me while I put some false moustaches on those."

d) "Don't be frightened, young man. You should see my perineum." ➡

7 Tinky Winky is:

a) a terrific name for a child's private parts, right up until they leave home.

b) sailor slang for semaphore messages.

c) a bit of a nancyboy and that's the way we like 'em.

d) an 8-year-old rapper from Launceston.

8 The Parenting Anthem is:

a) "I Will Survive" by Gloria Gaynor.

b) "Feelin' Kinda Sporty" by Dave Graney and the Coral Snakes.

c) that lullabies compilation in the glove box with peanut butter on the underside.

d) "I Mashed the Pumpkin, But I Did Not Fool the Fussy One" sung to the tune of "I Shot the Sheriff, But I Did Not Shoot the Deputy" by Mr. Bob Marley.

9 When a child weighs approximately 40 pounds, a safe car restraint should:

a) be buckled up by someone in a less cranky mood than me.

b) come in a late model Mercedes provided by the government.

c) be constructed entirely from plastic dinosaurs that go "Raaarghhh."

d) be slightly less expensive than an aircraft carrier.

10 Discipline:

a) shmisipline.

b) should be consistent, persistent, and performed by trained robots.

c) shut up.

d) should never be humiliating or confusing to the parent.

11 What's the worst thing to say when you're dropping your child off at day care?

a) "We think of lice as our special little friends."

b) "Christ on a STICK, I could do with another vodka."

c) "Is this the child-care center?"

d) "If I'm not back by 7 or so, sweetie, make your own way home."

12 Reassuring phrases for your child can include:

a) "Don't worry, personality isn't always genetic."

b) "Don't worry, body shape isn't always genetic."

c) "It's true, the Secretary of Defense does look like a boiled turnip."

d) "When you're 18 you can leave."

13 You think fathers who look after their own children are:

a) fictitious.

b) marvellous, really quite marvelous.

c) married to vicious, godless, feminist, selfish, hairy harridans.

d) seahorses.

14 "Controlled crying" is:

a) when you can sob without getting snot on your face.

b) a method whereby parents can cry for 5 minutes at a time, for efficiency reasons.

c) when you cry and you look like the guy in that Scream painting, but no tears come out.

d) usually recommended by people who are not in your house at 8:20 p.m.

15 Sex is:

a) something done by people whose photos are in *People* magazine.

b) 'Huh? Wha . . . er . . . the . . . (snonk) zzzzzzzzzzzzzz.'

c) over.

d) ova.

16 The most important thing is:

a) love.

b) trust.

c) thinking of your child as your friend.

d) not starting to order the vodka by the keg.

17 Children's clothes should always be:

a) designed to make kids look like demented Italian supermodels in their thirties.

b) made of plastic wipe-down materials.

c) able to withstand being machine washed with knives and tumble dried in temperatures exceeding 32,000 degrees.

d) partly removed from under the bed before being placed on child.

18 The dog and the kid have both thrown up in the car at the same time. You:

a) pull over safely to the curb and scream into a pillow.

b) pull over safely to the curb and hose down the inside of the vehicle.

c) thank your lucky stars you don't own the car.

d) pull over safely to the curb, calmly exit the vehicle, go to the airport and fly to Antigua.

Answers Oh, who the hell knows? We're all trying to make this up as we go along.

kid

KAZ COOKE

wrangling

The real guide to caring for babies,
toddlers, and little kids

TEN SPEED PRESS
Berkeley | Toronto

While every care has been taken in researching and compiling the medical information in this book, it is in no way intended to replace or supersede professional medical advice. Neither the author nor the publisher may be held responsible for any action or any claim whatsoever resulting from the use of this book or any information contained in it. Readers must obtain their own professional medical advice before relying on or otherwise making use of the medical information contained in this book.

Contact details for organizations and website addresses frequently change: those included in this book were correct at the time of publication.

Copyright © 2004 by Kaz Cooke
Illustrations Copyright © 2004 by Kaz Cooke
Kazza Font Copyright © 2004 by Kaz Cooke

All rights reserved. No part of this book may be reproduced in any form, except brief excerpts for the purpose of review, without written permission of the publisher.

1⊜

Ten Speed Press
Box 7123
Berkeley, California 94707
www.tenspeed.com

Originally published in 2003 by Penguin Books Australia, Ltd.

Cover and text design by Sandy Cull, Pengiun Design Studio
Production work on the U.S. edition by Betsy Stromberg

Library of Congress Cataloging-in-Publication Data on file with the publisher.
1-58008-557-1

Printed in Canada
First printing, 2004

1 2 3 4 5 6 7 8 9 10 — 08 07 06 05 04

CONTENTS

Intro **1**

PART 1: BABIES **7**

PaRT 2: ToDDLeRS 257

PaRT 3: LiTTLe KiDs (3 to 5) 317

PART 4: PARENTING 356

PART 5: stuff 491

iNTRO

The information in this book is not meant to be taken instead of individual, professional medical advice. Nor is it a good substitute for a nutritional diet. The book will, however, prop up a bad window when you're not using it.

What should I do when the baby cries? What do babies eat? Is it like having a puppy? What's a good present for a 2-year-old's birthday? What do I do when my preschooler behaves like a supermodel? What do kids need to know before they go to school? Which is better: staying at home or using child care? Is immunization dangerous? Is that a carrot stain on my forehead? Will I get to a hairdresser before my first-born turns 6?

Grab a cup of coffee and take a load off, we'll get to all that.

A lot of the people who read my book *A Bun in the Oven: The Real Guide to Pregnancy* wrote to me and said, "WHERE'S THE SEQUEL?! HURRY UP YOU DEMENTED SLATTERN, I NEED TO KNOW WHAT TO DO NEXT!," which was quite rude but I understand they were sleep deprived and needed to know which end to put the diaper on. So I started to research what a parent needed or might want to know in the first five years.

The book ended up being fairly huge. (It also took a while because I had a toddler of my own, and I don't know whether you've heard but toddlers can be a tad time-consuming.) Please don't be appalled by the size of the book. Don't think "Oh MY GOD, I need to know all THIS?" because you won't.

Don't be freaked out by the Health chapter, for example. It's full of bugs your kid might catch, but it's practically impossible for kids to have all of them—and certainly not at the same time!

Some people say we shouldn't need a book to help us look after our kids—that we should follow our "instincts" like animals, who are automatically proficient parents. This is piffle. (Sometimes lionesses eat their own cubs, for heaven's sake.) We're not born with parenting instincts, we develop them.

"Some animals are lovely, and we can learn a lot from watching them, but as role models and guides to personal hygiene they're the dregs."
DAME EDNA EVERAGE, *VANITY FAIR*, FEBRUARY 2002

Anyway you don't need to know everything at once. Knowing only some things at a time is perfectly fine in the parenting department. If you're starting with a baby, it's years before you'll need any preschool info: this book should last you about five years. As you go on you'll almost certainly need less info so that's why the toddler and preschooler parts are shorter than the baby bit. And then there's a whole bunch of other subjects that can apply to more than one age group, such as pacifiers, health, food, immunization, siblings, parenting philosophy, safety, reading, TV, and lots more, which you can look up in the last two parts of the book when it takes your fancy.

Kidwrangling is designed to help the people who are madly in love with their babies and just need some nipple advice, as well as the people who haven't a clue what to do with a small person and keep accidentally folding diapers into attractive swan shapes and putting them in the freezer. And to help all the parents and caregivers in between. The whole book is for dads as well as moms, even though there's a special dads' chapter and there isn't much you can teach them about how to breastfeed.

It's a book designed to be used by busy parents who want information given as succinctly as possible. So if you try to read it in sequence like a novel, you may come across a few repeated facts because mostly we expect people to be looking up toddler development, party ideas for 4-year-olds, or stomach bugs in the index or the contents list as they need things. Don't think we were asleep at the wheel—we left in some repetition in case you only read one or two chapters.

This is not a parenting-guru book that represents one theory or the ideas of one person. I'm no expert, with a brilliant, one-size-fits-all theory. All parents and all children are different so wherever possible a number of solutions are given and there are pointers to further help. I didn't write this book because I had all the answers—I wrote it because I had to go looking for them.

Most of the quotes you'll see scattered in this book are from the parents (mainly moms) who responded to the Kidwrangling Survey, in which I asked a number of questions about being a parent. More than 900 people responded, and I'm grateful to everyone who gave generously of their time. The Survey wasn't in the least designed to be scientific or produce statistics; instead it provided a rich source of helpful hints, a base of advice from the real experts, and the feeling that we're not in this parenting caper alone. The quotes are on selected topics, not every one, because unfortunately the Survey questions couldn't go on forever.

Most chapters in *Kidwrangling* include a More Info section at their end, which includes book recommendations, and the phone numbers, websites, and addresses of services you can go to for further advice or research. The part called Extra Resources at the end of the book has other important services and contacts.

Don't be slow to get professional help: it's what we have now instead of a tribal society full of wise women. Right at the end of your phone line are networks of specialists in all sorts of baby-related businesses. I think I called about half of them three times each when I was a new mother so don't be shy.

Many of the books I've suggested are, by their nature, specialized, but your local bookstore will order them for you, and at the same time you and your child can get used to browsing in bookstores. A lot of the books should also be available at your local library, which needs your support.

Although *Kidwrangling* is pro-kid, it is also very much on the side of parents and caregivers. You can't do or be everything your child wants (otherwise they'd be eating Easter eggs every day for breakfast and you'd be dressed as a giant penguin).

This book doesn't make a big deal—or any sort of a deal—about different family structures or parents' sexuality because that's largely irrelevant to being a good parent. Here's a round-up of possible family groups parents might be in or their child might encounter as they make friends: Mom, Dad, and the kid; Mom, Stepdad, and nine kids; Grandma and kids; Step-mom, Dad, Dad's brother, Ron, and kids; Mom, Mom's girlfriend, kids, and offsite Dad; Dad, Dad's girlfriend, kids, and offsite Mom; Mom and kids in an apartment, and an aunty next door; Mom and the kid, with Dad and Dad's boyfriend offsite; Mom and the kid in a shared house with some friends and their kids.

The only thing that's relevant to the child in all these possibilities is that they're in a safe and loving home. Especially when they're under 5, kids just assume their home is normal ("Yes, my father sleeps with a cardboard cut-out of Barbra Streisand and he plays for the Niners." "Jeez! Mine farts like a tractor.") I mean, why should kids know what one gets up to in the privacy of one's room with a tin of golden syrup and a photo of Prince Charles? Okay, that's just me.

So I'm not going to bang on about all these different types of families except to say it's always worth remembering that sole parents—who don't have someone to share custody with—have a harder time than shared-custody parents.

Some people complain "Books never tell you how much you'll love your children." No—you can make that serendipitous, wonderful discovery for yourself. This book is supposed to help you with just about everything else.

I hope you'll find *Kidwrangling* reassuring, informative, and easy to read. I hope it becomes your friend, helps you to feel calmer and more confident about being a parent, and provides lots of fun on the way. If not, I plan to have a tantrum.

-kaz

1
BABIES

IF YOU'RE READING *PART 1: BABIES*, YOU MIGHT ALSO BE INTERESTED IN CHAPTERS IN OTHER PARTS OF THE BOOK.

in the beginning

So, you're home. Now what? If you had enough brain cells left you'd be wondering why everyone makes you babyproof the house, because here's this wee, tiny, curly-up creature wrapped like takeout fish and chips, who lies in whatever position you put them in and does nothing but blink, eat, poop, yell, and sleep, not necessarily in any order—and who isn't all that chatty.

hello!

useful things to know in the first days

You don't have to know everything right away
In fact you'll never know everything. You're starting a new, important job for which you have no qualifications. Treat yourself at least as kindly as you would a girl scout on the space shuttle, and accept that you'll be learning as you go.

Don't expect your baby to be the life of the party

Newborns shouldn't even really be out of the womb—they just come out because otherwise they wouldn't fit down the "birth canal" (oh please, can we start calling it a vagina again now?). So they're not like baby giraffes, who are up running around an hour after the birth. (Which is probably just as well frankly.) Newborn babies literally don't know where they are, sleep a lot, cry a lot, and need to fill their tiny tummies at irregular or regular intervals (like every 2 to 4 hours— closer to 4 if you're lucky).

Babies like baby talk

They like burbly-urbly, slightly high-pitched talk—and the voice of their mom, and any other voice they've heard during their time inside or are getting to know on the outside. Even though a baby can't speak or fully understand, hearing you talk to them is great for their own fun and development. If you feel weird talking to them, describe what you're doing as you go about the day, tell them things that are going to happen, or even sing silly songs. You'll be surprised how much babies understand from your tone of voice. And a sudden or loud noise will frighten them—they'll need a cuddle and some soothing words to calm down.

Babies love an animated face to go with life's chat

Make close-up surprised and delighted faces and smile as you chat (as long as they're not too tired, in which case if they could they'd tell you to bug off). You're their major source of visual entertainment. In the first few weeks newborns can see about the distance from their mother's breast to her face. They'll love you making wildly interesting faces, with mobile eyebrows—but not from the other side of the room.

Babies love a heartbeat

(Well, they've been soothed by their mom's for months.) Being cuddled against a chest can comfortingly remind babies of those floaty times on the inside.

You will probably never be this tired or clueless again

This is good news. I am not kidding you, it all gets better from here. Don't listen to gloomy nincompoops who say each stage of childhood has its own vastly worrying concerns (pause for violin music so you can take notice of their tragic lives): the newness and the sleeplessness set this time apart. The more communicative your child becomes, the easier it is to be a parent.

Let your baby know you understand it's all a bit freaky

Everything is new to babies: imagine landing on a planet where nothing, not even air or shapes or colors, is like anything you've experienced before. Imagine you've never felt anything on your skin or digested food—no wonder babies cry sometimes, especially at the end of the day. It must be so much to take in. Talk to them in a soothy, explainy, "It's okay, darling" sort of way when they seem discombobulated.

Your baby doesn't know which cry means what yet, either

After a while you may be able to tell whether your baby is having a little cry or is really distressed, whether they are hungry or just have something that feels wet and odd coming out of their bottom, or whether their tummy hurts while trying to digest all that brand-new milk. I reckon if you've exhausted possible reasons for crying (they're hungry, wet, poopey, cold, hot, overtired, or have indigestion: see the Crying chapter), then they've probably got a case of understandable, non-specific, I'm-not-used-to-the-world freak-out. All you can do is try to be comforting and as bouncy-rocky as a womb, and share the crying baby around as much as possible so if you go mad you all go mad together. You can get so worried about solving the crying it only occurs to you months later that some of it may have been unsolvable.

Babies are born with personalities

People who have a lot to do with babies know that some of them are placid and some are cranky, and some are intense and some are as alert as all get out. If your baby is clean, comfy, cuddled, and well fed and still cries, it isn't a reflection on what sort of parent you are. A crying baby may be much more a reflection on what sort of baby you've had. (Or what sort of baby they are TODAY.)

You don't have to let go of your baby yet

Sometimes in the early days you hardly want to let your baby go to anyone else's arms, let alone out of your sight. That's okay. (Conversely, you may have an immediately social or laid-back baby who is happy to be passed around, and you don't mind a bit. Do what feels right.)

GOOD THINGS TO DO FOR A NEWBORN BABY

✱ Start a baby scrapbook.

✱ Plant a tree against which to measure your child's growth—perhaps a photo in front at each birthday would be fun to take. (If you're not a green thumb, plant a spare just in case.)

✱ Write a letter to your baby to be opened when they're grown up.

✱ Pick a nice newborn photo, run off a heap of copies, stick a stamp, an address, and the baby's name on the back and send it to friends and relatives. Nobody should expect prose at a time like this.

✱ Put your baby's hands and feet into some non-toxic water-based poster paint and gently make some "paw prints." They'll only be this small for about a minute.

Never force anyone to hold the baby if they're clearly uncomfortable or frightened of dropping them—there's a lifetime of cuddles coming for family and friends. Let them sit down on the couch and have the baby on their knee if they feel safer doing that. But don't push it: there's no point making everyone tense.

As the weeks go on you'll know which people you feel happy to let hold or even look after your baby while you go shopping or have a quiet moment.

HOW TO PICK UP A NEWBORN BABY

This info is for everyone, but especially new moms and those dads who might think being female automatically means you know how to pick up a very new baby—it's just practice and you can be as good at it as any mom. (Many men actually have a major advantage with their bigger hands.)

In the first weeks just make sure that when you pick up the baby you pick up the whole baby so there aren't any bits (head, arms, legs) dangling unsupported over the edges.

The most important part to be careful of, especially in the first two months, is the baby's neck. That oversized baby head is so heavy for the little-baby neck, and the neck muscles have to be developed and trained.

As with almost everything you do with your baby, tell them when you are going to pick them up or put them down. This is also how they start learning to anticipate and communicate. They'll get to understand and not be too startled.

When you pick your baby up, slide your arm along the little one's back until your hand is supporting the head and neck and try to lift them in one steady movement (all early jerks should be accompanied by a soothing apology).

How to Hold a Newborn Baby

Once you've picked them up, you can go horizontal: transfer the baby to the crook of your other arm so that the head is cradled in your elbow and the body supported along your forearm. Or you can go vertical: pick the baby up gently, continually supporting the head and neck, and hold them so that the little head peeks over your shoulder.

Keep supporting the head and neck at all times until the baby has full control of them (usually at about 6 weeks old). Don't forget that babies love to be held close and to hear your heartbeat. Another thing you can do is sit down, put both your feet flat on the floor, and lay the baby tummy up, with their head and neck supported by your knees and their feet in your lap.

How to Touch a Newborn Baby

Gentle, stroking motions will probably soothe your baby. For centuries people have been touching and massaging babies without having to take lessons on baby massage or read books about it so don't feel you have to do anything special. Skin-to-skin contact between baby and caregivers, like cuddles and chat, is known to improve baby happiness and health, and it can help you fall in love with your baby.

Tell your baby when you're going to touch them. You can lay them on their back on the floor (to avoid a fall from a table), then sit down and lean forward to stroke them. Make sure your core is strong, your tummy is held in, and your back is braced. (This is no good after a cesarean obviously because it will be too painful.) Or try sitting in a chair and putting the baby in a basket on the table—with a rule that you never take your hand off them or wander away when they're up high. Babies also love to lie skin to skin on a bare chest. (For more on baby massage techniques see More Info at the end of the chapter.)

GOOD THINGS ABOUT BABIES

* Their head smells of Baby.

* Their tiny starfish hands.

* That little hollow at the back of their neck.

* Their excellent chubby thighs.

* The way they bend time when you're sitting holding them in a quiet place.

* They stare at you and you can stare back.

* They hold onto your finger.

* Their toothless grins.

* They have amusing hair or they're bald.

* They look kind of Star Trekky.

* There's so much potential in such a small package.

* They have hilariously short arms.

* You can read stuff into their faces: "wise," "bewildered," "flabbergasted."

* They mimic facial expressions.

* They snore, but not very loudly.

* They have a total body response when they're excited.

* You are keeping another human alive.

* You are creating new love in the world.

* The green poop stage doesn't last long.

WRAPPING a NEWBORN BaBY

Most young babies, particularly newborns, like to be wrapped firmly in a baby blanket or sheet cotton in winter and muslin in summer (when a blanket is likely to be too hot). They like having their limbs all wrapped up because it reminds them of being in the womb. Sometimes when a baby's arms and legs are loose, you can see them give a "startle reflex" because, it's thought, babies have a

15

hard-wired fear of falling. Most cultures have some version of swaddling (wrapping) and carrying small babies, which often helps a baby to calm down or go to sleep. Ask your midwife, doula, or the labor nurse nurse how to swaddle a small baby.

Usually by, say, 4 months old a baby will wriggle too much to be kept in their package and you can abandon the wrapping, either straight away or slowly, whatever the baby seems to prefer. Don't start to wrap a baby after 4 months and don't keep a baby wrapped all day: perhaps just for sleep or a winding-down time. Babies, especially those more than a couple of weeks old, need to practice wriggling around a bit, to stretch their arms and legs, and to feel the fresh air on their skin.

It's important not to wrap a baby too tightly or overheat them so only wrap a lightly dressed baby (undershirt and diaper).

Like all babies, a wrapped baby should be placed on their back to sleep. A wrapped baby on their side is more likely to roll onto their tummy.

more info

BABY-CARE BOOKS

I reckon the best books for babies to about 1 year are the ones written by nurses as they have seen so much. Unfortunately, all authors tend to generalize at least some of the time, and some only provide their own method rather than also discussing others.

What to Expect in the First Year
by Arlene Eisenberg, Heidi Murkoff, and Sandee Hathaway, Workman Publishing Co., 2nd ed. Nov. 2003.
The first in a series, it basically consists of a billion questions asked and answered. It's incredibly comprehensive, with pages on all the development stages, a section on stay-at-home dads and going back to work, and a brief introduction to special needs categories such as Down syndrome and

deafness. Has an oddly regimented approach to what a mother should eat. Many parents find this better to consult when and if they have a problem, as it covers so many possible concerns and illnesses that reading it like a novel is enough to give a worrying parent the heebie-jeebies.

The Baby Book: Everything You Need to Know About Your Baby from Birth to Age Two

by William and Martha Sears with (sons) James Sears and Robert Sears, Little Brown and Company, 2003.

This high-profile one-family industry of advice on all things baby advocates "attachment parenting" (see index) and their big range of books follows that philosophy encompassing gentle, baby-comes-first, breastfeeding a go-go principles. This book has a welcome emphasis on getting to know your baby's personality (yes, they already have one!). More targeted spin-off books include *The Family Nutrition Book, The Discipline Book, Parenting the FussyBaby and High-Need Child,* and *Nightime Parenting,* many of which are mentioned in various sections of this book.

Secrets of the Baby Whisperer: How to Stay Calm, Connect, and Communicate with Your Baby

by Tracy Hogg and Melinda Blau, Ballantine Books, Jan. 2002.

Has a lovely emphasis on getting to know and enjoy your baby, with everything flowing from there, and plenty of practical advice as well. Includes a routine for twins, and a fantabulous body language guide to what babies are probably signaling. A UK book.

The Contented Little Baby Book: The Secret to Calm, Confident Parenting

by Gina Ford, Random House, 2002.

More of your British nanny stricter than Tracy Hogg, Ms. Ford's a maternity nurse with lots of suggested routines and schedules from birth to eating solids (at about 6 months) and through to the end of the first year. These can be incredibly useful as long as you pick a routine to suit you and your baby instead of trying to fit yourselves to a schedule. There's a real emphasis on what bothers parents most: getting some sleep, sorting out feeding, and trying to impose some sort of vague order on life. Very practical, with a brisk tone and lots of case histories.

BOOKS COMBINING INFO ON BABIES, TODDLERS, AND PRESCHOOLERS

Your Baby and Child: From Birth to Age 5
by Penelope Leach, Knopf, rev. ed. 1997.

The book is broken into sections: the first few days, the first 6 months, from 6 months to a year, from 1 year to 2 and a half years of age, and from 2 and a half until 5, with lots of stuff about development as well as sleeping and crying for all those stages. Not to mention several sections called, as if we were in nurses' school in 1932, "excreting." Penelope Leach can be a little acerbic, perhaps without meaning to: "Babies in this age group [6 to 12 months] cannot have sleeping difficulties so if there are any problems they are yours, not your baby's" isn't the most reassuring or helpful thing to say to someone who hasn't slept more than 2 hours straight since their baby was born.

Complete Baby and Child Care
by Dr. Miriam Stoppard, DK Publishing, rev. ed. Feb. 2001.

A whacking huge hardback with lots of helpful pictures from babyhood to preschool, a great layout, Miriam's usually medical approach to most things and some curious information you wouldn't have thought you'd need such as "Look for clothes that are practical as well as smart to dress your baby boy" and (for girls) "You may prefer more feminine clothes for special occasions"—such as a bikini with a feather hat, perhaps. In Miriam's world (and probably most people's) fathers here "help" rather than participate in a partnership. There's a big section on babies and children with special needs. The book has an introduction to everything you need, including language development and how to show more physical affection. The pictures may be of special help to a first-time parent who's never had anything to do with babies.

Other books   See also the child-care books given in More Info at the end of the chapter Who's the Centre of the Universe? which starts *Part 2: Toddlers*.

BABY WEBSITES

These tend to have a lot of stuff about pregnancy as well as after the birth, and chat rooms galore (and see also the parenting websites in More Info at the end of the next chapter, Your Support Team—they usually include baby business too).

www.babycenter.com
Huge site covering almost everything to do with babies, and includes articles and advice from baby professionals.

www.babyzone.com
Gigantic website with heaps of question-answering and articles.

www.marthastewart.com/baby
Although everything looks too perfect in Hyperhomemaker Marthaland, this is actually a useful site with pics of how to bath a baby and hints on feeding and nursery decoration. Also has parent forums and advice. Other parts of the Martha site have tips on housekeeping and craft activities for kids.

www.babycentre.com
The UK sister of the preceding website.

www.essentialbaby.com.au
Aussie site with lots of sponsorship from various baby-related products. Also has discussion groups, stuff about guys, and an emphasis on pregnancy.

BABY MASSAGE

Baby Massage

by Dr Alan Heath and Nicki Bainbridge, DK Publishing, Feb. 2004.

Gives reasons why massage is good for a baby, plus lots of pictures showing how to massage and gently stretch your baby's limbs. Contains info on massage for premature babies, newborns, older babies and toddlers, children with special needs, and techniques that may help "colic" (gas stuck inside a baby causing tummy pain), constipation, non-specific cranky crying, teething, and dry skin. It also has sensible advice such as don't use nut oils in case your baby has an allergy to nuts, and don't always massage your baby to sleep because when they wake up in the night they can't get themselves back to sleep without another one.

www.infantmassage.com/contact.htm

Contains a directory of infant massage instructors and practitioners in the United States.

www.makewayforbaby.com/massages.htm

Has a nice section with step-by-step illustrated instructions.

your support team

You'll be needing a hand, then. Ideally you will have thought about this before the baby arrives and have lined up some home help, in particular with the cooking and cleaning, or a full freezer at least, for the first few weeks. Some people are lucky enough to have trusted relatives and friends close by who know what to do with babies. Your back-up team will probably also include the people mentioned in the following pages and a few butlers and footmen if you've married well.

midwives and lactation consultants

If you're given conflicting advice about the baby in hospital, pick the doctor or nurse you like and only listen to that one, or employ an independent private midwife or a doula (someone to help you with breastfeeding and baby care in the first little while at home).

Lactation consultants (or shall we call them Boob Ladies?) to help you with breastfeeding are often employed by hospitals and can also be hired privately: contact your nearest maternity hospital or the one where you gave birth (Women's Hospitals in Extra Resources at the end of the book gives contact details for the major ones), or look under Breastfeeding or Lactation in the Yellow Pages.

your pediatrician or general practitioner (gp)

Now you have a little one at home you'll be needing a pediatrician or general practitioner. If you're living in an area where there are very few kids and the waiting room is full of octogenarians, find out who's the nearest GP who sees most of the kids. This GP will be experienced, and they'll usually know what's "going around." It's always worthwhile finding out who's the parents' favorite. A doctor who really listens and thinks laterally is important. A doctor who is also a parent of young children can be a bonus, but so can one who specializes in pediatrics. (Many GPs specialize in children these days, others have special interests in women's health or geriatrics.) Doctors don't always get it right—a fever and non-specific symptoms could mean so many different things—but one who is thorough, experienced, and kind to children is a good start. I know it's harder to have a choice in a rural area: you may need to go to another town if that's possible.

Health insurance plans in the United States vary greatly. You may be unrestricted in your choice of doctors or you may have to choose from a list of participating doctors. Check with your insurance company and prospective doctor. If you don't have insurance, you need to know that there are many programs that you may qualify for to help you pay for your child's health care. See the More Info section at the end of this chaper to learn more about how to find programs in your state.

If you feel concerned about your baby's health, always have it checked out. It doesn't matter if there's nothing wrong. It will help get your child used to going to the doctor, and a check-up never hurts. If you're not happy with the outcome, find another doctor—you'd probably feel more guilty about changing to another hairdresser.

family and friends

Family and friends can be a great source of help or not much help at all, depending on how used they are to babies and kids. If they're not up to speed on offspring the age of yours, they can help in other ways, such as doing housework and hunter-gathering, provided they're willing and able. Someone who has a child a little older is always helpful as long as their ideas about children are similar to your own. Anyone with much older or grown-up children may be sympathetic and handy for babysitting, but will probably have forgotten the specifics of caring for a small baby or child: you may need lists on the fridge or other reminders to help them. Leaving this book around to be looked up when necessary may be helpful, unless you have a 98-year-old gran who's sure she learned everything she needed to know before 1953. (There's more on caregivers in the Child Care and Preschool chapter in *Part 4: Parenting*.)

Some family members, of course, will pop around every few months to wave from the other side of the room but otherwise won't be much actual use. The trick is to recognize the people who'd like to get to know the baby, and learn how to help look after and enjoy the babe as a developing person, and those who are genuinely not interested or are benign onlookers. Which is probably fair enough.

To be utterly candid, before I had a baby myself I used to be more interested in people's dogs than their babies.

Godparents or special adult friends can have more defined roles than others. Perhaps they can take the baby for regular outings and have preferred-babysitter privileges.

DOULAS AND NANNIES

If you have some hessian bags full of cash down the back of the couch, or you've saved up for some baby extras, you can hire a doula or a nanny to help you in the first few weeks. Some will live in, others will do shift work or just come during the day. To find one, try the Yellow Pages or ask friends who've done the same thing. Always check the legitimacy of an agency and personally check the references of the doula or the nanny. (See the More Info section at the end of this section for a list of helpful resources.)

PARENTS' GROUPS, MOTHERS' GROUPS, AND PLAYGROUPS

Ask your GP or local family services agency for the contact details of local groups of parents (usually but not always moms), with babies or kids about the same age as yours. These groups can be particularly good for moms who feel isolated and can be great for making friends and reminding you that your feelings and experiences are probably not so unusual

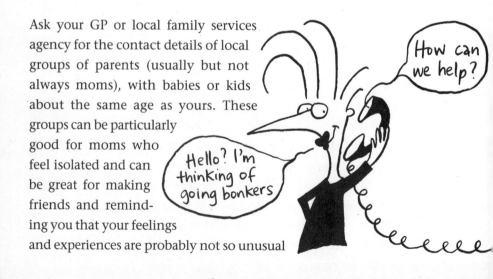

(although some parents find parents' groups nothing but a hotbed of judgmental remarks and dull conversation). Children for the first couple of years and even beyond, depending on the kid, really don't play together, but after several months babies are at least interested in looking at each other, and meanwhile you can hang out and chat.

Groups meet in local halls, each other's houses, or local parks. Remember to make a shared community space a child-friendly zone—for example, unplug and lock gates to the street.

Contact resources for playgroups are given in More Info at the end of the Baby Development (0 to 1) chapter.

MORE INFO

PARENT HELPLINES

Phone counselors can help when you are feeling at the end of your tether and phone advisors can give you practical and specific information. You can call anonymously.

There are lots of parent helplines and many of them are 24-hour lines or have 7-day daytime access, although the situation with any of them can change with the funding. Below is a list of parent helplines by state.

ALABAMA
CONTACT Helpline
24-hour crisis line.
1-800-239-1117

ALASKA
Anchorage Center for Families
Parenting education and support, services that come to your home, and a 24-hour hotline.
907-276-8511

ARIZONA
Parent Information and Referral Center
1-800-690-2282

Parent Assistance Program Hotline
1-800-732-8193

ARKANSAS
Jones Center for Families
501-756-8090

CALIFORNIA
Parental Stress Services
24-hour crisis hotline for parents.
1-888-829-3777

FLORIDA
Parent Help-Line
Provides 24-hour telephone
counseling, crisis intervention,
information, and referral to services
that can help children and parents
through difficult times.
813-234-1234

HAWAII
The Parentline
1-800-816-1222

ILLINOIS
Parent Hotline
For parents who need help with
prenatal and newborn care.
1-800-545-2200 or 1-888-727-5889

INDIANA
**Family Service Association of
Monroe County**
Offers counseling, parent support,
and workshops on child rearing.
812-339-1555

KANSAS
Parent Helpline
1-800-332-6378

KENTUCKY
Parent Helpline
24-hour hotline.
1-800-432-9251

**Health Access; Nurturing
Development (HANDS)**
Offers home visitation services for
new parents.
502-564-2154

LOUISIANA
Parent Helpline
1-800-348-KIDS

MARYLAND
Parent Warmline
Offers child-rearing advice.
301-929-WARM

MASSACHUSETTS
Parent Line
617-421-1789

Parental Stress Line
1-800-632-8188

MICHIGAN
Parent Help Line
1-800-942-4357

MINNESOTA
Crisis Connection
612-379-6363

Fathers' Crisis Line
612-874-1509

MISSOURI
Parental Stress Hotline
1-800-367-2543

ParentLink Warmline
1-800-367-2543

NEW HAMPSHIRE
Parent Line
1-800-640-6486

NEW JERSEY
Contact Crisis Line
856-795-2155

NEW MEXICO
Family Crisis Hotline
505-325-1906

NEW YORK
Parent Helpline
1-800-342-7472

NORTH DAKOTA
Parent Line
1-800-258-0808

OHIO
Family Link Line
513-946-LINK

OKLAHOMA
Parenting Helpline
1-877-446-6865

OREGON
Parent Helpline
1-800-345-5044

PENNSYLVANIA
Parent to Parent of Pennsylvania
1-800-986-4550

TENNESSEE
Parent Helpline
1-800-356-6767

TEXAS
Family Forward Texas Parent Heartline
1-800-554-2323

VERMONT
Parents Assistance Line
1-800-727-3687

Parents Stress Line
1-800-244-5373

WASHINGTON
Family Help Line
206-233-0156

WEST VIRGINA
Family Matters Hotline
1-888-983-2645

WISCONSIN
Florence County Parenting Warmline
Support for the day to day challenges of parenting.
1-888-432-6495

CANADA
Parent Help Line
24-hour tips and information on child rearing for Canadians.
1-888-603-9100

PARENT SERVICES

The services listed on the following pages can help you develop sleeping strategies, deal with exhaustion, and move on from a bad patch. They can help you develop routines, learn what to do about feeding, and cope better with crying. They may be able to help you over the phone or with group meetings.

The National Family Support Mapping Project

A website featuring an expansive national database of family support programs. You can search by service, expertise, state, or keyword. Go to the website and click on "National Family Support Mapping Project."
www.familysupportamerica.org

Child Help National Hotline

24-hour advice and referrals for parents who have questions or emergencies.
1-800-422-4453

Boys Town National Hotline

Provides crisis intervention, information, and referrals for children (girls and boys) and families. Spanish-speaking counselors are available.
1-800-448-3000

La Leche League International
24-hour helpline and resource for finding breastfeeding support groups.
1-800-LA-LECHE (525-3243)

National Association of Mothers' Centers
Meet other mothers in a supportive place. Share your experiences and learn more about your child's development. Check out the website for a mothers' center near you.
64 Division Ave.
Levittown, NY 11756
1-800-645-3828
www.motherscenter.org

Parents Anonymous
Offers parenting support groups and tips. Check out its website or give them a call to find out about meetings in your area.
1-800-345-5044

Postpartum Support International
Runs support groups across the country for parents.
927 North Kellogs Ave.
Santa Barbara, CA 93111
1-805-967-7636
www.postpartum.net

PARENTING WEBSITES
If you like the Internet, you could find these sites useful or reassuring (and see also the baby websites in More Info at the end of the preceding chapter, In The Beginning). There are lots of US websites that give parenting advice. Watch out for ones that may be religious-based and not share your values, or those that exist mainly to sell you baby and kid equipment and a bersquil-lion other things you may not need.

www.parenting.com

Comprehensive website of *Parenting* magazine so has lots of resident experts and advertising. Lots of info about sleep, budgeting, cooking, all the usual helpful stuff.

www.forparentsbyparents.co.uk

A UK website where parents give advice to each other: there's moms on moms, dads on dads (you know what I mean), and lots on common questions to do with caring for babies.

www.badmothersclub.co.uk

A very naughty website, with high entertainment value, about how parenting's not all beer and skittles. Has good links and includes articles such as "Pregnant, Confused/A Bit Thick? Don't Panic!" and "10 Things I Hate About My Fourth Child."

www.brainchildmag.com

Subtitled "The Magazine for Thinking Mothers," this is a quarterly magazine that includes essays, forums, and personal stories.

The following websites also have mommying and daddying advice listed by subject:

www.parentsoup.com

www.parenthood.com

www.parenting.org

www.about.com/parenting

NEWBORN WORRIES

In the first days our babies are so new to us we hardly recognize them. And they're so teeny tiny and so unlike the big, robust babies crawling around on TV ads smiling, grabbing things, and signing modeling contracts. It's easy to stress out about newborns. What follows is some stuff we tend to worry about that is probably, actually, usually okay.

Ask your obstetrician or midwife about any anxiety while you're in hospital, and after you've left bring it up with

calm down...

your obstetrician at your 6-weeks-after-the-

birth appointment or make an appointment

with your doctor. You're beginning to

develop a parent's instincts. If your baby is

fine, you've learned something and no harm

was done. Never be afraid to ask questions.

WORRIES ABOUT HOW THE BABY LOOKS

Because of the birth experience babies may have a squashed or bruised face; puffy, closed, or even bloodshot eyes; scrunched-up ears; or a pointy head. Almost all weird-looking stuff disappears quickly: ask your doctor if something worries you.

Fetal pozzie

Babies have been in that womb for so long and have been so cramped at the end that they keep their fetal pozzie for a while, and they like their little hands closed tight. Things gradually uncurl by themselves: you don't need to stretch or pull any bits.

Eyes

GUMMY ONES Squirt on some of your own breast milk (a traditional remedy) or squeeze some sterile saline from the pharmacist onto clean cotton balls (a new one for each eye) and wipe gently. The problem should clear up: if not, see a doctor.

REASONS TO GET MEDICAL HELP WITH A NEWBORN

Call 911 if:

✱ the baby has difficulty breathing or has stopped.

✱ the baby has a convulsion.

Go to the doctor if:

✱ the baby seems to have a fever and/or is distressed or floppy and uninterested.

✱ there are signs of dehydration (dry, pinched skin, sunken eyes and fontanelle, fewer wet diapers than usual, dark, stinky pee).

✱ the baby has been repeatedly vomiting.

✱ the baby seems in pain or otherwise screams for a long time no matter what you do.

✱ the baby suddenly doesn't want breast or bottle.

✱ there's something that looks yucky or pussy oozing or coming out of somewhere.

✱ there's something you haven't seen before such as a rash or lump.

✱ the baby has a wheezy cough.

✱ you are worried about anything.

See also the Health chapter in Part 5: Stuff.

DRY ONES Little babies sometimes don't cry tears, and sometimes the tear ducts are blocked. These should right themselves in the first few months. Babies should be able to produce tears by about 2 months old.

WANDERY, SQUINTY ONES   Babies don't really focus their eyes when they first come out into the world. This should sort itself out by 6 months. If one eye doesn't move from a certain position, see a doctor right away so that it can be fixed.

CHANGING-COLOR ONES   Some people claim all babies change eye color in their first year. Utter nonsense. And all babies are not born with blue eyes despite what they tell us in lots of Anglo-Saxon textbooks. Some babies change eye color, some don't.

Skin

BIRTHMARKS   Many babies have "stork marks," a red, rash-like mark on the forehead, eyelids, and back of the neck. (The idea that a stork's beak made the marks dates from the days when people pretended babies were brought by storks to avoid any mention of s-e-x. Can you believe it?) The stork marks are visible blood vessels close to the skin and usually fade quickly. But they can hang around or reappear as the blood vessels bulge away harmlessly when a kid holds their breath, yells a lot, or is hot or stressed. I've heard of some that last until towards the end of primary school or perhaps longer, despite some books saying that they all disappear in the first months.

Some babies of Asian heritage or dark skin are born with bluish grey pigment spots on their buttocks, back, and sometimes arms and legs. These spots fade.

Other birthmarks can be more permanent, although most are removable by laser treatment later in life if that's important to the child. You should talk about the marks with your doctor and have them identified. If in doubt, get your doctor to give you a referral to a pediatric skin specialist.

DIAPER RASH   This is usually caused by pee or poop irritating the skin under a diaper. Wash everything off with a baby wipe or a cotton ball soaked in a bottom-cleaning lotion or water, pat or air dry, and apply a barrier or diaper-rash cream. Disposable diapers are less likely to cause diaper rash. (For more on all this see the Bottoms chapter.)

CRADLE CAP   You can remove this rather crusty layer on top of a baby's head, but it may keep coming back for a few weeks or even months. Don't ask me why, but they say it's caused by oily, not dry, skin. To get rid of it try a paste of 1 teaspoon of baking soda and about half a teaspoon of cold tap water. Make the paste a consistency you can apply with a cotton ball. Rub it into the baby's scalp lightly and leave it on for 5 minutes, then wash the head with baby shampoo. Gently comb through the baby's hair if it is combable or rub the scalp gently to loosen the flakes so they fall off, or wait for them to fall off by themselves. If you only rub them with olive oil, as many recommend, it will get on everything and have to be wiped off. The cradle cap is often over that soft bit of your baby's head, the fontanelle. It's okay to massage it gently.

THRUSH   This is a horrid white rash, usually in the mouth or on the bottom, and is caused by a fungus. Try an over-the-counter treatment from a drugstore or get your doctor to prescribe a cream.

ACNE   Little pimples, whiteheads, and other acne are pretty standard for babies, and often last for about 3 months. You just need to make sure they're not insect bites (in which case you'll need to use screens, a mosquito net, or another non-chemical strategy in the baby's bedroom) or something else. See your doctor for a diagnosis.

SUCKING BLISTER   Some babies get a small blister on their lip from sucking. It might make the baby a little antsy while feeding, but should heal by itself.

VEINS   The thinner a baby, or the thinner the skin, the more you may be able to see veins or a bluish tinge where the blood vessels are close to the skin.

Private parts

Well, there's nothing very private about a baby's bits, but "genitals" sounds so po-faced Doctor Weirdy. The festival of hormone production that happens at birth can lead to some rather swollen parts on boy and girl babies, and even a slight, period-like bleed from a baby girl's vagina—just some of her own tiny, tiny womb cells coming away. This will right itself in a few days. If anyone is proud that their son has an enormous pair of testicles they should know it's temporary. And feel free to roll your eyes.

Hair

Some babies have a headful, some have none. Others have baldy patches where their head rests in the crib. The first baby hair sometimes falls right out and is replaced later. Body hair (called lanugo), which is often found on the back and shoulders, is normal and will fall out.

Fontanelle

This is the squishy bit on your baby's head where the skull plates haven't meshed together yet. It makes it easier for your baby's head to go temporarily pointy when coming down the vagina during birth. It will grow over (sadly unlike your vagina in the early days) and you won't notice it in a few weeks' time—although the plates don't fully fuse until the second year of life. The fontanelle requires the same amount of careful handling as the rest of a tiny baby. If it looks higher or lower than the rest of the head, see a doctor: it could be swelling or a sign of dehydration.

Head

Babies' heads are big compared with the rest of them: this lasts well into childhood. Babies who were pulled out with a vacuum device or forceps may have heads that look a bit pointy or dented. Ask your obstetrician how long this is likely to last. It's usually very temporary.

Arms

Yes, well spotted: babies have short arms compared with us.

Heartbeat

Okay, it's got nothing to do with how they look, but you may want to know that babies' heartbeats are faster than adult ones.

Teeth

Apparently some babies are actually born with teeth. Let's hope they keep them to themselves during breastfeeding.

Jaundice

If a baby is jaundiced, their skin and the whites of their eyes look a bit yellow. It's just that the liver should have broken down some extra red blood cells by the time baby was a few days old, but it's going a little slowly. Sometimes the getting-rid-of-the-yellow process is given a kick along in hospital by putting the baby under bright lights. Some experts dispute that this helps, insisting that jaundiced babies sort themselves out in their own good time, which can take days or even weeks. In the maternity wards jaundice is generally considered ho-hum unless the baby is lethargic and not feeding well. If it's an unusually severe or long-lasting case, a pediatrician should investigate.

Umbilical cord

What a strange little stumpy thing they send you home with on the front of your baby: the blackened remains of the umbilical cord fastened with a plastic, well, peg. It looks absolutely revolting. At some time during the first couple of weeks, perhaps even after a few days, the cord stump will fall off, plastic peg and all. Usually you just clean the tummy button and stump with tepid

temporary pointy head

stumpy bit

tap water, and gently pat and air dry afterwards. If there's a bit of blood after the stump falls off, continue cleaning the area in the same way once a day and it should be good in a few days. See your GP if there is pus, or inflamed redness around the area, or it's smelly.

Ears

Drinking breast milk can help protect babies against ear infections. Don't squirt anything into the ear to try to combat an infection: it is on the other side of the drum so nothing will get through. And if it did, through a hole in the drum, it could cause further infection. Don't poke anything inside: it cleans itself in there. (For more info look up ears in the index.)

WORRieS aBOUt MeaSUReMeNtS

Early days weight loss

Newborn babies are supposed to lose weight. They do it—losing up to about 10 percent of their birth weight—in the time after they're born and before your proper milk comes in several days later (see the Boobs chapter for all the guff on milk and getting the hang of breastfeeding). Coincidentally, at the time the milk comes in you sometimes have a big, weepy hormonal crash. (Helpful, isn't it?) So worrying about whether your baby has lost too much, and scampering about with your bosoms akimbo trying to make up the loss super fast, is just going to cause you stress. Medical staff and midwives really shouldn't say anything about your baby losing weight unless it's really a problem, and it so rarely is. Mentioning it just leads to thousands of parents worrying and women wondering if their baby is fading away and it's their fault.

Multiple birth babies, because they have to share the womb, and preemie babies are often at the lower weight end. The biggest babies are usually boys.

Most babies are back to their birth weight in a week or two.

Weight and length

I know that doctors and nurses have to weigh and measure babies but unfortunately, instead of resulting in a public health tool that reassures parents, this tends to produce graphs and lines and sets of numbers for people to worry about. If your baby is diagnosed as "failing to thrive," you may have to change your approach to feeding. Apart from that the numbers are just facts that nurses write down. They're not nearly as interesting as what sort of personality your baby is developing.

Some babies are darling roly-polies with dimply buttocks, others can be surprisingly lean yet healthy: this is mainly a matter of genes. It doesn't necessarily bear any relation to their eventual grown-up size and shape—although it is sometimes exactly that, an indicator of a child's natural body. As long as the baby is not distressed, lethargic, or undernourished, weight is not a problem.

Babies should steadily put on weight—but not so steadily that you need to weigh your baby yourself or constantly have their weight checked. Some weeks there'll be more growth than others. Suddenly going backwards may indicate a problem, but growth spurts are pretty normal. Regular visits to your doctor will pick up any problems. If your baby is anywhere on the chart they're somewhere in the normal range.

Head size

Don't even think about taking notice of the head circumference measurement unless a nurse or doctor tells you there might be a medical problem (extreeeeemely rare).

Worries about preemie babies

Bringing home a tiny baby can be awfully daunting—especially after seeing so many tubes and machines doing things to and for your baby in the hospital. Sometimes it can help to be introduced to great, hulky, galumphing teenagers who were once as preemie as your wee baby. Your hospital should have a handbook or at least a pamphlet on preemie babies, which you can take home; or contact your nearest major city hospital (see Women's Hospitals in Extra Resources at the end of the book).

Find out from the doctors whether your baby needs special handling, but don't be afraid to touch your little one, no matter how fragile they seem. Almost constant skin-to-skin contact and soothing, comforting soft songs and voices are known to perk up a preemie baby in the early days. They may have a specially pale or red skin, a distressing thinness and prominent veins, but when they put on weight these will disappear. Very early babies may be covered in the tiny hairs (lanugo) that all babies have in the womb: it's temporary. Your baby may have difficulty with sucking so if breastfeeding isn't possible don't stress.

You mustn't be hard on yourself about being emotional or feeling overwhelmed: after what you've been through that's absolutely normal. Many people feel scared of their preemie babies and daunted by the responsibility. DO get help if you feel that the difficulties are constant and never-ending (see the parent helplines and parent services given in More Info at the end of the previous chapter, Your Support Team, and also More Info at the end of this chapter).

you're early...

oops

These days so many babies are born prematurely and survive and thrive that doctors and nurses know a lot about them. La

Leche League has phone and booklet help for moms who want to express milk for or directly breastfeed their preemie baby (see More Info at the end of the Boobs chapter).

Early arrivals can have physical difficulties, including lung trouble and pooping problems, and might always be a smaller size than other kids of the same age. Ask your obstetrician to recommend a pediatrician who specializes in preemie babies. Make sure you fully understand from your midwife or doctors, including your ongoing pediatrician or GP, what to expect. Some preemies never have a problem: it often depends on how preemie they are.

Most of the small sizes in baby clothes may be too big at first. Your baby will soon grow into them, but in the meantime you'll need the softest cotton things you can find: little hats are particularly important to keep a tiny head warm. Many hospitals are given clothes especially made or knitted for preemies by wonderful volunteers. Be careful that any wool isn't causing an itch the baby can't tell you about. Most of the large department stores and maternity hospital shops carry a limited range of clothes for preemie babies in their baby-wear department: you should be able to mail order with a credit card over the phone.

WORRIES ABOUT NEWBORN BEHAVIOR

Noises
Babies often make odd snorky breathing sounds, just getting used to breathing with their little tubes and lungs. Sneezes, hiccups, grunts, and general snonkiness are all perfectly normal.

The baby has slept longer than normal
It's probably just your baby's first big sleep. Most parents know the blind panic, on the first morning the baby misses a night feed and "sleeps through," of racing in to find a hungry but healthy baby. As

long as the breathing seems regular and untroubled, and there is no fever, it's almost always best to "let sleeping babies lie." They can be quite cross at being woken up.

Is my baby hurt?

Happily babies are very resilient. Many have been dropped. Usually everything's fine, but of course if you do drop your baby, or they receive a knock, go to the doctor immediately. A baby who's floppy or sleepy after a drop or knock is a worry, and if they can't be roused, stop breathing, or have a convulsive fit call 911.

ROUGH PLAY   Some parents and relatives—often older men—think it's a great idea to throw babies up in the air and catch them: they must be stopped. This shouldn't happen to babies at all until they're at least a year old, and certainly never to newborns, whose brain and eyes can be badly damaged by being rattled about. This is the same damage that can be done by shaking a baby.

Is my baby sick?

You'll find info on stomach bugs, colds, fever, and convulsions, in particular, in the Health chapter in *Part 5: Stuff* (and you can look these up in the index).

Is my baby too hot?

By this I mean too hot because of the weather, not too hot because of a temperature caused by an illness. Signs of a too-hot baby include crying, a red rash, and dehydration. Make sure your baby has lots of fluids on a hot day. (This usually means breast or bottle milk. Some people suggest a few teaspoons of cooled boiled water, while others scoff at the boiled water business: it seems to go in and out of fashion.) To cool down an overheated baby, get their gear off and lay them on the floor or bed, sponge them with tepid water, and perhaps use a fan—but not directed right at them—to move air around. The change should be relatively gradual so don't use ice or cold water. A hot bedroom at night can be cooled by air-conditioning (if you have a thermostat about 68 to 72 degrees Fahrenheit is standard); by wetting towels and hanging them over the edge of the crib; or by using a fan not directly pointed at the baby.

Professor David Brewster, head of pediatrics at the Royal Darwin Hospital in Australia, says the important thing to remember is that a baby born in the tropics will be acclimatized to warm weather, while a child who is not used to high temperatures will need to drink more, be watched more closely (monitor the number of wet diapers) and perhaps be sponged with tepid—never icy—water if they're hot and cross.

Babies in the tropics, especially visitors, are more susceptible to skin problems such as infected scratches, thrush, rashes, impetigo, and prickly heat. Don't overdress them.

Is my baby too cold?

Most of the cases of prickly heat in American babies don't occur in the tropics, but in cold areas where the babies have been so bundled up to the eyebrows in woollies that they're sweating under all their layers. This particularly happens with babies who are dressed for the cold outside and then brought into shops or homes that are heated. This is the time when a lambskin underneath the baby in a stroller, with a small blanket (polar fleece or woolen) over the top, rather than extra clothes, may help.

Hats are good for keeping a baby warm outside: the general rule is if you need a long-sleeved shirt, a small baby needs a hat. Remember that while you walk with the stroller you're warming up, but not so the baby being wheeled about. Small babies can't run around to warm up, or throw on more clothes, so you need to be aware that a too-cold baby may start out crying but then become very quiet and still.

Dr. Graham Bury, the medical director of the women's and children's department at the Royal Hobart Hospital in Australia, says, "I can't remember when we last saw a case of hypothermia." But if babies do get too cold, he says, "they get lethargic and don't feed or cry. Anyone would know there's something wrong. Windchill is the most obvious problem." According to Dr. Bury, the general rule is that little babies need at least one extra layer than we do to feel comfortable outside. (When they're toddlers and they're on the move they can start having the same number of layers as we do.)

To check how cold your baby is, feel their face: if it's cold, check their tummy, and if it's cold too that's unusual. Warm up a too-cold baby (or toddler or small child) with a hat and direct skin-to-skin contact under blankets pulled around you both, in a warm room—but not directly in front of a heater and not with a hot-water bottle, which is too much heat too suddenly.

A baby's room on a cold night should be kept warm, not hot (at about 68 to 72 degrees, as mentioned above). Make sure that the room is aired well between sleeps (and that the baby is too!). If it's not possible to heat a baby's bedroom, they need a hat and mittens, appropriate covers (blankets, not a duvet, which can cause overheating and suffocation), and their feet covered with one more layer than adults would have.

WORRieS aBOUt SUDDeN iNfaNt DeatH SyNDROMe (SiDS)

It's normal, but awfully tiring, to keep waking up and creeping next to your baby to check whether they're still breathing. In the past few years there's been a steady drop in the number of babies dying from an unknown cause that makes them stop breathing called sudden infant death syndrome (SIDS). (It used to be called "crib death.")

It is believed that the babies who die have a respiratory problem that means they can't fight for air if they have trouble breathing or their mouth or nose is blocked; and of course very young babies are unable to move their bodies at all by themselves. Most SIDS deaths happen before the baby is 6 months old. At about 6 months babies start to move in their sleep, which means they will almost certainly be able to shift to a better position if they can't breathe, unless they have a respiratory problem.

The marked drop in SIDS cases is attributed by doctors and researchers to the publicity campaigns warning parents about the risk factors for SIDS. Researchers and doctors now recommend a checklist (coming up) that emphasizes babies sleeping on their back.

There is no causal link between vaccinations and SIDS and there is no causal link between breastfeeding (or not) and SIDS. Awake babies can be regularly placed on their tummies to help them strengthen their necks and kick against the floor, although some babies hate this so just do it for a minute or two a day until they're cool with it.

Research is continuing: America's biggest SIDS research foundation is SIDS Alliance. They have info and counseling services for grieving parents (for contact details see Sudden Infant Death Syndrome (SIDS) in Extra Resources at the end of the book.)

WORRieS aBoUt CiRCUMCiSioN

Male circumcision is the removal of part of the penis foreskin with a scalpel. This is usually done in the first few hours or days of a boy's life. About 65 percent of newborn babies is the United States are circumsised each year. It is performed because it is believed a religion requires it; for cultural reasons; because the parents mistakenly think it will be cleaner; or because they want the boy's penis to look like his father's.

Circumcision is a very painful and shocking procedure for newborns when done without anesthesia. It's common for doctors to

ANTI-SIDS CHECKLIST

✱ All babies should be put on their back to sleep, not on their tummy. (As babies get older and can move their head to the side themselves and shuffle around changing position in bed–at about 6 months–they might choose to sleep on their tummy themselves. This is usually not a problem.) If your young baby tends to vomit during sleeps, talk to your doctor about sleep positions. When your baby's lying on their back for a sleep, roll their head to either side, alternating from time to time otherwise a slightly flat-back-of-the-head situation can arise (this usually fixes itself before school starts).

✱ Avoid overheating. Try to keep the bedroom at a mild, pleasant 68 to 72 degrees Fahrenheit.

✱ A sleeping baby should never have their face covered, and shouldn't have a duvet or any other puffy paraphernalia such as pillows. They should be firmly, not tightly, tucked in at the bottom of the crib because babies wiggle up, away from where their feet are pointing, when they're asleep. Babies can be "dressed" in a sleep bag, which ends in a square bag instead of separate feet. Babies in hot climates can drift off in an undershirt and diaper, and all babies who like it can be wrapped (from the neck down) in muslin or a cotton sheet until they are old enough to wriggle out of them.

use local anesthesia, but this does not necessarily make the procedure or recovery pain free. Results of the operation done without anesthesia include severe pain, shock, hysterical crying, and, in some cases, infection and bleeding. Reclaim-the-foreskin groups say circumcision will result in the penis having up to 75 percent less sensation during sex.

Sometimes boys are born with a fusion of the foreskin to the penis that in time will cause pain or friction, requiring surgery to

* The baby's mattress should be firm, not something their nose or mouth can sink into. To keep the airflow going and to cut down on the chance of smothering, avoid bumpers (padded crib liners), fluffy toys, and similar objects. Babies don't need fluffy toys when they're tiny; they need the comfort of having a parent or caregiver nearby and on call.

* If the baby is sleeping unattended, they should always be in a modern, safety standard crib (see cribs in the index).

* The baby should never be left to sleep unattended in a car, a car baby seat, carriage, or a stroller.

* Don't let a baby sleep on a couch whether someone is there or not.

* There should be no smoking by anyone near the baby or inside the home, car, or any other environment. The parents of the baby should be non-smokers. If either of the parents smokes, or the mother smoked during pregnancy, the baby should not sleep in their bed. If any parent or caregiver is drunk or drugged, the baby should not sleep in their bed.

* Parents need to keep an eye out for any breathing or rousing problems and see the doctor about them right away.

correct it, which is the same procedure as a circumcision. Doctors almost always recommend that babies be 6 months or even older when they have this operation so they can have general anesthetic (evidence is increasing that anesthetic should be avoided as much as possible with children because of brain cell damage). There is no other medical reason for circumcision.

Female circumcision is the removal or mutilation of the clitoris, usually with a knife or razor blade, sometimes accompanied by a process called infibulation: the vagina is stitched closed or mostly closed. It is rarely performed in the United States (and then usually by people who are not doctors and because it is believed a religion requires it or for cultural reasons). The aims are that the girl will grow up to be an "acceptable" wife because she is unable to enjoy sex, and that her stitched-up vagina will only be penetrated by her husband.

The results of female circumcision variously include shock, severe pain, mutilation, permanent sexual disability, possibly septic wounds, deep psychological trauma, menstrual and childbirth complications, and severe pain with penetrative sex. There is never a medical reason for female circumcision. Education is believed to be the strongest factor leading to the decline of female circumcision in some countries.

The practice of male and female circumcision, which causes pain in the most sensitive parts of the body, is widely regarded as unnecessary and outdated. Many religious parents who want their son circumcised are now waiting until a general anesthetic can be safely used or until the child is 18 and old enough to make his own decision. There are growing movements, in all the religions associated with male circumcision, that say the practice is traditional and cultural but not actually required by the rules of these religions. It is not mentioned in the Koran, or in some versions of the story of Abraham (other translations of the Bible have suggested circumcision is a way for Abraham's descendants, the Jewish people, to identify themselves to God).

WORRieS aBout feeLiNg aNgRy aND fRuStRateD WitH youR BaBy

Most parents know the inexplicable rage that sometimes comes over you when you're spectacularly tired, you've tried EVERYTHING to make the baby happy but they're still crying. I can remember shouting at my baby to shut up (you don't see that on the diaper ads, do you?), which was just nutty but I was at the end of my rational self. It's not as if it's the baby's fault, and in normal circumstances you'd never take out your frustration on a baby. But in these days of isolation and lack of sleep, your coping skills are sometimes hard to find.

You must not shake or hit the baby. The Feeling Overwhelmed or Depressed chapter has suggestions for dealing with your anger and frustration (look up rage in the index), but you must immediately get help because the situation will probably happen again, and you'll need a strategy to get you through the next time. (Parent helplines and parent services are listed in More Info at the end of the second chapter, Your Support Team.)

a gRaB-Bag of woRRies

Strange baby dreams

Remember those strange baby dreams you had when you were pregnant? Dreams are a way of processing what's been going on, and when you have a baby there's a lot going on in your brain at once. (I once dreamed I was panicking in a huge library because my baby was a flat, baby-shaped bookmark and I couldn't remember which book I'd left her in.) Don't take the dreams too literally, and if you're really worried about a recurring or distressing one ask your doctor about seeing a counselor.

Worries about not being a good parent

Are you doing it "right"? Probably, most of the time, particularly bearing in mind THERE'S NO ONE RIGHT WAY to do everything. You'll learn. It's okay. Nobody knows what to do at first: even people who've been midwives get a shock when the baby is their own and they can't go off shift! And don't forget that magnificent parental motto: near enough is good enough. Throw away any books or people who make you feel guilty or inadequate. If you're reading this book, you care enough to find out the right things to at least try. So guess what? You're already a good parent.

Fears that something awful will happen to the baby

We all get those. They fade with time. If you find that they're the focus of most of your waking life, see your doctor.

Magazine envy

Well yes, don't the babies in the magazines look adorable! Aren't their clean little nurseries so full of gadgets and pale gingham flouncy French things and perfect furniture and expensive toys! Nobody really lives like that. Magazine people have teams of stylists running around deciding what a baby's room should look like, and many of them have had nothing to do with babies since they were one. If it makes you feel better, use the magazine to light the fire. One homewares mag I read suggested bolting a raffia basket to the top of a chest of drawers for a change table. (Anyone for hints on how to get liquid poop out of raffia?)

And can celebrity mothers please shut right up? Oh, they're all so radiantly happy and say such stupid things about how sexy they feel with a new baby and how unremittingly marvelous it all is, and never mention their postpartum depression or their 24-hour team of nannies and how they have nothing else to do all day except stomach crunches. Ignore them! And if necessary stick pins in the eyes of their photographs, for they be the Devil.

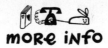

more info

PREEMIE BABIES

Twins: A Practical and Emotional Guide to Parenting Twins by Katrina Bowman and Louise Ryan, has a practical section on looking after preemie babies and coping with the realities and emotions of the situation (for full details and review see More Info at the end of the Multiples chapter in *Part 5: Stuff*).

www.preemie-l.org

A website for parents of preemie babies with discussions, answers to common questions, fact sheets, and links to other relevant sites.

New mom Health

You and your baby will have a check-up with your obstetrician about 6 weeks after the birth. (I recommend you wear pasties on your nipples and a sombrero, just to indicate you're doing fine.) While being concerned about your baby, don't forget yourself: you are a child of the universe. Or at least a confused woman in a ludicrous track suit.

...that can't be right, surely?

Recovery from the Birth

Childbirth is still a big health risk for women. Don't be surprised if body and soul take a while to recover from such a stressful event. Even if your experience was relatively easy, your mind and physical self will still need time to heal.

After your baby is born, you have a kind of period (known as the lochia) so that all the blood and tissues from the wall of your uterus, which nourished the baby, can come out. This will go on for 2 to 6 weeks, and starts off as a heavy period with some small clots, then gets paler and paler and eventually stops. Don't use tampons because they are more likely to cause an infection as the cervix slowly closes. Tell your obstetrician immediately if the bleeding doesn't happen; it suddenly turns bright red after being paler for a while; there are large clots; or it has a yucky smell. As your uterus contracts to help expel the lining and shrink down to its normal size, you may feel some cramps like period pains.

You should be healing well: any bruising or stitches should be dissolving. If you can, have therapeutic massages. Treat yourself as you would your best friend who's just been through the same thing. For heaven's sake don't be leaping about with a hockey stick trying to prove you can do it all.

Women who have had a difficult labor—or an emergency cesarean—will probably need to talk and cry about it, and then move on when they are ready. You can do this with your friends and family, mothers' group, midwife, doula, or a postpartum counselor at the hospital or one that your doctor can refer you to.

Recovery from a Cesarean

The injuries caused to your body are at least as severe as those caused by a serious car accident: they've cut through about seven layers of your body. Your scar will be itchy and may heal as a ropey line: some say massage with vitamin E will help, some say take vitamin E capsules, and others say nonsense to both ideas. Good, healthy food will speed recovery. Having a cesarean makes it much harder to look after a baby in the house. You'll need help: ask for it. Go easy on yourself.

Make sure you find out from your doctor what you can't do: usually no picking up of anything except your baby for 6 to 8 weeks (that includes the shopping and the washing basket); no reaching above your head to lift anything at all; no driving for a few weeks—that sort of thing. Don't tire yourself out. Do half as much each day as you think you "should." You'll be shuffling about from the pain of your wound. Make sure your obstetrician or GP gives you some effective pain relief for the first week or two at home.

NUTRITION

Eat as well and heartily as you can, particularly if you're breast-feeding. Special breastfeeding or women's vitamins are probably a good idea, although they're not as well absorbed by the body as nutrients from food: your pharmacist can advise you about reputable brands, or you can carefully read the labels at the supermarket and choose an appropriate one. Basically try to keep up with your body's needs, which will be higher if you're breastfeeding. Have things you can eat in the middle of the night if you get ravenous, snack-monstery feelings: soy milk and a banana perhaps, or a vegetable muffin. Or indeed a block of chocolate. Sorry. Try to eat different kinds of veggies and fruits every day—don't get stuck on just carrots and zucchinis. Try to get some protein in at every meal: cheesy omelette, tuna sandwich, tofu mountain. Rice with protein and veggies is filling and quick, as is a potato or a sandwich. Chicken and veggie soup is sublimely useful. And great hunks of toasty, crusty bread can be dipped into oil and dribbled on a passing sailor.

SEE YOUR DOCTOR AT ONCE IF

✳ you have a worry.

✳ anything is swelling up or getting redder.

✳ you have any stinky or yucky discharge from your vagina or your cesarean wound.

✳ you have a high temperature.

✳ you ha\ any shortne of breath.

✳ you find a lu in a breast (this lead to mastitis).

✳ you're depressea

✳ you're never hungry.

postnatal fitness

Hospitals all have physical therapists on board, and many have post-partum exercise classes that teach the basics. Your hospital should have already given you a pamphlet or some sort of information on exercise and fitness (and see More Info at the end of this chapter). There will be different stuff to do, depending on whether you had a vaginal or a cesarean delivery. A physical therapist can help you work out what exercise you can do to recover from a cesarean. Physical therapists are listed in the Yellow Pages, or ask your doctor for a referral.

If you take up or resume exercise, it's imperative that you are taught and supervised, initially by a specialist in postpartum exercise, so make absolutely sure the person you choose is not just a general instructor. Take any exercising slowly, with an approved trainer, or a community group or a class run by someone trained in post-pregnancy yoga or Pilates. Tell the instructor you're recovering from the birth. Do not under any circumstances buy celebrity or supermodel exercise tapes or DVDs.

Sneezy pee

You may have noticed that your pelvic-floor muscles are so weak that you pee a little if you sneeze or laugh. The pelvic strain is caused during pregnancy by the weight of the baby on your trampoliny pelvic floor.

To avoid a small pee, try tensing, sitting down, or crossing your legs before the sneeze or laugh. The only way to really stop it permanently from happening is to tighten your pelvic-floor muscles by exercising them.

You can find your pelvic-floor muscles by "holding it" for a minute before you pee, or stopping the pee midstream and then starting again. That's what you need to do without the pee factor: tighten and hold those same muscles for as long as you can, then repeat until you're sick of it.

Current wisdom (which keeps changing) is to do the exercises as often as you can until it's tiring. Some people put red sticker dots around their house and do the exercises every time they see one. (In a similar exercise you can scream every time you see the chairman of the federal reserve on TV. It does nothing for the vagina, but I find it passes the time.) If all else fails, you can buy thin panty pads in case of unscheduled pees, and get an obstetrician's referral to a specialist.

Your back

The most important priority for you is to protect your back, especially after a cesarean (see the Recovery from a Cesarean section earlier in the chapter). Your core muscles—your abdominal and lower back area—may now be very weak, leaving you vulnerable to lower back injury or strain.

Core muscles can be built up using specialized yoga, Pilates, or other exercises. You must not be doing any abdominals such as sit-ups if your rectus muscle has separated during the pregnancy (a common, hernia-like condition): ask your obstetrician, GP, or personal trainer to check.

Make sure all your equipment such as the baby bath and changing table are at a good height. Always lift heavy things with bent knees, and squat down instead of bending over for actions such as picking up your baby from the floor. (If you have a toddler, squat in front of the stroller to fasten or undo the straps: don't bend forward from your position at the handles behind the stroller.) Your baby is just going to get heavier so start strengthening your back now, or at least avoid injuring yourself.

Resuming sex

A fall in libido is probably a mixture of hormonal changes and wanting a rest for your body, or more sleep, or George Clooney. Many women feel that their body has been through enough, and has enough to do, and want a rest from sex. Some women are worried about what their body looks or feels like now—please believe your partner when they say they still find you sexy. Sex should be mostly about how we feel, not whether we look particularly like Uma Thurman. Otherwise only Uma would be doing it, to herself.

If you don't feel like sex, talk with your partner about why: the best way to keep the relationship working is to talk about your feelings. And work out ways you might become less tired.

COMMON FEELINGS ABOUT SEX

* Never again.

* I'm too tired.

* Leave my body alone: someone's already getting milk out of it and it's recently been inhabited. I want it to myself for a while.

* I may have sex again if I ever want another child.

* I can't see the point now I've had a baby.

* It's fine with me as long as you don't wake me up.

If vaginal dryness (caused by an estrogen drop in breastfeeding women) is a problem, use a lubricant—olive oil is good (you can even use extra virgin!).

Ask your obstetrician when you can have sex again after the birth: usually you're told 4 to 6 weeks. (Some guys say they've been told it's 4 to 6 years.)

Contraception

Please use it unless you want to get pregnant again. Breastfeeding is NOT a guarantee you won't get pregnant: some people ovulate in the first few months and get caught out.

Some forms of contraception can have the effect of lowering the libido. Many breastfeeding women are prescribed the Mini Pill as it's less likely than the stronger Pill to cancel out the hormone prolactin and so interfere with the breast milk supply. By the way, women on this sort of contraception should still look out for the symptoms of ectopic pregnancy, which happens when the fertilized egg implants itself outside the uterus (usually in a tube). Symptoms, which tend to occur at about 6 weeks, may include abdominal pain, either on one side of the abdomen or more generalized and which come and go; spotting or bleeding; dizziness, faintness, paleness and sweating; nausea and vomiting; sometimes shoulder pain; and sometimes a feeling of pressure in the rear.

Please have condoms near the bed and use them if you suddenly get frisky unless you're just so fine with the idea of two kids under 3 (or more if you have twins!). Talk to your GP about contraceptive options.

mom's weigHt

While you might be feeling proud about every weight gain of your baby, and loving kissing every funny, pudgy baby roll on their thighs, you might be feeling the exact opposite about yourself—well, unless you're one of those moms who snaps back to pre-pregnancy weight without thinking about it.

Moms who have trouble keeping weight ON after pregnancy, and especially those who want to breastfeed yet keep losing weight so much they can't keep up a milk supply and feel rundown, need to see a nutritionist or their GP to get help to maintain a weight-gaining, nutritional diet.

Right. Put on a lot of weight during pregnancy? Can't believe what you look like now? Heck if you know how to start getting it off?

1 Don't read women's magazines with stories about celebrities who are the shape of Chupa Chups with gravity-defying bosoms a week after the birth. They're freaks. Rich, pampered, freaky freakified freaks who are just a little too on the freaky side. And this is no time to be concerned about what Elizabeth Hurley did with her ass.

2 Banish all full-length mirrors from the house. Either put them in the shed or tack some dark fabric over them. You won't be needing them for a while.

I used to be a pear, now I'm a quince

3 Search through your clothes and make a big space in your wardrobe for the stuff you can wear right now—maternity, stretch, wrap, whatever. Just make it so every morning you're not searching through clothes you can't wear to get to things you can.

4 You are officially not permitted to worry about your weight for at least 4 months after the birth unless your obstetrician tells you you have a serious health problem that must be addressed by weight loss in that time.

5 Exercise. You need to be fit and strong to do the things a mom has to. Don't think of exercise as being only about weight loss. If you are self-disciplined, set yourself some goals and work towards them. Day One: walk around the block and sit in the park. Day Two: walk around the block twice. Week Seven: briskly walk 1 or 2 miles, depending on you. Start at your own pace and work towards being "puffed" for half an hour to an hour every day. Or you might prefer the idea of walking the stroller solo while listening to a personal tape or CD player or enjoying the sounds of nature. Try to avoid traffic and stressful areas if possible. If you've had a cesarean, make Day One getting to and from the mailbox, and proceed more slowly with the suggested build up of exercise.

If you'd rather have company, plan to exercise with a friend or join or start a moms' exercise group, which could be part of your moms' group in the neighborhood. Your group could employ a yoga teacher or personal trainer very cheaply by all pitching in. A trainer could set up a few "circuit" programs and then you could run them yourselves. (Supervision is always important for new things such as weights and yoga-style exercises.) Or do without by just getting together to walk once, twice, three times a week.

An everyday routine will soon have pounds you won't miss coming off. I know walking quickly is much harder when you have a baby *and* other children. If you can't use a double stroller, you can maybe arrange with a friend to mind each other's kids so that you can take turns to walk. Or do your exercise before your partner goes to work or after they return, or on your way home from work.

6 Don't even think about dull or fad exercise programs, such as walking around the kitchen table a berzillion times, because you "can't" leave the house, or ridiculously expensive exercise "machines" bought off latenight TV that look like they're made out of a bike frame and a rubber band and would have your back hurt and your eye out.

7 Fresh air, a change of scenery, and social interaction are all good blues busters too.

8 Forget about fad short-term diets with low calories. If you need help to work out a healthy, long-term eating program, ask your GP for a referral to a nutritionist. (See also More Info, which follows.) Get outside

9 Keep reminding yourself that any sensible weight-loss scheme means that losing 2 pounds a week, max, is realistic. (It may need to be even less for you—check with your GP.)

P.S. They say breastfeeding causes weight loss, especially after the first 4 months of it: this doesn't work for everyone. Don't believe claims such as "Breastfeeding burns 500 calories a day" because (a) it's crap and (b) this is no moment to find the time to count calories.

MORE INFO

POSTPARTUM FITNESS
www.babycenter.com
Has specific postpartum exercise and nutrition tips (search postpartum exercise). Other baby websites do too and there's a list of them in More Info at the end of the first chapter, In the Beginning.

www.storknet.com

Includes a great section on health and fitness with illustrations and a day-by-day postpartum exercise routine. Click on the "Nutrition for Two" link, then scroll down to find the link to "Exercise After Pregnancy."

MOM'S WEIGHT

If Not Dieting, Then What?

by Dr. Rick Kausman, Allen and Unwin, 2004.

A book about weight issues and a realistic and self-friendly future. There is a "little book" version called *Calm Eating*.

www.ifnotdieting.com

This is Dr. Rick Kausman's website. An anti-dieting website, with fact sheets, helpful information about weight loss and details about No Diet Day (May 6).

BOOBS

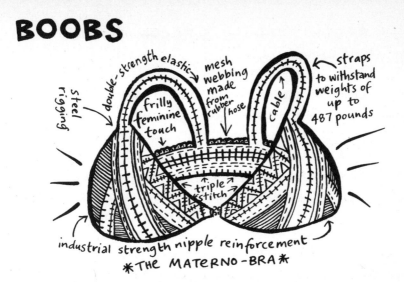

steel rigging
double-strength elastic
mesh webbing made from rubber hose
frilly feminine touch
cable
straps to withstand weights of up to 487 pounds
triple stitch
industrial strength nipple reinforcement
✳THE MATERNO-BRA✳

Whether you're breastfeeding or bottlefeeding (of which more in the next chapter, Bottles), remember that a newborn baby is as new to this as you are. Their digestive system has never worked like this before. It may take some time. They've never had air trapped in their insidey bits before, and until they burp that air up or fart it may hurt their tummies—a most unpleasant feeling they never had before they were born. Together you'll work it all out.

WHy BReastfeeding is Recommended (if you can)

Breast milk has so much good stuff in it the scientists haven't even worked out all the benefits yet. Not only is it full of exactly the right combination of vitamins, minerals, fats, and other compounds for optimum health, but it also has stuff that boosts a baby's immune system. Literally hundreds of elements are all packaged perfectly to be absorbed properly and quickly by the baby's body. Babies need special fats and cholesterol for growth and development, all of which breast milk has. It's got anti-infection stuff and agents to help digestion, and it doesn't have things in it that a baby's kidneys find hard to process. Many of these components can't be reproduced in formula milk.

The current expert line is that babies will get some of breast milk's benefits even if they're only breastfed for a short time, but they will probably benefit fully if they breastfeed for at least 6 to 12 months.

Good points about breastfeeding
★ Breast milk has all the necessary ingredients.
★ Breast milk has important health and immune system benefits.
★ Breast milk is portable and on tap.
★ Breast milk is free.
★ Breast milk is always the right temperature.
★ There are no hygiene contamination problems.
★ Breastfed baby poop smells better than bottlefed baby poop.
★ The baby won't be allergic to breast milk.
★ The baby usually doesn't get constipated.
★ There's an immense feeling of pride in being able to, just with your own body, keep your baby alive and healthy.

"I am lucky—breastfeeding came very easily to me and is a part of babyhood I savored, and missed dreadfully once they were weaned. [But] it's your decision alone, and nobody else's business!"
TIFFANY

Possible drawbacks of breastfeeding

★ The baby is totally dependent on you: some people love this idea, others don't.

★ It can cause problems such as the infection mastitis.

★ Breast milk will carry drugs or illnesses from you, which can affect the baby.

★ People assume that breastfeeding is a contraceptive. For some women this is true for about 18 months, for others it is never true. If you want to avoid another pregnancy for the time being, make sure you use condoms: you can't be on some of the Pills as the hormones will go through your breast milk to the baby (ask your doctor).

★ Your breasts can leak at embarrassing moments.

★ If you want someone else to feed the baby, you'll have to express the milk.

★ You have to wake up (sometimes barely!) for every night-time feed. In the early days this can be incredibly draining and put you into a brainless, starey state that only gradually, gradually gets better as you start getting more sleep.

★ You get short-term memory loss, extreme fatigue, and other symptoms such as putting the car keys in the freezer.

★ You really need someone to look after you in the first weeks by feeding you nutritious things and taking the housework weight off your shoulders.

"Breastfeeding is something you both need to learn to do."
LIBBY

65

Bad reasons to continue breastfeeding

★ Guilt: a feeling that you'll be a lesser mother if you stop.

★ Pressure from partner, friends, or family.

★ You think it will help you lose weight (it depends on the individual: for many people it makes no difference).

★ Your baby is more than a year old and wants to wean but you love breastfeeding too much to give up.

★ You think it will affect your child's future health or intelligence: there are many factors that come into play for that, not the least of them genetics.

"I ended up doing it to keep my husband happy, even though my son and I would both be in tears trying to get it right."
MOTHER WHO BREASTFED FOR 6 MONTHS

Bad reasons to stop breastfeeding

★ It didn't work the first time.

★ You can't be bothered.

★ All your friends have stopped.

★ You reckon it would be easier to use bottles (it isn't necessarily).

★ Partner or family pressure.

Some reasons why it might not be a good idea for you to breastfeed

★ You can't make enough milk to keep your baby growing and happy. Some women don't produce enough prolactin, the hormone that controls the milk supply, so they can't make enough milk for their baby (luckily this is rare, and you could well be able to combine breast- and bottlefeeding).

★ Your baby can't suck effectively: some babies have a real problem with learning to suck properly, and a few are never going to get it together.

★ The difficulties you have experienced trying to breastfeed are affecting your relationship with your baby, which is more important than your baby's relationship with your boobs.

★ You've tried everything, received help from all sorts of groups and individuals, and it still isn't working.

★ You are so against the idea of breastfeeding that if you do it you will resent the baby.

★ Breastfeeding or its side effects (such as chronic mastitis) are consistently making you ill or depressed.

★ You have an illness such as HIV that could be passed to your baby through the breast milk.

★ You smoke, drink alcohol, or take other drugs: even if you don't do this often, you shouldn't be breastfeeding. Some people have an occasional glass of wine—but even this does affect the baby.

★ You've had breast surgery: any kind can make it physically difficult or impossible to breastfeed.

★ You need to be on a medication that will go through to the breast milk and won't be good for your baby, or which

MEDICATION AND BREASTFEEDING

Many drugs are okay to take while breastfeeding, but **always** check with your GP and pharmacist about **any** medical or herbal preparations, whether prescribed or off the shelf. Many herbal preparations as well as drugs can be very dangerous for pregnant or breastfeeding women because of possible damage to the baby.

Pharmacies can tell you which drugs go through to breast milk and whether it's a problem for a baby (see More Info at the end of this chapter).

interferes with milk production. This is especially true for women who need to be on a high-dose antidepressant or anti-psychotic drugs—it's so much better for the baby to have a happy, sane mother and a lovely bottlefeed.

If you've decided to bottlefeed, tally-ho on to the next chapter, Bottles.

"I encountered a lot of opposition when I gave up, but both kids were lactose intolerant and had to go on lactose-free formula."
AMANDA

"I ended up with acute mastitis, a temperature of 107 degrees for 4 days, and a hospital stay to have the lumps surgically removed. And still the do-gooders insisted I should feel guilty for not wanting to continue breastfeeding."
MOM WHO BREASTFED FOR A MONTH

"Every woman is capable of breastfeeding her baby and you should try to do so." A BOSSY BABY BOOK

"Oh shut up, you bossy baby book!" ME

tHe fiRsT DaYs

Colostrum

Breast milk doesn't come in until 3 or 4 days after you've given birth, as your body switches from baby-inside-you hormones to baby-outside-you hormones and pumps out its new, large output of pro-lactin, allowing your body to make breast milk. But your little one still gets to snack because in the meantime some yellowy stuff called colostrum comes out of your breasts, which is really good for babies (body builders take formulas with animal colostrum in it—euww).

Human colostrum's full of antibodies and mysterious ingredients that help the baby's digestive system gear up for a totally new way of ingesting, now that the whole umbilical cord thing is out of fashion.

Newborns lose weight

Your baby will lose some weight before the milk comes in. So despite the fact that people in hospital run around weighing babies all the time and telling you they've lost a few ounces, you are not to worry! Unfortunately, the impression sometimes given is that babies have to be breastfed, breastfed, breastfed (no pressure) to get that weight back on, creating unnecessary stress for a new mom trying to work out how to breastfeed. Remember nobody used to weigh babies and know about 5 ounces here or there—and your baby is almost certainly fine.

getting started

Most people have some sort of trouble getting started: like anything, breastfeeding takes practice to find a successful technique. After all it's quite possibly the first time you've had to do tricks with your boobs—and the fact that it's "natural" to breastfeed doesn't mean that knowing how to do it comes naturally. We don't every day see women around us breastfeeding so don't blame yourself if you feel awkward! Most people take a while to get used to breastfeeding.

Moms who've had more than one baby say that breastfeeding depends on the kid: with some it's easy, with others it's hard. It doesn't seem to get easier or harder with each child—it's just the luck of the draw. So you mustn't blame yourself if it's difficult.

All the women I know had some kind of problem, and the ones who went on with it were only really hitting their stride and feeling fully comfortable at about 3 months: then many went on to breast-feed for a year or more—even the ones who had inverted nipples or painful breast infections. The first month or so will always be the hardest. Expect some hurdles and know you'll usually be able to get over them. If you can't, there's the bottle so don't panic, and always feel you've got the time to have a second or third go at a new technique: your baby won't starve as long as you are under the care of a good lactation consultant, doula, or GP (see the second chapter, Your Support Team).

There's so much new information to pick up when you're in hospital, don't be afraid to ask anyone to go over something once more or to sit with you and help you try again. Once you've left the hospital, it's almost inevitable you'll need further help or reassurance, especially with hospital stays getting shorter and shorter. It's a guaranteed recipe for getting into a state and results in many women giving up breastfeeding when all they needed was some practical advice.

It's always much better if you can have someone show you, and then just refer to written notes to remind yourself. Often midwives or well-meaning friends and relatives will tell you different things: one will recommend the "football hold," another will say wait until the baby opens up for a yawn and then whack them on the nipple. Choose one whose approach you like and only listen to them. I ended up getting a lactation consultant and just listened to her, which was the best thing I ever did. My theory usually is, when in doubt make sure you get a specialist.

The hospital where your baby was born has an obligation to help you with breastfeeding even if it discharges you before your proper milk comes in (which is appalling). If a hospital tells you its lactation consultant is busy or on vacation or can't come until next week, kick up a stink. If you're too tired, get your mom or your partner or an in-law or a friend to do it. Make enough fuss until it's worth the hospital's while to shut you up by obliging you. Call the supervisor, the hospital manager, your local member of state government.

Put the heat on. Threaten to call *20/20* if you have to. (But don't—it's too stressful.) Other than that, see the list of contacts in More Info at the end of this chapter. It's important to get help quickly before it all becomes too difficult, or before a milk-duct blockage becomes a serious mastitis infection.

> *"I went home on Day 3 from the hospital just when my boobs were lusciously sore and lumpy and me having no idea how to breastfeed. So 3 weeks was IT."* JANE

How often to breastfeed?

Newborn babies usually feed eight to twelve times in a 24-hour period. In the early days you will have to try to muddle through, but to give you an ideal "textbook" situation (I know, I know, we're not textbooks), your aim would be to feed the baby every 2 to 3 hours during the day and when they wake and cry during the night—unless they wake every hour or two, in which case they may just be feeling a bit freaked out about not being in the womb and need a rock back to sleep.

Some nutcases say you should feed babies only according to the clock (for example every 4.5 hours), no matter how long they cry. This does not account for the needs of individual babies or natural variations in a baby's requirements or growth spurts. On the other hand, although breastfeeding as often as you like in the first weeks will help you build up a constant, replenishing supply of milk, it will leave you a zombie if you wake up every couple of hours to feed the baby.

Try to give a complete feed at intervals of 3 to 4 hours rather than get the baby used to snacking or top-ups every 2 hours. This may be easier after the first 3 or 4 weeks. Sometimes a baby may genuinely need

snack time, please, oh bosom lady

a feed in 2 hours, but often this is just habit—it's impossible to tell but try not to feed every 2 hours as a regular habit. Be aware that you can get yourself into a vicious circle of feeding your baby little bits too often: you'll need to gradually extend the time between breastfeeds.

I finally worked out my baby wanted a feed pretty much exactly every 4 hours–which is the case for many babies by the second month (but not all of them!). Despite the fact that a telephone information-line Boob Lady told me to feed her if she cried (the baby, not the Boob Lady), any breast milk dispensed between the 4 hours was always projectile vomited a minute later. I just needed time to get to know my baby, and I was too worried to wait. I didn't know why she was crying and I wanted an answer on the phone NOW.

Sometimes it's just a matter of trying to be calm enough to let things happen. This is a philosophy that has always made me want to repeatedly strike hippies with a hockey stick. (How infuriating that on this issue they are absolutely right. Damn it all to hell.)

"Escape from the extremes of scheduled feeding has led some mothers into difficulties with the extremes of demand feeding."
PENELOPE LEACH, YOUR BABY AND CHILD

"Watch your baby, not the clock."
MARTHA AND WILLIAM SEARS, THE BREASTFEEDING BOOK

How long to breastfeed for?
In the early days feeds tend to take between 30 and 50 minutes in total (both boobs). The time usually gradually reduces. Eventually you'll probably be feeding only 7 to 10 minutes on each breast.

Incidentally the first weeks are no time to be going "back" to work or becoming the unassisted chief executive officer of a house—even though that's exactly what may be happening to you. If you've chosen to breastfeed you need to allow yourself time and energy to concentrate pretty much solely on that, as well as to get to know your baby, to give yourselves some fresh air, and to recover from the birth. Eventually your baby will develop a rhythm of feeds.

Breastfeeding privacy

It's possibly best for everyone in the first few weeks if you leave a crowded room so that you can concentrate fully on breastfeeding and have time alone with your baby. While totally believing breast-feeding should be allowed to happen anywhere, you may find that a quiet corner in another room or a discreetly draped diaper will allow you to avoid having to deal with distracting conversations (for you and the baby), ludicrous disapproving stares, or the under-standable embarrassment of male relatives, in-laws, and friends who don't know where to look because they're trying to be respectful but end up feeling dreadfully uncomfortable.

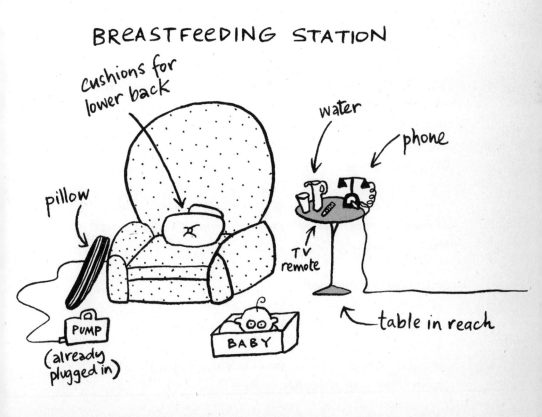

BREASTFEEDING STATION

cushions for lower back

water

phone

pillow

TV remote

table in reach

PUMP

(already plugged in)

BABY

LeaRNiNg How to BReastfeeD

After a few weeks you'll probably be able to breastfeed upside down on the monkey bars at the local park, but in the beginning you may need to set up a comfort zone at home. Choose a rocker or armchair as your breastfeeding HQ. Next to the baby's bed is perfect, especially for middle of the night feeds. Make sure the room is warm. On a side table put a big glass of water or a bottle of water and a glass. You need to drink a lot during the day if breastfeeding, and you'll sometimes feel thirsty during a feed when you can't get up.

You may also want a pencil and notebook if you're recording which breast you need to start on next time, and how long each feed is. You don't need to do this, but I found it quite useful when I was brain dead. (It hadn't actually occurred to me that if the baby fed every few hours I would have to be awake every few hours.) The lack of sleep makes everything harder–including trying to remember which boob you started with last time. After a while you'll gain confidence and forget to make notes. Later you can look back and laugh at your funny lists with "L 25 min." and "R 17 min." on them.

If you're out shopping and need to feed your baby, go to a large mall or department store and use their ladies' lounge or mothers' room, which should have a couch or armchair to sit on. Otherwise a corner of a café will do fine, or even a park bench or the car.

"If you're out, plan to be in the bigger shopping centers around feedtimes: these days they have excellent parenting facilities at most of them." YOLANDA

Breastfeeding equipment
You'll need:
* maternity bras—supportive, stretchy, your new size, and front-opening.
* a lanolin-based nipple cream or one that's okay for a baby to swallow—ask your pharmacist.

* breast pads—little disposable or washable pads to put in your bra to soak up any leaking milk.
* to carry a spare top and bra and spare breast pads in your bag in case you do leak those big, tell-tale wet circles on your front.
* pillows to help you support your baby and your back.
* hot wheat-filled fabric packs (many are designed for microwave heating) to help the milk come (or used cold to stop your breasts from becoming engorged).
* a hand pump in case your nipples are sore—you can express some milk (see the Expressing Breast Milk section later in this chapter) and give it in a sterilized teaspoon or bottle.

"Using a U-shaped pillow to support the baby for breastfeeds made it easier." AMY

How to breastfeed

Basically choose whatever works for you and your baby. Speak to your baby soothingly and encouragingly. Trying to get breastfeeding going can be stressful if the baby is crying with hunger, and I know it can be hard, but a calm attitude will help you both.

Take a few deep breaths. Sit up straight and make sure your lower back is supported. This means you need to bring the baby to your breast rather than hunching over, round shouldered, to deliver the breast to them.

Put a diaper or cloth over your shoulder in case the baby throws up a little during a break or straight after feeding.

You can try various feeding positions, including laying the baby sideways across your lap, face up, then turning them gently so the baby is facing you and tummy to tummy with you. Another common one involves holding the baby on their side, under your arm, and facing your body, then bringing them forward to the nearest breast, as if you're holding a hungry surfboard (this is the "football

BREASTFEEDING CHECKLIST

✱ Drink a big glass of water and have another one within reach.

✱ Put a cloth over your shoulder for when you burp the baby.

✱ To bring the baby up to the right level without your getting aching arms, and to help if you've had a cesarean, put a couple of pillows on your lap and lay the baby on this high, comfy "tray" (while still holding onto them so they don't roll off).

✱ Talk to your baby and explain what you're doing.

✱ Sit up straight.

✱ Find a feeding position for the baby that's comfy for you.

✱ Start on the breast you didn't start with last time or the one that is fuller.

✱ Get your baby to open wide, by tickling their cheek, so that they take a big mouthful of areola as well as nipple when they latch on.

✱ As your baby opens wide aim your nipple towards the roof of their mouth.

✱ Reattach if the attachment is not a big mouthful, feels wrong, or hurts.

✱ Let the baby have as much as they want on the first breast, and then however much they can take on the second.

P.S.   You don't need to wash or sterilize your nipples after a feed.

hold" or the "French loaf hold"—or any term suggesting carrying something under one arm–that is often referred to). Experiment until you find a position that feels good. Some people prefer to breast-feed lying down, but this seems an unduly restrictive position to have to be in every time.

Support your baby's body and neck, either with your arm or pillows. Remember that tiny babies can't hold their heads up by themselves.

Start with the breast you didn't start with last time. After a while you may be able to tell by feel which is the fuller one; otherwise jot the info down or put a safety pin on the side to start on next time to remind yourself. If being seen in public with a safety pin above one boob worries you, why not substitute a priceless ruby brooch in the shape of a small squirrel?

Tickle your baby's cheek to create the sucking reflex: their mouth will open. Try to get the breast in when the mouth is open wide, wide: if you need a visual idea, go to the supermarket, lurk furtively in the breakfast cereal aisle and look at the curve of the K on the Special K box. Think of your baby's mouth as that K curve. The baby needs to get a big mouthful of areola (the colored circle around the nipple) as well as nipple, not just to suck on the nipple itself, which will be painful for you. If the baby latches onto only the nipple, slip your little finger into their mouth and gently dislodge it. If you just pull the nipple out, it can really hurt.

HOW LONG ON EACH BREAST Let the baby suck for approximately 20 minutes or more on the first breast. Some advisers say there isn't any point in going much over 20 minutes on each breast, but others say a newborn can take up to an hour to get everything they need while they're working up those jaw muscles and swallowing skills. Helpful, ain't it? Some babies suck faster and the milk is squirted out more quickly. (I remember in those first few days it was half an hour each side, and then by 3 months it was about 15 minutes.) So it's probably best to be guided by what your baby seems to want to do, and ask for help if you still feel bamboozled. The baby will pull away when they've finally had enough, and then you can burp them (or not) and snap them on the other bosom until they've had enough there.

BURPING A lot of babies don't need to be "burped," and it's unknown in many cultures. If you want to, you can burp the baby when they have a rest during the feed and then get back into it. After the feed or between boobs, hold your baby upright, peeking over one of your shoulders, and rock and pat until there's a burp–but don't worry if there isn't one. The theory is that burping stops gas from causing tummy pain.

BRAAAP!

lovely

Foremilk, middlemilk, and hindmilk

In the first few minutes at the breast the baby gets a big thirst-quenching, tummy-filling squirt of "foremilk," and then, several minutes in, there are other goodies, followed in the middle part of the feed by different stuff, and at the end there's some important fatty, vitaminy elements that babies like and need, sometimes called the "hindmilk." Look, it's not all that scientific, I know, but basically don't worry. This just explains why you don't do only 5 minutes on each breast, and so you know that over a full day of breastfeeding your baby gets fore-, middle-, and hindmilk without your having to measure anything or be concerned. And even if your baby only does 5 minutes, it's still not panic time—according to some experts 80 to 90 percent of milk volume goes in in the first 4 minutes on each breast!

"It's practically an art form, and takes ages to master it."
ALEXIS

"With both children it worked like a dream—both were keen feeders from the word go." ANN

Breast-milk supply and demand

Unless you have a problem, the more a baby sucks, the more milk your body will produce. This is how people are able to feed twins, and were able to become "wet nurses"—women who fed other people's babies as well as their own. If you stop breastfeeding for a few days, the milk will "dry up" and you may not be able to get the flow going again, although breastfeeding organizations will help you to try: many moms have been very successful.

Anecdotal evidence suggests that older moms, especially those over 40, may have difficulty with supplying enough milk. At this age the reproductive system is winding down and the body produces fewer eggs, so it makes sense. Women who conceive using scientific methods can also find their body isn't geared up for maximum milk supply.

BREAST SIZE   Boob size is irrelevant to breastfeeding—even the tiniest ones are up to the task. All breasts get bigger for breastfeeding.

Getting in a tizzy

You're tired, your brain's on strike, your new baby's crying, you're crying, you feel like you're the only woman in the world who can't get her boobs to do the right thing, and nothing seems to be going right. You feel you might as well start on bottles today, although you're too tired to work out what to do and you'd feel so guilty. But please don't give up without having another shot. You might regret it later. What you need is a fresh eye on the problem. Call someone from one of the breastfeeding support groups (this should be free)

for a private visit from a lactation consultant (usually paid per visit). For heaven's sake, don't mind about calling complete strangers to advise on boob business: that's what they're for. Then, if you do give up, you will always know you did your best and got the best help you could: there's no shame in that.

And get some sleep: sleep between each feed at night and between some during the day. Take the phone off the hook and put a sign on the door saying not to knock (you might like to photocopy the sign supplied in the Sleeping chapter). Or express some milk for someone else to give in a bottle; although some babies are fussy and don't like a nipple, most will take it when they're hungry. It's impossible to make rational decisions when you're very sleep deprived.

A WISH LIST FOR EASY BREASTFEEDING

* As much rest as possible.

* No other commitments apart from baby, at least for the first 6 to 8 weeks.

* A healthy diet.

* Extra food. (Everyone I know got the munchies at 4 a.m. in the early days.) Soy milk and bananas are good.

* No obsession with low-fat products and losing weight— you need fuel for breastfeeding, although you shouldn't be actually gaining weight. Your protein requirements are higher now than they were in pregnancy.

* Lots of fluids–but not coffee, tea, or gin.

* Support from family and friends.

* Perseverance: nearly everyone has early problems to overcome.

* Help: even champion breast-feeders can come across temporary problems.

* Luck: you need to be one of the people who can do it.

Perseverance

Everyone bangs on about perseverance but perseverance itself won't get you through. You need perseverance and good technique (as well as no physical problems) or you just keep persevering with something that isn't working. But it's true that, all going well, what feels clunky and by the book at first becomes, simply with repetition and practice, something you can do without even thinking about it.

The other problem with perseverance is that when you're in the middle of a difficult time, every hour seems to drag and every feed can bring new tension and anticipation of pain and trouble. I can remember someone telling me at 6 weeks that it would all be sorted out by 3 months, and I wanted to hit them. Three months! They may as well have said 2017, it seemed so far, far away. This is a Baby-land situation where you have to take one day at a time, even each hour at a time.

COMMON PROBLEMS

Temporary supply problems

The reasons can include a mom not getting enough fluids and nutritious, filling food; going back to work; being rundown, tired, ill, or stressed; smoking; taking some medications (always check the fine print and talk to your doctor and pharmacist about the effects any medication might have on breastfeeding); starting the Mini Pill (and look out for the signs of ectopic pregnancy: see contraception in the index); using cabbage leaves too much to reduce engorgement, which can have an adverse effect on supply. Or the baby could be ready to eat stuff and want less milk—some time between 4 and 6 months babies show signs of wanting more in the food department.

Home remedies to increase the milk include the rather stinky fenugreek tea or less stinky fenugreek tablets, raspberry-leaf tea or tablets, and blessed thistle herbal tablets, but you must check all these with a lactation consultant or your GP before using them. Make sure you get a mainstream brand, subject to national safety laws, and read the label to check all the ingredients and additives. Feed your baby more often to encourage the supply, and have good nutrition, REST, and lots of fluids.

> *"The best tip I have had for bringing milk in was: while showering direct the shower as close to your nipples as possible and blast them with the warmest water you can stand. Doing this for the first three days of your baby's life seems to help get it going. That and drinking water like there's no tomorrow."* SOPHIE

> *"When at 4 months he started crying for no good reason after every feed I knew something was up. Of course the experts said, 'Just persevere, mother.' Meanwhile he was nearly starving as the quality of my milk decreased. Although clinic nurses have their place they are not always right."* HELEN

La Leche League has a pamphlet called *Establishing Your Milk Supply* (see More Info at the end of this chapter).

Very zingy or buzzy pain in the breast

This is a normal feeling early on in your breastfeeding career and is caused by your body doing as it should, creating a "let-down" of the milk—and telling you you're full of goodies and ready to go. In the first days you may feel contractions of your uterus while feeding as it shrinks. If you have sharp pains in your breasts or under-arm area, especially accompanied by a temperature, you may have a blocked milk duct causing the infection mastitis.

Milk not coming

Try thinking about babies, thinking about your own baby, listening to a baby cry, smelling a baby's head, and/or putting hot washcloths on your breasts and drinking lots of water. My friend Miss Kate used to let down her milk in the supermarket if she heard someone else's baby cry. "It's my 'feed the world' reflex," she would say.

Blocked ducts and mastitis

A blocked milk duct may cause a red mark or lump on a breast: treat by pressing warm packs on the spot and massaging the area before and after a feed. Run warm water on it in the shower. If not cleared, it can become mastitis, a quite common infection, which is often accompanied by a temperature and flu-like aches. Treatment includes cold compresses to alleviate pain; warm compresses or a warm hot-water bottle to maintain the flow; painkillers (check with your pharmacist or GP); keeping the breast empty by offering the baby frequent feeds or by expressing; REST (yes, that means no housework); and, in serious cases, antibiotics to clear the infection: the doctor will prescribe one that doesn't harm the baby. If you have mastitis, you must see your doctor. It can lead to high fever, severe pain, and unconsciousness.

Cracked, sore nipples

These are almost always caused by the baby not being attached with a big mouthful. It will NOT help to "toughen up" nipples by scouring or pinching them! The only real cure is to get the baby positioned in a different, mouthfully way. This is best done with a lactation consultant, midwife, doula, or GP watching you and advising. The most common methods of treating the pain and keeping breastfeeding going are rubbing on naturally based ointments from the drugstore; using nipple shields; massaging breast milk into the cracks and sores; briefly exposing your bosoms to sunlight (but most certainly not to sunburn); and resting your nipples from feeding for 24 hours and expressing milk for your baby instead.

Most breastfeeding experts warn against nipple shields, and say only the thinnest silicone ones should be used and only at the beginning of a feed. The conventional wisdom is that they should be used by women with very flat or inverted nipples to make it easier for the baby to get hold of something to suck. Shields can cut down the milk supply a little because they cut down the sensation of the baby sucking, which stimulates the milk supply, but they work well for some people.

Inverted nipples

It may be difficult to coax those shy, inverted suckers out at first, but most people can breastfeed successfully after some initial nipple pain. Lactation consultants and breastfeeding groups have heaps of hints on how to "pop out" your nipples so the baby can really latch on. The underarm hold is often recommended for women with inverted nipples, and shields and creams are commonly used to try to reduce soreness in the early weeks. According to a friend who had stubborn inverted nipples, medical staff often presume your nipples will just pop out when required, but some people with severe inversion should investigate as much as they can the sorts of techniques or equipment that may help. Don't accept "it will all be fine" if it isn't fine for you, and expect some pain when establishing feeding because your nipples need extra coaxing to come out to play.

"Against advice I used nipple shields the entire time. I guess once he got used to this he wouldn't do it any other way." JOANNE

Thrush

This common fungal infection loves warm, wet areas such as babies' mouths and bottoms, and moms' breastfeeding nipples. It causes a painful red rash. Your pharmacist will have over-the-counter creams and drops, but the rash should be seen by a doctor.

Painfully full breasts

This is also known as "engorgement." Don't worry, most new moms get this rock-hard, possible-exploding-boobery feeling while the breasts are trying to find the right amount to keep in readiness for the baby. After a few weeks the boobs will settle down and feel quite normal in between feeds instead of being all hard and bursty just before each one. As with mastitis, you can relieve the pressure by putting a warm washcloth on your breasts and leaning over the bathroom basin to let a bit of milk dribble or squirt into it; conversely a cold (not icy) pack should calm things down. A cold cabbage leaf cupping each breast is also said to work wonders, but using cabbage leaves all the time can reduce your milk supply.

> *"Cabbages, cabbages, cabbages. Let's be honest, your chest starts to take on the appearance of a bad renaissance painting by the time your milk starts coming in."* TRACYLEE

One breast not behaving
This needs professional help. You can feed with only one breast if you absolutely have to.

Baby pulls away from the breast and cries
There can be a number of causes. "They" say babies may balk at the taste of your milk if you've had an unexpected curry, onions, or garlic—but presumably this doesn't happen in a culture full of that sort of food. Having different tastes in breast milk is a way babies get to know variation. If something you've eaten doesn't agree with them, babies may show distaste but are more likely to have farty problems, indigestion, or diarrhea. Chocolate and citrus upset many newborn babies, according to lactation consultant Margaret Callaghan (see also the later Crying chapter).

The baby might have something making their mouth or throat sore. Check for baby health problems such as thrush.

Some newborns come off the breast at the start or during a feed when they get big squirts of milk (this could be messy so keep a cloth handy). Your supply will sort itself out and your baby will get used to it.

"For lunch in the hospital they served coleslaw and I chose not to eat it because I'd been told it caused problems with gas in babies: mine was the only baby in the ward not screaming during the night and I had a midwife ask me what on earth I had done to have the only angelic baby on the ward. When I told her she was amazed. I found the following to cause problems: cabbage, broccoli, onion, cherries, kidney beans, spicy food." MAREE

Your baby may have a blocked nose so can't breathe very well on the breast—in which case try to clear the nose very gently by taking the baby into a steamy (but not hot) bathroom, putting a vaporiser (from the drugstore) in their bedroom or dabbing some eucalyptus oil on a hanky and waving it under their nose (but not blocking it).

The baby could just be so hungry they're cross and confused, or they may be feeling pain caused by a gassy tummy, a tooth coming, or something else (haven't you developed ESP *yet?*). Use the usual calming techniques, including burping, soothing chat, swaddling, and going to a quiet, dim room for a slow, rocking cuddle. Not easy, but you're supposed to stay calm. (Like when they say "Relax" just before a Pap test—yes, such a soothing atmosphere!)

If your baby continues to pull away and cry, get some advice from your doctor or a lactation consultant. La Leche League has a pamphlet called *How to Handle a Nursing Strike*, which has hints for encouraging a baby back to the bosom (see More Info at the end of this chapter).

"I'd advise perseverance. For me it was mastitis and cracked and bloodied nipples early on, but this sorted itself out in due course and the convenience of not having to prepare countless bottles countless times a night is a good trade-off." KARINA

IS MY BABY GETTING ENOUGH BREAST MILK?

A baby should be growing and putting on a certain amount of weight each month (depending on their individual size). This is one of the reasons you go to those regular weigh-ins at the doctor's office. Babies shouldn't stay the same weight or go backwards between visits.

The other major sign of a problem is screaming or listlessness. Basically a baby who is hungry will tell you by yelling. Unfortunately, the baby doesn't know how to yell so specifically that you get the picture immediately. A baby who is really starving will stop yelling and become lethargic.

A young baby should need six to eight nappy changes in a 24-hour period, and have regular poops as well throughout the day (look up poop in index).

Babies do go through hungry periods and growth spurts, when they seem to want more, and then the rate drops back a little. If you have any doubts or worries, see a lactation consultant or your GP or call a breastfeeding support group.

"My GP told me to stop breastfeeding at 3 weeks because I was so tired, so I stopped cold turkey, got blocked milk ducts and mastitis. I ended up in hospital on a drip and sicker than before (when I was just tired). In the hospital the midwives encouraged me to go back to breastfeeding even though it hurt like hot pokers and sharp needles being jabbed into my nipples but I went on and we made it to 10 months." JULIA

getting Help with Breastfeeding

Some hospitals, like lactation consultants or postpartum doulas, should be able to help. Contact your local one and ask whether they have breastfeeding clinics you could attend. You don't have to have had your baby at the hospital to go to the clinics, but you might have to pay a fee. At these you can put your feet up, have instruction on breastfeeding or expressing milk, troubleshoot any technique problems, and talk to other moms and staff.

The National Women's Health Information Center (NWHIC) has teamed up with La Leche League to provide a toll-free, national breastfeeding helpline. The phone counselors are La Leche League–trained "breastfeeding information specialists" who can offer support, help you with breastfeeding questions, send you free breastfeeding information, and provide referrals to resources and breastfeeding support groups in your area. Their website is filled with helpful information

Lactation consultants can help:

Those things on your front are boobs

Aieee!!

and has links to free downloadable publications. See More Info at the end of this chapter for contact details.

You can become a member of La Leche League, join their local breastfeeding support group, and get lots of newsletters and catalogs for breastfeeding books and paraphernalia and other baby-related products, which you can mail order, often for a lot less than in-store prices. You may have been given their pamphlets in the hospital, and they have a popular book called *The Womanly Art of Breastfeeding*. You can order inexpensive pamphlets for all sorts of breastfeeding situations: inverted nipples, cosmetically altered breasts, cleft palate, Down syndrome, and other special needs, you name it. Their website is a useful source of help and information. (See More Info at the end of this chaper for the details.)

YOUR BREASTFEEDING BODY

What do your boobs look like?

Breastfeeding boobies can look like a road map of Indianapolis, with the veins pushed closer to the surface by all the milk ducts and milk in there. Large breastfeeding boobs hopefully don't get *too* much larger, but expect to go up a full size plus two cup sizes. That is, if you start out a 36 you're likely to be a 38 in a maternity bra. What that will settle down to after breastfeeding is anyone's guess. Some breasts get smaller than before.

Pregnancy itself makes the breasts bigger—everyone has floppier, softer, less pert and pointy-out breasts afterwards, whether they breastfeed or not. Cosmetic surgeons who want your money call this "deformed." Billions of partners around the world beg to differ and love you and your bits just the same. Celebrities who claim pregnancy made their breasts permanently bigger, firmer, and perkier deserve only one reply: liar, liar, pants on fire. And probably boobs as well if they get too close to a naked flame.

Nipples

Nipples have lots of holes, like a sprinkler, for feeding. The aureolae appear darker (they will stay darker forever now) so it's easier for the baby to zero in when the light is dim. Your nipples will stay more prominent.

Some boobery issues

Partners can find the transformation of breasts from sexual objects to life-giving boobs needs a little adjusting to. Some of them don't like to hear breasts referred to with new words that relate to babies and children only, such as "booby" (as in "Do you want some booby?"), "boo-boo" or other baby-talk expressions, and prefer to have them more formally referred to (although presumably not as the divinely romantic "fun-bags"). I'm not saying you have to indulge a partner on this one, but I am saying you may need to be sensitive to the issue if it arises. A good indicator of attitude to breast-feeding is gained by "accidentally" squirting your partner with breast milk. Initial shock is fine, but you may have some psychological work to do if, instead of eventually laughing, they freak out and think it's revolting.

Some partners and older kids want to have a taste of breast milk. It won't do them any harm. But don't do it unless you feel comfortable. You may well feel one (or two) recipients is quite enough.

Does breastfeeding make you lose weight?

Yes. No. Depends. Some breastfeeders start to lose weight after 3 months, some snap back into pre-pregnancy weight within weeks, and others hold onto every extra pound with a white-knuckle grip no matter how much they breastfeed. The best way to lose weight after a baby is slowly, with self-respect, and by walking briskly with the pram. Most of the celebrities who miraculously lose 27 zillion pounds in the first three weeks after pregnancy don't breastfeed. Come to think of it, half of them don't even have a pregnancy, and the other half live on lettuce ends and Peter Stuyvesants.

expressing breast milk

Moms who want to go out or go "back" to work can "milk" themselves with a handheld or electric breast pump that can be rented or bought from lactation consultants, pharmacies, hospitals, specialty stores, and even online. Do compare prices of pumps, which can be wildly different. Some hospitals and HMOs and La Leche League have cheaper deals than stores. If you're going to be expressing milk a lot, get an electric pump. The machine will make a noise (sort of a cross between a sucking noise and a vibrator, from memory, but that can't be right—you'd sound like a porn movie). You can hook yourself up and read while it's rhythmically pulling a nipple into a soft silicone nipple shield attached to a bottle. The electric business seems quite contraptiony, but it's basically very simple. A lactation consultant or instruction pamphlet should be able to help you learn how to use a hand pump or an electric one. The hand pump can give you a very

sore hand from repetitive action. The electric pump is hands-free. Although it's hard not to say "moo." You usually pump both breasts, one after the other, to keep them "even" as you would if you were breastfeeding directly. Or you can purchase a double pump to pump both at once.

The collected milk can be put straight into a sterilized bottle and then the fridge and warmed for the feed in the next few hours, or poured into a plastic freezer bag that can be frozen and later thawed by someone. Drugstores have special bags for breast milk, which funnel into a bottle when it's time to use them and which you can write the use-by date on. Your baby will need to accept a bottle nipple—something many babies reject. Some parents give a bottle of expressed milk a day, or in the nighttime to serve the dual purpose of giving mom a rest and getting the baby used to a teat. Some breastfeeding advocates say this can cause "nipple confusion," with the baby not wanting to go back to the breast, which can be harder to suck on. If you do use a bottle, use one designed to avoid creating bubbles of air (see the next chapter, Bottles).

Try to build up a store of frozen milk for emergencies—for instance, if one is spilled or you can't get home in time for the next feed. (Always carry breast pads for milk leaks and feel free to squirt some milk out if your breasts get too painful—probably not into the air on a bus but, say, into the basin of a locked bathroom.) Remember that the more you express, the more your breasts will think they need to make extra milk, so don't go overboard and try to fill heaps of bottles, freezer bags, or sachets all at once.

Freeze or store the breast milk in single-breastfeed amounts to avoid waste or having to use part of a thawed, second freezer bag for a feed. The bottles you express into will have markings on the side so you'll know when to stop.

Do label the milk properly and let everyone who uses the freezer understand not to tamper with it. Write "BREAST MILK" and the date you pumped it. You may also like to put a sign on the freezer saying "Keep Freezer closed as much as possible! Breast milk inside!" if it's used by lots of people.

> *"Angus is now 6 months old and while breastfeeding we have listened to [as audio books from the library]* The Hunchback of Notre Dame, *a variety of the Brontë sisters' works, lots of Agatha Christie radio plays, and Robert Hughes reading* The Fatal Shore."
> KATE

> *"*The Bold and the Beautiful *can easily be watched in one feeding session when you fast-forward the ads."* HOSHI

Storage times for breast milk

Breast milk should always be immediately put in the fridge after it's been expressed if you're not sure when you'll use it or you're not using it in the next little while, and especially if you live somewhere hot and humid. Stored expressed milk will "separate," but it's still okay—you just need to shake the bottle gently (turn it upside down once or twice, don't treat it like a cocktail shaker) before giving it to your baby.

According to La Leche League, breast milk can usually be kept:

- ★ at room temperature (68°F–72°F) for up to 10 hours.
- ★ in the fridge, stored at the back in the coldest part, for up to 8 days (they describe this as 32°F–39°F or lower).
- ★ in a freezer compartment inside a refrigerator for up to 2 weeks.
- ★ in a self-contained freezer with separate door for 3 to 4 months
- ★ in a deep freeze (maximum of 0°F) for 6 months.

The League also says:

- ★ if milk has been frozen then thawed at room temperature, use within 4 hours.
- ★ if milk has been frozen then thawed in the fridge, use within 24 hours.
- ★ if milk has been frozen then thawed, do not refreeze.

These guidelines are conservative—others will give you up to a week to store breast milk in the fridge. Milk that will be used within a day is better off in the fridge than in the freezer because "the antimicrobial properties of human milk are better preserved with refrigeration," the League says.

Thawing breast milk

- ★ You can take a batch out of the freezer and leave it in the fridge overnight to thaw.

★ Or you can put the frozen container into a saucepan, bowl, or sink of warm water to thaw. Boiling water will curdle the milk and it will be spoiled.

★ Don't use the microwave to thaw or heat breast milk: "research suggests that microwaving changes the immuno-logical and nutrient quality of breast milk," according to the Australian Breastfeeding Association. It can also heat the milk unevenly and cause burns.

★ Don't boil your breast milk. The milk should be thawed and brought gradually up to room temperature, and not made any hotter. Some babies are happy to take milk at room rather than body temperature. This is handy if you're out.

La Leche League has a cheap, useful booklet called *A Mother's Guide to Pumping Milk* (see More Info at the end of this chapter).

Breastfeeding and going back to work

If you want to work outside the home and continue breastfeeding, you'll need to be very organized, and very careful about not getting overtired. Breastfeeding support organizations have lots of hints and info about how to accomplish this. Some workplaces provide a place for mothers to express milk so they can lock the door and don't have to be in a bathroom. (It's about time!)

Breastfeeding twins and bunches of babies

I know it sounds daunting, but lots of people do it and have milk to spare—it's amazing how most women's bodies can keep up with supplying the milk demand, although if your multiple birth was the result of IVF and you are an older mom you may not have the milk supply you would have had when younger.

And if you don't want to do it, here's official permission: you don't have to. It's more important that you're well rested and enjoying your babies and coping well. Anecdotal evidence suggests moms with twins usually give up in the first couple of months or get the hang of it and go on to feed for a year or more.

See the Multiples chapter in *Part 5: Stuff*, which has the contact details for National Organization of Mothers of Twins Clubs for locating clubs and information for parents of multiples. They can put you in touch with people who have done it. The La Leche League website has FAQs (frequently asked questions) and other info about breastfeeding twins or more, and a local leader may be able to get you in touch with other moms who are doing the same thing. (See More Info at the end of this chapter.)

DROPPING BREASTFEEDS

As your baby gets older the feeds will become further apart. The first feed to "drop," if you can manage it, is obviously a night-time one. When people say a baby "slept through" they mean the baby stayed asleep from, say, a 10:30 or 11 p.m. feed until, say, 6 a.m. Eventually many moms get down to just a breastfeed in the morning, the time when their breasts are fullest, or perhaps one in the evening as a comfort before the baby goes to sleep (obviously that one can become a hard habit to break).

The chapter "Possible Routines for Babies" has suggested feeding schedules for babies of various ages, which could suit you. Talking at playgroup to other moms with babies the same age, or to your doctor, can also help you to establish a routine that fits your and your baby's needs and is adjustable as time goes on. Some babies sleep through as early as 6 weeks old, others at 3 or 4 months, 18 months or later—which is why people seek help (see the Sleeping chapter).

95

weaning from the breast

> *"I'm still breastfeeding at 20 months much to the disgust of parents/in-laws who have been encouraging me to wean since she was 9 months old."* NICKI

Everyone who breastfeeds will need to wean their baby—end breastfeeding—eventually. Some experts and people who say "weaning" use it to mean starting on solid foods. This book uses it to mean the end of breastfeeding, or coming off the bottle. (See the Learning to Eat chapter for the other business.) Many moms have the luxury of weaning gradually, others have to wean suddenly because of illness or another reason. Some babies wean themselves gradually—or stop suddenly with no warning.

Most moms in the Kidwrangling Survey suggested that if you're happy to breastfeed until, say, 10 months or more, wean the baby directly onto a cup. You can buy special ones with lids so that the baby can start with a spout, then progress to a straw and finally to a normal open cup. Older babies and toddlers can also learn to drink from those little bottles with pop-up tops like the ones on sports drinks, although you may have to be in charge of the opening and closing. This way you can avoid bottles with nipples altogether.

If you know you'll be weaning onto bottles, try beforehand to get your baby used to the artificial nipples—and someone else feeding them—by giving a bottle of expressed milk or formula once a day. This is when a companion or a full-time live-in nanny (with her own Rolls Royce) comes in terribly handy.

The most common reasons given by moms in the Survey for weaning their kids were:

★ the baby gave up themselves (many mothers described their reaction to this as "horror at the feeling of rejection").

★ the baby got teeth and bit a nipple (some breastfeeding encouragers say you just need to say no sharply, but some babies find this simply hilarious).

★ the moms reached their breastfeeding goal—most often set at 1 year.

★ another baby came along and they didn't want to feed two.

A feeling of "wanting my body back" was mentioned by many.

Expect to have an emotional response to weaning, which may or may not be affected by hormonal changes. Some women feel an aching sense of loss and disappointment, others rejoice in a new-found freedom and independence.

Everyone does it differently. As you'll see, there are a lot of ways to choose from. Do remember that if you wean a baby from the breast before 12 months, you'll need to get them onto formula bottles, not straight onto cow's milk, or they won't be getting everything they need. Any weaning should be done after a chat to your GP about how to replace the breast milk.

Self-weaning babies

US kids with parents who care have a fabulously varied and nutritious diet and access to plenty of yummy food and drinks. It's not surprising that many wean themselves. Try not to take it as a rejection or the end of close, good times with your baby. You're still your baby's most favorite mom of all, and they shouldn't be made to feel they're doing the wrong thing when they tell you they're getting enough nutrition elsewhere and it's time to take your boobs away. If your baby weans independently, feel exultant—you've done your job brilliantly. Self-weaning can happen as early as 8 or 9 months, although it's most common at about 1 year, but some babies will happily go on breastfeeding into their second year or longer. If you definitely want to continue after 8 or 9 months and your baby loses interest, you may need some strategies to continue (see More Info at the end of this chapter for breastfeeding help groups).

When you talk to your GP about the self-weaning, they will be able to make sure your baby hasn't temporarily lost interest in breast milk because they have a sore mouth or some other physical cause.

Many babies wean themselves when their mom is pregnant with the next one. This could be due to the supply, the taste, or other factors being affected by the mom's different hormones.

"I was devastated when my baby self-weaned very abruptly at 11 and a half months. I wasn't prepared for it at all." JILLIAN

"One day he just thought my breast was the funniest thing he'd ever seen and kept laughing when I tried to give it to him. I can take a hint." JULIE

"My baby self-weaned at 10 months much to my disgust and heartbreak!" FRAN

"We swapped for a tricycle." CHRIS

"He got a tooth and two bites later the breastfeeding stopped." LEANNE

"Follow the baby's lead." SHANTE

"She cut back to one feed a day herself, eating more food so not wanting the breastfeed." MELANIE

Fast weaning

If you have to wean immediately or relatively quickly (over 4 or 5 days) for any reason you may spend a couple of days with rock-hard bosoms, wearing a one-size-too-small sports bra to "bind" them, and standing over the basin in the bathroom a couple of times a night with a warm washcloth compress, letting out just enough milk from each nipple to stop the painful pressure, but not enough to let your body think it still has to feed a baby.

The danger of fast or sudden weaning, apart from the possible shock all round, is that it leaves the breasts mightily engorged and vulnerable to blocked milk ducts and mastitis, so keep an eye on yourself. To help breasts during sudden weaning:

★ massage any lumpy bits.

★ use warm compresses to let a little milk leak out to relieve the pressure.

★ use cold cabbage leaves to help relieve engorgement.

★ wear a tight bra, or a very tight shirt over a handtowel wrapped around your breasts—the pressure can help to relieve the pain and some milk can leak into breast pads or the towel.

"I expressed in the shower every morning, just enough to take the pressure off. I massaged my boobs during the day to push lumps out. Sometimes I leaked a bit in my bra. It took about 10 days to be really comfortable and about 3 weeks for the milk to totally dry up." FIONA

"Freeze newborn-sized disposable diapers and put one in each bra cup. Initially (30 seconds) it's freezing, but after that it is pure heaven." JOHANNA

"I weaned my son at 4 months when he was admitted for surgery. I told numerous hospital staff (doctors, nurses, nutritionists, etc.) but no one told me how to go about it. I thought you stopped cold turkey. Even when my son was recovering in intensive care he refused a bottle for three whole days before finally giving in. This was the most horrendous way to wean a baby imaginable. I was very distressed (as was my baby) and was left with hard and painfully engorged breasts. No one told me how to relieve my discomfort or even seemed to care." ELIZABETH

Elizabeth's story above is so heartbreaking. It reminds me that we should all keep talking to each other about how we do various aspects of our child care—not so we can give unsolicited advice with the assumption it will be taken, but to keep discussions going and to keep reminding people there is more than one way of doing something. Nobody should have to go through what Elizabeth did. I'm so sorry she didn't know she could call any number of parent helplines and services for instant help and support.

Semi-fast weaning

Lactation consultant Margaret Callaghan says the following method, compared with fast weaning, is much kinder to you, your boobs and your baby. It involves dropping one feed every 4 days and replacing it with a bottle feed.

★ On the first day of dropping a feed, express a little bit of milk until you feel more comfortable.

★ On the second day of dropping a feed express a little again if you are not comfortable enough.

★ On the third and fourth days don't express.

★ Then drop another feed, but not one on either side of the first one you dropped.

After the last breastfeed is stopped:

★ express on the first day to comfort level.

★ don't express for the next 48 hours.

★ express again to comfort level.

★ don't express for another 3 days

★ express again, then don't for the next 4 days, and so on.

When you get down to only being able to get less than an ounce from both breasts in total, you can "leave the rest to nature to reabsorb."

Marg says that when your baby hasn't had any formula before you wean, you're less likely to have the bottle chucked back at you if the first bottles you give them contain expressed breast milk, or half expressed breast milk, half formula. Gradually increase the ratio of formula until your baby's happy to have 100 percent formula. (For the whole palaver about preparing formula milk see the next chapter, Bottles.)

> "I realized it would be much easier to wean them onto a cup and bypass bottles if I fed them till around 12 to 15 months. There seems to be a crucial point at which you can wean them and they'll forget about breastfeeding altogether, whereas friends who continued till the child was older, say 18 months to 2 years, found that even after they were weaned the kids still wanted to comfort suck." MERONA

> "Be prepared to get really clucky because your hormones go haywire." WENDY

> "Have smaller bras ready for the deflation of your boobs." KIMBERLEY

> "After 3 days of not feeding I felt as though I had postpartum blues again and cried for a while–I guess my hormones were settling down. I wasn't expecting this." SARAH

Gradual weaning

Most moms who weaned gradually suggested dropping a daily feed—say, the middle of the day one—for a week, then dropping the late night one, then the evening one, then the morning one. This way you cut down gradually over a few weeks and the supply adjusts without your bosoms getting a fright. Many moms advised only giving the breast on request, apart from a morning or before-bed feed, then phasing those out too.

> "All the books tell you to take it slowly . . . it still hurts." SAIGE

"Just before her first birthday I was feeding around four or five times a day. I decided to drop a feed every two weeks starting with breakfast. Instead she had a cup of cow's milk. Then 2 weeks later I dropped lunchtime feeds and so on to the dinner feed. By her first birthday she was weaned onto three bottles of cow's milk a day." ALISON

"I weaned his early morning feed at 8 months, his lunchtime feed at 9 months, and his 4 p.m. feed at 12 months, and then his 7 p.m. feed at 13 months." BRENDA

"Try and drop the later feeds—you will still need to do the morning as your breasts will be full. Get Dad to handle baby during a normal feedtime." SUE

"The cuddles continued, the closeness, the holding, so it was just the menu that changed." MAREE

"Unless there is a great rush, drop a feed every 2 weeks."
CAROLIN

"I found that introducing a cup or sipper cup to my children at about 9 or 10 months helped them wean." LIBBY

"Basically I needed to have my body back." KATHY

"Late" weaning

Moms tend to agree that if you don't wean by about a year, either by baby's or mother's choice, it becomes much harder later as toddlers start to use the breast for comfort, often demanding a breast to suck or fondle in social situations when they feel a little uneasy and Mom least wants to participate. But of course, some moms are happy to go on and on.

Every mom who breastfeeds a kid old enough to walk, talk, get themselves a sandwich, and have a chat on the phone, and tall enough to breastfeed standing up when their mom is sitting down, knows the disapproval and shock this causes. Some relish it and encourage their kid to do it as long as possible. Many regard it as an act of defiance against parents and parents-in-law, who see it as a discipline or social acceptability issue. Others are embarrassed and wish they could find a way to stop.

"Some people found me feeding a 2-year-old who hopped off the nipple to join the conversation quite disconcerting." SARAH

"At 18 months the poor kid was getting bruised cheeks trying to elicit moisture from my little breasts. It was obvious it was time to move on. From 12 months we were down to three to four feeds a day, by 18 months it was down to two a day. She was getting adequate liquid from a cup so it was really gaining the courage to accept my daughter was growing up, and being ready in my head to move to the next stage." LISA

"Cold turkey. He would have gone on until he was 18 given the choice." LUPE

"Don't talk to me about breastfeeding . . . mine was still having her 'booey-boos' at the ripe age of 3 and a half . . . I am very sorry to say that the little buggers make their own minds up before you have a say in it at all." PENNY

"I breastfed all four of my children until they were 2 years or more. I found it a beautiful way of mothering. They all weaned themselves when they were ready. They are all adults now but those years were some of the happiest." MARGARET

more info

MEDICATION AND BREASTFEEDING
American Association of Poison Control Centers
1-800-222-1222

GETTING STARTED AND LEARNING HOW TO BREASTFEED
The Breastfeeding Book
by William Sears, MD, and Martha Sears, RN, Little, Brown, US, 2000.
She's a nurse and lactation consultant, he's a pediatrician and between them
they're a parenting advice phenomenon. They're really into breastfeeding,
but also have a great troubleshooting section, a guide to products, and a
chapter on moms and babies with special needs.

Breastfeeding: How to Give Your Baby the Best Start in Life
by Sheila Kitzinger, Penguin Books, 1998.
Bask in the bosom of Sheila, birth and mothering guru from England.
Common-sense, rah-rah breastfeeding advocacy and lots of reassurance.
A general reference.

Getting Started with Breastfeeding video
A useful video for beginners from the Northwest Georgia Breastfeeding
Coalition. You can puchase it for $14.95 from La Leche League.

GETTING HELP WITH BREASTFEEDING
National Women's Health Information Centers (NWHIC)
A project of the U.S. Department of Health and Human Services office,
NWHIC offers a breastfeeding helpline and website.
1-888-220-5446
www.4women.gov

La Leche League

Has a swag of info on the hows and whys of breastfeeding.

www.laleche.org

Promotion of Mother's Milk (ProMoM)

A great site with lots of links to articles, tips, and support for breastfeeding and discussion forums.

www.promom.org

www.breastfeeding.com

Provides info, a newsletter, and downloadable instructional videos.

WEANING

The breastfeeding books given above should help with weaning schedules. La Leche League has a book on weaning called *How Weaning Happens* by Diane Bengson.

BOTTLES

While accepting that breastfeeding is the best possible start for a baby, it's very important to realize that if you're lucky enough to have access to a modern health-care system and access to a healthy lifestyle and fresh foods, bottle-fed kids are on a great track, too.

BOTTLefeeDiNg is YOUR OWN BUSiNess

If you decide to bottlefeed, for whatever good reason, it's important not to feel guilty about it. This is hard because of the constant pro-breastfeeding fanfaronade. Many studies have shown that kids who were breastfed are statistically less likely to get a range of illnesses, and even that breastfed kids "perform" better (I hope they brought their leotards) in IQ tests—but, to be honest, it very much depends on other factors as well, not least of them genes, lifestyle, and access to good medical advice and education. Who sets the IQ tests and what do they measure? What about studies that don't repeat the result? Who paid for the study? There are too many variables to unravel the reasons for how smart children are. How do you measure intellectual curiosity anyway? Bah, humbug! Many breastfed children have allergies and asthma, and many bottlefed kids are absolutely brilliant.

These statistics are not about your individual baby in your caring family in your environment. If you've given breastfeeding a red-hot go and it doesn't work for you, move on. As I said in my book about pregnancy, *A Bun in the Oven*: look at the adults around you. Can you tell who was breastfed and who wasn't?

Good points about bottlefeeding

★ The kid always gets the same thing (breast milk varies in quality and taste according to a mom's health and diet), and you can eat and drink anything you like—curry, onions, a glass of wine—that would otherwise go through to the breast milk.

★ Someone else can feed the baby and enjoy the loving bond and eye contact.

★ You can sleep through the night while someone else gives the night feeds.

★ You know exactly how much the baby has drunk.

★ Babies tend to sleep longer on formula.

★ Your body is now your own again.

★ Most people find it easier to teach a baby to bottlefeed than to get the breastfeeding right.

Drawbacks of bottlefeeding

★ Formula can't supply all the goodies that breast milk does.

★ Formula's harder for the baby to digest because it forms a curd.

★ You have to sterilize bottles and nipples.

★ You need to be careful with quantities and measuring, and it's easy to contaminate bottles. (Poor people in developing countries have made up formula with contaminated water or watered it down to save money, with predictably tragic results.)

★ A baby on formula has smellier poop.

★ Going out and traveling require more planning.

★ When you're away you're dependent on local water supplies and need to find somewhere to heat up a bottle.

★ It costs money.

★ It can take trial and error to find the right bottle nipple for your baby.

★ Formula is much more likely than breast milk to cause allergic reactions.

★ Bottlefed babies are more prone to constipation.

★ Some babies who are used to the breast reject the artificial teat and refuse the bottle for the first few tries: this is usually overcome by hunger and having someone other than the mom feed the baby. (The theory goes that a baby smells the mom and expects breast, if that's what they're used to, but they're more likely to realize they've never had any boob action from Dad or Granny.)

Many people who fear a lack of bonding when forced to give up breastfeeding are thrilled to find that, in the absence of stress about faulty breastfeeding, bottlefeeding is a tender time that can be spent quietly enjoying the moment, free from pain or worry.

"Don't let anyone make you feel guilty if you can't breastfeed. You can still maintain closeness with your child." WENDY

"I didn't have enough milk for my preemie baby and I was under a lot of pressure from health-care workers for him to put on weight. After realiing that he wasn't thriving at 12 weeks I tried a bottle on him and he looked at me with absolute marvel that I had finally given him a decent meal. It's a shame the breastfeeding wasn't a success as I really enjoyed it and am looking forward to trying again next time. I did find out from this, though, that I will never listen to the advice of people who are not directly involved with my children. I knew my son was hungry but I was told that I should never give up breastfeeding as it's the best thing for children. Didn't I try my best as it was?" AMY

Things you get from bottlefeeding as much as from breastfeeding

- ★ The baby enjoys the sucking reflex.
- ★ Intimacy.
- ★ Bonding with your baby.
- ★ The feeling that you're sustaining your baby.
- ★ The knowledge that you're doing your best for your baby and making sure they're as healthy as possible.

"I will not bottlefeed my baby in public because I get disapproving stares from other mothers who feel I am not giving my baby the best source of nutrition. When will society provide information to mothers who can't or choose not to breastfeed their babies?" AUDREY

equipment

Make some space on the kitchen bench: you're going to need some stuff. A large pharmacy in an area where there are lots of kids should be able to give you good advice about available products. Remember that some shops will only carry one brand, but there are several brands to choose from. Drugstores, some supermarkets, and some baby shops will have the best range of bottlefeeding paraphernalia, including sterilizers.

Formula

The important thing to know is that there are plenty of people who make squerzillions of dollars out of formula, the upside of which is that they have a lot of employees working for their companies trying to make the best formula and get it as nutritionally close to breast milk as they can, with some extras such as iron supplements. Formulas, obtained at the drugstore or supermarket, usually come in a big tin with a plastic pop-off top, a measuring spoon inside and instructions. Generally the tins are divided between formulas for babies under 6 months and those for babies over 6 months. After a year babies tend to come off formula and start to drink cow's milk, or a substitute such as calcium-enriched soy milk if necessary, as their solid food should be providing them with most of the nutrition they need. Toddler formulas sold in similar tins are really just vitamin drinks, not the whole nutrition package of a baby formula.

The instructions folded inside or printed on the side of the formula tin will tell you how much you need to give a baby of a certain weight or age (weight is always a better indicator as some babies are tiny and preemie, while others are great hulking cuddlers). Follow the instructions carefully.

Some companies do a ready-made liquid formula. It's much more expensive and needs to be used within 24 hours of opening. Travelers or parents on the go may also like to buy formula packets, which can be added to boiled cold water en route.

WHICH FORMULA? It doesn't really matter: you can even pick the tin you like the look of best. Just make sure it's for the right weight and age of your baby. If your baby has been diagnosed by a nurse practitioner or a GP (not by you or a relative) as having an intolerance, you can use a special formula such as a lactose-free one or one based on soy or goat's milk. Ordinary formulas are based on cow's milk, but have a reduced salt content as a baby's kidneys don't cope well with salt. Formula has more iron and vitamin D than breast milk does, but this doesn't make it better than breast milk. (All babies over 6 months old need iron in their "solid" food or formula.) If

---

DON'T MESS WITH THE FORMULA

You must not try to second-guess dosages. Too little formula powder can result in hunger and distress; too much in an overload of calories and a tummy upset. You are not doing more for your baby by adding more, and babies should never be put on a "diet" of watery formula. Chucking in an extra spoon or putting in less than the recommended amount in the long term can make your baby very ill. Babies on properly prepared formula—or on breast milk—are never too fat. They are supposed to have those lovely jubbly rolls, or not, depending on their individuality.

And you must use a commercial formula made especially for babies. Do not ever try to make up your own formula by using cow's milk or soy or rice milk—or anything else. Your baby's life depends on it: babies have died when people with good intentions have made their own "formulas." It's not like the old days when a Dickensian crone mixed a bit of rice water and flour together to see if a baby could survive long enough to do a spot of chimney sweeping. Millions of babies have been brought up healthy on modern commercial formula. Have a look at the ingredients so you know what a complex lot are going into your baby.

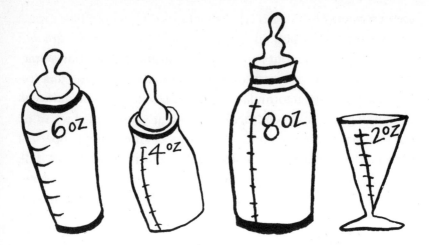

you are opposed to genetically modified foods, make sure you purchase certified organic products. There are no animal hormones in formulas as they are destroyed by the manufacturing process.

Bottles

If your baby will need, say, six bottles a day (see the tin instructions), buy those and a couple of spares in case of emergency or loss. Get all the same brand so the parts are interchangeable. There's no point in buying tiny bottles—soon enough you'll be going up to 8 ounces of milk so get the full-sized ones. Buy bottles with a wide neck as these are designed to reduce the air bubbles that can be gulped down and cause tummy aches.

Nipples

Check out the age-related nipples—there are ones with tiny holes for newborn babies, and ones with bigger holes that allow slow, medium, and fast flows, with maximum flow for older babies. Also check nipples regularly to make sure they don't have bits falling off, especially after your baby gets teeth. Buy as many nipples as bottles plus a few extras.

Sterilizing equipment

You'll need the biggest saucepan or pot to sterilize the bottles, tops, nipples, and anything else that will touch the formula, plus some tongs to fish them out with. If you're going to be doing this for months or even weeks and you have access to money, buy a plug-in electric steam sterilizer. It looks like a big lettuce spinner and acts like a mini-dishwasher that sits on the bench and does the lot and then drains them dry. There are also microwave sterilizers. For traveling or emergencies you can get sterilizing tablets to dissolve in water, but they make things taste nasty and chloriney.

Once a baby starts crawling around and getting a nice supply of immune-system-building germs, there's probably not much point in sterilizing everything that goes into their mouth—but make sure to use very hot water and detergent to wash out all skerricks of milk.

Bottlebrush

Use this to scrub all traces of milk out of bottles, tops, and nipples before they go in the sterilizer.

How to make formula milk

Look on the tin's label to see how many bottles a day your baby will probably need. Keep checking the label as your kid grows because they will need more formula milk. It will still be essential to get the proportions of water and powdered formula right as directed, but your baby will drink more of it—it's not like throwing a good-looking amount of Nestlé Quick into a glass of milk and stirring.

- ★ Sterilize all equipment—if you are using a saucepan for this, the water needs to boil for 5 minutes.
- ★ Boil a kettle of water for making up the formula for 5 minutes, then let the water cool down.
- ★ Wash your hands with soap and wipe them on a newly washed towel.

★ When the bottle or bottles are cool enough, take them out of the saucepan or sterilizer, using sterilized tongs.

★ Fill a sterilized bottle with the number of ounces of freshly boiled water recommended on the formula label (for example, to the 4 ounce mark).

★ Spoon in the exact amount of formula powder recommended on the label, using the measuring spoon provided. Scoop the powder up and then, without packing it down, level off the top with a sterilized knife. (You can just pour some freshly boiled water over the knife to sterilize it, if you like.)

★ Fit the sterilized nipple through the plastic bottle ring using the sterilized tongs, then screw this combo onto the top of the bottle, and snap on the protective see-through bottle cap.

★ Shake the bottle until the formula is well mixed.

★ Immediately put the bottle in the back of the fridge so that it cools down as quickly as possible.

★ Keep all formula powder in the fridge once opened.

★ Warm a bottle just before you serve it. Prepared bottles should only be heated up once.

★ If a bottle is not used within 24 hours, throw the milk away.

I think it's probably nutty to waste time making up bottles as you need them. Most people have a nighttime ritual where they sterilize the used bottles from the day in the six-bottle steamer thingie (which takes 10 minutes or less) or a boiling cauldron of some description. Then they make up the bottles for the next day, plus one with just boiled water in case they need to go out and make one on site somewhere.

> *"Being the mother of twins I found it easy to make up the formula all at once in a jug and then pour it into individual bottles and keep them in the fridge until feedtimes."* TRACY

114

How to warm formula milk

Formula milk should be at body temperature when it's given to your baby—you can check by squeezing a little onto the inside of your wrist. If the milk feels cold, heat it up a little more and test again. If it's too hot, allow it to cool down and test again before giving it to your baby. The milk should be gently warmed up to the right temperature and should never be scalded, cooked, or boiled.

The best way to warm formula milk is to place the whole bottle in a saucepan, bowl, or sink with hot (not boiling) tap water up to about the level of the milk in the bottle if possible, and then let it sit for a few minutes. Shake the bottle gently or turn it upside down once or twice to distribute heat through the milk, without causing bubbles—or let any bubbles subside before testing.

AVOID THE MICROWAVE Heating a bottle in a microwave isn't a good idea: it can lead to hot spots in the milk. If using a microwave is unavoidable because no hot water is available, make sure the milk is left to stand for a minute, then turn the bottle upside down ten times (rather than shaking it as that will create air bubbles). Test the milk's temperature carefully: the formula should feel tepid, not warm or hot.

Never give a bottle without testing the temperature. It can be a good idea, in case you're ever caught short, to give a baby a bottle that is not really cold but not quite tepid either. If your bub is used to this happening occasionally, it will increase the chances of them accepting a colder bottle, warmed under your arm, in an emergency.

> *"My firstborn was a preemie and couldn't suck. My milk didn't even 'come in.' Both of my children were lactose intolerant so they had to have a special formula."* TRACEY

How to Bottlefeed

★ Sit down comfortably, holding your baby in one arm. You may want to "balance" your baby on one or two pillows (holding onto your tike all the time!) to bring them up higher: this can be particularly helpful in the early weeks if you've had a cesarean.

★ Support the baby's head and neck.

★ Tickle the baby's cheek to make them open their mouth.

★ Hold the bottle on enough of an angle so that milk always totally covers the inside of the teat to make sure the baby is sucking milk and not air.

★ Let the baby suck at their own pace, resting as many times as they'd like during the bottle. (Sucking is hard work when you're new at it, or if your parent has put on a teat with a too-small hole for your size.)

★ Immediately the baby has had the last drop of milk, gently disengage the teat from their mouth with your little finger so they don't suck on air.

★ After a pause in the feed or at the end, put a tea towel or a cloth diaper over your shoulder and, letting it hang down your back in case of a little vomit, hold your baby upright, looking over the covered shoulder, and rock and pat them until there's a burp (or not). The theory is to stop that gas from causing pain.

> *"When I was ready to bottlefeed the twins—for me it was about 3 months—I put each baby in a rocker/bouncer and sat between them with my back resting against the settee and a bottle in each hand and off we went. It took the stress out of listening to one baby cry while I fed the other and it was a real milestone for me."*
> JENNIFER

"Make it a quiet time to cuddle and enjoy rather than have the TV blasting." SUE

The sleepytime bottle

Older babies who can hold their own bottle still shouldn't be left with one to leisurely suck on when they go to bed. Give the bottle in another room, then put it away. Do something else such as washing your baby's face or reading a story before finally going through the sleepytime ritual in the bedroom. Otherwise when you want to wean your baby, this bottle part of the nummy bedtime tradition will be hard to give up. Bottles that kids carry around and drink over a long time contribute a lot to tooth decay as the milk swishes against the teeth for ages.

"I found my baby slept better through the night as the formula is thicker and fills tummies better." SHARON

tRaNSPORTiNG fORMULa MiLK

Because warm milk is a breeding ground for germy nasties, it's best when you're out or traveling to heat a bottle right before a feed rather than carry a warm one around with you like a Thermos. Before you go out, take a bottle from the fridge, wrap it in ice or a cool pack from the freezer and a tea towel, with a rubber band around it (you might want something more groovy-looking such as a wine insulator), and place it upright in your handbag or baby bag.

In case of hunger spurts, an accident to the bottle or the original bottle being rejected (if you've already heated it once, you can't reheat it), you could take an extra bottle with just the right amount of sterilized water and add a packet of formula (according to the package instructions) when needed. Because a packet is always the right amount for a big bottle, pour some of the made-up milk out until it's the right amount if your baby is very young. (A few packets could be left in the baby bag at all times, just in case.)

You'll get used to asking café kitchens to sit a bottle in a saucepan of hot water for 5 minutes—always with the cap on to protect the sterilized teat. If people are reluctant (very unlikely), smile sweetly and say "Oh come now, you really don't want this baby screaming with hunger in your café, do you?"

> *"I would fill a bottle with quite hot (sterilized) water, put the right amount of dry formula into another, wrap the water one in a tea towel, then, while I was shopping, when my son was ready for a bottle the water had cooled to the right temperature. Saved me from having to get a shopkeeper to heat the water for me."* KARYN

tRouBLeSHooting

If you are having trouble with bottlefeeding, don't hesitate to check in with your doctor. There may be other resources available to you in your area. (See also More Info at the end of the Your Support Team chapter.)

Constipation

This sometimes happens when bottlefed babies are little or you've just made the switcheroo from breast milk. Also check you're not putting in too much formula powder. A small spoon of sugar in the bottle is an "old wives' cure," and shouldn't be used regularly.

Diarrhea

This is most likely caused by a tiny speck of unclean milk or other agent contaminating the milk—or it has nothing to do with the milk. Step up your cleaning and sterilizing procedures. Also make sure your formula is not too weak and watery. (Look up diarrhea in the index.)

weaning from the Bottle

As your baby gets close to 1 year talk to your doctor about when's a good time to cut formula milk out.

As when weaning from breast to cup, those baby cups with a detachable spout top, and a straw for later, are good to start your kid on, before they graduate to a cup with one or two handles. It's also not a bad idea to teach your baby to drink from a small bottle of water or juice with a pop-up top, or even from a spill-proof bottle of water, such as still mineral water, that can be resealed. This gives you more options when you're out and about. Don't take milk drinks around with you—they spoil quickly and are more likely to result in hideous cleaning-the-vomit-in-the-hot-car scenarios, not to mention very-bad-bus-incidents.

"I changed from a bottle to a non-spill cup at 18 months (or I'd do it earlier) before they became emotionally attached to the bottle."
KATRINA

"One night she went to sleep without her bottle, and didn't wake during the night for it, so I just stopped giving it to her and she didn't miss it." RACHAEL

"My child thought he was a very big boy using a cup, not a bottle."
SUBHA

"By accident I gave the 20-month-old the newborn nipple. He threw it at me. I did this again and he did the same thing, so I thought he no longer wanted the bottle, just his cup . . . I finally realized but I had gone this far so I just left him with his cup." HEIDI

It's not necessary to give a child fruit juice if they eat lots of fruit. And juice, because it lacks fiber, shouldn't be substituted for bits of fruit. Juice should usually be diluted with water by 50 percent as the acid can attack tooth enamel. Watch out for commercial juices in little packs with a straw attached—some are chock full of sugar and many other dubious-sounding things with numbers instead of names (look up drinks in the index).

"The more pressure I put on myself to breastfeed the worse I felt, and in the end I put my babies on formula and never looked back." JEANETTE

"I was worried to tell the nurse that I had decided to bottlefeed, and she was wonderful." DONNA

"I cried for a year because I 'failed' [to breastfeed] and it was such a waste of energy!" JOANNE

more info

www.askdrsears.com/html/0/T000100.asp
Breastfeeding advocate and pediatrician Dr. William Sears answers questions about formula milks and bottlefeeding.

www.avent.com
This commercial website from Avent—one of the companies that sells bottles, nipples, breast pumps, and other paraphernalia—has a list of frequently asked questions and hints for bottlefeeding. Call customer service at 1-800-54-AVENT (1-800-542-8368).

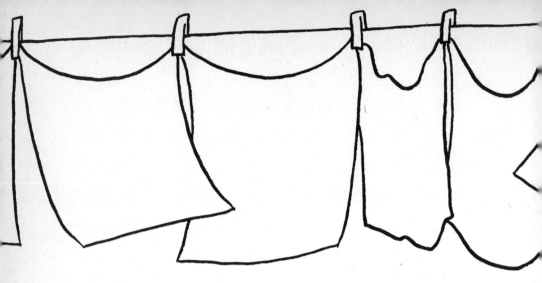

Bottoms

Suddenly you need to deal with someone else's bottom. A baby can go through six to eight diapers a day (that's nearly sixty a week). A toddler just before toilet training will have perhaps three to four a day and, once toilet trained, some kids may still need one at night until they're 4 or older, especially if it's a long, cold trip to the john. According to *Mothering* magazine, more than 90 percent of diapered bottoms in the US are swathed in disposable, rather than cloth, diapers. That's 5,000 to 8,000 disposables in two and a half years for each baby.

HOW OFTEN BABIES PEE

All babies are different but generally really new babies pee a lot—often more than twenty-four times a day in the first 6 weeks. Most are little pees. A slightly older baby pees in larger amounts about every 3 hours, in between each feed, and has quite pale pee. If yours doesn't, they could be dehydrated (look up dehydration in the index): give them fluids and see a doctor immediately.

CLOTH DIAPERS

Cloth diapers are usually flat-weave cotton (always used for newborns) or more absorbent toweling.

Good points about cloth diapers
★ They're reusable for first and subsequent kids.
★ They're the cheapest option, after the initial outlay.
★ Clean ones can be thrown over shoulders to catch baby vomits or turned into rags when finished with.

★ They get uncomfortable more quickly so toddlers are more likely to want to use the toilet, although they will still get there in their own time.

★ Diaper services will take away dirties in a sealable bucket each week and reissue you with clean ones (this makes the cost higher than for disposables).

★ The first few weeks of diaper service is sometimes paid for by friends, relatives, or colleagues as a present.

Bad points about cloth diapers

★ They require *far* more labor.

★ Soaking and washing them is an unpleasant, tedious task.

★ They need to be washed in very hot water. Some folks also use very hefty antibacterial chemical washing powders and if the diapers are poop stained they use savage bleaching products to get rid of the skid marks. Polluted water is the by-product. And if diapers are dried in a dryer, they also use a lot of electricity.

★ They require folding.

★ A couple of days' worth of diapers can become a seething, space-munching, stinky monster in your laundry, which you have to deal with because you're running out of clean ones.

★ It's hard to cope unless you have a whizzbang washing machine and dryer. Although front-loading washing machines use less water and so are better for the environment, they're a lot less suited to soaking and washing loads and loads of diapers, not only because of their lower capacity but also because you usually have to squat down to drag out heavy, wet loads.

★ Cloth diapers are slightly trickier to fasten.

★ They require plastic overpants to stop leaks, and these need to be thoroughly rinsed, soaked in something antibacterial, rinsed again, and hung out to dry or, in an emergency, towel dried. (It may seem obvious to some, especially those who aren't sleep deprived, but don't put plastic pants in the dryer.) Plastic pants can lead to hotter and rashier bottoms.

★ If you have to take your washing to a launderette, I really think using cloth diapers is asking way too much of yourself—most launderettes won't let you wash them there anyway for health and hygiene reasons.

Choosing cloth diapers

You'll need:

★ about 30 to 35 diapers.

★ about 6 to 8 plastic overpants—newborns can dispense with these as their volumes of pee are small.

★ fasteners: either plastic snap-on ones or antique-becoming safety pins.

★ rubber gloves.

★ a special plastic spatula or brush for scraping off poop.

★ 2 big diaper-soaking buckets with close-fitting lids kids can't get off (to avoid accidental drowning).

★ a washing machine with a hot function.

★ antibacterial laundry detergent.

★ lots of clothes-line space and fine weather or a big clothes dryer (clear the lint after each load because it's a fire hazard).

★ 2 waterproof undersheets for the crib (one for the wash, one on the bed).

DISPOSABLE DIAPERS

Good points about disposables

★ They're stupendously more absorbent so don't need to be changed as often and cause fewer rashes. The diapers' absorbency means wetness is drawn away from the skin.

★ They're much less fiddly to put on than cloth ones.

★ Because the bottom stays much drier, the baby sleeps longer.

★ They're ready to go from the package—no folding required.

★ You don't have to deal with the contents of the diaper— just put it in a plastic bag and trash it. (When the big poops start put the contents in the toilet.)

★ The sticky tabs that fasten the diaper can be reused so you can check a diaper quickly and refasten.

Bad points about disposables

★ They're expensive, and cheaper brands are usually not as absorbent.

★ They add hugely to the problem of solid waste (the Environmental Protection Agency estimates they total 1.5 to 2 percent of urban waste; diaper manufacturer Kimberly-Clark points out that food and garden waste makes up 55 percent).

★ Most disposable diapers contain chemicals to make them absorbent: the long-term effects of these chemicals next to the skin are unknown.

★ Even buried biodegradable diapers will take hundreds of years to decompose, and the plantations used for the diaper material may be taking the place of old forests.

★ Disposable diapers get more expensive as the baby gets bigger.

★ You have to empty inside bins often as the discarded poopy diapers are stinkeroo, and by the end of the week the outside bin is pretty on the nose to say the least; deodorized plastic bags to put dirty diapers in cost extra and add to the waste problem.

★ If you see little squishy balls in a wet disposable diaper, that's absorbent crystals leaking out: just wipe them away and change the diaper.

Choosing disposable nappies

You'll need:

* ★ 2 packets of the right-sized diapers (the size is marked on the package). Different ones are sold for boys and girls—something to do with the spouty effect of a willie no doubt—but in a shopping emergency it's not a big enough difference to matter.
* ★ 2 waterproof undersheets for the crib (one for the wash, one on the bed).

CHOOSING BETWEEN CLOTH AND DISPOSABLE DIAPERS

The fab folk at *Ohio State University Extension* magazine worked out that a month of diapers washed in an electric washing machine and dried in an electric dryer cost parents about $40 (not including the original outlay buying the diapers); a month of disposables cost about $50, and a week of diaper service was about $40 to $60 a month. (You'll find diaper services listed in the Yellow Pages.) Personally, I think if you have even a hint of feeling overwhelmed or depressed after having a baby, the cloth diapers should be metaphorically the first thing out the window, then the housework. (I don't mean you should live in a disaster area, just that you should try to lower your standards and get lots of help.)

Your decision will probably be based on your philosophy. It is useless to try to argue that disposable diapers, cloth diapers, or more children are good for the environment. But it is also useless to argue that a disposable diaper is anything but a boon to parents and babies. They are far and away better than a cloth diaper and that's why they're now so much more popular. The only two reasons not to use them are philosophical and economic: both very sensible reasons. (See More Info at the end of this chapter.)

If you want to use cloth diapers, that's fine—but not a word to individuals, letters to newspaper editors or columns, or calls to talk radio about how everyone else should too. No one is in a position to judge what other people need to do to get by and be kinder, more cheerful parents.

It seems to me that women at the most stressful time of their lives shouldn't be taking the blame for environmental pollution or being turned into drudges because corporations haven't got the biodegradable thing right yet. It's worth thinking about what women (it's almost always women) have to do if they have to use cloth diapers day after day: scrape poop of all colors and descriptions into the toilet; then cart the diapers to the laundry and soak them in heavy chemicals; then wash them in boiling hot water; then drag the heavy, wet diapers out and peg them on the line, praying for good drying weather, or run them through an electricity-sucking dryer; then get them down from the line or out of the dryer; then fold them; and then do it all over again a grizillion times.

One way to rationalize choosing disposables is to say that our water is very precious, whereas we have more room for landfill: oh, I know it's not a perfect solution, but then I'm not a perfect mother.

If anyone tells you off about using disposables and ruining the environment, ask them if they'll do the washing. Ask them if they have any idea how much water and how many pesticides are used to make cotton fabric. Then ask them if they ever ride in cars.

If they still give you a hard time, hit them gently on the nose with a rolled-up newspaper, or try a firm, stern, disapproving voice and a water pistol.

And as for those women who wash diapers themselves for years, and I'm utterly serious about this: what's the point if they don't get a medal?

WHEN TO CHANGE A DIAPER

Change your baby's diaper when you smell the poop or feel the wet-ness. Check it every now and then, and change it if there's been any action, even if your baby is happy. Diapers should be changed promptly, no matter how super-absorbent they are.

Babies can sometimes pee or poop right after you've changed them: never assume they're dry because you only changed a diaper 5 minutes ago. A baby, especially one in a cloth diaper, may cry to let you know it's wet and uncomfortable.

A diaper can be changed when a baby is asleep. This prevents the diaper being really wet and nasty when the baby wakes up later.

If you are in someone else's home, double-bag your dispos-able diaper and take it home with you. Needless to say cloth ones shouldn't be left behind either: peuwww.

HOW TO CHANGE A DIAPER

Keep within reach of the changing table or the bench or table you use for changing diapers:
- ★ new diapers.
- ★ baby wipes or cotton balls, and other bottom-cleaning needs such as baby lotion or tepid water.
- ★ a barrier or diaper-rash cream if required.
- ★ a lined bin or other container for the used diaper.
- ★ clean clothes for the baby.

Lay your baby on the changing table, always keeping a hand on them. Open the soiled diaper and clean the baby's bottom with a baby wipe or cotton balls dipped in baby lotion or tepid water. Throw away the baby wipe or cotton balls and put aside the soiled diaper. Pat or air dry the bottom. Many people also use baby powder or smear on some babies' barrier or diaper-rash cream before fastening the new diaper. Deal with a poopey cloth or disposable diaper as soon as you're free to do so but don't leave the baby alone on the table while you go to the bathroom, laundry, or trash bin.

If the baby has done a ballistic poop, give them a bath after a thorough wipe down.

DiaPeR RaSH aND SKiN iRRitatioNS

Diaper rash is most common in older babies who spend long hours at night in diapers. Some people say cloth diapers are better for preventing diaper rash because they allow more airflow, but most people agree disposables draw the irritating pee away from the skin more. Heat and moisture create a great rash environment. An allergy to washing powders may also be a cause of diaper rash.

When washing your baby, use a soap substitute (soap is very drying) on the bottom bits; and use baby wipes that contain an oil or lanolin but not alcohol. A barrier or diaper-rash cream will protect the baby's skin from the worst irritation caused by pee. Let the bottom run free as much as possible, and be vigilant about changing a diaper as soon as you can after your baby has peed or pooped.

OH my god, it's someONe else's POOP

Yes, well, just make sure you don't talk about it to other people unless they ask. There's nothing worse than a parent banging on about their offspring's poop unless it's to another interested or gobsmacked parent, I say. If you must know, here's a rundown (sorry).

★ Breastfed newborns can poop six to eight times in 24 hours, and this can go on for up to 3 months.
★ Breastfed babies can happily go a week without a poop, but bottlefed babies have a poop once or twice a day.

FREE THE BOTTOMS

Whenever possible—say, when your baby is lying on a blanket inside, with a towel folded underneath, or outside under a shady tree or umbrella—let their bottom run free and give them a rest from the heat and padded feeling of a diaper. But don't put a baby in direct sunlight because they're likely to end up with sunburn as well as diaper rash (look up sun care in the index).

* If the baby cries when pooping, the poop is hard, there's blood in the poop, or there's any other poop worry, see your doctor.
* Breastfed baby poop is that classic orangey "baby poop" color; surprisingly it doesn't smell too bad.
* I am sorry to say that sometimes baby poop is green, and I don't know why and I'm not going to ask. All I know is it's not a problem and I'm happy to go with that.
* Bottlefed baby poop is usually bigger, browner, and smellier than breastfed baby poop. Constipation is not unusual when you switch to a bottle: as suggested in the previous chapter, Bottles, try a scant teaspoon of sugar in a bottle of formula.
* See your baby's doctor if diarrhea—frequent, watery poops—goes on for longer than 24 hours. (There's more info in the Health chapter in *Part 5: Stuff*; look up diarrhea in the index.)
* Huge, stinky poop? Your child is now on solids, possibly meat.

Oh, what a charming and whimsical way to end a chapter! Do pass me a martini, Lady Georgina, and we'll stroll down to the ornamental ocean.

more info

www.ConsumerReports.org

Consumer Reports rated disposable diaper brands and found that many store brands tested as well as some premium brands. (You must be a member or subscriber to access their article online or you can look at your local library for the article published in their March 2004 magazine.) You can subscribe to their online service by the month and access up to 4 years worth of archived articles including numerous baby product reviews.

www.mothering.com

Mothering magazine has several articles about diaper choices and calculates the cost of two and a half years of disposables at about $2000 (at 2003 prices), not including pull-ups, baby wipes, or deodorized diaper bags, and of cloth diapers at anywhere between $400 to $1200 depending upon which products you decide to purchase, not including your time spent laundering.

www.kimberly-clark.com

Kimberly-Clark, a disposable diaper manufacturer, has a Environmental Question and Answer page on their website answering questions about their policies.
www.kimberly-clark.com/aboutus/env_qa.asp

THROWING UP

Baby books call baby chuck "spit up" because it sounds so much more refined, dahling. Usually throwing up happens straight after a feed or in the middle (or during burping). If milk is vomited later, it can be partially digested and smellier.

Parents and caregivers get really used to this and usually have a tea towel or cloth diaper over one shoulder for a year or so.

Most of us have unwittingly gone out with baby chuck down our back. And we'll

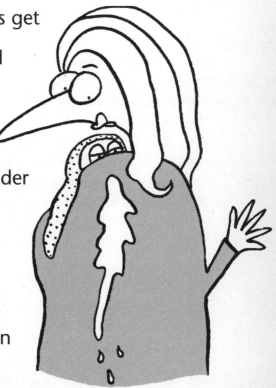

never know how many of the non-initiated
we freaked out. A woman once said to me
"And then her baby threw up on me and
I realized, euwww, that was just in her breast
a minute ago. Yuuuuck." If she thinks that's
yuck, thank heavens she hasn't had to deal
with green poop.

WHy DO BaBieS THROW UP?

A baby usually vomits because all the bits of their digestive system
aren't in foolproof working order yet. Or because they drank too
much milk at once (they're still learning how to take the right
amount). Repeated throwing up associated with what seems to be
a rejection of the milk can indicate an intolerance and in any case
can be very tedious for all concerned, so if you're sick of sick see
your doctor.

iNSOUCiaNT VOmiTiNg

The state of mind of some babies can best be described as la, la, la,
happy, happy, enormous vomit, la, la, la, happy, happy. In other
words, there is a kind of vomiting the baby doesn't mind in the least,
and which poses no threat to anything but your patience, ambitions
to wear something without chuck on it, and the warranty on the

washing machine. It's annoying but not actually a problem for the baby unless they're losing weight because they're vomiting up lots of food (when you hear "food" in relation to a baby under 6 months, it really just means breast milk or formula milk). Most babies vomit a tiny bit when burping.

Some babies also seem to be on a hair-trigger and vomit if they choke slightly on some milk, or later on solids, or someone puts a finger too far into their mouth to check for teething action. It makes perfect sense for babies to be quick to vomit in this way as nature is preventing them from choking. I know a baby who is like that. The only doctor who listened to the mother's warning is the only one who doesn't put a depressor on the baby's tongue to check her throat, and is consequently the only doctor not to get utterly chucked on every time.

BaBies WHO THROW UP a LOT aND CRY (RefLUX)

Some babies cry a lot or are unsettled—find it hard to get to sleep or stay asleep—because they have a valve problem in their esophagus that means milk rushes back up from their tummy, causing heartburn-like pain. Sometimes it rushes up so regularly that the baby seems to constantly vomit a lot after each feed. This condition is called "reflux."

It's important to remember that lots of babies throw up a bit after each feed, but it doesn't mean they have reflux. Reflux needs to be medically diagnosed before being treated.

If your baby is diagnosed with reflux, a breastfeeding consultant can help you learn to feed with the baby held somewhat upright rather than lying down—bottlefeeders can try the upright position too. A refluxing baby will probably prefer smaller feeds, more often. Medical treatments include thickening agents in formula; anti-vomiting drugs (which seem to be out of fashion due to doubts about whether they make much difference); and heartburn preparations: ask your doctor. (See also More Info below.)

La Leche League has a pamphlet called *Breastfeeding the Baby with Reflux* to help moms who've had their baby's reflux medically diagnosed, with advice about the condition and coping with it (see the contact details in More Info at the end of the Bosoms chapter).

more info

REFLUX SUPPORT GROUPS

http://groups.msn.com/LivingWithRefluxUK

Has helpful tips and an online support group based in the UK.

REFLUX WEBSITES

www.reflux.org

This gastroesophageal reflux site has frequently asked questions, parents' stories, discussion groups, and links to other resources. They also have a helpline you can call and leave a message for someone to return your call or send you free materials: 301-601-9541 or 760-747-5001. Check to see if there is a chapter in your area sponsoring meetings, discussion, and lectures.

www.gut-instincts.com

Sponsored by Pediatric and Adolescent Gastroesophageal Reflux Association (PAGER), which runs www.reflux.org. You can register online to receive free information and support about reflux.

www.kidshealth.org

Search for GERD for helpful information in diagnosis and treatment of reflux in infants.

SLeePiNg

The sleeping habits of a newborn baby are perfectly logical and sensible—unless you're not a newborn baby, in which case they're completely and utterly insane. And luckily temporary. Babies usually wake up when they are hungry, which is far too often because they have such tiny tummies. They really should stay in the womb for longer and do the umbilical thing, but then they'd be too big to come out in the time-honored fashion.

Ape babies are carried by parents until they learn to swing from trees themselves. The babies can sleep any time they need to, wake up for a breastfeed or to check out a leaf, and then fall asleep again when it suits them. Unfortunately, there is no research on whether this makes the parent apes put the peanut butter in the freezer, sob hopelessly on occasion, and sometimes wonder whether they could leave the small apes at a mall and get the next flight to Freakoutistan.

your baby's attitude to sleep

All babies are different. Pediatricians tend to be able to spend some time with a baby and know whether they're a sleepy, placid bub or an alert sort of a little tyke who will always fight sleep. You'll need to get to know these things too because your baby is probably not an exactly average sleeper—so any sleeping strategies from a textbook or "sleep school" will have to be tailored to you and your baby, usually by a bit of trial and error and time expenditure.

> *"I don't want to take a 'nap,' goddamnit. I want to SLEEEEEEP!"*
> ME

NeWBORN sLeep facts

Newborn babies will go to sleep just about anywhere. Once they're asleep they're initially very deeply asleep, then they have peaks of being easily roused before going into deeper sleep again.

Some babies are born with a pregnancy-induced pattern of being soothed to sleep while you're walking around (amniotic bouncing) and waking up when you're still (asleep). That's why lots of people end up rocking their baby in their arms, pushing a carriage backwards and forwards, renting or buying some kind of bouncy, hammocky thing for their baby to sleep in during the first few months, or driving around aimlessly in a car trying to get the baby to sleep.

Newborns love to hear a heartbeat. If you don't mind them sleeping in a strap-on baby carrier, you can do other stuff—but this is not the answer if you need to sleep when they do, early on. Do get the best one you can so the weight is distributed properly across your shoulders, back and waist: your baby will get heavier all the time (look up baby carriers in the index).

Don't worry about being tight-lippedly strict about routines in the early days. (Come to think of it, that's probably to be avoided at any stage.) But if you want to, it doesn't hurt to start heading towards some sort of pattern to make more sense of your days, as long as you know it goes out the window on the whim of a newborn and almost always in later days if a baby or toddler is sick. (See More Info at the end of this chapter, and the Possible Routines for Babies chapter.)

Baby Sleep Patterns

In the first 6 months the "average" baby wakes two to three times a night, then between 6 months and 1 year they wake one to two times. Most babies after 6 months will be having one long stretch of sleep, perhaps 6 to 8 hours, and will be getting sufficient milk during the day and evening not to need a night feed. It's good to try to manipulate this long sleep to last until the dawn or early morning feed. Most babies over 6 months will have a morning and afternoon nap, and then just the afternoon nap from whatever age it suits them—say, 10 months, 3 years, 4 years, or 5 years. Depends on the kid. Older baby and toddler naptimes usually range from about 45 minutes to 2 and a half hours. I reckon they often sleep longer when they seem to be having a growth spurt and eating more too, also known as "on the fang." Others have observed that babies learning to crawl get more restless in bed.

What a Baby Needs to Get to Sleep

Your baby may need a few or all of the following elements:
* ★ a quiet wind-down time.
* ★ a feeling of comfort and safety—often a firm tucking in or swaddling (ask your doula, lactation consultant, or doctor how to wrap a baby for sleep). But don't swaddle a baby who seems to detest it: that's your little individual!
* ★ a dry bottom.
* ★ a full tummy.
* ★ a ritual—words, pats, music, swaddling.
* ★ a blackout blind.
* ★ a dim night-light.

"Tips to encourage sleep? Read them the **Financial Review.***"* TOM

SIGNS OF BABY TIREDNESS

* droopy eyelids.

* the slow blinks.

* stiff and jerky movements, like a clockwork figure.

* the long-distance blank stare.

* whiny and irritable.

* yawns.

When the baby is a bit older, add:

* rubbing their eyes.

* pulling their earlobes or hair.

* hyper-style hysteria or aggression.

* mood swings.

* clingy behavior.

* going to bed and getting in (well, you can hope).

DO NOT DISTURB

Ritual

Remember, though, that babies can get hooked on the back pat or rub, the soothing music, the pacifier, Mom or Dad lying down with them, or a breastfeed or a bottle. This may be fine with you or it may pose difficulties now or later.

A bedtime routine for an older baby can include a story, a catch-phrase—"Sleep tight, I love you," "Sweet dreams, my little farter," (maybe not)—and a firm but loving exit.

Products

Many baby gear shops have baby hammocks and a full range of bassinets and cribs, as well as other bouncy things for settling a baby, although not necessarily settling them to sleep (the Equipment chapter in *Part 5: Stuff* has all the info on safety requirements). Remember that a baby that's used to sleeping only in a bouncy bed will require a few days to adjust to a flat crib.

There are mail-order products and sleep techniques offered on the Internet, but geez, Louise, some of these are as shonky as all get out. Do be careful about what you send money away for—you're almost certainly better off talking to a real person on the phone or face to face, or getting one of the books mentioned in More Info at the end of this chapter.

Sleepy music

Most sleepy music for tots has a picture of a sleeping baby on the front. Often it comes as two CDs or cassettes, or CDs only. I'm convinced that in about 10 years a generation of young adults will be easily and instantly hypnotised by Brahms lullabies. Some say any old drifty classical music will do; others insist the magical ingredient is a beat that's like the human heartbeat. Some babies like the white noise of an electric fan or other machine. A rug or curtains will make a room quieter—fabric soaks up sounds while hard surfaces bounce them around. (See More Info at the end of this chapter for some CD titles.)

A blackout blind

It's a big call—I don't usually say anything's essential unless it involves a health or safety issue. But if you want your baby to get as much sleep as possible, my sister-in-law Emma gave me the best tip ever: get yourself a blackout blind or curtain—not just a dark or heavy one, but one that doesn't let in a line or chink of light from outside. (I'd say paint the window black and nail it up, but light and fresh air are good between naps!)

The expensive version involves pelmets on the top and the sides of the window, a fabric-lined blackout roller blind, and heavy fabric-lined blackout curtains on each side to stop light creeping around the edges of the roller blind. For a cheaper version, paint a roller blind black or get an inexpensive black or navy one. Attach the roller blind high up, a little above the window, put a wood Venetian blind over the top or tack on a wide piece of heavy cardboard as a pelmet—anything to stop light spilling in around the top of the blind. Put loops of masking tape or a pliable adhesive around the bottom and side edges of the blind, and stick it to the window frame or wall to cut out all light. Pull curtains across the edges.

A blackout blind means your baby isn't up with the dawn, when the outside light changes, unless you have really loud birds outside or that's when they insist on waking anyway: no doubt it's what lots of humans are programmed to do.

English newborn-nurse Gina Ford also recommends an elaborate curtain system in her *The Contented Little Baby Book*: she is so strict about this that she "will not take a booking unless the nursery has both curtains with a blackout lining and a special blackout roller blind." Ooh, my gawd.

If there's a handyperson in your life, this can make them feel they are contributing something crucial. If you haven't a handyperson, use your life savings to get the window covering up to blackout standard. Those extra hours of sleep are worth it.

Kids will usually go to sleep in the afternoon in a dim, not black, room but may wake up earlier if they're in a lighter, unfamiliar place. Take blackout fabric with you when you and your baby are away overnight.

A night-light

Lots of kids like a dim night-light that throws out a consistent light so they can see if they wake up. It also lets you see to feed at night. Don't put it near your baby's head—under the crib, or any other spot where it will be as diffuse as possible, is good. Hardware shops sell a light that plugs into a power point and is the size of a double adaptor. A dimmer switch can also be used for low light.

make a safe, familiar sleeping place

Subject to safety considerations, your baby's bed in the early days can be your bed, a bassinet, a cradle, a specially designed bassinet that snaps out of a carriage, or a crib. For the first couple of months many people sleep with their baby, who then graduates to a crib. Other babies are still co-sleeping at toddler stage or moving on only when a new baby is taken into the parental bed.

Okay, let's get the stern, rulesy bits out of the way: babies must never be left alone in a car, even if they're sleeping peacefully, in case of overheating or theft. Babies in a locked car can overheat and die in a matter of minutes even on a seemingly mild day—you may be unavoidably delayed. Apart from this, a baby in a car seat can droop their head too far forward—for most babies this won't matter, but a very few can cut off their air supply and not be able to revive.

Always put the baby somewhere safe for naps, such as their own crib: it will be familiar and they may resettle themselves if they wake up rather than be startled, and if you fall asleep or are somewhere else you won't have to worry about them getting lost under, for instance, a couch cushion.

In case they wriggle into a suffocating position, babies should not be put to sleep and then left alone out of sight in a carriage, a stroller, a baby seat (either in the car outside or brought inside), or a couch or a chair.

It's dangerous to leave a baby sleeping unsupervised in an adult-sized bed: they can become tangled in adult bedding, wedged between the bed and the wall or caught under a pillow; they can also roll out and fall at an earlier age than you think.

"Makeshift sleeping environments are dangerous," according to the SIDS and Kids research organization. Don't make adjustments to carriages, beds, or devices not designed for babies to actually sleep the night in. Follow construction and operating instructions exactly.

Bed safety requirements

Buy cribs that meet the safety standards set by the Consumer Projects Safety Commission (CPSC) and the voluntary standards set by the American Society for Testing and Materials (ASTM) and are certified by the Juvenile Products Manufacture's Association (JPMA). Spaces between slats should be no wider than $2^3/8$ inches (about the width of a soda can), and corner posts should not be higher than $1/16$ inch high. Cribs built before 1989 may not meet the basic safety standards and should be considered unsafe. It should have a tight-fitting mattress. If at all possible get a new mattress made from cotton or another material that "breathes" rather than hard foam. The crib should also have cotton sheets and cotton cellular blankets, but no duvet until the baby is 1 year to 18 months old.

It's better to heat the room a little bit in winter if you can afford it; otherwise use light woolen blankets. A sheepskin underneath the baby is a nice idea unless the room gets too hot; they are machine washable (but not meant for the dryer). Crib "bumpers" restrict the flow of air in and around a crib, and babies can get their heads stuck underneath them. Any waterproof undersheet should be a plastic-backed fitted cotton one so the baby doesn't get too hot. Spares of everything are important in case of a washing emergency (although towels can be substituted during a bedding shortage). Babies don't need pillows and they're not recommended until at least 2 years. (Older kids move around so much in bed they're often off the pillow too: it's not a problem.) If you use pillows and other foofery to "dress" the crib and make it look nice, take it all out before the baby goes down to sleep.

CO-SLeepiNg OR SLeepiNg apaRt

In an effort to snatch as much sleep as possible, parents often choose to sleep with their baby in their bed so they don't have to get up to crying or for breastfeeding (although they need to wake up enough to change diapers). For the same reason (maximizing sleep) many parents choose to have the baby sleeping near the bed in a bassinet. Others have the baby sleep in a separate room and get up whenever summoned by a cry in the night. Any of these options is a legitimate choice. One is not necessarily better than any other, and it is very annoying to have people rudely insisting that you do what they did with their children. The important question is "Which suits *us* better, co-sleeping or sleeping apart?."

Proponents of co-sleeping insist that "babies sleep better" and "mothers sleep better." If you like the idea and this seems to be true for you, then go for it. It certainly seems to make sense, especially for moms who have had a cesarean, unless someone else gets up and brings them the baby for feeds and cuddles each time. And it must be easier for some single parents.

But in my case if my baby was in the bed I woke up so many times in response to the tiniest snuffle, and had so many experiences of a recurring nightmare in which I had lost her under the duvet, that to continue would have led to madness. I started to sleep better when she was in her own crib, and the nightmare went away. So co-sleeping isn't for everyone. (I recently read, to my surprise, an account of virtually the same recurring dream experienced by another mother: as usual, any thought you have as a parent is unlikely to be unique, no matter what you believe at the time.)

People who go to bed drunk or drugged, smoke, or have a disorder that makes them sleep very heavily should not sleep in the same bed as a baby because there is a higher risk of suffocation or sudden infant death syndrome (see the earlier Newborn Worries chapter). Some studies show a higher SIDS risk when babies are in another room, some show a greater risk when babies are in bed with a parent, particularly if the babies have a respiratory illness at the time. Co-sleeping or not co-sleeping is still a personal choice that isn't supported one way or the other by medical advice and it depends on your individual situation. A baby's crib or bassinet right next to your bed is a middle ground if you're worried about sleeping too heavily or rolling on the baby. (Co-sleeping fans say parents always sleep lightly enough to wake if this happens—which sounds like a possible recipe for sleeplessness for some.)

An unattended baby in a bed is always at risk even if their parent hops out for only a moment or so.

YOUR YOUNG BABY WAKES CONSTANTLY

Some babies, especially ones who sleep with their mom, can train themselves to take little bits of milk, often, at the all-night milk bar lying next to them, which means that instead of feeding every few hours, the mom has to wake up every hour or so for snacktime. And some babies are picked up whenever they make a little cry or snuffle during the night, which is quite normal behavior for babies. Instead wait and see if they'll settle themselves, and always try to soothe them back to Dreamland, with a soft word or ritualized pat. Of course if it's the usual time for a feed, they probably won't settle. Even with their baby in the next room, some moms have to wear earplugs to cut out the little snuffles, grunts, sighs, and snorky noises in the night. If the baby definitely needs someone or is really awake and needing attention, the noise is quite different—and louder. And even through the earplugs most moms hear the sounds first and are out the door before the dad is aware of the slightest noise. Here's a brilliant suggestion I heard: reverse the baby monitor, if you have one, so the baby can hear their parents snoring or chatting (but perhaps not doing erotic folk-dancing practice). This means you can't hear the little grunts and snuffles, but you'll hear them yell out if they really want you.

Developing a pattern for night and day

Help your baby understand daytime and nighttime. Nighttime feeds should be a sleepy, quiet, darkened affair, with no play and straight back to sleep. Daytime feeds can be animated and chatty, with a play afterwards.

"Never wake a sleeping baby"

Generally it's a good rule. If the baby's asleep, they probably want to be. Certainly never wake a sleeping baby at 2 a.m. for their usual feed—this may be the night they drop it! Yes, but what if it's the 11 p.m. feed they sleep through? If you let them stay asleep and go to bed yourself, the baby may wake at 12.30 a.m. for a feed. I reckon you should wake the baby up at 11 p.m., but expect possible dreadful grumpiness.

What if the baby is asleep in the car and you have to go inside? Take the baby. What if you need to move your baby from stroller or baby car seat to crib so they can keep sleeping and you can get on with something somewhere else? Put the baby in the crib (or safely on the floor) every time, but try to be so gentle that sleep isn't much disturbed.

Hints for more parental sleep

Sleep when the baby does: forget housework and take the phone off the hook if you need sleep. Of course you need sleep. You have a baby. (Unless you have a 24-hour live-in nanny and a weekend nanny and go to the hairdresser every day to get your hairdo, in which case you wouldn't be reading this book because you'd be getting your 24-hour live-in nanny to read it while you had Tumultuous Mauve painted on your fingernails by someone whose name you don't know.)

You may find yourself getting hysterical when your baby is just a few days old, and sobbing that there's no point in going to sleep if you only have to wake up in 2 to 3 hours for another feed. If you're anything like me, you'll be a lot less hysterical if you take all the catnaps you can in those early days.

If you have a partner, get them to do half, or some, of the night feeds (using expressed breast milk or formula). Also get them to settle the baby to sleep sometimes so the baby doesn't demand you every time.

I know it seems obvious, but there are some things you can do or not do to get a better sleep. If you sleep better with your baby in the bed, do that; if you sleep more deeply with them elsewhere, do that. Avoid stimulants such as coffee, tea, and cigarettes, and a cocaine habit. Drink warm milk with honey in it, have your own rituals such as a warm bath, make your room dark, make rules about other people being quiet if you need to; wear earplugs. Taking sleeping tablets is *not* a good idea for the same reason that you must not sleep with your baby if you're drunk or stoned, and because they will go through to your milk if you're breastfeeding.

You may find you need to readjust to sleeping through the night once your baby decides to!

Daytime Naps

Some people say day sleeptimes shouldn't be unduly quiet so the baby learns to sleep through any noise. Really it depends on the baby. At certain times in their sleep babies can sleep through anything loud, but a sudden noise such as a slammed door will always wake them at other times. You may want to put a sign on the front door asking people not to ring the doorbell or knock (there's a sign on the following page you might like to photocopy). You'll probably need to also ask people if they would call beforehand to get the go-ahead for a visit. And why not unplug the phone when your baby is asleep? The result will be the baby sleeps as long as possible, and so will you. And quite frankly unless you're expecting George Clooney to pay a call, what could be more important right now? ("George! Take off your trousers! Now fold that laundry!")

SHHHHH!
PLEASE

DON'T KNOCK OR RING BELL

BABY ASLEEP

COME BACK LATER
OR
LEAVE MESSAGE IN MAILBOX

THANKS

© Kidwrangling: The Real Guide to Caring for Babies, Toddlers, and Little Kids

"SLeePiNg tHROUgH"

This is the holy grail: the baby finally drops a feed between 12 a.m. and dawn so they sleep through from an hour or so before midnight to 6 or so in the morning, to take a random example. Be aware that a baby might do this once and then not again for days or weeks. The first sleep through is often a big surprise to the parents, especially a breastfeeding mom with explodey-feeling boobs. If the baby is old enough to be getting all the milk they need during the day, sleeping through can be encouraged by having a non-lactating person go in to the baby to try to settle them without a feed, although perhaps with some cooled boiled water in a sterilized bottle. (The baby is supposed to think "Oh perlease, water instead of milk, how boring, I'm going back to sleep.") If the baby goes back to sleep without minding, it can herald the start of sleeping through. Your doctor or a book on sleeping (see More Info at the end of this chapter) can help you with likely routines at various ages (see also the Possible Routines for Babies chapter).

HeLPiNg a BaBy LeaRN to go to sLeeP By tHemseLves

Basically your baby will adjust to whatever bedtime or naptime ritual you decide to use. Many people develop one unconsciously, although this might not end up being the most useful one for them; for example, exhausted mom breastfeeds, then baby and mom flake out on the bed together, and so baby only learns to go to sleep when mom is there.

When babies are little you must always go in to comfort them if they cry or call out: only nutty, fundamentalist, baby-disliking theorists would dream of recommending that a baby should be left alone in a crib to cry, without your patting or soothing them, before the age of 6 months. But it is good to be able to comfort a baby back to sleep without picking them up (of course they may have made a particularly irritating poop and need to be changed).

The usually recommended way to help a baby get to sleep on their own is some sort of variation on the following.

- ★ Have some wind-down time.
- ★ Wrap your baby firmly, but not too tightly.
- ★ Place your baby to sleep on their back.
- ★ Give them a pacifier if you want to.
- ★ Pat their back or bottom gently, with a slow rhythm, a few times until they're sleepy.
- ★ Leave the room before they actually fall asleep.

You can train your baby over time to understand that they are being put to sleep by themselves (always in a darkened room, with a comfy temperature, familiar smells and blankies, a comforting back rub, and the same catchphrase such as "Nightie-night, possum"), but that you'll return reassuringly if they need you so that they realize they're not being abandoned. The idea is to get the baby to realize that it's safe and fine to go to sleep by themselves in their own bed without your being there, rocking the side of the crib for ages or breastfeeding them to sleep. It will go a long way to setting up good habits that you will be grateful for later.

The key is that after comforting rituals, the baby is left in the room calm, happy, safe, hopefully sleepy, but still awake, and learns how to go to sleep independently without your obvious presence so that if they wake during the night and don't need a feed they can go to sleep again without your help.

Yes, I know it sounds like an impossible dream when you're in the mad, sleep-deprived early weeks. It isn't, but I fully admit I was in a tizz and to get the hang of it had to go to a day-visit sleep school at 4 months (a lovely Australian institution), and then we needed to refer to a book to practice. After we learned some patting and settling techniques, our baby could go to sleep herself, knowing that if there was anything wrong she could yell and someone would respond to her.

There is an exultant joy in having a baby who can wake up and then happily settle back to sleep. In our case it eventually took the added assistance of a pacifier and a loop tape of classical music, but it worked. (At least until the tape slowed down and started sounding like the Eeyore Boys Choir and then broke.) If you are consistent (and lucky), your baby will be happy with the arrangement too.

Think of it as you and your baby learning together. And if another way suits you, then for heaven's sake use that. It's just that most people eventually don't want to have to rock their baby to sleep or breastfeed every time, or lie down with their toddler until they're asleep and then again if they wake up during the night.

There may be many resources in your area to help you with establishing or altering routines, or you can talk with your doctor. You can call one of the parent services to see if there are groups in your area that run classes or give phone advice on establishing a routine and settling a baby, toddler, or even preschooler. Talking with other moms in a parents' or breastfeeding support group can be a great help as well (see the contact details in More Info at the end of the second chapter, Your Support Team).

"Controlled crying" or "controlled comforting"

Most babies will cry when you're trying to get them to go to sleep by themselves. "Controlled crying" and "controlled comforting" are the terms used for a structured way of getting these babies to sleep without a parent. They're the same thing, only controlled crying sounds a bit scary and controlled comforting is what you want to feel you're doing. It's not recommended that this approach be tried on a baby under 6 months old: talk about it with your doctor if you're unsure when or how to begin. Basically some time is spent letting the baby cry and some spent comforting them. The aim is to slowly change the sleeping habits of your baby if these are disrupting family life or driving you bonkers.

The approach is to reassure the child that it's time to go to sleep, institute the ritual, and then retire to outside the door while they yell at you. Depending on whose theory or book you follow you wait, say, 30 seconds, then go in and reassure them again and resettle them. The next time you stay out for 1 minute, then progressively make the margin wider—but never longer than 5 or 10 minutes. A baby left to cry for a long time will wind up being very distressed.

While practicing this routine, parents will often sit in the corridor looking at their watch, crying, and taking turns not to let the other one in until the right number of minutes has elapsed. Sole parents really need someone to help: it's much harder for them, I reckon.

The people who subscribe to the attachment parenting theory (described in the Parenting Philosophy chapter in *Part 4: Parenting*) think that controlled crying is cruel because it teaches babies not to expect comforting on demand (look up attachment parenting in the index). Others say that babies need help to understand how to put themselves to sleep, that it's kinder to teach them how to go to sleep instead of getting constantly overtired and distressed, and that this can be gradually achieved without actual trauma.

This may be one of those times when you start to learn to distinguish the kinds of crying: heartbreakingly sad, outraged, or try-ing it on (see the next chapter, Crying). Sometimes it can be really useful to have the help of an outsider, who can be kind but more dispassionate (and is less shatteringly sleep deprived). Often the atti-tude of the baby is "Well, all right, I can see the way this is going, I might as well go to sleep." The baby can have changed habits in as little as 3 or 4 days: possibly 3 or 4 traumatic days, with a bit less trauma each passing night until there's none.

The *Secrets of the Baby Whisperer* author and maternity nurse Tracy Hogg doesn't believe in letting babies cry; she takes up to 2 weeks to train them. She says sometimes on the first night a baby will have to be laid back down to sleep many, many, many times, but then it's always less the second night and so on until the prob-lem is solved. (Mind you, those parents in her book had Miss Tracy in their house for days on end helping. So you'll need to be strong when it becomes your time to change a baby's habits.)

You *can* change your baby's habits

No baby's sleeping habit is set in stone: quite often a difficult habit happened by accident. It's important to know you're not stuck with it. Even very ingrained habits can be changed gradually—some within a day or so, some within 3 weeks. I'm not saying this is easy or that a person should be expected to do it alone. It takes loving firmness and lots of patience. This means the baby will be very cross occasionally but never afraid or desolate: there's a big difference. It means you as a parent have to take control rather than letting chance or a confused baby impose a way of life that doesn't work for you and is therefore not good for the baby either.

"Use an association with sleep other than yourself or any other person, for that matter: sheepskin rug, doll, musical toy. Must be carried everywhere so make sure it's not the size of an elephant."
KAREN

"Make sure they're full and if not settled after having a dry diaper pat them on the bottom until their eyes start to droop, and repeat if they stir." ANITA

"For me a baby's sleep routine was when they wanted sleep. The old tired signs of rubbing eyes, yawning, and generally getting grumpy work if you can catch them at the right time. But if all else fails be a sucker mom like I was and rock your baby to sleep: you never know, you might like it . . . if your child needs a cuddle or a story or just someone to be there then so be it. Enjoy that. They will only be little for a small amount of time." CHERRIE

"I found putting the newborn into the older siblings' routine to be the best way, especially for afternoon naps and bathtime." JALEESA

"Kids love consistency, consistency, consistency. My baby actually sighs with delight and relief when she is tucked in and usually lets us know (loudly) when we are running behind time." HAYLEY

"Be flexible! Accept from the start there is no such thing as a baby routine . . . Baby Number 1 slept from 6 p.m. to 5 a.m. from 6 weeks and still needs 10 hours' sleep at age 6. But he refused to sleep during the day for more than 20 minutes: no time to get anything done. Baby Number 2 used to sleep all afternoon and stayed up until 11 p.m. Baby Number 3 woke at 11 p.m., 2 a.m., 4 a.m., 6 a.m., for 5 minutes at a time. All three now go to bed on their own."
ANONYMOUS

"I hardly ever went anywhere in the afternoons so she could sleep. She is now 3 and still having an afternoon nap and I still haven't got a life. It worked for me!" BERNADETTE

"Despite all the anti-tummy sleeping, this is all my baby would settle with. I kept him on a firm mattress with a fitted cotton sheet, no bumpers, no covers, and checked on him constantly. At night we'd turn him onto his back once he was in a deep sleep."
KIMBERLEY

"In the first 6 months we adopted the seemingly usual routine of a relaxing bath, large bottle of formula and then 'restfully' pacing up and down his room till he fell asleep, then gently placed him in his crib—and ran like hell to get out before he woke up! It nearly killed us. So much stress, his awful incessant crying—we ended up at a family health clinic to learn controlled crying and establish a sleeping pattern—which thankfully has worked wonders." CORRI

moRe iNfo

SLEEPING ISSUES

If the situation's not urgent, see which one of the books below might fit your style.

Silent Nights: Overcoming Sleep Problems in Babies and Children
by Brian Symon, Getty Center, Apr. 1999.
Written by an Australian doctor who has made sleep difficulties his specialty. An easy-to-get-into book that identifies problems and possible solutions, starting from earliest breastfeeding and the first 6 weeks through to toddlers and special disruptions such as daylight saving, moving house, relatives who sabotage your routine, and first nightmares. At the stricter end of the scale.

Solve Your Child's Sleep Problems
by Dr Richard Ferber, Simon & Schuster, Reprint, 1986.
Dr Ferber is the director of the Center for Sleep Disorders at the Children's Hospital of Boston. He's against co-sleeping and is known as the "controlled-crying guy." Many sleep schools in Australia use variations of his methods. This dense book, with annoyingly small type, also covers nighttime carry-ons, bad dreams, how daytime naps can help nighttime sleeping, and how to get past nighttime feeding.

Other books Gina Ford has a priority of sleep routines in that British no-nonsense way in her *The Contented Little Baby Book*. Tracy Hogg's *Secrets of the Baby Whisperer* advocates a gentler, slower form of "controlled crying" tailored to your baby's personality, and calls babies left to cry "Ferberized" (after the author of *Solve Your Child's Sleep Problems*, above). *Baby Love: Everything You Need to Know about Your Baby's First Year* by Robin Barker has a helpful section that can help you to develop a routine from your baby's birth on and to understand the sleep needs of a small baby. Her follow-up, *The Mighty Toddler*, has several mentions of sleep plus a section that is her version of controlled comforting, and there are also tips on other side issues and common problems, from night frights to early morning waking. *How to Stay Sane in Your Baby's First Year: The Tresillian Guide* has all the lowdown on sleeping. (More Info at the end of the first chapter, In the Beginning, has full details and reviews of these books except for *The Mighty Toddler*, for which see More Info in the Who's the Center of the Universe? chapter in *Part 2: Toddlers*.)

Websites   Most of the general baby and parenting websites listed in the More Info sections at the end of the In the Beginning and Your Support Team chapters have hints and sometimes forums on sleeping issues.

CO-SLEEPING

www.askdrsears.com
Search for "co-sleeping". Authors and pediatrics experts Martha and William Sears advocate co-sleeping. His page on sleeping is here. If you decide to co-sleep, this crew can tell you lots of good things about it.

SLEEPY MUSIC

Most big music shops have baby-soothing selections.

Bach at Bedtime: Lullabies for the Still of the Night
Philips
Includes music from Bach, performed by the English Chamber Orchestra.

Lullaby: A Collection
by various artists, Music Little People
A very popular collection of soothing songs.

CRYING

Newborn babies have only a few ways to communicate: the most useful one for them is crying. You might like to regard this as a design fault. If only they could scribble little stick-on notes to let us know exactly what's going on. Babies are used to being in the womb, minding their own business, and hanging out at the Umbilical Cord Café, when suddenly they're thrust into a world full of touch, taste, smell, sound, and light, with a digestive system that has never had to work this way before. Everything they see, hear, taste, smell, and feel is new, every second of the day. No wonder they burst into tears every now and then, especially at the end of the day. The very experience of living is an overload for those first few weeks. The baby is not crying because you are a bad mother, or an incompetent dad, or a lousy babysitter.

The baby is crying because the baby is a baby.

THINGS a BABY'S CRY MIGHT MEAN

Don't feel that you should be able to automatically interpret a baby's cry. In the first few weeks and months, a baby's cry can sound the same, yet mean ⊚ I'm hungry ⊚ I'm too hot ⊚ there's a weird feeling in my diaper ⊚ I'm all floppy and I used to be snug ⊚ that was a scary noise ⊚ I'm grizzly and a bit cranky ⊚ I'm annoyed ⊚ I am damn furious ⊚ is everything okay? ⊚ stop waking me and poking me and picking me up ⊚ if that's my grandmother, let me out of here ⊚ my sister stood on me when you were out of the room

◎ where's that nice smell I'm used to? ◎ I'm tired but I don't know what tired means ◎ I'm tired and I don't know how to go to sleep ◎ I just found out about Britney Spears ◎ there have been too many new feelings and sounds today ◎ ouch! ◎ I'm not used to doing this so I don't like it ◎ I'm scared in the bath because it's floaty but I'm not scrunched up ◎ there's something wrong with me and I can't tell you what it is ◎ my tummy hurts ◎ what the *hell* is THAT? ◎ something squishy is coming out of my bottom ◎ I need a cuddle ◎ I was just checking if one of my people was nearby ◎ I'm tired and you keep picking me up instead of letting me go to sleep ◎ pick me up! ◎ I don't know why I'm crying—it's just everything seems so overwhelming sometimes.

Possibly helpful hint

Baby development expert Lise Eliot says a hungry cry is likely to be "rhythmic and repetitive," an angry cry is "loud and prolonged," and a cry of pain is "sudden in onset, punctuated by breaks of breath holding." Gina Ralston, crying-baby expert from Tweddle Child and Family Health Service in Australia, says "Most cries sound the same, but the behavior gets more predictable."

You will get to know each other over time.

Crying peaks

"They" say there's a crying peak at about 6 weeks old, and some of these "theys" say there's one at 8 weeks as well. Don't panic if your baby suddenly seems to cry a lot. If you've ruled out a hidden illness, it's quite possibly just a phase, like a mysterious growth spurt that makes them need more milk more often than usual. Being with a baby is about constant little shuffle readjustments.

Babies who cry a lot usually cry even more towards the end of the day, and even some otherwise placid babies do too. This is what's known as "arsenic hour." It can really bring everyone to the end of their tether and often coincides with the partner who works outside the home coming back to scenes of utter despair. I sometimes

cuddle me!

leave me alone
(no, don't)
(oh, I don't know)

I'm cross

shall I cry?

I'm not tired

feed me!

ouch!

I can't remember
why I'm crying

I couldn't be
more shocked

where's my teddy?

...Sounds like...

I saw a great
big DOG

wonder if it's babies just being fed up with all this new word business late in the day: sensory and neurological overload. I think I'd cry too. Come to think of it, I did cry every day during arsenic hour for the first couple of weeks: big, tired tears—not hysterical, just quiet, exhausted ones.

> *"It's okay to let a baby or child cry for a little bit. If it is the worst that happens to them in their life, then they are very lucky."*
> KAREN

THiNGS THaT MiGHT STOP THe CRYiNG

There are lots of things you can try to stop the crying when it happens.

★ **Food:** is a feeding due? Or could the baby be needing extra? (Careful: they might just be overfull, in which case only time and comforting will help! I don't know how you tell the difference either—unfortunately it's trial and error, which takes time.)

★ **Sleep:** is the baby overtired and needing help to go to sleep?

★ **A diaper change:** the baby might have a wet or poopey bottom.

★ **Security:** the baby, if under 4 months, might like to be wrapped up snugly to remind them of womb living.

★ **Soothing:** the baby might just need a pat, a cuddle, or a pacifier.

★ **A carry:** the baby might want to be carried around so that they can hear a heartbeat like the one that ticked away near the womb—a strap-on baby carrier, or older children, can save your arms.

★ **A quiet time:** the baby might be in sensory overload and need to be away from visitors and busy places.

★ **Someone else:** everything may have gone into a vicious circle, with you being tense and the baby being tense— after you've tried for hours, a baby may be quite suddenly comforted by someone else (don't feel too demoralized by this, it happens to us all!).

★ **A big burp:** the baby may have tummy ache and need to have a burp or be comforted until the pain subsides. Hold the baby upright and gently pat or rub their back. Prevent the baby from swallowing air when they feed, especially likely if you're bottlefeeding: hold the bottle so the milk, not air, covers the inside of the nipple as the baby sucks. If you're breastfeeding, take note of any foods you've eaten that seem to cause gassy problems.

★ **A medical check:** the baby may have a medical problem— have your baby checked out by your local doctor or a pediatrician.

★ **A gentle massage with an edible oil:** most people avoid nut oils in case of allergy (look up baby massage in the index).

★ **A lullaby:** your voice, no matter how untuneful, is very soothing to your baby. You can even read an adult book aloud, as long as it isn't Stephen King or anything else spooky that makes your voice sound worried.

★ **Quiet music:** CD stores have lullaby compilations.

★ **Time in a carriage or stroller:** this might even just be being wheeled back and forth, although fresh air is a bonus for both of you.

★ **A warm bath:** babies often enjoy a deep one with a hands-on adult.

★ **Rocking:** this can take the form of a trip in the car, jiggling the crib, or a go in a safe hammock (look up hammocks in the index).

★ **A comfy temperature:** a room somewhere between 68 and 72 degrees Fahrenheit will be fine. This doesn't mean you need to strictly maintain a "perfect" temperature in your place. After all, millions of babies are brought up in the tropics and the Arctic Circle. (Actually I don't know how many babies live in the Arctic Circle. Possibly I mean moose.)

★ **Fewer clothes:** a lot of babies are overdressed. For little babies a general rule is one more layer of clothes than you need yourself as you move about.

★ **A daily routine:** after the first weeks naps at customary times can prevent a baby from being regularly overtired (see the next chapter, Possible Routines for Babies).

And as the baby gets a little older:

★ distraction, distraction, distraction. Older babies' moods can change in an instant. "Look at those vastly interesting pillowcases flapping on the line!" "Look, wicked old Aunty Beryl's making a hilarious noise!" "What is that funny face Mommy is making?" "Let's look in this book, check out this rattly thing here, play and chat with your older brother/sister/cousin/passerby at the bus stop."

It may take a while but, unless your baby is in pain or sick, you can build up some strategies that work for you. It's a matter of trial and error.

Some people reckon babies should be picked up straight away if they cry because otherwise they get distressed and then it's harder to settle them again. Others say leave babies to cry for a minute or two. One thing to keep in mind is to try soothing methods other than picking up every time (singing, rocking, a comforting voice, a rhythmic pat) as your baby may just need to know you're there so they can go to sleep happily. If you pick them up every time, they can get very irritable because they're not getting a chance to sleep or lie about.

Newborn babies need to sleep a lot. Respect this, and don't try to keep them up all day entertaining visitors, no matter what the visitors want. You're the one who'll end up with the wound-up, blubbering flummery baby at the end of the day.

Crying problems and sleeping problems are almost always tightly linked, so have a look at the previous Sleeping chapter and don't hesitate to get professional help to set up a sleep routine or learn settling techniques.

BaBies WHO CRY foR HOURS (OtHeRWise KNOWN as COLic)

If nurses and doctors can't find anything wrong with a baby who cries all the time, the diagnosis is usually colic. What does this mean? That you have a baby who cries all the time. Some people find it comforting to give the problem a name. There's no cure for colic, but it's a diagnosis that says it isn't the parents' fault, they simply drew the temporary short straw and got a colicky baby.

Generally colic is supposed to be a digestive problem—a pain in the tummy that causes a baby to make a screamy sort of cry—which generally lasts for 2 to 4 months depending on which book you read or, more to the point, what sort of baby you have.

Medical suggestions for colic include preparations that are supposed to reduce gas and, as a last resort, sedatives: see your doctor. Off-the-shelf herbal remedies are not a good idea because they are not formulated for babies. If you feel it's hard to know where to start, contact one of the parent services listed in More Info at the end of the second chapter, Your Support Team.

Babies who vomit a lot as well as crying may have a physical problem called reflux (see More Info at the end of the Throwing Up chapter).

"Difficult" Babies

If you have checked out all the possible causes and your baby still cries, keep in mind that you have done everything you can—everything a good parent could do. Your baby may be a "crier," also known as a "difficult" baby. This doesn't mean that your baby is naughty or trying to be difficult. (Happily a "difficult" baby can grow up to be a strong, resilient person who can stand up for themselves.) It just means you'll need some longer term strategies to cope in the next weeks or months—the most important being to rustle up as much help and babysitting as possible to give yourself breaks.

Getting some help

I used to call up for professional help quite a bit when I felt bamboozled—no doubt I would have been less bamboozled if I could have had more sleep. I'm sure sometimes I sounded completely mad: luckily they're used to it, and nobody ever minded a bit. And there's no such thing as a silly question when you're learning to be a parent. Others have found their mothers' group or playgroup very useful for sharing stories and strategies (and providing babysitting swapsies).

If you can afford it or wangle it, get some child care, either from a professional or a friend or relative, so you know there's respite coming. Even if someone calls in every evening for a while and holds the baby so that you get some things done or go for a walk (try a roster system!), it can be crucial time out. (See the Coping Strategies for Parents chapter in *Part 4: Parenting*.)

And if you're absolutely distraught and frightened that you might shake, hit, or harm your baby in some other way, see the suggestions for dealing with these feelings (look up rage in the index) and get help because this situation will probably happen again.

If you need help now, call one of the specific parent helplines (many run 24 hours a day) listed in More Info at the end of the second chapter, Your Support Team. That's also where you'll find contacts for parent services, which may provide counseling, classes in settling and sleeping, and residential stays. You can also contact your GP.

"Controlled crying"

"Controlled crying"—the approach of letting babies cry over set periods—is described in the previous chapter, Sleeping. Only people who care more about theory than real babies suggest using it for

WHICH BABIES CRY?

* Babies in stressful homes cry.

* Babies in calm homes cry.

* Babies with good moms cry.

* Babies with good dads cry.

* Lonely babies cry.

* Babies who are never left alone cry.

* Smart babies cry.

* Sick babies cry.

* Healthy babies cry.

* Babies at about 6 weeks cry (for up to an hour and a half).

* Babies who are carried around by their mothers in slings all day in small African communities cry.

* First babies cry.

* Second and subsequent babies cry.

* Safe babies cry.

* Babies who grow up to be delightful children cry.

* Babies of self-assured parents cry.

* Babies of nervous parents cry.

* Babies of child-care experts cry.

babies under 6 months. That doesn't mean you are helpless against the crying before 6 months. Try the strategies already suggested, look at the specialized books given in More Info at the end of this chapter, or call one of the parent services.

tHe Bottom LiNe aBout CryiNg

If a physical problem is ruled out, your baby's temperament is the biggest factor affecting whether they cry a lot. It has nothing to do with your skills or aptitude as a parent. You can learn tricks that may help. Do everything you can, but treat yourself with special kindness. Don't try to do it alone: traditionally babies have been brought up in gigantic extended family situations, with lots of help, and a collective approach. Besides, when you're sleep deprived, you sometimes can't see solutions, and that isn't your fault. Above all, take it day by day. This hard time will end.

more iNfo

All the baby-care books in More Info at the end of the first chapter, In the Beginning, address crying. The following books are also very helpful.

The Fussy Baby Book: Parenting Your High Need Child From Birth to Age Five
by William Sears, MD, and Martha Sears, RN, Little, Brown, 1996.
The gurus of attachment parenting weigh in with their kid-friendly approach (look up attachment parenting in the index for more on the theory). Like the Pinky McKay book (following), they don't recommend controlled crying.

100 Ways to Calm the Crying

by Pinky McKay, Lothian Books, July, 2002.

Dear Pinky is an Aussie mum and baby fancier who has written a baby-friendly book that looks at the reasons for crying and a range of simple, possible solutions to each kind of crying without having to use the controlled crying approach.

Websites   Many of the general baby and parenting websites listed in More Info at the end of the In the Beginning and Your Support Team chapters will have hints and forums on crying.

POSSIBLE ROUTINES FOR BABIES

A routine is basically a daily schedule for when to feed, play, sleep, have a shower, clean out the cutlery drawer, that sort of caper. So put down "Eight years from now—clean out cutlery drawer." Having a daily routine when your baby is very new, though, is a bit like your birth plan: the little one might have other ideas. Babies are not necessarily going to take to a pattern, and even those who do may not

time for morning snack, bub

gorp

like it all the time. Babies going through growth spurts may wake earlier for feeds, and any baby can do unpredictable things such as suddenly change their sleep habits for no obvious reason.

After a few weeks you may well be able to work out a bit of a pattern, but you'll have to be ready to abandon it at any point. Little babies can't be fed on a strict schedule that follows the clock or in between precisely timed meetings. Sometimes they will be extra hungry earlier than usual, and sometimes they'll be in a transition period from, say, three big sleeps a day to two big sleeps, and that will take some adjusting.

customizing your routine

A routine isn't a set of rules to follow day and night. It's a flexible plan to make things a bit more structured, to make a baby feel secure, and to make a little more sense of the day for you and help you grab a bit of time for yourself even if you've never been a fan of routines.

new baby routine:

Later on keeping a very strict routine can make it hard for you to go out unless you can organize it so the baby sleeps in the car while you're traveling, in the stroller, or at someone else's house—some babies are too interested in the world to be able to sleep away from their non-stimulating bedroom, but most will sleep in the soothingly mobile car (although this can create a problem in itself if they automatically wake up every time the car stops). Some people really need to stick to their routine because they know otherwise they'll pay for it with an overtired, grumpy child later that afternoon or even in the night. Others can fiddle around the edges of their routine quite happily. And others would rather eat a placenta than have any routine at all.

arsenic Hour

Arsenic hour—that delightfully reassuring term for the late afternoon, early evening time when everyone's overtired and cranky and the baby reaches what seems to be a peak of crying—happens, somewhat infuriatingly, anywhere from 4 to 7 p.m. rather than for a strict hour. By anticipating it in your day and experimenting with solutions, you may be able to keep crabbiness to the minimum. Strategies can include getting the baby down for a late afternoon catnap; enlisting help with the baby, a sibling, or the cooking; and drinking vast quantities of gin. I beg your pardon, that's not a strategy, it's a typographical error.

feed, PLay, SLeeP

Many of the sleep schools and parent help centers in Australia talk about the idea of a baby having a feed, then a play, then a sleep, then a feed, then a play, then a sleep; or, in the case of newborns, a feed, a cuddle and a chat, then a sleep. "Play" for a young baby over 6 weeks old means chatting, being sung to, being taken out for a walk, and looking at things they can focus on. This is designed to let the baby have a feed, enjoy a social or interesting time, and then get enough rest to be able to do it all over again. Importantly it separates the feed and the sleep as many babies get so used to a breast- or bottlefeed being part of their sleep ritual they reach a point where they can't nap or go to sleep without it. There is an exception: unless your baby when older has developed an association with feeding and sleep that you are trying to change, it's fine to give a feed immediately before the big night-time sleep, after about 7 p.m. The feed is often a deliciously comforting wind-down ritual for both baby and caregiver.

POSSiBLe NeWBORN ROUtiNe

Baby wakes up.
Feed: breast milk or formula.
Play: diaper change; chat, fresh air, cuddle, pre-sleep ritual pat, rock, or words.
Sleep: as long as the baby wants to.

This feed–play–sleep block can be repeated eight or more times in a 24-hour period.

In the first few weeks the awake part of the feed–play–sleep routine will probably last only an hour or an hour and a quarter, but watch for your baby's tired signs rather than the clock (see tired signs in the index). When a baby shows classic tired signs, pop them down to sleep. In the very early weeks they often nod right off wherever and whenever they feel like it, and if a baby takes a laid-back 50 minutes to feed that will eat into their playtime as well.

Many newborn babies tend to want to stay awake for more like 2 hours in the late afternoon or at the end of the day, contributing to arsenic hour when everyone's fed up. If your baby is showing tired signs at this time, try to get them off to sleep. If they're alert and seem to need the extra time awake, try using a sling to carry them around in or having a relaxing sing, bath or massage routinely at this time to help things stay calm. Difficult if you've dinner to prepare and others such as a toddler to attend to, but perhaps someone else could help.

The feed–play–sleep routine can be repeated as needed into the night, but remember that nighttime feeds in dim light need to be followed directly by everyone going back to sleep, instead of playing, to get the baby used to the most excellent idea that there are no playtimes at night.

Remember, sleep all the times your new baby sleeps at night and some of the times during the day too, and be careful that you let them sleep when they want to, instead of keeping them awake to amuse you or your Aunty Norma, who's due to visit at 3:15. Try to keep visitors flexible: make sure they call before they come so that you can adjust their arrival time with them if need be, or make sure visitors and other kids understand the baby must be allowed to fall asleep and not be disturbed. And watch for those tired signs.

POSSIBLE BABY ROUTINE FROM 3 MONTHS

Continue the feed–play–sleep routine and again watch for your baby's sleepy signs, not the clock. Basically, though, the daytime awake periods will get longer—say, 1 to 2 hours—and there will probably be three big sleeps during the day.

Baby wakes up.
Feed: breakfast (breast milk or formula).
Play.
Sleep.

Feed: morning snack (breast milk or formula).
Play.
Sleep.

Feed: lunch (breast milk or formula).
Play.
Sleep.

Feed: afternoon snack (breast milk or formula).
Play.
Arsenic hour: introduce a restful activity if the baby is cranky or overtired.
Sleep: possibly short or the baby may want to stay awake, but watch for tired signs.

Bath, wind-down.
Feed: dinner (breast milk or formula).
Sleep: about 7 p.m.

Adult dinner and relaxation or sleep.
Feed: supper (breast milk or formula).
Sleep: through the night (hey, it's a plan!).

Playtime sessions can involve outings, walks, visitors, reading a board book, looking at cars swishing past outside the window, singing, chatting, and cuddling. Remember that when a baby wakes for a nighttime feed there's no playtime and the light is kept dim.

Put your baby down to sleep at about 7 at night, then wake them gently for a non-stimulating, business-only feed about 10:30 or 11 p.m. This should see you through for a longer period of sleep, until 5, 6, even 7 a.m. If you are not getting a longer nighttime sleep of 5 or 6 hours by the time your baby is 6 months old, ask your doctor or call one of the parent services for help with adjusting your routine (see the contact details in More Info at the end of the second chapter, Your Support Team).

POSSIBLE BABY ROUTINE FROM 6 MONTHS

The feed–play–sleep routine continues, with the baby moving toward, two big sleeps during the day—a big morning and afternoon nap—and probably a catnap at about 4:30. Catnaps usually last 20 or 40 minutes.

At 6 months a baby will need four or five milk drinks, and tastes of solids (see the Learning to Eat chapter). By 1 year the emphasis is on solids and about 20 ounces of milk throughout the day or the equivalent in dairy products such as yogurt and cheese.

Baby wakes up.
Feed: breakfast (breast or formula milk and a taste of solids such as rice cereal or a bit of fruit).
Play.
Possible sleep for a baby closer to 6 months than 1 year.

Feed: morning snack (breast milk or formula and maybe a taste of solids).
Play.
Sleep.

Feed: lunch (breast milk or formula and a taste of solids).
Play.
Sleep.

Feed: afternoon snack (breast milk or formula and maybe a taste of solids).
Play.
Possible catnap if there are tired signs.
Arsenic hour: a restful activity.

Feed: dinner (a taste of solids and a drink of water).
Play (may be longer than usual, but watch for tired signs).
Bath.
Drink: breast milk or formula.
Nighttime ritual.
Sleep: about 7 p.m.

Adult dinner and relaxation.
Possible feed: supper (breast milk or formula) or start phasing it out.
Sleep.

Put your baby down to sleep at 7 or 7:30 at night. After the baby is 6 months old you can experiment with the late evening feed. Drop it and see what happens. If your baby wakes up at 3 a.m. starving, then it isn't time to drop that feed yet. But maybe the baby will sleep through until 6 or even 7 a.m. It's not unusual for babies to sleep 10 or 12 hours before morning. The solid food introduced at this age helps babies stay full through the night. By about 9 months the late evening feed should be gone and you should be getting a big sleep yourself at night: if you can't quite seem to manage it, ask an adviser at one of the parent services to help you adjust the schedule or talk to your doctor.

POSSIBLE BABY ROUTINE FROM 9 MONTHS

The same sort of pattern is followed but the late afternoon catnap is usually dropped, leaving just a morning and afternoon sleep; and you can move to getting a longer sleep at night if you haven't already.

Baby wakes up.
Feed: breakfast (solids and breast milk or formula).
Play.

Feed: morning snack (a snack and a drink in a cup).
Play.
Sleep.

Feed: lunch (solids and breast milk or formula).
Play.
Sleep.

Feed: afternoon snack (a snack and a drink in a cup).
Play (watch for tired signs but a very late afternoon sleep may interfere with bedtime).
Arsenic hour: a restful activity.
Bath.

Feed: dinner (food and a drink in a cup).
Nighttime ritual.
Drink: breast milk or formula.
Sleep: about 7 p.m.

Adult dinner and free time for exciting housework.
Sleep: everyone until the morning (fingers crossed).

going from two Daytime naps to one

At around a year (maybe earlier, maybe later) your baby may start routinely showing no interest or little interest in the second, afternoon sleep, and want to just faff around. This probably means they're ready to go to one sleep a day, which traditionally is an afternoon sleep. You'll need a transition period, which will probably last about 3 weeks, while you slowly winch the morning sleep later until they're having one daytime nap that eventually starts at midday or 1 or 2 p.m. As they're making the transition you might find them getting crankier at the end of the day; if so put them to bed an hour or half an hour early. (Splendid news: in most cases this makes absolutely no difference to the morning wake-up time.)

By 18 months most kids are down to one sleep a day, and this can last right through until your baby starts school. Others drop the afternoon sleep somewhere along the way, although it's always useful to pick it up again briefly during those stressful or exciting times when they're sick, they're overtired in the first days or weeks of day care or kindergarten, or they've been to see Dorothy the Dinosaur on stage in the morning.

Can I have a nap too?

Daylight Savings

Spend a few days before each daylight-saving changeover gradually altering your routine so that by the time you get there it's a 15-minute adjustment rather than a whole hour. Or you can start the day an hour earlier by the clock in summer.

More Info

BOOKS WITH BABY ROUTINES

Tracy Hogg's *Secrets of the Baby Whisperer* has something called the E.A.S.Y. plan—eating, activity, sleeping, you—based on those four principles. She makes suggestions for a kindly routine that is tailored to your baby's inclinations, and also suggests routines for twins. She believes that even small babies like to anticipate and get into a rhythm of life. Gina Ford's *The Contented Little Baby Book* says babies shouldn't be overstimulated at least 20 minutes before a sleep, and that part of playtime can be baby exploring things on their own. ("Hey, what's that thing on the end of my arm? I think I shall have to stick it straight in my mouth!") She's pretty much Mrs. Strictypants when it comes to baby routines, but some people and babies will like that idea. (See More Info at the end of the first chapter, In the Beginning, for full details and reviews of both books.)

WASHING THE BABY

Babies were not traditionally washed every day until the scientific cleanliness mania of the 1950s had nutty doctors insisting that mothers wash their tiny tots in rubbing alcohol and other antiseptic solutions every day. This, along with soap, contributed to many children developing dry skin and eczema, and also made any existing skin problems worse.

Bathing your baby once every day or two, or even occasionally, is plenty if you're absolutely scrupulous with bottom cleaning after diaper changes. It's not like the tot is playing in puddles.

NEWBORNS AND BATHS

Here's my big tip: if your newborn baby doesn't like the bath, just put them on a couple of layers of towel and give them a going over with warm, wet, soapy cotton balls, then rinse them with warm, wet cotton balls or use a very soft flannel, and dry them well by patting them with a towel or let the air dry them if it's a warm day. In other words—avoid stress, no matter what the textbooks might say about bathing.

Newborn babies, used to being curled up in the womb, get all stretched out for a bath so it can be strange for them the first few times. It always helps to explain to your baby what you're up to as you bath them. If your baby still dislikes it, don't continue but reintroduce the bath now and then: most babies eventually love it—at least when they can start splashing about.

BATHING YOUR BABY

Many people use a plastic baby bath but, as long as you can warm the room, a cleared kitchen sink is fine. Baby baths can be so heavy to lift and empty and a pain to fill from kettle and jug, especially as you'll have to put the baby down safely somewhere else if you're dickering about with kettles. Make sure any faucets are moved out of the way, turned off tight, or disabled.

Assemble everything you need on the bench next to the filled baby bath or sink:
* cotton balls, or flannels you wash after in antibacterial powder and hot water every bottom contact.
* a soap substitute—however often you wash your baby it's safer to use a non-soap product to avoid dry skin (ask your pharmacist to recommend one).
* a soft towel (some fancy ones come with a baby hood).

183

★ a new diaper, and diaper-rash cream if necessary, plus a clean outfit (cut these out if you carry your baby in the towel to the changing table to be dressed).

The bath water should be a temperature that feels pleasantly warm, but not hot, on your elbow. Don't let the baby get too cold as the water cools: you want to replicate the relaxing amniotic fluid feeling rather than plunge them into a bracing trough.

Make sure you have one arm under your baby, supporting the neck and head during a bath, and use the other one for washing.

A two-person team bath can be had by one adult sitting in the big bath with the baby bath on the bottom of it. The baby is bathed in the smaller receptacle by Person One, then removed by Person Two, who is also instructed to bring Person One a pineapple daiquiri.

Eyes and ears

If they look mucky, eyes should be washed separately, with a cool sterile saline solution (look up eyes in the index): don't hold eyes open to wash them.

Don't poke anything smaller than your elbow into a child's ear. This means you can wash any bits you can see (the outside), but *not* inside in case you damage the eardrum or introduce infection.

Willies and girly bits

Babies and toddlers with penises don't need to be washed under their foreskin. Between the ages of 3 and 5 the foreskin will usually become moveable, and you can teach your boy to clean underneath himself, and eventually to understand the importance of doing so for the rest of his life. Until then, don't try to roll back the foreskin. It's tight when he's little because it's there for protection against grit and infection. Just clean the outside of the penis with a cotton ball when he's an infant, and normal soap and a flannel washcloth will do in the bath as he gets older. A circumcised penis isn't necessarily cleaner and, despite rumors, is definitely *not* a protection against infections, sexual or otherwise. When he gets a lot older, if you're worried about him getting sexually transmitted diseases, tell your son about condoms.

The folds of a girl's private parts also need to be washed carefully and gently, and this skill passed on to her.

safety

Needless to say (but you're not always logical when you're sleep deprived), keep a hand on your baby *at all times* in the bath: this is a hard and fast rule and means you can never leave them or turn away for the mere seconds it can take a baby to drown. And remember, a baby who likes water, or even an inquisitive one, can fall into a bucket or a sink, a pond, a dam, a pool, or a puddle. Babies' and toddlers' big heads make it hard for them to right themselves. All water, however shallow, is potentially dangerous to a baby, toddler, and preschooler. Always pull the bath plug or empty a baby bath the second that it's possible: don't wait until later.

Get a non-slip rubber mat for the big bath as soon as your baby is ready to go into it.

washing yourself

In the very early days after the baby's born it's sometimes almost impossible to get time to have your own shower. Take advantage of visitors who can hold the baby or put your baby securely in a stroller or a floor basket while you shower. Climbing out of jammies and getting clean can help you feel refreshed and more in control of your life.

Bath toys

Newborns don't need any bath toys: wait until your baby is reaching for and grabbing things before you introduce a rubber ducky or a floaty plastic anything.

Cheap baby toys that last into toddlerhood and beyond include safe, colorful, soft plastic shell and sea creature shapes; old shampoo bottles that become squirters; sieves; plastic cups and other containers for pouring water into; food coloring; all manner of plastic dollies and boats; and toweling glove puppets.

Every few weeks you may like to give all the plastic bath toys a good jooshing with a wash brush in a bucket of water to which a cup of white vinegar has been added, and then dry them in the sun to make sure there are no germy bits. On the other hand you might figure they get washed every night so get a grip. Regularly squeeze out the old water that splooshes around in the squirty toys because otherwise it gets pretty swampy in there.

BONDING

We hear so much about the wonderful joy of having a baby that if we don't feel it ourselves immediately we think there's something wrong with us, whereas the "slow bond" is just as legitimate an experience. Some things take practice and experience. It's okay to have negative or blank feelings: it just seems particularly awful if they're not balanced by a few good feelings. This chapter gives you some options for helping the bonding process along.

some ways people respond to their new baby

★ Immediately you see your baby for the first time you feel a rush of protective love and never want to be parted.

★ You look at the baby and wonder what all the fuss is about and feel nothing. Gradually you learn to love your child.

★ As a guy, when you see your baby being born you realize you want to protect and love them and their mother every way you can.

★ The first time you put your baby to your breast you feel that it's all perfect and natural.

★ The first time you hug your baby to your breast you remember you're a man and feel a bit useless.

★ When the cesarean drugs or the shock of labor wear off, you slowly begin to marvel at and feel connected to your baby, whether you breastfeed or bottlefeed.

★ As time goes by, you feel more and more loving and confident in your relationship with your baby.

★ After a period of confused and depressing thoughts, you get help from counselors, a doctor, a support group, or some prescribed drugs perhaps, and you begin to learn how to look after your baby and you begin to care. You understand that this feeling will build, and doesn't come immediately or without effort for everyone.

★ The thought of anyone affronting, let alone hurting, your baby makes you instinctively furious.

With almost every other relationship in life love is earned. And yet we are expected, through miraculous hormones or somehow automatically, to love and bond with our children. This can make us feel terribly guilty if we don't experience great surges of love and bonding straight away, or even in the first weeks.

The process of birth is such a huge thing (and one that we've probably been concentrating all our thinking and learning on for so long) that we may need to stay with our own body recovery for a while and not just snap into the "next episode" immediately. It is very common to feel quite disconnected or helpless when the baby is born, just as it's common to feel a great rush of relief and love. Because as first-time mothers (and fathers) we are often not experienced with babies, we are quite overcome and shocked by how tiny and defenseless our babies look, and this can make us feel frightened to cuddle, frightened of responsibility. And for many of us the birth of a baby (especially the first) can mean giving up and grieving for the permanent or temporary loss of a whole lot of really good things such as independence, cocktails on a whim, an income, and our former kept-to-itself body. All these legitimate thoughts and conditions can give us pause, and get in the way of feeling joy and attachment.

Although the first moment a mother or a father is left alone in a room with a new baby, they may feel complete bewilderment, even fear, this will pass. Even if it doesn't pass by itself, people can get help to move on from feeling empty or frightened to gradually falling in love with their babies and having a happy future together.

getting Help With Bonding

Be patient with yourself and make sure you go to the source of any negative or blank feelings and find a solution. While you're still in the hospital, if you feel that you're not equipped to look after your baby, tell the nurses: if you are in a good hospital, they'll help you learn the new skills needed or get you in touch with resources in your area that can help. (You don't have to be perfect. You just need to try.) If you feel a bit indifferent and as if you don't know what to do with the baby, it may well be the sheer physical and mental shock of the labor and birth or the dulling effect of cesarean and recovery drugs.

COMMON REACTIONS

✱ Oh, my GOD. Did it really come out of me?

✱ I've never felt such a strong love.

✱ Can I touch him?

✱ Give her to me!

✱ They're not expecting me to actually feed that, are they?

✱ I can't wait to try breastfeeding!

✱ Don't take my baby out of my sight.

✱ I really need to sleep: can you look after her for a while?

✱ I won't know what to do because I'm a guy.

Common feelings include:

✱ bewilderment.

✱ pride.

✱ blank exhaustion.

✱ exultation—a high.

✱ fear of Doing the Wrong Thing.

✱ anxiety about the baby's health and safety.

✱ inadequacy at the thought of parenthood.

✱ calm bliss.

✱ a maelstrom of different thoughts and emotions.

✱ shock.

Tell the nurses if you're feeling ambivalent about the baby. They've seen it all, believe me, and they know you don't need to panic.

If you're home and having these feelings, your first point of contact for help is your doctor. Don't worry—that's why they have tissues in their office, they're used to this sort of thing. They'll be able to refer you to a specialist in this problem.

You might also like to talk to other mothers. Your hospital, doctor, or local family services agency should be able to help you find a local parents' group.

If you need a voice on the phone right away there are parent helplines, and lots of parent services, listed in More Info at the end of the second chapter, Your Support Team. And see the next chapter, Feeling Overwhelmed or Depressed, for the lowdown on general, non-specific "blues" and full-on postpartum depression.

"If your maternal instinct doesn't kick in (mine never did), then read books or seek help from family services." AUDREY

ways to increase bonding

Don't forget to take photos and spend time flaked on the couch just looking at your baby and having as many calm moments as you can. The newborn time feels endless now, but when you look back it really will (cliché alert) seem to have gone in a flash. The only way to get to know baby cries and baby body language is to spend relaxed time together.

★ Sit quietly and inspect your baby from top to toe.

★ Chat to your baby face to face up close.

★ Name your baby and start using the name a lot, or use lots of special nicknames.

★ Sing to your baby: anything will do.

★ Watch your baby's expressions and try to guess what they mean.

★ Think about what you'd do if someone tried to hurt your baby.

★ Tell your baby you're going to get to know each other over time.

★ Have lots of skin-to-skin contact.

★ Be very still and listen to your baby breathing.

★ Feel your baby's heartbeat.

★ Look at your baby's feet, hands, back of the neck.

★ Hold the baby to your chest when standing or lying down.

★ Gently massage your baby (look up baby massage in the index).

★ Watch your baby sleeping.

feeLing overwheLmed or depressed

Parenthood isn't always wonderful: the first weeks will be tiring and stressful. As well as being fascinating—"Look at those darling starfish hands!"—your baby will scream and poop and not explain themselves at all. This is probably your training ground in unconditional love and devotion, and some- times it's a pain in the butt at best and absolutely maddening and exhausting at worst. The hard aspects can be balanced by the pride and joy of keeping your little one alive and well, and the thrill of getting to know your baby. But for

some people the good feelings get pushed
to the background or swamped completely,
either for a few days or weeks or in tough
cases for months: professional help is a must.

a perfectly sane response

To be honest I can't quite work out why anyone *wouldn't* come crashing down after the ultra-stress of birth, the lack of sleep, the realization that this isn't for the weekend but for life, the sore aching girly bits, the carry-on and sometimes early pain of first-time breastfeeding, and the anxiety about whether you're doing ANYTHING right. (I wish I'd started using disposable diapers in the hospital—they would have been one less damn thing to fold properly.) Plus you may be astonished to find that you feel like a worn-out old couch instead of a supermodel.

And that's if everything's going fine. If you are also dealing with outside relationship problems, a sick baby, or unhelpful relatives, it can all seem a bit of a disaster. I think parents at this stage can sometimes feel terribly alone, especially sole or single parents and parents whose partners go back to work leaving them—aarrgh, surely some mistake—in CHARGE. And the house looks terrible a day after getting home from hospital and how are you supposed to eat fresh, healthy food when you can't even get out of your PJs by 5 p.m. and I can't cope, and shut up. Which often leaves partners not knowing what to do to help and be supportive (see the Dads chapter in *Part 4: Parenting*).

All this is not helped by the amazingly intense attention that newborn babies need—feeds every 2 to 4 hours, diaper changes, comforting—while you're trying to snatch bits of sleep here and there. Honestly, I think if you weren't feeling a bit demented at least once a day there'd be something wrong with you.

And you're allowed to have negative feelings about your new role: some of it is hard and tiring and revolting work. That's why sensible societies share the care of a newborn baby, and rich people have full-time nannies. Every other mother (and father) is having the same insecurities—I can guarantee you the first-timers are. And the others are wondering why the things that worked with the first baby aren't working with this one.

All the pictures of mothers and fathers in those baby books are of well-groomed, tidy, rested-looking people reading books and smiling contentedly at chuckling 6-month-old babies, or at least newborn babies who aren't screamingly red as if they've just been lightly parboiled and shouted at.

One of the contradictions I remember feeling through the newborn days was wishing that somebody would turn up and say "There's been a terrible mistake, this isn't your baby and we're going to take them away and have them looked after by more competent folk," while simultaneously knowing that if someone did actually try to take my baby away from me I would kill them with a swizzle stick. Or some dental floss.

Sometimes it's hard as hell, and sometimes we're all bad parents who would so fail an audition for one of those margarine ads. I reckon it's time we admitted it to each other and helped each other stumble through, instead of pretending to be superparents who know everything.

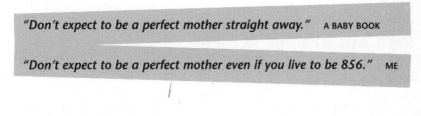

"Don't expect to be a perfect mother straight away." A BABY BOOK

"Don't expect to be a perfect mother even if you live to be 856." ME

Somebody get me a helicopter

These days women are more educated than they ever were, and the United States is one of the best places to live if you're a woman (and a mother). There are employment opportunities, civil rights, high quality health care: it may not be perfect but it's about as good as it gets for most women in the world. The flip side of this is that many of us are smart, educated women who gave up school or work to have a baby, large numbers of us are used to striding about being independent, spending our own money, and demanding that unfairnesses be corrected and equality enforced, and if there's a problem we nail it down and fix it, or get somebody else to fix it. Being a mother, especially in those first weeks, means that no amount of scheduling meetings, rational thought, or rope ladder will solve the problems. In most cases we just have to ride it out: we can't walk away or fix it right NOW.

Make important decisions when we haven't had more than 3 hours' sleep in a row for 9 days? Not be able to get dressed all day? Not be able to walk out for the afternoon and have it all solved when we get back? Can't send the crying baby back to the shop for an adjustment? A problem without some sort of immediate solution? We're so not used to that. We'd never start a job and expect that we wouldn't receive any training—yet we expect to somehow be great as parents right away, even though we haven't trained for the job, or spent weeks and months getting up to speed. Not to mention most new jobs are not 24 hours a day, with no deep sleep for weeks. Call the union!

THe eaRLy Days BLues

The third or fourth day blues

All those lovely, floaty, hippie pregnancy hormones shut off like a tap just about day 3 or 4 after the birth as your prolactin hormone levels gear up for milk delivery. (Progesterone, estrogen, cortisol, and beta-endorphins fall away.) This is often what's called the "baby blues" or the three-day weep.

Recovering from a traumatic birth

Maybe the labor or the cesarean didn't go the way it was "supposed to." Traumatic births very often result in feelings of sadness, shock, or distress that are played out in the open, or suppressed, in the first few weeks of a baby's life. Recovering from a particularly exhausting or surgical birth is a factor often overlooked by people, who simply assume you're fine once the baby comes out. Sometimes many tears need to be shed, and the birth story told or considered over and over, before you feel able to move on.

You need to be patient with yourself about recovering, and you need to understand that having a healthy baby is really all that matters now. It's important to acknowledge the trauma, but also to realize that it wasn't your fault the way the birth turned out. It's the luck of the draw.

Ask your doctor to refer you to a therapist if you need extra help to work through your feelings.

A health problem with the baby

Sometimes babies are born with minor or severe health problems, which can trigger depression. In the intensity of focusing on your child, don't forget to pay attention to the mental health of the rest of the family, including yourself. Don't be afraid of asking for help.

Coping when you first get home

One thing that does seem to help people cope in the early days at home is prioritizing: letting the housework go, not caring too much about your hairdo, and just making sure food goes into everyone and sleep is grabbed whenever possible. In the early weeks that's all you can do.

Another thing that helps is getting outside into the fresh air and seeing the sun in the sky: otherwise you live in a twilight world ruled

by feeds every few hours, regardless of day or night, experiencing something like self-perpetuating, hideous, endless jet lag.

Support from a partner (if you have one), family, or friends is crucial. In the Kidwrangling Survey, the number of women who ran to their moms and were grateful for them was matched by the number of women whose moms were critical, or had forgotten what it was like to have a baby, or had old-fashioned advice and were offended when it wasn't followed. A lot of people had difficulty with mothers-in-law. And sometimes the child's grandparents can be more of a burden than a help because they are too elderly or out of touch to actually make things easier. It may be that you need to look elsewhere for supportive help.

I realize now that I should have had more visitors to help and chat and normalize things, but I was so tired and felt so inexperienced and down that I didn't want anyone to see me. It's a big mistake to think you have to put on a show of any kind for visitors. If we all pretend, everyone will continue to be

24 HOUR CHART

look out window
sleep
change top
think about sleep
sleep
bosom wrangling
Ms Zombie-pants
sleep
can't remember
EAT
or not
something

shocked by the reality. Believe me, other parents of young children understand.

Although routines can make your life easier at this stage, if part of your routine is Thursday afternoon clean the toilet maybe just go out and have a cup of tea and talk to some adults for a while instead. (And see the Coping Strategies for Parents chapter in *Part 4: Parenting.*)

"You're swimming through the day. I don't think I articulated anything. I don't think I showered. I don't think I ate anything unless it came out of a box and fit in my hand. People would say to me 'Let's go out to dinner' and all I could think was 'How cruel.'"
TERRI, QUOTED IN *MARTHA STEWART BABY* MAGAZINE

"I felt like a cross between a milking machine and a washing machine." LESLEY

"Having worked as a private maternity nurse and nanny, I really thought that motherhood would pose no problems for me. How wrong I was. In those first few weeks, with both my children, I had serious doubts as to whether I was really cut out to be a mom. When I finally expressed my concerns I discovered that 99 percent of the mothers I knew had experienced the same physical and emotional problems . . . There I was thinking that there was something wrong with me because it wasn't 'coming naturally.' Turned out I was perfectly normal: it's just that you apparently have to become a mother before you get let in on that particular piece of secret women's business." TRACEY

"When family and friends come over get them to fold a load of washing." BENITA

"I'm an A type personality and it was hard not having the control over my life that I used to have." GARDA

"If you are tempted to look at the stay-home full-time moms of yesteryear and wish for their capabilities, remember that they often had four generations of helpers. Don't compare yourself to a situation that bears no resemblance to your own."
MICHAEL

"I wish other moms would stop putting up walls and saying that everything is okay and life is wonderful. Because that is garbage. Having children, a husband, and a household is plain hard work. At times enjoyable work, but most of the time just hard work. And part of the time it is frustrating, exhausting, upsetting, and stressful. I really didn't know what stress was until I had two kids and a husband." JOANNA

THINGS THAT MAY HELP HEAD OFF THE BLUES

✱ Understand that the tiredness and stress of a new baby will only get better as time goes by, and that it's okay to be bored, impatient, or annoyed by aspects of parenting, as long as you don't take it out on the baby.

✱ Get out into the open air as much as possible—a half-hour walk a day with the stroller will reduce stress and make you feel better. It doesn't matter what you look like.

✱ Talk to women who've been through it and come out the other side.

✱ Ask for help—from anywhere you can get it: partner, family, friends, postpartum depression support groups, doctor (see More Info at the end of this chapter). If you have spare money hire a cleaner and doula or babysitters.

✱ Get away as much as you can: maybe to a movie that takes you into another world.

"I was desperate for a baby, and I think I couldn't see past that, and saw the life through rose-colored glasses. I was quite shocked by how hard it can be and also by how mundane it can be at times." LOUISE

"I think that some people just need to be allowed to feel overwhelmed, I think that we should all be taught that childbirth is a real effort for a lot of women and may not come easily to you."
CATHY

"My baby was nearly 7 weeks premature so I was sent to a Tresillian home in Sydney, where they taught me calm, sensible ways to look after my baby. Before that I knew absolutely nothing."
ANNE

✱ Understand that you may feel alone in your house but out there there are thousands just like you, about to go into it or going through it, and thousands who have come out the other side.

✱ Have a long, hard look at what you're expecting of yourself. If a friend came to you with your problems, what would you advise them? Why be harder on yourself?

✱ Cut off from people who are critical and negative without actually helping very much: you really don't need them, even and especially if they're related to you.

✱ Go to a mothers' group, parents' group, or playgroup, even if your baby is too young to really play.

✱ Learn yoga or another relaxation technique. Look for a special postpartum class or an instructor who is experienced in postpartum exercise.

"I was so dumb I thought I wasn't allowed to take the baby for a walk after 3 p.m. (I was very taken with a local maternal nurse—she of no children and about 68 years old). The best advice in my experience was to make new friends, even if you never would have liked that type of person. Invite them for morning tea. You will have to get out of your pyjamas and so will she. Go to the local mothers' groups . . . get the baby outside even if he screams for the entire walk. You have achieved something, and it knackers them if they cry for two blocks." SOPHIE

"Sometimes you have to have a good cry and try and remember that the bad days will end." JILLIAN

"What a nightmare those first 6 weeks were. I tried to take everyone's advice, which was contradictory in most cases, and ended up tying myself in knots. Luckily my family ignored my breezy, confident "I'm fine!"s and were wonderfully supportive." KELLIE

"I found joining a playgroup very useful. It was good to meet other moms going through the same types of things even if their children were a bit older." HEATHER

"My firstborn being a preemie scared me a lot. I hated anyone touching him and breathing near him. I was too scared to put him down. I spent a whole day without eating because I couldn't leave him. It didn't occur to me that I could hold him (in a sling) while I made a sandwich! I think I lost half my brain when my baby was born!" TRACEY

"Accept all help offered whether it be a meal, the ironing, or somebody to watch baby for 15 minutes while you ENJOY your shower." LINDA

"Ignore housework TOTALLY, eat takeout and frozen foods, ask friends and relatives to do the washing, cook the casserole, or have the other kids. Nobody shows up to help these days, we're so busy: you have to ask, and make sure you show your appreciation later when you are on your feet, bake them a cake or buy them a lottery ticket. Don't read too many books by 'experts.'"
HALONA

"Get your husband/partner involved from day one. Teach him the ins and outs or you are setting yourself up to be the only one that settles, feeds, etc. Maintain contact with the outside world and delegate, delegate. Have one day a week that is yours." TRACY

"I make it a point to have a shower, put on make-up, and dress before 9 a.m. For me it has been important to dress in my trendy gear, not house clothes, even if I am not going anywhere or expecting visitors. It makes me feel good." MARY

"Wear your track suit to bed, and then if you don't have time to dress/shower in the morning, you still look like you have!" ANN

"Screw the housework." MELANIE

"If you can afford a cleaner, go for it." STEPHANIE AND PAM

"Newborns are so portable. Get out of the house." MARY

"Call a parent helpline if you're worried about anything. Nothing is a stupid question and they have heard them all before. They also don't mind if you cry while you're talking to them because you're sleep deprived or worried. Many times I would call them when absolutely beside myself and I never found them to be anything other than fantastic and wonderfully supportive." AMANDA

"In the end it comes down to this: if the baby is fed, clean, warm and loved, then you're doing just right." EMMA

"I didn't get out of my PJs until 3 p.m. every day." CHRISTINE

"Buy an answering machine: your message should be very long and tell the listener everything you might possibly be doing that is stopping you from reaching the phone—hopefully they will either come and help or LEAVE YOU ALONE." ROBYN, MOTHER OF THREE UNDER 3

ONGOING LOW-LEVEL BLUES

A more specific level of ongoing blues is often felt by women who take a baby home to a family that already has a young child or children. Again a totally rational reaction to such a situation, I would have thought, but one that needs help as depression is—well, dammit, it's depressing, even if it comes and goes. You need help in a situation like this: perhaps coping strategies and the allocation of specific jobs to partners, relatives, or friends. Routines might help.

Mild depression usually comes in small doses such as a few days or a week or so at a time. Symptoms include mood swings, crying, crankiness, and tiredness. For parent services that can help see More Info at the end of the second chapter, Your Support Team.

RAGE

It's common to feel angry with a baby, particularly a baby who won't stop crying, even when you know how irrational that is—babies can't be "naughty" because they have no idea what they're doing. What's important is that when you feel angry you do something about it that doesn't involve blaming—or harming—the baby.

If your frustration with your baby rises to boiling point and you think you might shake, hit, or otherwise harm them:

★ put the baby in a safe place—a crib is best—and walk out of the house (into the garden, if you have one) to calm down.

★ or pop the baby in the stroller and go and sit in the park— the baby might still cry, but you'll be outside and in public and less likely to do something awful.

★ or call one of the parent services or a parent helpline (see More Info at the end of the second chapter, Your Support Team).

A very experienced person in the field of distraught moms tells me a good quickie soother is to stand with your hands palm down in a basin of warm water and breathe slowly.

If you have got to the stage of feeling at the end of your tether you will probably feel that way again, and it may get worse, so it's a good idea to seek some help at this point. I think many, many parents have shouted rather uncontrollably at a baby who "refused" to go to sleep or to stop crying. This can frighten both of you and make everyone cry even more.

POStPARtum DePReSSiON (PPD)

Postpartum depression can turn up straight after the birth or unexpectedly some time in the first couple of years, and often comes on gradually. Even though many people don't talk about it, PPD affects thousands of US women each year, and some men too. The depression can be hormonally caused, psychological, or even a recurrence of depression from another time. In some cases PPD can recur with the birth of each child. This is the black hole from which you can't see a way out: you think it's never going to get better.

PPD seems utterly unrelenting to those in it: you don't have any good days, or you have more bad days than good days, and you feel no optimism or enthusiasm for anything. The feelings are intense or constant, and you can't "shake yourself out of it" or "pull yourself together." This, my friend, is completely treatable, and so many moms have been through it: you must tell your partner or someone you're close to and see a professional about your feelings now.

Symptoms of PPD
These are common symptoms:
- ★ feeling tired.
- ★ feeling cranky.
- ★ crying.
- ★ appetite loss.
- ★ black moods.
- ★ feeling worthless.
- ★ feeling that somehow your "self" has gone missing.
- ★ overwhelming despair or pessimism.
- ★ feeling numb or blank.
- ★ anxiety attack symptoms such as sweating, palpitations, shaking, terror.
- ★ insomnia.
- ★ feeling bad, guilty, ashamed, or inadequate.
- ★ thoughts about harming your baby or yourself.
- ★ memory blanks.
- ★ exhaustion.
- ★ feeling uninterested in affection or sex.

Risk factors for general depression
These factors for general depression may or may not contribute to PPD:
- ★ having a history of family breakdown or unhappiness.
- ★ poverty.
- ★ being a victim of some kind of violence or emotional abuse.
- ★ a whole bunch of stressful things happening at once (pregnancy or childbirth counts) or one or two big-stress events.

★ previous depression.

★ low self-esteem generally.

Added risk factors for PPD

These factors are more related to PPD than general depression:

★ low self-esteem caused by feeling inadequate as a parent.

★ having little or no support with a young baby.

★ depression during pregnancy.

★ problems with a partner.

★ a difficult labor or unexpected or unwanted cesarean.

★ being a sole parent.

★ a baby who cries a lot.

★ wanting to make things "perfect" or to be "perfect."

★ being a pessimist.

★ having a depressed partner.

Some people with PPD have experienced none of the above risk factors.

"I ended up with postpartum depression, which is when I stopped trying to do fifty things at a time. I stopped worrying about working, school, about fixing up our house." JUNINE

"I had quite bad postpartum depression after my second son was born and I found just going out in the garden and sitting was wonderful. Just to physically leave the inside of the house and get out. I also sew and found the days when I gave myself time to do a bit of sewing made me more settled and peaceful with myself." KARYN

"I always thought it only affected mothers who felt no bond with their baby or who had a 'high maintenance' baby. I found out at 4¹/₂ months it had nothing to do with any of that. My baby is a happy little fella generally and I had an instant bond with him . . . I could not fathom how I could go from being a fearless and capable professional to an anxious, fearful, blubbering heap of misery in a matter of months. I couldn't sleep, my mind would not shut off. I started spending the entire day watching TV, regardless of what was on. When I yelled at my baby because I couldn't hear the TV, I was certain I was in need of help. I called my doctor and she did a PPD questionnaire on me. I came up trumps and got all the help I needed. It was the best thing I ever did, reaching out to the doctor. You should never feel you are a 'bad mother' if you're feeling anxious and/or depressed—get some help, and with time, things will improve." MOM

"I suffered from postpartum depression after my first child and found it very hard to relax and enjoy him. I also thought I should be superwoman and get back to my before-baby life as soon as he was home. I think the best thing you can do is accept that life has changed and go with the flow rather than stress out about what you can and can't get done." LIBBY

Partners of people with PPD

Partners can be terribly stressed and worried about the whole situation, and need to get away sometimes too. Dads can suffer from a form of PPD. You can end up in a double depressed situation, which needless to say is really bad for babies and children. For their sake as well as yours you need to get professional help from someone trained specifically in postpartum depression.

Treatment for PPD

Treatment may be a combination of any or all of the following:

- ★ counseling—on your own or with your partner (see More Info at the end of this chapter).
- ★ group support or therapy.
- ★ antidepressant drugs, which should always be used with other treatments such as getting practical help at home and counseling (drugs usually mean an end to breastfeeding, but this is not necessarily a bad thing).
- ★ hormone-balancing drugs.
- ★ discussing and developing a plan for improving your life and routine.
- ★ talking to moms who have been through it and are back on an even keel.

POSTPARTUM PSYCHOSIS

This is a mental illness that affects a handful of mothers in every couple of thousand. It comes on in the first month or two after the birth, or even almost immediately, and is characterized by terribly severe depression, hallucinations, and other scary business such as wanting to harm the baby or yourself. There is often a known or unknown genetic predisposition, or a family or personal history of bipolar disorder (meaning the wild high and low feelings formerly called manic depression) or schizophrenia.

Some people who develop postpartum psychosis have no history of warning signs at all. Some recover quickly, others need ongoing medication to control the condition. Postpartum psychosis must be treated with drugs to help restore a balanced brain chemistry—this may take some time to get exactly right, and may or may not involve rest and recuperation in hospital until the drugs have kicked in properly. It's very important that the focus is on treating the mental illness. A caregiver must be found for the baby and breast-feeding will have to stop so the drugs won't affect the baby.

It's possible for mentally ill people to maintain normal and loving lives as moms; but they must have an understanding that they are sick and an insight into their disease that means they keep taking their medication—indefinitely, if necessary. They also need understanding and support from family and friends. Uncontrolled and untreated mental illness can be one of the most lonely and terrifying things for both parent and child. Postpartum psychosis isn't something people can just snap out of by free will. Like other mental illnesses it is made worse by alcohol and all non-treatment drugs. It is very likely that counseling and special explanations will be needed for the child as they grow, to understand ongoing problems and that their parent's illness is not the child's fault. The child will also need an easily accessible, safe haven with friends or relatives.

If you have dark days of depression all the time, serious thoughts about harming yourself or your baby, you are hearing voices or experiencing unusual urges, or you haven't slept for days, get someone to be with you *right now*. Call your doctor. Tell them there's a baby involved and you need help straight away. If it's after hours, get someone to be with you *now* and call one of the parent helplines listed in More Info at the end of the second chapter, Your Support Team, or call 911.

If you feel you can wait a day, you can make an appointment with your GP to talk about the best way forward, and who to be referred to. You will need to be referred to a specialist psychiatrist so don't be dismissed off with the usual antidepressant drugs without knowing the exact nature of your illness.

moRe iNfo

A PERFECTLY SANE RESPONSE

Life After Birth

by Kate Figes, Penguin, UK, 1998.

Kate Figes has an honest look behind the pretty picture of what many people expect from motherhood: she tackles health and exhaustion; common fears; adjusting to motherhood; the notion of a "good" mother; relationships with the father of the baby; how sex goes out the window for most people; what motherhood can do to your notion of the world, including your sense of self and your circle of friends. An antidote to those pictures of grinning celebrities with new babies saying "I never felt so sexy" and "I love it. I just want to be a mother all day for the rest of my life! (although I do need to pop over to Cannes for my latest premiere)."

> *"Sleeping during the daytime with more than one child is usually out of the question, unless you know that someone else is looking after the baby. Often mothers of one child find that they cannot sleep during the day because they know that at any moment their baby could wake up."* FROM THE 'EXHAUSTION' SECTION OF *LIFE AFTER BIRTH*

POSTPARTUM DEPRESSION

You can ask your local PPD support group to recommend a good book on PPD for you. You can also call a parent helpline listed in the More Info section at the end of the second chapter, Your Support Team.

According to the National Women's Health Information Center, a woman's first point of contact is her doctor who can refer her for therapy. Some insurance companies require a doctor's referral; others may require the patient to choose from a list of providers; some plans do not cover counseling. Services for women without insurance coverage varies by community. Even if there are no local resources (rare), there is a plethora of information and online support groups that can help.

There is a range of community organizations that provide support, with some communities overflowing with wonderful resources and volunteer-run programs and others with very few. Local family services agency, social services office, or health department should be able to provide a list of what services are available.

Here are some of the major national postpartum depression resources:

Postpartum Support International
Includes listings by state for local support groups and organizations and a comprehensive list of other postpartum depression support websites. They also provide excellent information and suggestions about how new mothers can build their own support system.
www.postpartum.net/

Postpartum Stress Center
Very helpful site, including a FAQ, links, and helpful information for husbands and family.
www.postpartumstress.com/

Online PPD Support Group
Has excellent resources including a Dad's page. Hosts a postpartum depression online chat several times a month.
www.ppdsupportpage.com/

parentsplace.com
Hosts an online postpartum depression discussion board (and parenting discussion boards about almost every imaginable topic).
www.parentsplace.com

National Women's Health Information Center (a project of the Office on Women's Health in the Department of Health and Human Services)

1-800-994-9662

www.4woman.gov/faq/postpartum.htm

Helpful information and links. Moms can call the national helpline for more information. They will be referred to their doctor or the following organizations:

Depression After Delivery, Inc.

1-800-944-4773

www.depressionafterdelivery.com/

Postpartum Education for Parents

805-564-3888

www.sbpep.org

ALL KINDS OF DEPRESSION AND MENTAL ILLNESS

American Psychological Association

800-374-2721

www.apa.org

National Institute of Mental Health

301-496-9576

www.nimh.nih.gov/

National Mental Health Association

Provides free information on over 200 mental health topics including bipolar disorder, depression, bereavement, post-traumatic stress disorder, and warning signs of mental illness. Referrals to local mental health services. Distributes free national directory of local mental health associations, and offers low-cost materials. Advocates removing stigma of mental illness and for mental health benefits.

1-800-969-6642

National Institute of Mental Health Information Line

Automated phone system that takes orders for free brochures on depression.

1-800-421-4211 (publications)

301-443-4513 (information and referrals)

National Mental Health Services Knowledge Exchange Network

Refers callers to many mental health organizations nationwide.

1-800-789-2647 or 800-THERAPIST gives referrals to local therapists.

Learning to eat

Sorry, I couldn't bring myself to call this chapter Solids as that sounds quite industrial and disgusting— especially since in the beginning "solids" should be called "mashes" anyway. Basically it's about when your baby starts to eat (and throw) some mushed-up stuff as well as drinking breast or formula milk.

← NB if you see a high chair that looks like this don't buy it

WHeN to start

"They" (those shadowy child-nutrition figures in the shadowy Child Nutrition Bunker) used to say you needed to start giving babies mashed-up things at 4 to 6 months; now their latest guidelines suggest 6 months is the best time.

Many reasons for the change are given (maximizing breast-feeding time, minimizing allergies), but probably the really sensible reason is that this is about the time when babies begin to need more than breast milk or formula can give them. Fundamentally, they start to need more iron so that their bodies can make more red blood cells. Also babies at this age start wanting to try real food—sometimes looking at you intently while you're eating or reaching out a chubby fist to try to grab something as the fork goes past.

So beginning on solid food should be when your baby starts looking interested in what other people are eating—it shouldn't be because a book, friend, or relative tells you at 3 or 4 months it is time to start shoveling it in, regardless of what the baby seems to want. When you first start it can seem incredibly stressful and worrying—sometimes because parents think they must force the issue or must feed their baby all sorts of things to keep them healthy. "Nonsense!" I hear my inner-Nanna snorting.

Science experiments

While babies are still being mainly fed on breast milk or formula, any beginner's food business is all about experimenting. You don't suddenly start cutting down on milk feeds. In the beginning eating is just part of life's big adventure for your baby, and you get to be there to see amazing facial expressions the first time they try strawberry yogurt (wooooow!) or something they hate (they make a face like Queen Victoria's). Enjoy those expressions—they're probably the same ones you'd make at a dinner party if you hadn't been taught manners.

In those first weeks of trying mushes don't think of the food as sustenance or keeping your child alive. It doesn't matter if they spit it ALL out, it just means you should put "solids" away until your baby's interested. They're not ready, no matter what the books or charts say. It will just make you all miserable if you push it. Some kids, especially breastfeeders, might hold out longer than 6 months. At this point you're conducting fun experiments in taste—not nutrition.

As long as they're getting lots of breast milk or proper formula milk, you are hereby instructed not to panic about food. Up to 1 year old, babies should still be getting about 32 ounces of breast or formula milk each day. (I know you can't measure your breast milk if it's coming straight out of your nipples, but if your baby is putting on weight and pooping and peeing as usual the amount will be fine.) If you're worried about quantities, talk to your doctor (and see More Info at the end of this chapter).

Try one new food at a time in case of an allergic reaction—then you'll be able to pick the culprit right away. And babies will enjoy the unadulterated individual tastes.

The theory goes that the more varied a diet you give your baby and toddler, the more they will experiment with new foods. It's worth a try and makes nutritional sense, but it's not a foolproof way to get adventurous eaters. Another theory, which also makes sense, is that when kids start to walk they get more conservative about trying new foods because evolutionary survival instincts stop them from the equivalent of wandering into the bush and eating an unfamiliar food that's poisonous. Most cheerfully excellent of all, this means you don't have to take rejection of your spoon personally and can't blame the kid or yourself because it's just pointless to expect an instant overriding of in-built tribal survival instincts.

At 6 months a baby should be quite happy buckled into a highchair with their own useful tray for eating off and other fun (for safety details look up highchair in the index). Highchairs also have the advantage of being a safe place for a baby while you move around—the baby can amuse themselves with a toy or a finger food such as a zweiback.

The following things will mysteriously get food on or in them as your baby spits, flings, squeezes, and pats some mash: your hair, the baby's hair, the baby's nostrils, your back pocket, the mailbox, the front of what you're wearing, the back of what you're wearing, and the pillowcase in the laundry basket. All I can say is stock up on sponges and tea towels.

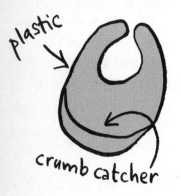

plastic

crumb catcher

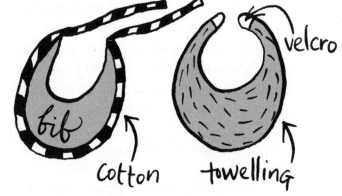

bib

cotton

velcro

towelling

some foods to start on

Put the baby in a highchair, or somewhere else wipe-cleanable or hoseable such as the backyard, and try a teaspoon or two of one of the following:

★ iron-fortified rice cereal for babies (home-made recipes can be found in baby cook-books but will be low in iron, or try the supermarket baby aisle): this is usually given first because of the iron and because you mix it up with breast or for-mula milk so it's not too wildly differ-ent a taste for the baby, and it's all runny and easy to swallow

★ cooked, puréed fruit flesh (some raw fruits can be rough on very new digestive systems)

★ mashed ripe, raw banana or avocado (but some babies hate the slimy texture)

★ puréed cooked pumpkin or sweet potato

★ full-fat yogurts, with live cultures

★ tiny pinches or totally squished-up bits of chicken, fish, beef, lamb, or tofu

★ zweibacks—homemade or from the supermarket baby aisle: good for a teething baby when the baby teeth are breaking through the gums.

Development expert Lise Eliot says, "While taste perception is well developed in infancy, the understanding of what is edible is largely learned." Every kid has their own tastes. Some people give a few veggies before they try fruit because they think babies will otherwise just prefer the sweeter fruit. Babies and children do have a natural preference for sweet things, but some babies love sucking on lemons.

Your baby may be more enthusiastic about a taste they haven't liked if you leave it for a couple of weeks and then try again. Or they may need a new food to be offered up to ten or more times to accept the idea of eating it. And if you don't introduce a food at all during the baby stage, toddlers are likely to be very suspicious of it—unless of course it's candy!

NUTRiTiONaL NeeDS

Babies are so individual and such different sizes, have such different appetites, and change so much from month to month and during growth spurts, that it's very hard to say what yours needs in the way of "servings." Basically "listen" to your child and be guided by their interest in food or rejection of it. As long as they aren't offered solids straight after a big breast- or bottlefeed, and as long as they're not sick, they'll probably eat enough to keep them going. And remember, in the first few weeks the "eating" is just experimenting and up to the age of 1 year the real nutrition is still coming from the breast or formula milk. Gradually you can build up the amount from a few teaspoons: ask your doctor what's right for your baby's size, weight, and interest in food.

The baby and toddler cookbooks listed in More Info at the end of the Food chapter in *Part 5: Stuff* have menu plans that can get you started. You could even photocopy a few of those pages at your local library if you check with the librarian about copyright issues. Any of these sources will show you a picture of the healthy diet pyramid, which has all the (unrelentingly badly drawn) things you're not supposed to eat a lot of in the pointy bit up the top (sugar and fat as in chocolates, cakes, pounds of butter) and goes down through the next level (the "eat moderately" gang of proteiny things such as fish, eggs, yogurt, nuts, meat, and cheese), and then to the bottom slice of the pyramid (where you get an open-slather selection of the stuff you can eat the most of—bread, grains, fruit, and veggies). I shall

spare you a picture of a healthy diet pyramid because it is blindingly obvious and because I can't draw chicken legs, which somehow always appear on level two.

Beth Martino, who is the head of the nutrition and dietetics department covering the King Edward and Princess Margaret hospitals in Perth, Australia, sent me the following list of requirements for babies 1 year old and over (I've rejigged it slightly—she would probably never say "proteiny things"). Don't forget that babies won't eat exactly the same amount at each meal on each day or the same amount each day. Most parents recognize an erratic lurching about rather than a pattern: their child, say, one day munching away, the next not so interested, the next having a huge breakfast then nothing much else, and so on. The cup Beth refers to is the standard measuring cup, but the amount suggested doesn't have to be exact, it's just a guide. She says "These are minimum requirements: to have more would be fine!."

There's no need, once you get the hang of portion sizes, to weigh and measure food. Life doesn't work like that. Feeding kids isn't a perfectly calibrated science, and besides it will send you screamy la la mad. As long as you have fresh and varied food on offer from the groups listed and your kid is putting on weight, you're doing fine.

Daily needs for babies 1 year old and over

1½ SERVINGS OF CEREAL-TYPE THINGS   A serving is 1 cup of pasta, rice, noodles, or porridge; or 1 slice of bread.

1 SERVING OF FRUIT   A serving is a bit of fruit or bits of different fruit adding up to the size of 1 apple; or 1 cup of canned fruit.

1 SERVING OF VEGGIES   A serving is ½ cup of cooked veggies; or 2 large scoops of mashed veggies; or 1 potato; or 1 cup of salad veggies.

⅔ OF A SERVING OF PROTEINY THINGS   ⅔ of a serving is 1 chop; or ⅓ of a cup of cooked ground beef; or 2 to 3 ounces of any other meat (a thin slice about the size of an adult palm); or 1½ eggs; or ⅓ of a cup of beans.

2½ SERVINGS OF DAIRY STUFF   A serving is 1 cup of milk or custard; or 2 slices of cheese; or 1 small (8 ounce) tub of yogurt.

Studies consistently show that people pick up more nutrients from fresh food than from vitamin supplements, but if you think your child needs a vitamin boost talk about it with your doctor.

Things to be wary of

Current guidelines from child nutritionists (and these do change, so keep up by asking your doctor about them) say you should delay giving some foods to children.

They suggest holding back on:

★ straight cow's milk (but not formula based on cow's milk) until after age 1 because there is not enough nutritional value in it.

★ honey until after age 1 because it may have bacteria in it.

★ eggs until after age 1 to avoid early allergy.

★ nuts up to age 4 in case of allergic reaction (particularly with peanuts), which is easier to treat in an older child.

There's a section on allergies (and ones on vegetarian and vegan eating) in the Food chapter.

BABY DEVELOPMENT (0 to 1)

Babies—and kids—develop skills at different rates. Think of the age ranges given in this chapter as a kind of average. Your baby may roll over very early, but take a little longer than most kids to walk. Honestly there's no need to be worried or ashamed if your kid takes their time: in the vaaaast majority of cases it has no bearing on future development. Of course if you feel your child is consistently

$E = mc^2$

slow in several areas, ask for a special check-up with your GP or pediatrician. Some kids miss "stages" altogether: there are plenty of kids who turn up their nose at crawling, one minute doing a funky butt-shuffle or that commando tummy crawling, and the next standing up and wobbling about.

NOTES ON DEVELOPMENT

Much of what seems like straightforward development, such as being able to grasp a toy, helps kids learn other skills as well, such as hand-eye coordination. Every time your baby topples over they are learning what not to do in order to stay upright. So "mistakes"or everyday events and movements can be very important for kids learning how to use and enjoy their bodies. Many of their skills are not innate, though; for example, a baby doesn't know how to roll a ball until somebody shows them or they have a ball to experiment with. There are lots of fun and important things you can do to help them develop in their own way.

Your baby could develop at about the pace outlined in the lists that follow—but they're at least 50 percent likely to get to the milestone sooner, or later. This doesn't mean they're "advanced" or "backward." It means they're in the normal range. It's important to think of your baby enjoying the pleasures of experiencing, and not to get hung up on whether they're "excelling." It's impossible not to compare your child's progress with that of others, but all kids are different. How your child develops and which milestones are reached when depend on a complex interaction between their genes, their prior development, and their environment: a kid in a sporty family of nine who live on a beach in Florida will probably be very different from an only child in a family of oboe players who live where it snows most of the year and whose home is full of books. Unless they're the same.

And there's no point in trying to hurry things along: especially when they're babies they need to mature naturally to certain levels before they can acquire more skills. Giving lots of encouragement, praise, and cuddles goes for every stage of your child's life and development.

Along with an outline of the various types of activities babies are up to at each age stage, there are sections on things you can do that might be fun and help development. With all these activities the point is for the child to enjoy them and then move on to others when they feel like it.

By the way

★ "Development" in this book is divided into physical, emotional and mental, and communication categories but sometimes there's a crossover, and I just had to choose one category.

★ For preemie babies it's important to adjust the milestones range to the age they'd be if they'd been born on their due date; that is, if your 3-month-old baby was 1 month premature, check out the development range for a 2-month-old baby in the list below. In some cases their abilities may be a little curtailed by the fact they have so much catching up to do. See a pediatrician about when they'll catch up.

★ Each age given is simply in the middle of a range: it's an average time for a developmental step—it isn't a deadline!

★ Girls often reach milestones, such as talking or wanting to use the bathroom consistently, before boys.

★ The suggested activities under the headings What Can You Do? are fun things to do in a leisurely way together or as a family. It's not a race to teach anything, it's all about experience and exploration. Being home with your baby at this age is the perfect excuse to have dreamy, drifty days. And if you sometimes get bored, make sure you get time off so you can come back refreshed. Sometimes people forget that mothers (or dads) at home looking after kids full-time need their time off too. Part of your child's development is learning to be with other caregivers, relatives and children. Playgroups (see More Info at the end of this chapter) are one way, but you usually have to be there too.

★ See your GP or pediatrician if you're concerned about your child's progress.

Don't read old, borrowed books about children because they have outdated and often wrong ideas on child development and breezily say things such as babies are toilet trained between the ages of 0 and 4 months, and repeat other complete stuff and nonsense from Dr. Arrogant-Pants of about 1958.

"Babies want to be enthusiastically enjoyed by other people from the beginning of life. When that happens they feel good about themselves, with a healthy pride and good self-esteem and secure attachment." FRANCES THOMSON-SALO, CHILD PSYCHOTHERAPIST

Newborns (first 6 weeks)

Physical development
Your newborn:

★ sees faces that are close up (about the distance between a mother's and a baby's face when breastfeeding; they go

cross-eyed trying to see anything closer and simply can't
see anything further.

★ will look towards a light if there isn't an object they can
focus on.

★ makes movements that are all a bit random and jerky, with
sudden kicks and out-of-control arms.

★ needs their neck supported as their head's still too big for
their body and the neck muscles aren't developed.

★ will stay in the position you put them in to sleep.

★ sees the world mainly in strong contrasts of light and dark—
bold black and white shapes and patterns are good to look at
but, let's face it, newborns didn't have these until the last
few years when people started selling special mobiles and
other marketing ideas—so don't worry about it.

★ can smell breast milk and see the dark areola on the breast,
and will turn their head and home in.

★ loves skin-to-skin-in-the-nuddy contact.

★ is just starting to touch, smell, taste, hear—everything,
in fact.

★ has a curled-up body and curled-up hands; don't try to
fight against this—it will not help development and will
distress your baby.

★ can't hear as well as adults; there's no need to shout, but
just speak when you're near them or speak a little louder if
you move away—if they startle, it's too loud!

★ tends to need quiet, especially if they're preterm, while
their hearing develops to cope with louder sounds.

Newborn reflexes

Reflexes are involuntary movements; the newborn's reflexes are
unique to babies and disappear over time.

★ **Stepping:** for about the first 2 months when you hold a
baby vertically, and their legs touch the floor or another
surface, they'll look as if they're trying to walk.

- ★ **Rooting:** a tickle of a finger, a breast, or a nipple on a baby's cheek will make their mouth automatically open for a feed.
- ★ **Startling** (also known as the Moro reflex): a baby throws out their arms and legs automatically when they are startled or feel lost in space.
- ★ **Sucking:** for months everything available goes in the mouth because it's the baby's means of checking things out.
- ★ **Grasping:** a baby curls their fingers around an adult finger, but otherwise keeps them in a fist.
- ★ **Survival:** a baby should turn their head if their mouth and nose are covered, to get more air.

Emotional and mental development

Your newborn:

- ★ can't really organize their brain to tell their limbs, or any other part of them, what to do.
- ★ is fresh in the world so is easily startled (imagine if you'd never seen any colors, shapes, people, or objects before—frankly I think I'd lose my mind), and needs a soothing environment.
- ★ is learning to trust you and to be soothed by "their people" (family and caregivers).
- ★ likes relaxing music (think classical or reggae, not thrash metal) and their mother's and father's (or other caregivers') voices (especially when pitched higher) and listening to baby talk with exaggerated vowels (babies do love it and people do tend to speak to them like that, but you need to get over it, or at least mix it with normal words and chat, as time goes on or your toddler won't learn to speak anything but baby talk).
- ★ can recognize the face of their mother, father, and other caregivers if they have a lot of contact, and prefers expressive, but not wildly changing, faces to ones that stay still.
- ★ will have some unconscious and some experimental facial expressions as days and weeks go by, and will learn how to

react and how to fit expressions to feelings and mimic the faces they see. This is why an expressionless, depressed face is not something a baby needs to see all the time.

★ can recognize their mother's voice and prefers it, although in the very early days they like it muffled as if they were hearing through amniotic fluid (you don't have to talk underwater, it's just interesting to know). In only a few weeks they can get to know their dad's voice, or another caregiver's. It's believed that babies who hear their dad's voice in the last few weeks of pregnancy would know it too after birth.

★ has a fairly rudimentary system of feelings (as far as we know), which breaks down into hungry, tired, overwhelmed, and uncomfortable, and satisfyingly full, alert, and cruisy. It takes them a little time to develop more complicated emotions. At this stage your baby doesn't love you, but needs to feel your loving touch and kindness. Your baby knows you, needs you, and feels comforted by and interested in you, and will learn to love you along with getting all this brand-new eating, digesting, sleeping, breathing, moving, seeing, hearing, and other stuff down.

★ dreams—it's now believed that babies probably dream even before they leave the womb. Their dreams will develop as they get older. Some observers think that after a bad day (lots of crossness and tension) babies may have disturbed sleep.

Communication development

Your newborn:

★ communicates by crying. You will often be told this is the only way newborns can communicate, but they can also let you know how they are feeling by being suddenly still and wary, shaping themselves to your body or relaxing with skin-to-skin contact and breastfeeding; or even by staring hard when trying to understand or make a connection with you.

What can you do?

Try lots of baby talk, lots of cuddling, songs, and baby massage, which is believed to be calming, especially in the first 3 months, and also helps a baby become aware of their body and feelings of touch and movement (look up baby massage in the index). Don't think you have to do anything special to entertain your newborn: sitting still in a chair having a cuddle and a chat for a while before a sleep is good for them and doesn't cost a cent.

When you're talking to your baby, pause for responses: pretend they've answered. This is more entertaining for you, and the baby has time to develop reactions, even facial expressions, that will show you they're trying to keep up and communicate.

If you have had a grumpy or stressful day, try to start afresh the next hour, after a nap or at least the next day so your baby is reassured.

Staring at a baby a lot of the time or being silent with them is not stimulating enough: they need a lot of chat and interaction (interspersed with quiet times and sleep of course: see the earlier Possible Routines for Babies chapter). It doesn't matter if neither of you has a handle on exactly what the other one is thinking: it's important that you both know that an effort is being made. Sort of like different planets in a *Star Trek* episode trying to make contact. (Well, at least you don't have to wear a velour jumpsuit.)

aвout 6 weeks

Physical development

An awful lot seems to go on at 6 weeks. One day researchers will probably work out why. Some people say it's also a peak time for crying for many babies. Your baby:

* will probably cry real tears because their tear ducts should have started working.
* probably smiles at things (before this age "they" say the smiley lips are due to gas, but parents know better, I reckon).
* stares, fixated, at things—maybe a person, maybe an object. Sometimes this is because their eyes aren't yet used to doing what the brain wants them to do, and they just get kind of stuck. If you think this has happened, and it's causing your baby distress, move the whole baby so their gaze is broken from the object.
* is less floppy, and can hold their head up independently—there's more head and neck control now.
* responds to faces and other things up close, but also notices things further away and more to the side rather than right in front or above.

Emotional and mental development

Your baby:

* has fleeting "emotions," shown by gurgling happily or crying inconsolably, although these episodes are over and forgotten practically immediately. But if the same thing makes the baby cry each time—a particularly loud and bumptious relative, for example—the baby will learn to cry when that person picks them up and speaks to them in a shouty voice, and will "remember" the nice smells and feelings of being rescued by their mom or dad.

Communication development
Your baby:
- ★ is steadily practicing all those newborn ways of communicating with you.

What can you do?
Give your baby more of those cuddles, chats, and songs, but also lots of "tummy time" to develop their arm, leg, and abdominal action: put baby on a blanket on the grass (always in the shade) or the floor. They might get cross at first: it's good to wait until they can hold their head up a bit so they're not just lying there looking at the blanket or floor! This is also a counterbalance to babies being put to sleep on their backs—one of the recommendations to help avoid SIDs (for more on this look up sudden infant death syndrome in the index). If your baby doesn't like tummy time, try it on your chest instead of the floor, giving them the "reward" of seeing your smiling, encouraging face if they lift up their head.

Let your baby uncurl and straighten out at their own pace, but feel free to move and bend their arms and legs gently if they enjoy it. Put a rattle in their hand and let them learn what it's for (there may be some preliminary accidental eye-whacking so make it a light-weight plastic rattle).

ABOUT 2 MONTHS

Physical development
Your baby:
- ★ still usually has closed fists most of the time—although they will curl them around a finger or other object, they don't really get it that those hands belong to them.
- ★ is following an object with their eyes more smoothly, with fewer jerks.

★ can focus more easily on things to the front and center, as well as peripherally, now that their initially blurry vision has sharpened.

★ waves their arms around trying to get control of them.

★ is starting to distinguish colors as well as light and dark.

Emotional and mental development

Your baby:

★ is trying to make sense of so many things at once they can get tired; that's why having lots of naps is a good thing.

★ is learning emotional responses, taking their cues from you.

Communication development

Your baby:

★ wants to make contact and talk with you.

★ smiles more in response.

★ makes extended, babbly vowel sounds and has very early, totally incomprehensible chats. Excellent conversations can be had, with each party enjoying themselves immensely. This babbling will get a little more complicated and sophisticated in tone until actual words start to come out (at about 9 to 12 months or just after).

What can you do?

Your baby is learning conversational tone from you so be amazed, serious, thrilled at what they're telling you, and tell them lots of stuff too, even if it's descriptions of mad things happening outside the bus that they can't see. They'll be riveted. Be lively but not frightening (that'll be when they cry or look freaked out). Sing to them.

Repeat the sounds your baby makes so they can practice the sounds with you.

If you are depressed, get help. A depressed caregiver, especially one with an impassive face and in a non-interactive state, can have a sad effect on a baby: introduce someone to your baby who can stimulate them and be genuinely enthused, chatty, and interested in them. If you get help from a doctor or counselor, that person can be you.

ABOUT 3 MONTHS

Physical development
Your baby:
- ★ may have a growth spurt that requires feeds more often for a day or so. Sometimes a baby really does grow during the night.
- ★ definitely seems to have worked out their hands are attached to themselves and practices doing stuff with them.
- ★ continues to use their mouth to explore the world so puts everything they can in it—this is fine as long as the thing is bigger than a small film canister.
- ★ lifts their head to look around while lying on their tummy—maybe with a slight "push-up" action of the arms
- ★ sits when propped up and held.
- ★ continues to watch things intently now and again.
- ★ grasps something put in their hand.

Emotional and mental development
Your baby:
- ★ can suddenly laugh or giggle.
- ★ recognizes familiar people.

Communication development
Your baby:
- ★ is more sociable.
- ★ smiles at voices, faces, and things.
- ★ has funny little noises that more obviously seem to be attempts at making a connection.

What can you do?

Most babies are social and, when feeling secure, love to have new experiences and see new people, places, and objects. Keep it simple and don't introduce too many things: learn your baby's tired signs (see tired signs in the index) so you'll know when there's been a little too much stimulation and it's time for a nap. Put your baby on the floor a lot, continuing tummy time.

Give your baby shakers and rattles, safe plastic toys in bright colors, soft toys with furry or silky sensuous textures to play with. Dangle things for them to whack and eventually grab.

Keep up the chat and songs and show them simple board books you borrow or buy. Give or pack away your black and white mobiles. Colorful, dangly, musical, revolving mobiles are a hit at this age.

ABOUT 4 TO 5 MONTHS

Physical development
Your baby:

- ★ is now able to see colors, not just black and white shapes.
- ★ may roll from their tummy onto their back.
- ★ holds up and moves their head independently.
- ★ can grab something dangled within reach and may start to try to get toys that are out of reach.
- ★ is becoming stronger and pushes harder with their legs and arms.
- ★ is feeling things with their hands, but most discoveries still go straight into their mouth for "oral exploration."
- ★ often drools a lot—some babies need frequent bib changes.

Emotional and mental development
Your baby:

- ★ laughs when you pull funny faces.

- ★ likes looking in a mirror.
- ★ shows their enjoyment of, for example, music and delight at leaves blowing in the wind; and also shows concern at stressful, shouty situations.

Communication development

Your baby:

- ★ is learning how to interact with people more as time goes on.
- ★ is working out how to communicate using their face, body language, and babble. Their feelings can be clearly seen in their facial expressions. Until they are much older, maybe even preschoolers, young children don't know how to "fake it"—all emotions are pure.

What can you do?

You can help your baby to stand and "walk" by holding their hands if they enjoy it—but "baby walker" contraptions won't help them walk any earlier and are dangerous. Let your baby have a clear view of their own feet, and take their shoes and socks off as much as possible so they can feel things with their toes: this applies to babies of all ages.

Rattles or bells on their wrists and feet can help your baby work out that those bits belong to them and can be manipulated. Try tummy time in front of a mirror so that when they lift their head up they can see their reflection (although they may not yet recognize themselves).

Keep showing your baby simple board books. This will be the start of all sorts of language and understanding development. Kids love stories and pictures even at this age. And don't worry, they all chew the corners.

Play peek-a-boo, make funny noises, blow raspberries on their belly. Play different kinds of music and dance with your tot—but not spooky, scary classical or frenetic hard rock: babies and kids are very sensitive to the mood music creates. Try some boppy songs or some songs especially for babies or kids.

Find time to do some things you like by yourself or with a partner or friends. A trip out of Babyland is a helpful break and you can come back refreshed (see the Coping Strategies for Parents chapter in *Part 4: Parenting*).

aBout 6 months

Physical development

This is another big time in a baby's life (oh, they all are, I know). Your baby:

★ gets their mouth around anything available and is reaching for and grabbing things. They still use their mouth more than their fingers to feel and explore objects.

★ can stick their toes in their mouth.

★ checks things out solemnly.

★ can maybe pass an item from one hand to the other, but usually can't hold things in two hands at once.

★ may find peek-a-boo a big hit because they're learning some things that disappear can reappear.

★ is starting to enjoy having a real effect on items that can be whacked, thrown, picked up, and so on.

★ recognizes their own name and perhaps other names ("Here's Mom back").

★ is now, like an adult, hearing high-frequency sounds better than low-frequency ones, but is still not hearing softer noises as well as an adult. By this age a hearing test should have been done by your doctor if the hearing wasn't tested in hospital. (We were told it would be terribly hi-tech, but a woman just stood behind our baby, first to one side and then the other, and rattled a spoon in a metal cup to see if they turned their head.) Babies found to have partial or total deafness—and their families—need to immediately start to learn sign language and other ways of communicating: the sooner the better (look up hearing test in the index).

★ can sit unsupported for a few moments.

★ is ready to experiment with solids—otherwise known as mashes—and to learn lots of new tastes. The more you give, the more the baby will get used to. Even small babies can enjoy bits of olives, asparagus, rose flavoring, and other fancies. Most babies will show a preference for naturally sweet foods and a distaste for very bitter tastes, which may be a poison safety instinct. (Unfortunately, not all dangerous substances are bitter, and some babies don't mind the taste of anything, so don't rely on this instinct.)

★ may have their first teeth starting to come through (see the Teeth chapter in *Part 5: Stuff*), just as they get interested in food.

★ may put their arms out as if to say "Lift me up."

Emotional and mental development

Your baby:

★ after 6 months will simply be much more engaged with the world around them: this is the time when babies get cast in commercials, dressed for baby fashion catalogs, and become more attractive propositions to some wary friends and relatives who figured newborns were too fragile to hold and not much fun to be around.

★ will develop emotionally much more between 6 months and 1 year, and will become aware of more sophisticated feelings (outrage, contentment, astonishment, doubt, amusement, a scoff, cheerfulness, jealousy).

★ finds their mirror image fascinating and it may now be recognized by them as "me."

★ may start getting clingy in the second 6 months of life, which sometimes builds to a peak around 18 months. They show a clear preference for the close family circle. A baby (or a toddler) is never happier than when fed and in a group, looking as if they could say smugly "These—these are my people!." A baby can be fixated on one parent, or two, or a carer, or a combo of parents and caregiver, depending on how "primary care" is divvied up.

Communication development

Your baby:

★ mimics facial expressions and sounds.

★ can probably have a funny baby chat with indiscernible words, often seemingly to themselves.

★ matches sounds and actions to events—waving is for bye-bye; a ducky goes quack.

★ continues to respond to chat from others with facial expressions, body movements, and sounds.

What can you do?

Over the next few months your baby will enjoy doing things they seem to have control over: batting at things that make a noise or pop up, or fiddling with objects. Give them lots of interesting food they can hold and feed themselves with: zweibacks; cheese sticks; a banana; some apple in a stocking or cheesecloth that they can chew and suck without swallowing big pieces; cooked veggies (not hard raw ones, which can be choky).

Songs and nursery rhymes help babies learn tone, rhythm, and words. Play together with simple musical instruments–a lot of these, like most things, can be homemade. Try a saucepan and wooden-spoon drum (but don't go mad and make yourself a tambourine!).

Flop down on a blanket in the shade in the garden or a nearby park and just relax: look at butterflies, blades of grass, talk about the clouds, and people going by.

Showing your baby photos of special friends, caregivers, and relatives and talking about them can help to widen their circle when the immediate family are not around for a while.

Encourage and praise independence in your baby, while making them also feel secure. (Yes, sorry, in other words be perfect and do two opposite things at once.)

about 7 months

Physical development
Your baby:

- ★ can sit up without being propped.
- ★ continues to hone their reaching and grabbing.
- ★ will try to see the source of sounds.
- ★ tries to move to see something or be nearer something, and will stretch out or angle their head to see better or be part of the action.
- ★ still throws up if they cough or cry a lot or something gets caught in their throat or put well into their mouth. This is the gag reflex that babies have from birth, which may last for years: it can be annoying but it's actually a great survival technique.
- ★ may be an early starter for crawling or butt-shuffling (some babies miss out on the crawling stage: it's not a problem).

Emotional and mental development
Your baby:

- ★ remembers what certain toys are built to do.
- ★ points at things to indicate "I want that."

★ plays swapsies with you (you take it—now give it back).

★ has worked out how to get your attention.

Communication development

Your baby:

★ is becoming more and more social and taking increasing interest in their world and understanding more of conversations and atmospheres.

★ as always, loves a chat.

What can you do?

Make things available for your baby to grasp and listen to (this applies to all baby ages).

Don't be alarmed if you see your baby adopt strange sleeping positions, even curled up on their tummy with rear in the air and head to the side. If your baby can roll onto their tummy to sleep they should be able to roll back if they want to: the tummy position is more of a worry for younger babies who can't move themselves. This new mobility is a sign of your needing to worry less—not more!

Make baby sounds such as "bub bub bub" for your baby to copy, and listen to their attempts to communicate, responding as if in conversation. Repeat the names for things and put them in sentences, so that "hat" is associated with that thing that goes on the head, and "drink" is the wet yummy stuff referred to in "What would you like to drink? Milk? Rightyho." Repetition is the key to building a vocabulary of understood words. Explain to the baby what's going on around them. Read simple storybooks to them and explain the pictures. Babies this age love animated conversation: play with facial expressions and body language. Let them watch you dance, and "dance" them in your arms.

Over the next month or so, introduce paper and big crayons and pencils, things with wheels such as large plastic trucks, and building blocks (knocking down might come before building up so get in there and help).

Roll a ball to your baby and encourage them to roll it back. Keep giving them toys they can have an influence on—especially those they love where something pops out or makes a noise when they press a lever. Also introduce them to shape-sorting toys or other toys that provide putting in and taking out opportunities; and to a sturdy cart or toy to push along.

Give them careful swings and slides at the park, where they can also watch kids playing.

about 8 months

Physical development
Your baby:
- ★ may start to crawl from now on.
- ★ can look for and find a toy you hid.
- ★ likes to fill things up and empty them—any game of now you see it, now you don't.
- ★ can sit alone but might fall over once in a while.
- ★ should turn their head to locate the source of a noise, but the turning may be slow.

Emotional and mental development
Your baby:
- ★ may start to develop separation anxiety and attachment to certain people and things, although they also start to understand that if you go you come back.
- ★ can discern your mood by your tone and body language.

Communication development

Your baby:

★ is developing more control over the babble and their "words" sound more like real conversation.

★ in the next month or so will develop greater powers of concentration and learning from what they've seen. This means if they've always had milk in a green cup they may be dubious about a yellow one.

What can you do?

Gently broaden your child's circle of caregivers. Help your baby with the idea of something going away and coming back—hide a toy under a tea towel and let them reveal it.

Continue to build up that group of toys that they can have an effect on: blocks to build up and knock down and banging and shaking things such as musical instruments. Toys that can be pushed, pulled, or go on wheels will help your baby learn to get mobile themselves. Lift the flap or other hiding and revealing games and toys are also perfect for this age.

Walks with lots of pointing out of things and chats with neighbors and shopkeepers can be fun: remember what's mundane to you may be perfectly thrilling to a baby. (Which is why you can be infected with the delight, but need to have the odd morning and afternoon off so you can do adult things! You can only go ga-ga over a dandelion so many times when you're a grown-up.)

9 moNtHs to 1 year

Physical development

Your baby:

★ is crawling or shuffling.

★ is climbing over or going around things (but they usually prefer to go right through them if possible!).

★ can pull themselves up to a standing position, look confused, and fall down on their bottom.

★ can "walk" when an adult holds their hands, may be able to totter from, say, a piece of furniture to a nearby knee and back or may walk alone.

★ drops things for you to pick up.

★ can pass things from hand to hand.

★ loves to throw things.

★ claps hands.

★ can wave bye-bye.

★ wants to use a spoon or a fork, hold a cup, clutch food

★ can pick small things up; by about 1 year they've mastered the true "pincer movement," using their thumb and first finger.

★ starts to phase out putting everything in their mouth (but this will continue as part of the repertoire until 2 years old or so).

Emotional and mental development

Your baby:

★ will show more of their "personality" and quirks will become recognizable—even if you don't realize this until later, when your child is older and you look back.

★ becomes an alert observer.

★ even though they can't see an object, they know it still exists ("object permanence"— a friend of mine says this never works with her ex-boyfriends).

★ knows where things "belong" on a shelf and which way up they should be.

★ is grasping simple concepts and explanations

★ enjoys familiar songs and rhymes or sets of words.

★ may become more clingy as they gear up for crawling and walking—evolution's way of keeping babies safely close to home instead of pootling off into the woods.

★ might show a preference for a fluffy toy (some kids never have favorites, or they rotate them).

Communication development

Your baby:

★ can follow simple instructions and sentences ("Find Nanna," "Can you give me the book, please").

★ can respond to their name or familiar words, and more and more loves babbling words.

★ recognizes familiar voices and copies sounds and words.

★ is making sounds that are definitely more like words, some with several syllables.

★ may, at about 9 months, start practicing sounds that start with a consonant and end in a vowel, such as "dada" and "fa," building up new words as the months go by.

What can you do?

Allow a crawler to crawl as much as they like, but make sure you babyproof their environment first. Help them to "dance," whether standing, sitting, or lying down. As with any new skill, the more they have the opportunity to do something, the better they get at it, so they can move on to the next step. Provide an opportunity for them to do their stuff but don't prod a baby to do something or "teach" them to crawl or walk. It doesn't happen that way.

Hand your baby things to hold in their shopping-cart seat, and help them to reach for some things on the shelves.

You can respond to their "Barbufdubbadubpaddca" with "Oh well, yes, I shouldn't be at all surprised." It helps to teach the art of conversation and is a more amusing way for you to pass the time.

1 year

Physical development
Your baby:

* ★ stands up from a sitting start.
* ★ may be toddling.
* ★ is learning to drink from a cup.
* ★ can put things into a bag or box and take them out again
* ★ will try to fit the noise to the item, such as an animal or a car.

Emotional and mental development
Your baby:

* ★ is very fascinated by and enjoys other kids but is not into sharing toys with them.
* ★ may be clingy.
* ★ enjoys interacting with you—passing objects and looks.

Communication development
Your baby:

* ★ understands many more words.
* ★ is building on their vocabulary every day, but at this stage uses far fewer words than they actually understand.

What can you do?
Help your baby to do things for themselves: pass them objects to hold and experiment with. Continue to roll balls to them and have some soft ones they're allowed to throw. (See the Being Active chapter in *Part 5: Stuff*.)

Make jokes by using funny voices or doing odd things such as putting a shoe on your head. Enjoy favorite songs and books together, and introduce new ones. Keep playing disappear and reappear games with toys and your face.

Use new words and practice familiar ones. Give them room to reply or react in conversation.

You might like to take your 1-year-old to a playgroup: they'll probably enjoy the play and watching other children, and it's also a chance for you to see kids at different stages of development, regardless of precise age.

The Toddler Development (1 to 3) chapter in *Part 2: Toddlers* carries on from here. (And see also More Info below for books on baby development.)

MoRe iNfo

Your Baby and Child by Penelope Leach has great sections on development for each age group, broken into physical, speech, playing, and mental development. She recommends ways of speaking to a baby and toddler, and play activities and toys for each stage. If you're not used to babies, the book gives you a good idea of what they're up to. (For full details and review see More Info at the end of the first chapter, In the Beginning.)

What's Going on in There?: How the Brain and Mind Develop in the First Five Years of Life
by Lise Eliot, Bantum, Oct. 2000.
A full-on, huge, doorstoppin' hardback on children's brain development, with lots of really fascinating info on what babies and kids think, what they can do, and the experiments that helped work it out. Includes everything from memory and perception to hearing, the effect of genes on brain development in the womb, and the social impacts on intelligence of position in the family, nutrition, and school. Intriguing bits about what touching and bouncing babies does to the brain. It's written by a neurobiologist and mom of three who combines chatty anecdotes with research. She has lots of information that I've never read anywhere else.

Mind you, "Prenatal Vulnerability of the Vestibular System" is the sort of heading you definitely want to skip when you're sleep deprived!

Your Child at Play: Birth to One Year: Discovering the Senses and Learning about the World
by Marilyn Segal, Newmarket Press, 2nd ed., 1998.
The first in a series by a psychologist and early childhood researcher who also had five kids (so I figure she'd have some great ideas on keeping them busy). Yes, but just get on with the fun activities and don't worry too much about your baby's intelligence at this point!

PLAYGROUPS

Online Playgroup
A website for finding or starting playgroups.
www.onlineplaygroup.com

Mommy and Me
You can register to this site and search their National Playgroup Directory.
www.mommyandme.com

toys and games for babies

Toys and play are fun for babies, and they're also an essential part of their development and learning process. You'll see from this suggested list—based on info from parents who responded to the Kidwrangling Survey—that I've edited out most of the merchandizing or brandname favorites. I figure they don't need the advertizing. Lots of the suggestions are low-budget options. All kids will have different favorites: some kids never get turned on by dollies, others never really like cars.

Keep a small swag of toys—say, enough to fit in a laundry basket—in the cupboard and rotate them every few days or weeks so that your baby always has a fresh lot of things to be interested in. (Obviously real favorites such as special comfort or sleepytime toys can't be whisked away.) A huge selection of toys leads to a jaded baby.

Always check the safety and age-appropriate labels on new toys (look up toys in the index). Make sure toys that are safe for one age group don't get used by younger babies. Look out for damaged or elderly toys, with bits coming off. Anything that fits into a plastic film canister can be a choking hazard for kids up to about the age of 3.

Didn't Incy-Wincy spider get BORED?

ideas from parents

Use your common sense for safe versions of all these suggestions. (See also More Info at the end of this chapter.)

Good toys for babies (0 to 1 year)

◎ Dangly toys to hang on the stroller or above the baby to swat at— if they make noises so much the better ◎ small things that are easily grabbed, such as cars or blocks ◎ floor mats with interesting patterns, for tummy play ◎ "touch and feel" books ◎ balls too big to swallow, easy to grasp with two hands and not too hard or full ◎ rice in a tightly sealed plastic jar to rattle ◎ a teething rattle or teething ring that plays music ◎ crackly packaging for grasping (but be careful: it will be eaten if possible) ◎ a baby photo album with photos of family and friends for you to look at and "talk" about together ◎ a safety standard bouncing harness ◎ little toys with wheels, which they can pull or push, or a small trolley or doll's stroller to push along if they're toddling already ◎ stacking cups ◎ a ball with a bell inside ◎ a low toy shelf rather than a box so that they can see things better and learn to take them off and then, you hope, put them back ◎ plastic chains or rings ◎ soft toys with long ears or tails for sucking ◎ plastic ware and cooking utensils ◎ net bags used for oranges, filled with scrunched-up paper ◎ tightly sealed plastic bottles filled with colored water or rattly dried beans ◎ broken or toy phones (battery removed from old cell phones) for pretend calls and button

ball with a bell in it

Knitted thingo

different-sized plastic doovers

pushing ◎ a packet of chips (unopened) to pulverize ◎ blocks ◎ board books ◎ an activity play center ◎ teddies and fluffy toys (some babies and kids never really get into fluffy things, although they're often given heaps) ◎ a yogurt container, with a plastic block in it ◎ books that have little flaps to open and look under ◎ a musical mobile ◎ unbreakable plastic spoons ◎ a xylophone ◎ a hammering game (pegs or balls are pushed or whacked through holes with a hammer) ◎ cloth books ◎ a cloth dolly with a rattle inside ◎ a battery-operated piano-style keyboard ◎ a cardboard carton to be sat in, to put things into, and to be pulled along in down the corridor at warp speed ◎ cardboard tubes (not toilet ones, sturdier cling-wrap ones) ◎ an inflatable ball ◎ sticky tape half-stuck on something for the baby to pull off and put on (but don't let them eat it) ◎ a babyproofed cupboard for unpacking and packing contents ◎ the saucepan cupboard ◎ foam jigsaw bases with numbers or letters that pop in and out ◎ a napkin or tea towel for playing peek-a-boo with ◎ a tissue box with bits of ribbon, material and different-textured things to put in and take out ◎ large plastic animals ◎ a small squirting animal ◎ a set of key rings with lots of keys ◎ pegs either by themselves or pegged onto something ◎ a baby-sized plastic watering can for bathtime ◎ balloons (but make sure the baby doesn't eat bits when one pops or deflates—get it straight into the bin) ◎ empty plastic yogurt containers to experiment with (babies love to stick their hands in, roll them, put other things in and rattle, and tip things out of) ◎ a stuffed caterpillar ◎ a toy wagon ◎ a safe mirror ◎ a large rubber bath plug

≡tight≡ ≡lid≡

beads in a bottle

253

⊚ a tambourine and anything else musical ⊚ a broken calculator, phone, or anything with buttons to press ⊚ a sturdy plastic potato masher ⊚ old paperbacks or magazines with pictures of kids and animals ⊚ a clothes basket and pegs ⊚ a squeaky duck ⊚ finger puppets (big ones can be scary).

Scrunched-up paper

Good games for babies

Child-care workers (and maybe some relatives) will know lots of baby games and rhymes: ask them to teach you some for your baby's age. Most large bookshops have compilations of nursery rhymes. ⊚ Peek-a-boo ⊚ hide something and make it reappear ⊚ the baby throws and you catch (they won't be able to catch yet) ⊚ rhyming games or songs ⊚ "What noise does a duck, cat, truck (or whatever) make?" ⊚ Pat-a-cake ⊚ blow bubbles for them to look at and try to catch ⊚ flap a crib sheet or colored fabric gently above the baby, cover them with it, and remove immediately ⊚ Round and Round the Garden.

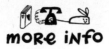

more info

www.huggies.com/na/fun/index.asp

Diaper-company-sponsored ideas for activities.

www.mamalisa.com/world

Children's songs and rhymes from around the world.

www.collingsm.freeserve.co.UK

Lists 500 nursery rhymes.

2
TODDLERS

IF YOU'RE READING *PART 2: TODDLERS,*
YOU MIGHT ALSO BE INTERESTED IN CHAPTERS
IN OTHER PARTS OF THE BOOK.

PART 4: PARENTING

Parenting philosophy
Unpaid work and paid work
Dads
Coping strategies for parents
A you-shaped family
Teaching kids how to behave
Helping kids understand grown-up concepts
Child care and preschool

PART 5: STUFF

Equipment
Home safety
Clothes
Teeth
Food
Health
Being active
Immunization
Reading
TV, videos, and films
Art and music
Travel near and far
Insidey activities
Birthday parties and presents

EXTRA RESOURCES

WHO'S THE CENTER OF THE UNIVERSE?

The toddler years are roughly those from 1 to 3, depending of course on when your cherub first takes to their tootsies. It's all so sudden— the baby months seemed to stretch on forever when you were in them, but now they're over. No more just plonking baby somewhere and expecting them to stay put when you turn your back for a moment.

Your little baby isn't such a bubba any more. They still have their baby face, but they're

TODDLERS: SHOW 'EM WHO'S BOSS

by DR GUESSYPANTS MD

BOSS

IN

growing into their own little person and trying to balance how much they need you with how much they want to feel independent and in control. Wanting to be a "big kid"—to use the toilet, for example, or be able to do up buttons for themselves— may cause great frustration until their capabilities catch up with their desires and ambitions. (Maybe that's why some politicians look so pouty and petulant.)

WHat's a toDDLeR?

Although "toddler" refers to a new physical stage, it is also a time for lots of mental and emotional action. Toddlers are growing into little people who, depending on their personality traits, will observe the world keenly, adore a chat, explore objects and places, and make and take a joke, although be careful with that one. Kids under 5 are not able to fully understand sarcasm, it's just confusing or hurtful. But they may love some elementary contradictions or slapstick: your putting an umbrella in the fridge, spilling a cup of water into the bath, or pretending to eat their galosh.

When kids get mobile, a new lot of safety issues come into play. Reorganize your house along toddler-safe lines (see the Home Safety chapter in *Part 5: Stuff*) and be extra careful about pools, ponds, baths, buckets, puddles, and other watery dangers at your place and elsewhere. Kids are programmed to be curious so it's safer to remove anything dangerous rather than expect them never to touch it.

Your new (eventually) all-talking, all-walking kid will soak up as many experiences as they can from social interaction, books, art, and music. They'll probably have firm ideas about what they want to eat, do, and perhaps even wear, and be more interested in playing with other kids their own age than they were. Toddlers are also building on their communication skills and will communicate with you not just through words, but through behavior and body language. You may find that varying the way you explain things—by using facial expressions, drawing a picture, acting out the physical effects of a feeling, allowing the child to thoroughly examine something new with their fingers, even if it's gloopy or disgusting (jelly, not dog poop)—will help you work out which ways your child most enjoys learning and communicating. Their curiosity is insatiable and their capacity for mimicking and copying almost endless.

When you've heard "Why?" for the 678th time, you may have to be creative. Surf the Internet with them. Take them to the library. Keep a promise to go on an excursion that will help explain something, such as to the zoo or the museum. Get your child to ring up Nanna or Grandad and ask them if they know. It's good to answer a query with "What do *you* think?" and then be positive about the answer—"Yes, that could happen." And if you're really stumped, I suggest you feign unconsciousness. Or perhaps I mean incompetence.

Your toddler's personality is developing and they're experimenting with how to get what they want. This can turn into an ongoing fight between a little person and a big person over who gets total control of which bits of life; or into continual push-me, pull-you negotiation. You'll need to show them (sadly by example mostly) how to react to frustrating situations. For instance, I like to lie on the floor, kick my legs, and swear in a shouty way.

GOOD THINGS ABOUT TODDLERS

* Toddlers are growing out of their baby face and into their own face, and personality.

* Toddlers want to learn to do things for themselves.

* A toddler's laugh is a wonderful sound.

* Toddlers listen to you carefully, even if they don't "get" it all.

* Toddlers' attention spans vary, but can be surprisingly long.

* Toddlers can entertain themselves for short periods.

* Toddlers think housework is fun (hee, hee, hee).

* Toddlers are fun to watch when they're determined (to get a sock on, for example).

* Toddlers force you to slow down to their pace (yes, I know this can be infuriating, but it's probably good for you).

* Toddlers can kiss and cuddle you— for a possibly short period between not being big enough to and not wanting to any more.

=HUG=

* Toddlers are amazed by things you have come to take for granted.

* Toddlers' emotions are all out there in pure form—sheer joy and terrible misery—so you usually know how they feel.

Giving your toddler as much control and as many choices as possible when the outcome doesn't matter ("Do you want pineapple or mango?," "You be the boss: shall we go to the beach or the park?") will allow you to get away with other negatives and absolutes ("You can't touch that because it will burn your hand and hurt a lot," "We are tidying the room now, but after that you can choose whether to go to the park or the shop"). If you give in

✱ Toddlers are so adorable when they're asleep (or quiet and not bouncing off the walls).

✱ Toddlers often bond with their attentive family, friends, and care-givers but warm to others slowly. This is wise and safe behavior, and not to be criticized as being "too shy."

✱ Toddlers say unexpected things that make you see the world from a new angle.

✱ Toddlers get excited and show it, without trying to act cool.

✱ Toddlers' fatty-diapered bot-toms are Teletubbie-cute.

✱ Toddlers have reached the last years when you can kiss their bottom without it being annoy-ing or weird.

✱ Toddlers are easier to pick up and carry than when they get older.

✱ Toddlers usually still have an afternoon sleep so you can too.

✱ Toddlers love books and the idea of stories.

✱ Toddlers pretend to read.

✱ Toddlers love songs.

✱ Toddlers start to imagine and pretend.

✱ Toddlers so intensely care about what they're doing that they remind you that little things can be as important as the "big" stuff in life.

✱ Toddlers don't want to borrow the car yet. (Actually they probably do.)

to tantrums, the toddler learns that they're a good way to get what they want.

Hints on how to avoid these and other potential battlegrounds (move to another country) can be found in the Teaching Kids How to Behave chapter in *Part 4: Parenting*. And, nup, it's never too late to change your expectations and your kid's behavior as long as you explain the change, help them to make the transition and then consistently stick to your approach. (I know it's easy for *me* to say!)

Now that your toddler is mobile and exploring the world, you'll need to dress both boys and girls for normal days in ways that allow them to get dirty, fall down, and climb things at the adventure playground, and although everyone likes to spruce up for a party, a long skirt or bowtie is not conducive to play. Prepare to face the reality of what happens to the clothes and bodies of normal, healthy kids. Kids get dirty. They need to get dirty so they can learn stuff about themselves and the world around them.

wobble

wobble

Despite the fact that girls and boys often (although not always) show different traits, you may want to ask yourself how much is genetic and how much is suggested by the reactions and expectations of grown-ups and by the opportunities that are given to them. Are the boys always first to the construction toys at playgroup so the girls do playdough? Are the boys allowed to have a cry if they hurt themselves or told to be a "brave little man"? (Look up gender in the index.)

Make allowances for children as individuals: if someone isn't keen to play a contact sport because they're scared of getting hurt, that should be accepted—it doesn't matter whether they're a boy or a girl. Everyone deserves some leeway, patience, and understanding.

Always ask for professional medical advice if you think development in a certain area has stalled. It probably hasn't as there's a very wide range of kids' capabilities at any age—in almost all cases everyone "evens up" eventually.

These are the bridging years between baby and preschooler, a time when you can make firm friends with your kid; get to know them really well; help them experiment; rejoice that they have a longer attention span and can amuse themselves for—oh—whole minutes on end; and perhaps launch them a little way into the world even though they, and you, know they can run back to you for comfort any time.

For many people this is also the stage when they have a new baby so they have to attend to their special needs as well as those of the toddler, who might wonder why they're no longer the center of the universe (see the A You-shaped Family chapter in *Part 4: Parenting*).

Not to mention parents wondering why *they're* no longer the center of the universe . . .

> **"Some fairy dust will be lost after washing."**
> **LABEL ON TODDLER UNDERPANTS**

more info

TODDLER-CARE BOOKS

As well as the toddler-care books that follow, see the child-care books, such as *Your Baby and Child* by Penelope Leach and *Complete Baby and Childcare* by Miriam Stoppard, reviewed in More Info at the end of the first chapter, In the Beginning, in *Part 1: Babies*.

The Mother of All Toddler Books

by Ann Douglas, Wiley, John & Sons, 2004.

A mother of four gives a down-to-earth run-down of all toddler related issues you're likely to strike: from everyday challenges and discipline to the life-changing decision whether to have a baby while you have a toddler.

What to Expect in the Toddler Years

by Arlene Eisenberg, Heidi Murkoff, and Sandee Eiseneberg Hathaway,
Workman Publishing Co., 1996.

It has the same huge Q and A format as their *What to Expect in the First Year*,
and everything from getting shoes fitted to immensely detailed food lists
and step-family issues.

TODDLERS AND EATING

Some days your toddler will not be interested in much food, the next they'll be "on the fang." Don't get too worried about lists of servings or measuring and weighing foods. Toddlers like to "graze"—have little snacks here and there. It's too long between three meals a day for them to last.

DAILY NEEDS

Basically keep the food choices as varied as possible. Every day offer full-fat dairy food, meat, veggies, fruit, and cereals or bread. The Learning to Eat chapter in *Part 1: Babies* has the food requirements for babies of 1 year and over. Here and there you can throw in the chance of different foods such as turnip chips, strawberries, or something new in season. Your job is just that: to offer it. If your kid doesn't eat it, offer maybe one alternative but don't jump through hoops to provide fourteen other options. (See the Food chapter in *Part 5:*

Stuff for info on cooking for babies, toddlers, and the family, general nutrition, and books with things such as weekly meal plans, if that's the sort of person you are.)

Don't stress about what your child should be eating—you can get lists issued by children's hospitals and nutritionists, although they're mostly for kids over 4 years old, and the suggestions can change from professional to professional and in the time between your having one baby and the next (see More Info at the end of this chapter for a good book on this).

When in doubt, talk about your child's eating pattern with your doctor and have a reassuring weigh and measure so you know your kid is thriving. Gaining weight slows right down after the first year. Babies by about 5 months have usually doubled their birth weight and by 1 year have normally tripled it, but after that they only gain 5 pounds or so in the next year.

Be extremely cautious about people who recommend exclusion diets for children such as wheat-free, dairy-free, or low-fat programs. These diets can be *very* dangerous and are, in a HUGE majority of cases, unnecessary. They can exclude a range of essential vitamins and minerals for brain and physical development so do at least please check them with a qualified dietician. (Look up vegetarian kids and vegan kids in the index.)

yum

"Junk" or "fast" food is fine once a week, but is virtually useless for giving kids the nutrients they need. It would be faster and easier to stay home and open a can of soup, make a sandwich, and hand over an apple. It's a good idea to get kids used to seedy whole-grain bread at this age or they'll only ever want white bread, which usually has about as much fiber as a piece of fuzzy felt—and probably half the vitamins. (Also look up drinks in the index.)

The main thing is to cover the basic food groups and to keep offering as many different foods as you can. Not always cheese sticks; sometimes

SOME TODDLER EATING TIPS

✱ Eat together as a family, then you don't have to cook for two sessions of dinner (or even three if you have other kids). Also the "How was your day? What's new?" aspect of the family meal is great for developing children's conversational skills and a comforting family vibe.

✱ Give toddlers morning and afternoon snacktime. Toddlers need to have little snacks here and there.

✱ When your kid seems to be getting too big for the highchair, say at 2, let them use a plastic booster seat, which sits on top of a normal chair; cushions are not stable enough (see booster seat in the index).

✱ Let your kid start using a toddler's utensil set—although just a spoon is still the easiest implement, especially when they're tired. Sets are available at supermarkets, drugstores, and baby shops.

✱ Listen to your toddler: don't be strict about a food "routine" if they're getting genuinely hungry at different times. Remember if overall they're eating a wide variety of foods (stop laughing), they should be getting all they need.

yogurt with fruit in it. Not always chops; sometimes stir-fry. Not always Mom; borrow Madonna's personal chef. That sort of thing.

things to try if your kid won't eat

First consider the possibility of a physical problem such as a sore throat, mouth ulcers, or an illness coming on. Or your child might just be having a day when they don't feel like eating as much as usual, and it will even up the next day.

Understand also that fussy eating is really evolution at work. The theory is that toddlers are hard-wired to refuse food until they're really familiar with it—when they've been served it up to ten times, for example. This instinct is designed to kick in when babies start walking and prevents them from wandering away from the tribe and eating unfamiliar, poisonous berries. And doesn't explain why they still won't eat spinach after 456 offerings.

★ Many kids simply feel already "full"—of juice or milk—before a meal. Cut out commercial juice, which is often just sugary water with a dash of vitamin C extract, and once they're weaned from breast or formula milk only give three cups of cow's milk a day after meals, not before.

★ Explain that the bread in their tummy is having a party and the carrots want to come. And the zucchini is all dressed up, with its cheese hat on, ready to go too. Give them a choice of a few foods they can invite or not invite. In other words you choose what to offer and they choose which of those foods to eat. This makes toddlers feel as if they're making decisions.

★ Shout and pull at your hair and lie on the floor and hold your breath and drum your heels on the floor. No, sorry. Maybe do some exercise with them to try to work up their appetite, and try to interest them in food again at the next meal. Or the next day.

★ Offer smaller helpings: it might be that you're expecting a toddler to eat a larger serving of food than is actually needed—toddlers don't grow as fast as babies. Many people experienced with toddlers say parents give servings up to four times larger than necessary.

★ Don't take it personally. If painstakingly prepared food is chucked around or ignored, skip the painstaking stage. Offer something simple, even raw, instead. That's what fresh fruit and veggies—and now and then things that come in packets—are for.

★ Make a game of eating little bits of different colors—a green snowpea, a piece of orange carrot, a grey mushroom, a white potato cube, a red cherry tomato. Bonus: this usually makes better nutritional sense than eating three scoops of the same thing.

★ Get over it. Your kid's not a prize-winning eater. Keep offering stuff on the plate and don't fuss about it or push the issue. When they're hungry, they'll eat. They can survive and thrive on such teeny amounts as to raise the eyebrows on the statue of Venus de Milo. Or even the arms.

The Little Kids and Eating chapter in *Part 3: Little Kids* has some further ideas for "fooling" the fussy eater.

"Kids tend to be grazers. They eat a little bit, regularly." SHELLEY

"We realized that she wanted to be independent and feed herself. She was quite happy when given a spoon of her own." JENNY

"Give it to the dog." CHI-HUI

"Put hundreds and thousands on vegetables." SALLY

"At 1 he pushed food away. If I held the bowl down so that he could see what he was eating, and how I put it on the spoon, he was happy." WENDY

"Friends ask how I get my kids to eat whole-grain bread and I just say they didn't know there was anything else." FIONA

"Let someone else feed them." LILIAN

"Send them to day care. We have many children who won't eat at home, but put them at a lunch table with five or six others and suddenly the attitude becomes 'I'm doing what she's doing!' or 'I'd better try this or miss out!'" KAREN

"Don't worry. They won't starve." HEAPS OF PARENTS

"Make a smorgasbord plate of six or seven different things (we call it 'Sixes and Sevens') and say the game is they have to have at least one bite of everything (or two . . .). Help them count. Or try giving sticks of carrot, opened pea pods, or half mushrooms as an entrée while they're distracted with a book, game or video, then serve just meat and potatoes at the table." ME

more info

A BOOK ABOUT EATING

Eat Right, Don't Fight: A Practical Guide to Feeding Children from Birth to the School Years

by Gina Ralston, Jan O'Connell and Rosey Cummings, Random House, Aust., 2003.

The authors of this book, staff members at Melbourne's Tweddle Child and Family Health Service, have seen it all when it comes to mush and much more. They give the modern lowdown, simple nutritional guidelines, the recommended daily levels of vitamins and minerals and what levels are found in various foods. It covers breastfeeding and bottlefeeding and advocates starting solids at 6 or 7 months. The book is also about how to take the stress out of eating issues from birth up to 3 years old.

toDDLeRS anD SLeePinG

The toddler years are often the time when a battle of wills sets in between parents and a determined child who doesn't want to go to bed, screams, uses delaying tactics, and simply refuses to cooperate. It's a battle of wills that parents need to take control of without crushing the spirit of their child,

It's bedtime!

maybe for you

which becomes even more difficult when
a kid can get out of bed and open the
bedroom door. Not to mention stand on the
bed and shout until they throw up (you may
want to invest in a hazardous-waste-
protection jumpsuit and matching helmet).

Daytime Naps

Gradually the morning and afternoon sleeps become one, early afternoon sleep. The Possible Routines for Babies chapter in *Part 1: Babies* has the lowdown on this. Most toddlers need an afternoon nap when they're 1—and most phase it out before they're 3, or 4, or 5 (sometime before high school anyway). Some won't have a nap and are always falling-about tired before bed; some always have a nap; and some have an afternoon nap occasionally. You'll have to be guided by your child: if they're horribly crabby in the last 2 hours or so before bedtime at 7 p.m., they may still need to be persuaded to have an hour or so of sleep in the afternoon (look up afternoon nap in the index).

At this age you can explain to them how a nap means they get two sleepytime stories, or it makes them strong and gives them energy to play or to get ready for that party on the weekend. Keep the room dark and have a familiar bedtime ritual.

Even if your toddler doesn't actually sleep, it's almost always a good idea for them to have a quiet time in bed because it gives everyone a break. And you never know your luck—if you take the pressure off, the nap might happen anyway.

Nighttime sleeps

Some parents let their kids stay up until they maraud around the house, even to 10 or 11 at night. Others insist on a bedtime of 7 p.m., with stories until 7:30. You may find that a fairly early bedtime is best because toddlers need to get 10 to 12 hours' sleep a day and sleep-ins may not suit your mornings. And a toddler who always wakes at 7 a.m. almost certainly won't get enough sleep if they're going to bed at 10 p.m.

Introducing controlled crying or controlled comforting

This approach is explained in the Sleeping chapter in *Part 1: Babies* (look up controlled crying in the index). The principle is the same for establishing a bedtime and ensuring your toddler doesn't want to play in the middle of the night. It isn't too late in the toddler years to set a bedtime and stick to it. The problem is that, as well as yelling, a toddler is now physically able to get up and try to get out of the bedroom. Calm consistency from a sole parent, two parents, or caregivers is the only way to achieve a regular bedtime.

The difficulty with controlled comforting is that it makes some children go berserk and scream maniacally until they throw up over everything. But there is no doubt that the slow, patient version, with firm consistency, no cracking, and no going back to bad habits, can sometimes have a problem fixed in literally a couple of days, depending on the personality of your toddler. But patience is very hard to maintain evening after evening so it's good if someone else can help you to be utterly consistent about what's expected. To make sure the toddler always feels reassured, and to withstand the barrage of hot, tragic tears, it often takes at least two adults—one sobbing in the hall and stopping the other from going into the toddler for another 5.6 seconds, and then swapping roles the next evening.

Toddlers who can escape from their crib must be gently put back each time, otherwise they learn that tantrums and escapology will be rewarded. What about toddlers who can reach the door knob and then barge out of the bedroom? Remove the door knob and have a hook fastener on the outside, but reassure them that you will come in if they need you. (You will have to abandon or modify these ideas depending on your kid's personality.)

Nighttime ritual

A nighttime ritual will always help a kid understand it's time to go to sleep. This can include your toddler:

★ fetching a non-spillable drink and putting it next to the bed.
★ going to the toilet.
★ putting toothpaste on their toothbrush.
★ getting into jammies.
★ putting Mr. Whiskers (or similar) in the bed.
★ turning on the night-light (continue to make it a very diffuse light that isn't near their head or eye line).
★ singing a song with you.
★ hearing a story.
★ saying a special or traditional goodnight rhyme or well-known story with you.

STALLING AT BEDTIME   Head off any toddler stalling strategies by planning ahead and have counter-strategies that build up over a few days. Wants a drink? Make sure one's already placed next to the crib or bed. Needs the bathroom? "You went just before you got into bed. You can go on the potty next to your bed."

BaD DReamS

Toddlers will need to have dreams explained to them: they're things you see in your sleep, but they're not real. Sometimes you have a good dream, and sometimes a bad dream. If you have a bad dream, you can wake up and the dream is gone. (See More Info at the end of the Reading chapter in *Part 5: Stuff* for some good kids' books on the subject.)

Some parents like to resettle their toddler in their crib or bed after a bad dream. Others bring the child into their own bed. And some hop into the kid's bed until they are "dismissed." But if you sleep with your kid you might create a habit and a new problem for yourself.

In cases where a bad dream is recurring or prompted by a traumatic event or ongoing stress, talk to your doctor about seeing a child psychologist. It's important to understand that a toddler in a stressful family situation will have disturbed sleep and nightmares that can only really be "treated" by an improved home life.

Monsters and night fears

If your toddler says "I'm frightened," talk about why and deal with those specific fears. Being in a dim or dark room on your own can be a very frightening experience for little kids, although some will use it as a stalling tactic.

Make sure there isn't a pile of toys casting a scary shadow on the wall or an open closet that looks as if it might have monsters in it. Try to distract your toddler with a funny goodnight song, one verse or bits of which they have to make up.

Some props can help you get rid of monsters: a torch, a garden sprayer with lavender water, labeled "Monster Spray," to frighten monsters away with; or a dolly that is put on guard to tell monsters not to come near. You will need to work out something psychological that suits your child's personality.

You might like to tell them "Tomorrow we can ring up Aunty Gail, who knows where monsters go, and she can explain there's none in the Northern Hemisphere." That sort of thing. One mother I know sat her little boy down while she dialed the "Monster Department" on the phone and told them in no uncertain terms her son insisted they not send any more monsters. The trick is to find something that makes your child feel empowered.

from crib to bed

Traditionally a kid goes into a bed when they've worked out how to climb up and fall out of their crib. (You can postpone this if you have an adjustable crib by putting the mattress at a lower level, once your baby can stand up.) Most kids go into their own bed at about 2 to 2 and a half years old.

To prevent falls you can buy a bed guard for a single bed at baby equipment or bed shops, or you can put the mattress on the floor for a while.

Give your toddler plenty of warning about the change. Talk about getting a new bed being a fun, grown-up thing to do. Saying that there's a little baby somewhere who needs the crib is usually very persuasive when swapping it for a "big girl's" or "big boy's" bed. But try not to do it at the same time that a new baby arrives at your home.

"My daughter is 22 months old and ever since about 3 months old she has had Barry, a small soft toy with a bell (unfortunately), that she goes to bed with. When it's time for her to go to bed or naptime we get her to call Barry and we wander around the house until we find him (surprise!). This works 90 percent of the time: lately we've had Barry and Elmo waiting for her in bed: she can't wait to get there generally. All of this happened by accident." KELLIE

night-drink, night-book, night-light, night-night

more info

BOOKS ON TODDLERS AND SLEEPING

The books *Silent Nights* by Brian Symon and *Solve Your Child's Sleep Problems* by Dr. Richard Ferber all have useful information on toddlers (More Info at the end of the Sleeping chapter in *Part 1: Babies* has full details and reviews). These two are probably at the controlled crying end of the spectrum while books by attachment parenting style authors such as William and Martha Sears have their own solutions.

POSSiBLe ROUTiNes fOR TODDLeRS

Oh, toddlers do LOVE a routine! You might like to copy good child-care centers, which have built-in times for a morning snack, lunch, an after-lunch sleep or quiet time, and an afternoon snack, and spaces throughout the day of not more than an hour long dedicated to learning about something, outside play, music, cleaning up, and art projects. You can add cooking; running, and jumping in the park; going to the beach or for a walk, with stroller time if they get tired; going to the shops or the post office and chatting to every-one on the way; doing housework; having a time for the self (yours and your toddler's); feeding the pets; and bath, stories, bed.

I sometimes wonder if the love toddlers have for a routine and familiar things isn't almost perfectly balanced by the fact that for all their life so far they've been learning new words, new actions, and new concepts and analyzing their world every day. The things we see as commonplace are discoveries for them as they understand more and more. This means a new song or phrase will tickle and delight them, but you'd better not try to move their bed to face another direction without consultation and preparatory chats. You may not want a routine of course—in which case go read another chapter!

getting a routine going

Base your routine around your individual lifestyle while you can: when morning child care or preschool starts, you probably won't be able to put a toddler to bed at 10 p.m.: kids this age need 10 to 12 hours sleep a night and most kids tend to wake up at 6:30 to 7:30 a.m., especially if light comes into their room. Below are suggested routines to use as a base, to cut up and rearrange—or to ignore entirely.

By age 1 your child may have dropped one of their daytime naps or be on the way to doing this, as outlined in the Possible Routines for Babies chapter in *Part 1: Babies*.

POSSIBLE toddler routine from 1 year

7 a.m.   Breakfast, chat.
8   Play and usual morning activities.
9   Possible morning nap.
10   Play.
11   Morning snack or lunch.
12 p.m.   Play.
1 Possible afternoon nap.
2   Afternoon snack.

2:30 Play, visit, or adventure, including some physical activity.

4:30 Possible 20- to 40-minute catnap if two daytime sleeps have dropped to one.

5:30 Dinner.

6 Bath.

6:30 Stories or quiet time.

7 Lights out.

POSSiBLe TODDLeR ROuTiNe fROm 18 mONtHS

7 a.m. Breakfast, chat.

8 Play and usual morning activities.

10 Morning snack.

11 Play.

12 p.m. Lunch.

1 or 2 Afternoon nap.

3 Afternoon snack.

3:30 Play, visit, or adventure, including physical activity.

5:30 Dinner.

6 Bath.

6:30 Stories or quiet time.

7 Lights out.

Kids approaching 3 years old may be dropping a daytime nap altogether (look up afternoon nap in the index).

DaYLiGHt SaViNGS

Some parents keep to "real" time so the day always starts at 7 a.m. (which reads as 6 during daylight savings) or 8 a.m. (7). Or you can take a week or two before daylight savings starts (or ends) to change the bedtime by quarter of an hour every few days.

using the toilet

Children don't even know they're peeing until about halfway through their second year. Because we're so used to them doing it, we often forget to explain to them what's happening.

I'm not going to call using the john "toilet training" because there's no point in training when the trainee couldn't give a toss, and before the kid is physically ready to identify the warning signs of an imminent pee or poop. It hardly ever comes together

fascinating

reliably before the age of 2. I remember thinking what if the neighborhood kids learned to use the bathroom before mine? Would that mean I had a slow learner (and after proudly producing such a gifted vomiter)? In the end I think it dawned on me that I was worried about bottoms that weren't even under my jurisdiction. So—no big deal.

WANTING TO GRADUATE TO THE TOILET

Don't listen to grandparents and other parents about when kids should be fully "toilet trained." In the olden days (like when you were a kid, maybe, even) children were more often in smellier, much wetter and more uncomfortable cloth diapers and couldn't wait to get out of them. These days disposables are so much easier for kids and parents that the in-diapers period is bound to go on slightly, especially in colder areas where children can't run about, bottom out, in the garden for much of the year. And so much of what grandparents and parents reckoned was toilet training was actually them chasing after a kid with a potty and whacking it under at the first sign of any action.

There is absolutely NO POINT in trying to teach your child to use the toilet each time they need to do a pee or a poop if they're not interested. They just humor you for a while and then it turns into a nagfest or a carnival of wet bottoms. Actual interest is when they ask you questions about it and want to see what's going on when people go to the bathroom. Any work put in earlier than this will probably end up being a colossal waste of time.

Basically by the time they're interested, they'll be able to tell when they're going to pee or poop and be physically able to use the potty or toilet: it just takes practice to get it all together.

WHeN aRe TODDLeRS ReaDY To LeaRN aBOUT THe TOiLeT?

Signs include being interested in reading a book with you about using the toilet; being interested in hearing about where poop and pee come from and go to after you flush, and what the flush is; asking about other aspects of the toilet and pee and poop, and watching older or other kids and family members going to the toilet; talking about, and looking forward to, no more diapers, and about being a "big boy" or "big girl"; and being interested in undies generally or a special pair in particular. (See More Info at the end of this chapter for books for kids.)

Sometimes interest wanes, or a kid regresses temporarily because a new baby in diapers is getting so much attention. Don't fall for the old-fashioned assumption that teaching them about the toilet has to be a frustrating battle to get the idea into their head. Every now and then try to spark some interest—a story about where pee goes; "Look at what Mommy's doing"; "Here, sit on this toilet seat"; "Wow, won't it be good when you can wear undies!" Wait until your kid is really interested and wants to do it, then help them—much less stressful for everyone and also much more successful.

Most of the books I've consulted say kids are ready between the ages of 1 and 3, and the average age is before 2 years old. Out in the real world I've NEVER heard of a kid having sustained interest before about 18 months and hardly anyone before 2, and the average seems to be somewhere between 2 and 3, with plenty saving it for 3 or 4.

There's a common perception that boys generally start and finish learning to use the john later than girls. There's no way of knowing whether this applies to your little individual so, hey, forget about it: it's really not useful info. Some kids get it all over with very quickly; others foof along in fits and starts until some time after their third birthday.

It's usually easier for a toddler to know when they're going to poop than pee. Pee doesn't herald itself so obviously to a child and can come too quickly in times of excitement or great interest in something else. Nap and then nighttime control take the longest to get the hang of: almost invariably after age 3. It's very, very common for kids to be in nighttime pull-ups at age 4, or using a potty next to the bed. It's a long trip down the hall to the toilet at this age.

HOW LONG DOES it take?

Learning to go to the bathroom regularly can take only weeks, or even a few days if your kid is really interested. Otherwise months and months. Be prepared for potty and toilet using to go backwards at unexpected times or to take a sudden leap forward.

HOW to explain the gig

It's always useful to explain to your child that their body takes all the food and drinks they have and uses these to make them grow and be strong, and the stuff the body doesn't need comes out as pee and poop; and that pee and poop are a bit stinky (though not a big deal, heavens no) so we need to flush them down the toilet (but *kids* can't ever be flushed away—and toys shouldn't be!). Making a poop often makes us feel more comfy and as if we have more energy.

It's also a good idea to explain what happens to pee and poop after we're finished with it: that they drop down into the water in the toilet, and then we push the lever and the water goes whoosh, whoosh, and then the wee and poo disappear down all these pipes, go into other big pipes, and finally into a big smelly pond in the ground a long way away, and eventually are spewed into our surf spots by governments that need to be slapped around. Well, maybe not that last bit, it's a little complex. But sometimes explaining the whole process demystifies the experience for kids, otherwise it's quite abstract.

TOILET PHOBIAS   If kids are scared about what's in the thing (sharks, monsters, the Unknown), explain where all the poop and pee goes, and that it's like the plughole in the bath: stuff goes down, but nothing comes up.

WHat you might NeeD

You might like to use:
- ★ a plastic potty in the bathroom—and one next to the bed might be a solution if your child finds it hard to get to the toilet in time in the middle of the night when they reach that stage.
- ★ a smaller-sized toilet seat to fit on yours.
- ★ a stool or a step for access to the big toilet.
- ★ "training wipes"—flushable wipes that a kid can use to take care of more poop than toilet paper would
- ★ pull-on half-diaper, half-undies things (see below).
- ★ a nighttime diaper for a while (a toddler before using the toilet will have needed three or four nappies a day).
- ★ a properly fitted waterproof mattress cover—this has waterproof plastic underneath with cotton on the top so they're not nasty, sweaty, and uncomfy to lie on. One on the bed and one for emergencies is a good call.

Pull-on half-diaper, half-undies things

These are a kind of final diaper—one that pulls on and off like a pair of undies. If you find one full of poo, lay the kid down and tear down the papery side bits, then take it off like a diaper (and put the poop in the toilet). They are often used as transitional pants when a child is learning to use the potty or toilet, and when a kid is using the potty or toilet except at night.

Some parents want their kids to go straight from diapers to the potty or toilet—and it's true that many kids are likely to poo or pee in a pull-on diaper because it's convenient, although a big poop isn't any more pleasant in a pull-on than a diaper.

Potty or toilet?

Some kids start on the potty and graduate to the toilet. Some parents like to start with the potty because a kid doesn't need help to get on; others take their kid straight to the toilet because they figure they want to start as they mean to go on.

Potties are cleaned by tipping the contents into the toilet, wiping them out with toilet paper, and then dousing them with disinfectant—if necessary, clean with a toilet brush before the disinfectant. (It's much easier to deal with pee in the potty than poop, so if you can manage it have your child poop in the toilet.)

some "toilet-training" ideas

★ Let your kid watch you on the toilet and have a look in the bowl afterwards to see what happens when you flush.

★ Keep talking to your child about why you're asking certain things of them. This will encourage them to explain to you why they're doing what they're doing or why they're afraid.

★ Some books suggest that kids should be put on the potty or toilet at regular times such as after each meal and first thing in the morning. (If I were a kid, I would find this far too prescriptive.) Others suggest trying to teach the child to get to know how it feels when they "need to go" and to tell a parent, who can take them to the bathroom.

★ Some people encourage reading or playing on the pot, others think this distracts from the business at hand.

★ Many parents suggest you wait until summer once your kid is interested, then let them run around the garden a lot with no pants on—they'll be more aware of peeing and pooping and any accidents will be easier to clean up.

★ Put a non-flushable floating target in the bowl for boys to aim their peeing willies at: corks and ping-pong balls are popular.

★ Some people swear by teaching boys to pee sitting down; others say the key is getting a bigger boy or man to teach them. A boy starting on a potty will have to graduate to stand-up peeing later.

★ Teach girls how to wipe themselves with folded toilet paper, from the front towards the back, so poop is not wiped forward as this can cause infections.

★ Show kids how to wash their hands with soap and dry them on a clean towel.

★ A sticker or star chart can be set up to show everyone the marvelous progress, and sharp, barking cries of admiration made frequently. (Okay, that was a joke. I don't want any complaint letters about children frightened by woofing noises.)

★ But avoid over-the-top, extravagant praise–buying full-page ad space in a newspaper to announce the first unassisted poop is likely to lead to a child developing weird ideas about the glamour and importance of waste management issues.

★ Try a smaller toilet seat that sits on the regular one if your toddler is worried about falling in or needs more comfort.

★ Use incentives: divinely pretty undies, or ones with pictures of their favorite character, are often a great bribe for the kid who can use the toilet.

★ Don't make a fuss or go on about the disgustingness of poop and pee: this can cause psychological problems. And I think we can do without references to "Mr. Poo Poo coming out," thank you very much.

★ Always treat an "accident" matter of factly, with a "Never mind, it's just a wee (ha!) accident."

★ Don't put a kid in overalls or tights that are hard for them to get out of quickly themselves.

★ Give your toddler lots of water, fruit, and veggies to help a hard poop or constipation problem. Giving fiber without extra water often only makes constipation worse.

★ Let a bathroom tap trickle in a pee-like way if your child is having trouble being able to pee; or sing a little rhyme or line that relaxes them such as "Pee, pee, pee, all the way in the pot."

★ Apologize for being grumpy if you find yourself getting angry or exasperated with "yet another" wet or poopey accident, or have a laugh with your kid about your grumpiness. If it's too late, make sure you're consistently nice about the next few.

★ Wanting to be like the older kids is often a big motivation. Child-care centers can be a great help, as can older siblings, cousins, or close pals.

★ An older toddler or preschooler can be mortified by accidents—don't add to the embarrassment, and remember "Never mind." Just help them to clean up in private if you're out, and hide the evidence in a plastic bag in your toddler bag or handbag.

★ If your toddler seems always wet, rather than sometimes dry and sometimes wet, check out with your doctor whether it means they have a urinary tract infection or any other physical leaky problem.

★ At night have a dim light all the way to and inside the bathroom, a rug on the floor if it's cold, and the smaller seat and stool in place, or the potty near the bed.

★ Always get the kid to go to the bathroom before you leave home, child care, preschool, a friend's house, or the shopping center. Little people have bladders that are also very little and they need as many opportunities to go as possible. (This is especially true when you're using public transport because it's always a longer trip than by car. You can carry a pull-up to slip on your toddler just for emergencies.)

★ If you're going to be peeing outside on a nature adventure, have them wear something on their lower half that can easily be pulled completely off and then put back on. Tights or shoes wet with pee after a squatting accident are no fun.

★ Always carry extra undies, trousers, wipes, and at least two plastic bags for accidents (one bag is for throwaways, another is for the dirty clothes).

★ Always stay with your child in a public restroom, and if there's no unisex parents' toilet, use the handicapped one as long as nobody disabled is waiting—the extra room is often a boon, and it can be much nicer for a guy who wants to avoid taking his little girl into the men's.

★ When you're out, help your child to balance on a grown-up seat.

Regression

A kid who's been using the potty or toilet for weeks or months and then suddenly isn't any more probably has some kind of common physical reason such as an infection, or a psychological problem caused by ongoing stress or a traumatic event (although it may not have seemed traumatic to you), so see your GP.

A kid who forgets to go to the toilet a lot is probably just not interested enough yet.

Nighttime accidents

Few children never wet the bed. (If it's an ongoing problem into the preschool years, look up bedwetting in the index).

Twins and the toilet

Most people in the kid business recommend waiting until all the twins (or triplets) are ready and moving on together—but if one toddler is determined to go ahead and it's not worrying the other, one at a time may be less work for you (although some say going through the process twice is worse). Just be careful that the praise given to one doesn't seem like something the other is missing out on because they're not good enough. Perhaps there might be something else to praise them for. Before you start, speak to as many parents of twins or triplets in similar situations as you can—but remember, you've got yourself a bunch of individuals in your family (there's more on them in the Multiples chapter in *Part 5: Stuff*).

"One Monday morning he said wearing undies was cool and by the end of the week he was completely trained much to my relief. [Toilet user at 3 years 5 months.]" ANGELA

"All my kids initially trained themselves ('How clever am I!'), then decided to regress to diapers ('That game's not fun any more') before they were properly trained. [Toilet user at 2 years 6 months.]"
MELISSA

"She did pretty well at 22 months until her brother arrived! Then she would demand a diaper like him. She used toileting as a way of controlling me and would demand to go to the toilet when I started feeding him or would just pee in front of me if she didn't get what she wanted. She managed eventually. I had him out of night diapers (2) before her (4). Every child is different." SARAH

"Children are scared of the flushing water and scared of 'What if I fall in.'" CHRIS

"Don't put a diaper on at night. While we had a diaper he wet. After I left off the diaper, I only had one or two accidents." JUDI

"We bought Wiggles undies and had very few accidents after that. The Wake Up Jeff undies took the brunt of it."
SAMANTHA

"They do it when they're ready and not before." JEANETTE

"I bribed him with candy for a poop and by God it worked! [Toilet user at 3 years 6 months.]" TRACY

"It felt like it was never going to happen for us. He or she will let you know when they are ready. Try pants during the day and regularly ask them if they need to go. They will eventually get used to this and go themselves. Still working on nights!" BIANCA

"At nearly 3 he is not interested in toilet training. I have tried special toys, stickers, stamps, cuddles, praise, and even candy bribery but nothing works. This has been the hardest of everything."
REBECCA

"My advice is to let them see what the toilet or potty is for, and pop the little tot into undies. When they wet themselves they will get very uncomfortable and decide they don't like it much . . . or in the case of one of our little boys he will run outside and cock his leg like our dog does." DALE

"Our son finally admitted he was scared of the toilet. My friend Debbie said she'd arrange for the Poop Fairy to come . . . Debbie and her three daughters all dressed in bright colors, tutus, fairy wands (homemade cardboard and stick) and fairy suitcase . . . my son said, 'You're Aunty Debbie,' and she said, 'Not today,' as she strode purposefully to the bathroom. She spent 10 long minutes in there with my son, anointing the toilet with stick-on stars and plastering the bathroom with fairy dust (very hard to get rid of). Without any other discussion, on the third day [after] he ascended the throne and hasn't looked back since. It would never have worked on my second son: the secret is acknowledging their fears and devising a scheme that will suit your own child." LESLEY

"He had a couple of times when he wet the floor and got very upset. I had a talk to him and said that if he was going to get so upset when he had an accident it might be better if we left it for a while and tried again when he was a bit older. He was very appreciative of this. When he did make the transition to the toilet (3 years 3 months) it was only a matter of a few weeks before we risked no night diaper and were off and running. Yay! No more spending $16 to $20 a week on diapers! It was well worth letting him do it under his own steam."
DIANNE

"Explain the body parts (kid friendly) and how things work and practice. Even after accidents we are just practicing, and we are doing so well. In my opinion, no potty if we are telling kids they're old enough to go to the toilet. That way they know the routine: wipe, flush, and wash hands. It makes them really feel like a big person."
CATHY, NANNY

"On hearing she wasn't toilet trained, my otherwise gorgeous nanna said, 'Oh, I'm so surprised. She's such a bright little thing!' Arrgh! Wise and experienced moms all say the same thing—if they aren't ready it will be months of agony. If they are ready, they'll do it themselves in a few days." KATE

"We made the stepping stool together, he painted it and decorated it with his mom and within 2 days had it down. [Toilet user at 2 years 6 months.]" JOHN

more info

BOOKS FOR KIDS ABOUT BATHROOM BUSINESS

What to Expect When You Use the Potty

by Heidi Murkoff, HarperFestival, May, 2000.

From the endless What to Expect franchise. Weirdly the author actually imagines you might decide to teach your child to call poop a BM (bowel movement). But the book does create interest in what poop is and where it goes.

296

The Story of the Little Mole Who Knew It Was None of His Business
by Werner Holzwarth, Chrysalis Books, Sept., 2001.
A picture story about a mole who was pooped on and goes in search of the animal culprit. Not a "how to," but a depiction of different poops. (Grandparents and the easily grossed-out may have palpitations.)

Everyone Poops
by Taro Gomi, Kane/Miller, 2001.
A picture book with animals and people. Who, I think you'll find, all poop.

Toddler Development (1 to 3)

By about 1 year your "baby" should have a repertoire of several emotions and will be influenced by your reactions to situations (drop glass on floor, say filthy word). They

plans for global domination

SHaKesPeaRe SocieTy

should be able to wave goodbye and associate other simple movements with situations (the word "Touchdown!" is accompanied by hands in the air).

If your kid is in child care, ask the professional workers, who are trained in this area, to let you know when they've checked your child's development for their age range. Professional child caregivers are often very reassuring because they see kids of all ages come along splendidly in their own time.

If you're concerned about the rate of development, see your GP or pediatrician. Some babies go straight from tush-shuffle to walking, without crawling; some walk months earlier than others—it usually evens up in the end.

1 year to 18 months

Physical development

Your toddler:

- ★ can see things in the distance and tries to get them.
- ★ is shuffling, crawling, bottom-dragging, just walking, or walking alone, perhaps moving with a tentative, stiff-legged totter, with feet wide apart for extra balance.
- ★ may be climbing onto ladders, chairs, boxes, tables, uncles.
- ★ can let go of something with controlled movement.
- ★ starts to stack things inside or on top of each other.
- ★ uses a spoon with greater dexterity.
- ★ is learning to get simple clothes off and to help to get them on.
- ★ starts to drink from a cup, a straw, or a pop-top bottle.

Emotional and mental development

Your toddler:

- ★ is bonded to one or two consistent caregivers at home and may want one or either parent primarily, depending on how the child care is divided.
- ★ may develop separation anxiety when they start walking or improve rapidly at walking. This can happen with other new developments, too.
- ★ is developing their memory—many girls are a little better at some aspects of remembering at this stage than boys, although this mostly evens out by about age 3 (women still do better than men on some short-term memory tests). A toddler may remember how to do a task or action they saw up to 4 months ago, and observe and copy actions seen on T.V.—but you can't rely on them to remember things you want them to remember.
- ★ often says "NO!" to test their control over things—and perhaps because they hear no a lot.

★ is showing great interest in books.

★ is starting to ask or look for things that are not in sight such as a drink.

★ is affectionate with familiar pals, but can be wary of new folk and strangers (sounds like an adult).

★ gets excited about something that is coming up such as unwrapping a present.

★ if frustrated might hit, kick, scratch, claw, or bite to show their frustration, even if they've never seen anyone else do these things.

Communication development

Your toddler probably:

★ begins talking, has a vocabulary of a few words (see if you can get "please" and "thank you" in as early as possible) and may even put two or more words together. Girls often progress more quickly than boys.

★ will start to pick up more and more words every day at some point near 18 months old, give or take a few months.

★ listens to and understands the gist of conversations and the particular meaning of words without having the skills to join in verbally.

What can you do?

Pull-along or push-along toys are good fun. Encourage outdoor play with balls, sand, and supervised water, climbing, swings, and slides: it helps them to develop physical skills and to exercise—and tires 'em out so they have a good sleep. All play involving objects with wheels, such as strollers and ride-on toys, or water needs constant vigilance and age-appropriate expectations.

Even "doing the dishes" in the sink is water play (always supervise the play, then pull the plug afterwards). Let them "help" you with chores: give them a feather duster, a sponge for rudimentary wiping work, a wooden spoon and bowl for stirring something safe while you're cooking. And they'll enjoy picking things out of the clothes basket to be hung up by you and passing you the pegs.

Teach your child early on to put their head back for washing off shampoo. Toddlers usually hate water on their face and eyes, which may be a survival instinct: this can be something to gradually work on in the bath or pool or at the beach.

As the kid gets more mobile and can reach to tabletop level and climb up bookcases, do another safety check of the house and places you regularly visit (see the Home Safety chapter in *Part 5: Stuff*). Find places where they can explore freely instead of being always restrained. Better to hide your heirloom vases for four years than have them smashed or a frustrated toddler who can't go anywhere near one corner of the living room.

Read your child simple stories and together look at picture books with images they can point to and name or flaps they can lift.

Play different kinds of music. Sing and dance together. Make up songs with familiar names and words in them. (See More Info at the end of this chapter for good books on having fun together.)

Don't put a kid in front of confusing or violent TV programs or stuff that isn't specifically made for their age group, including the news, which is distressing and disturbing for children this age, who cannot process the information (this will be the case for many years to come). Have videos handy rather than just turning the TV on. (See the TV, Videos and Films chapter in *Part 5: Stuff*.)

Talk to your child and give them space to talk back. Explain what you are going to do before you do it and why. Kids pick up an incredible amount just by listening and repeating. Their brains are making millions of connections, including the right uses and placement of words. This applies to all ages.

Don't "correct" a misuse of a word, instead use it correctly yourself. "I putted my hat." "Yes, you put on your hat." instead of "Don't say 'putted': that's wrong." If your kid isn't talking much, try not to anticipate their needs too efficiently so that they are encouraged to ask for what they're after, or offer them a choice to get a response.

Use simple terms to explain things, but now and then add some words that help them build a bigger vocabulary—kids of this age can understand words such as "bizarre," "fragile," and "ridiculous" in context—and it will stop you going mad from using only "cat sat on mat" type vocabulary.

Kids pick up on tone at least as much as words, and they won't understand irony for years to come: everything is taken literally. This means you can't do one thing while saying another, or say "Well, that's marvelous, isn't it?" when you mean "Ooh, I think we'd better clean this up."

Explain that kicking, biting, punching and, gouging are not good ways to solve a problem—reward other ways of behaving with attention and praise, and remove a child from interesting action if they behave violently. Say "Use your words" to encourage verbal expression of crossness. You can also begin now to say "It's not okay to push" or "We don't hit." Kids reinforce their learning by saying things back to you for confirmation such as "We don't bite, do we?."

Try to give choices so your toddler has to say yes to something and feels in control. Instead of saying "Put on your coat," say "Do you want your blue jacket or your yellow coat?." And try to let them do some things for themselves.

18 months to 2 years

Physical development
Your toddler:
- ★ is working on that stiff-legged walking style, getting more proficient, and experimenting with going faster.
- ★ runs straight-legged.
- ★ can see things in the distance—their eyes are working at full capacity now.
- ★ understands what the purpose of things is—a bowl is stirred, a page is turned, a shoe goes on a foot.

★ can throw a ball, although catching is more problematic—they hold out their arms but aren't able to anticipate the arc of the ball and move to where it will fall.

★ climbs stairs and other things—usually more up than down but can go down (usually on their bottom, rather than backwards, if they get practice on stairs in their home).

★ is still testing a lot of things in their mouth, although not doing it all the time.

★ can take off their hat and other clothes but is still not so good at putting them on.

Emotional and mental development
Your toddler:

★ has quite clear feelings of wanting to cuddle or wanting to be free and doing things by themselves.

★ as well as recognizing themselves in the mirror, experiments with moving their head and making faces. Kids often try out emotions in the form of face-making or crying into the mirror as if to say when I feel like *this* I look like *that*.

★ is terribly, terribly BUSY.

★ can amuse themselves for short periods at the same activity if an adult is comfortingly nearby.

★ will try to help with housework chores and grasps fundamentally what's required even though they couldn't get a job as a cleaner.

★ is affectionate.

★ is quick to feel frustration and possibly has tantrums.

★ as when younger, can be upset by a vibe evoked by bright or flashing lights, loud, scary, music or a tone such as sarcasm.

★ probably can understand simple directions and what's usually required for regular events, such as how to behave at dinner or at Uncle Roscoe's house (not allowed in the garden with the dogs without an adult), but can't be relied on to always remember the directions or instructions.

★ may remember or describe dreams more than in the past, and nightmares may happen.

★ may develop fear of things such as dogs, people in animal suits, water, being at the top of the stairs, or anything that it makes sense to be scared of, as a survival tactic.

★ shows sympathy for other children who are distressed.

★ wants to explore and touch everything.

★ cannot anticipate dangers or consequences but can learn from very specific events (the last time I touched that oven thing it hurt so I'm not going to touch it again—this heater looks jolly interesting, though . . . Ouch!).

★ can express jealousy and selfishness (which can also be interpreted as a survival technique).

Communication development

Your toddler:

★ is developing more words and language skills, such as using very simple sentences, as well as full-on "nonsense" chat. This is normal and healthy (also amusing).

★ is copying sounds, actions, and reactions from adults. This is often the age when you realize your reaction to dropping something is to say "Oh, buckety fuck" because your toddler says it in the post office to stunned silence.

★ is learning lots of names for things.

★ makes the right sounds when an animal is named.

★ learns bits of songs.

★ will tell you or show you if something is in the "wrong" place.

★ will show you how they are feeling and respond to the obvious feelings of someone else.

★ likes a 5-minute warning before a new activity ("Very soon we'll need to put the blocks away and go to the store," "Let's put on our shoes because we're about to go out to the clothes line to look for fairies").

What can you do?

Play chase with your toddler. Kick a ball together. Play throwing and catching games with the emphasis on them throwing and you catching. Toddlers (and preschoolers) find it easier to catch something that's not hard and unyielding, and not too small (tennis ball) or heavy (basketball). Try light, smaller-sized beach balls, not too tightly blown up, and, even better, adult-palm-sized beanbags.

Beg, borrow, or buy a ride-on "bike" without pedals for them to zoom around on.

You can start to teach your kid at this age actions that they'll get better at steadily as time goes on: washing and drying their hands; stringing large beads; sorting colors and shapes (this will be just an idea at first, but they'll get there); identifying everyone, including themselves, in family photos; playing in sand; stopping at the curb and other road safety actions; playing in safe water in the bath or outside (unless there's a drought); singing bits of songs; matching words to situations and feelings.

Help your toddler learn to dance on their own feet, although you may need to hold hands. Develop some favorite songs and make tapes or CDs for them (avoid the radio if possible because of distressing news breaks, stupid ads, and bad boy bands). Make music together with saucepans and rattly things. (See the Art and Music chapter in *Part 5: Stuff*.)

Read to them, look at picture books together and encourage independent looking at books. Make up and tell stories: toddlers often love to contribute, frequently trying to exactly copy your stories but eventually coming up with independent details.

As with a younger toddler, use lots of different words when you speak to your child; don't "dumb it down." A child of 2 can understand what "amazing," "completely loopy," and "schemozzle" mean, and using lots of words gives them a wider range of reactions and explanations. They also have fun saying them. You have to converse with kids for them to understand the language; you can't just sit them in front of a radio or TV and expect them to soak in what they hear like a sponge. They need to ask questions and use words in different contexts to see which ones fit.

Try not to say no all the time; instead try out some variations and distractions: "Hey, I've got a great idea! Why don't we do a jigsaw puzzle instead!"; "You know what, if you hold your cup with two hands instead of one you don't spill the drink inside"; "Instead of throwing Granny's mangy scarf in the bin, why don't we hang it up in the hallway where we can't see it?"; "Well, it's not an ice-cream day, but you can choose whether you want scrummy strawberry yoghurt or a banana milk-shake!" This expands their vocabulary and preserves their self-esteem; it cunningly gives them the illusion that they have more choice and are more in control than you because they get to choose stuff.

Child psychotherapist Frances Thomson-Salo says about the fears or phobias children may have from now on: "I'd try a mix of talking and reassurance and being very low-key about it. I think lots of children have these fears (and they probably served us well in evolution when we lived in natural habitats). Help the child deal with their own anxieties (rather than dealing with them FOR them). If they persist in a marked way and cause the child distress and giving some strategies doesn't help, I'd consider getting professional help." Strategies to overcome nighttime fears are suggested in the earlier Toddlers and Sleeping chapter.

Try to be patient as toddlers veer from rude independence to wrapping themselves around your neck when you drop them off at their beloved grandad's for a couple of hours.

2 to 3 years

Physical development

Your toddler:

* can jump up and down when asked.
* can stand on one leg.
* runs around confidently.
* may be showing signs of right- or left-handedness.
* can work out how to get the lid off some things and open some doors.
* is starting to get good control of a pencil or crayon and makes marks on paper that represent something, even if these are not recognizable to you.
* has all the fine motor abilities in place—little things can be picked up and put down deftly and pages turned neatly.
* can build a tall tower from several blocks.
* can feed themselves and use a fork, knife, and spoon correctly. As with all things this is not automatic but comes with practice. If a 3-year-old hardly ever sees a knife (or a chopstick), or isn't gently reminded how to use it, they won't suddenly be good at it.
* goes down stairs usually by getting two feet on each stair and then progressing, but is now going up one foot per stair (and probably needs to be reminded to use the stair rail or wall for support).
* may become very aware of diapers and want their dirty ones changed, but may not yet be making the leap to being interested in using a potty or the toilet.
* has a basically adult sense of taste, but still with a reflex against bitter tastes.
* can learn to ride a trike with pedals.

Emotional and mental development

Your toddler:

* ⭐ has a more developed sense of who "I" is.
* ⭐ is starting to understand more of your conversation and more simple concepts and feelings—"I'm cold," "over there," "falling down"—rather than just the names of things.
* ⭐ understands more than they can show. They are learning emotions and the way people interact as well as facts.
* ⭐ doesn't seem to recognize characteristics such as different skin or different-shaped eyes much at all, but may ask for explanations if they hear others referring to these details.
* ⭐ can understand simple explanations such as "Some people are always grumpy" or "Some people are not kind to everyone, and we just try to ignore them."
* ⭐ may have tantrums as a response to frustrating situations.
* ⭐ will work out the best ways to manipulate a situation to get what they want and use it (a tantrum will stay in the repertoire if rewarded).
* ⭐ remembers rhymes and information that are interesting to them.
* ⭐ understands more about the world—boats go on the water; the postal worker leaves letters.
* ⭐ likes to help and doesn't see routine things as boring—housework continues to be fun.
* ⭐ wants to be more independent and to get their own way
* ⭐ imitates sounds, actions, and reactions, with some of their own personal variations.

Communication development

Your toddler:

* ⭐ understands more words from listening to them in context.
* ⭐ will often repeat words several times or stutter as their brain races ahead and their vocabulary expands so quickly. The stuttering usually stops within a year or so.

★ wants to participate in conversations, singalongs, and group activities, and asks questions about the right terms and actions.

★ chats away, building daily on their vocabulary if given the opportunity, and works towards constructing more complex, complete sentences such as "Please go down there."

What can you do?

Obviously there's a big gap between 2 and 3 years old: don't see the suggestions as stuff your kid must be able to do by the stated age, but as something they may already be doing by that age—or may pick up in the next six months to a year.

Stick close to them, although this is never foolproof, because they want to investigate things all the time. (What's behind here? What happens if I throw this? What will it look like to take all this out of a jar and feel it on my hands?)

By the age of 3 your child might find a trike with pedals fun. And you can help them practice their "ball skills"—have fun with balls.

When reading together, ask your kid to point out and explain things in familiar books or to guess what's happening in new ones.

If your child—and you—aren't getting at least some fresh air and exercise every day, think about how to change this so they're not at risk of becoming bored or getting above a healthy weight.

Give them more music, more art, more nature rambles, more water play, more books, more jokes. Enjoy and share the small things in life that are fun for you to rediscover and all new for your kid: animal-shaped clouds, a big red truck, the way a squirrel moves. (See More Info at the end of this chapter for good books on all this.)

A kid this age might enjoy one quarter of a grown-up sports event such as soccer, but rarely the whole afternoon: try to see things from their point of view. Time is much slower for little people.

Rotate batches of toys so your kid sees them with new eyes. Give them crayons that have intense colors—better to buy one good set with strong colors or oil pastels, and look after them a little more carefully, than sets with pale, wimpy colors.

Understand that kids this age prefer to play next to each other rather than with each other (one with a truck, one with a spade, for example). Sharing toys can be a bit of a challenging concept.

Make TV, videos, and computer games occasional, not daily, activities. Kids need to interract with others to learn the listening and verbal skills essential for the first year of school.

Organize play times with other kids by using child care or swapsie arrangements with other parents: your child develops social skills and you get some time to yourself here and there.

Do lots of praising: if something isn't "right," praise something that is, or the effort, and try again later. Almost always, unless there's a safety issue, the experience and the fun are what's important.

Everything you do and say will be repeated or acted out, so if you blow up every time something goes wrong you're teaching tantrums, and if you punch the wall whenever you're angry they will too. If you hit them, they will hit their siblings, the dog, their toys, or you. As always, they will be guided by your example as much, if not more so, than your words.

more info

Your Child at Play: One to Two Years: Exploring, Daily Learning, and Making Friends
by Marilyn Segal, Newmarket Press, 1998.
Treat it as a resource for finding out what you and your baby might have fun doing together.

Your Child at Play: Two to Three Years: Growing Up, Language, and the Imagination
by Marilyn Segal, Newmarket Press, 2nd ed., 1998.
Rather than worry about "nurturing intelligence," which will happen anyway, you can find great things to do that will parallel your toddler's interests and capabilities.

toys and games for toddlers

The list that follows of fun toys and games for the 1- to 3-year-olds was compiled from suggestions by people who responded to the Kidwrangling Survey. As in the earlier Toys and Games for Babies chapter, I've selected them with a bias toward cheap fun, and kept away from brand names and merchandising toys, many of which are also lots of fun.

For further ideas about games for kids ask child-care workers and older people, and keep a lookout in thrift-shops for books about kids' activities, "parlor games" and indoor play. See what ideas you can get from books and activity days at your local library, which may have a toy-lending section, too.

iDeas from parents

⊚ Cars, trucks, trains ⊚ large click-together blocks ⊚ a plastic picnic set ⊚ baby dolls and a baby doll's stroller ⊚ playing pretend games (such as mommy mouse and baby mouse) ⊚ drawing and painting using non-toxic, washable poster paints ⊚ pasting using bits of fabric, paper, pictures torn from magazines, cut-up streamers ⊚ plastic tools and a construction hat ⊚ books ⊚ musical instruments, particularly bells and a recorder ⊚ printing with large potato stamps and paint ⊚ stickers ⊚ any dress-up clothes, for either sex ⊚ a box of Band-Aids, which can get emptied and filled, emptied and filled, over and over ⊚ colored wooden blocks ⊚ high-heeled shoes ⊚ a tricycle ⊚ a tea party set ⊚ playing pretend to fix things ⊚ kid-sized kitchen utensils to pretend to cook with ⊚ a wipe-clean magnetic drawing slate ⊚ a tent or cubby with blankets ⊚ biscuit cutters, rolling pin, and playdough (if using homemade add food coloring and see the Playdough box opposite for a note on safety) ⊚ a small train set ⊚ ladybird beetles in various incarnations ⊚ pretending to be dinosaurs ⊚ plastic frogs ⊚ bangles ⊚ wooden or plastic farmyard animals ⊚ balls ⊚ CDs and tapes ⊚ "sewing" enormous buttons onto a piece of cardboard with holes punched in it, or threading beads with a shoelace ◎ bubble blowing (but an adult needs to work with the child on this one) ◎ party whistles (the ones that roll and unroll when you blow them) ◎ coins and a money box ◎ letters and a mail box ◎ alphabet and number posters ◎ early jigsaw puzzles ◎ old purses and handbags ◎ colored chalk on the sidewalk ◎ toy phones ◎ cardboard boxes ◎ pretending to have a tea party or playing "cooking stuff" ◎ playing "store" with or without fake money and a cash register ◎ sanded offcuts of wood to stack or arrange ◎ soccer ◎ a toy hammer to hammer golf tees into styrofoam ◎ a spinning top.

PLAYDOUGH

Homemade playdough recipes usually have a large amount of salt in them. A high concentration of salt can damage a child's internal organs. Kids, especially babies and toddlers, should be supervised so they don't eat a lot of homemade playdough. The commercial stuff should be a major brand and labeled non-toxic: it shouldn't contain salt.

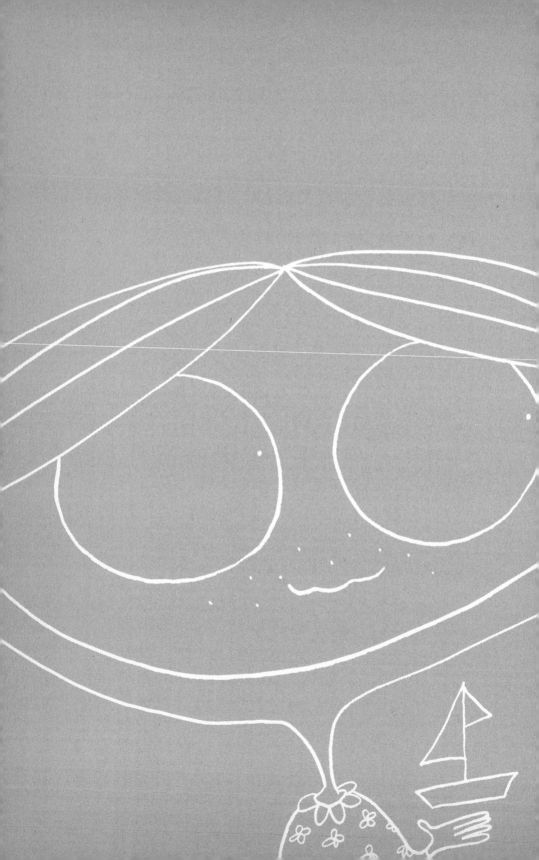

3

LiTTLe KiDS

IF YOU'RE READING *PART 3: LITTLE KIDS,*
YOU MIGHT ALSO BE INTERESTED IN CHAPTERS
IN OTHER PARTS OF THE BOOK.

No More Baby Face

Well, it's not as if 3-year-olds are ready for school—but they're almost certainly steady on their feet, probably at the very least starting to learn to use the toilet, and can be most indignant at being associated with babies and toddlers. And seemingly in a flash they really will be off to kindergarten, usually at the age of 5.

Your baby is now very much enjoying being their own person and physically changing from their toddler shape into a kid shape (leaving behind the Teletubbie-diaper-bottom is a good start). Physically and mentally they're making great leaps and bounds, and are ready to test themselves alone and with others in playgroups and 3-year-old and

4-year-old child-care programs.

goodBye to toDDLeR Days

Little kids can understand much more complicated concepts and situations than before, and continue to explore and to ask questions about how things work and why, and who and what and when (not to mention "Huh?"). Despite the fact that 3 to 5 year olds can be friendly companions, and enjoy being more grown-up, they're still the littlest of kids, needing to feel safe and that they always have a haven.

This is the time when kids build on their physical and mental skills, and the foundations for healthy self-esteem and confidence are laid down. They need to know they're wonderful and that it doesn't matter if they make mistakes or don't get things "right" all the time. And that there may be a number of correct answers to the same question. It's a time when they watch you very closely to see what being a person is about.

I Love you

Little kids will constantly try to push the boundaries of behavior, wriggle out of cuddles, and dash here and there—only to come running to you when they need love and reassurance. This is also often the time when your child first moves away from you, even temporarily—while still seeing you as the center of their world. So don't feel too sad that they're going off to preschool and eventually school—enjoy the fact that they still see you as clever, comforting, and the font of all knowledge. In a few short years they'll find you hideously embarrassing and roll their eyes a lot.

Your child may come home with new ideas and words you didn't even know they had, stories of new experiences or having heard about a terrible event close to home or elsewhere in the world. Talking about these, rather than getting upset or angry, will encourage your child to know they can be open and don't need to hide things from you.

Everyone bangs on about the terrible twos, but nobody seems to warn you beforehand that "discipline" issues go right into the 3-to-5 years because your little kid is still testing to see who's in control of what and needing to understand the balance between rights and responsibilities (see the Teaching Kids How to Behave chapter in *Part 4: Parenting*). They'll imperiously shout orders from another room and treat you as a slave if you let them.

And they'll also expect you to solve every problem for them. Even though it may be quicker just to do this most of the time, a child will really love it when you ask them what *they* think—and say "Yes, maybe" instead of "No, that will never work," and help them through discussions with grown-ups and other kids. Even more than when they were a toddler, you can help them arrive at answers to their own questions through "research," by talking to an "expert" such as an engineer friend, getting a book from the library, or seeing what happens when they're allowed to fill a cup to overflowing in the sink.

It's also time to rejoice that occasionally they'll listen to reason, at least in the morning before they get exhausted. Or if they're not in the midst of that seemingly endless period of colds and stomach aches caused by the inevitable gap between stepping up contact with other kids and building immunity against most low-level illnesses. Or you haven't caught them at a low ebb when they need something to eat or drink. (Oh, let's face it, sometimes they're unbearable for no apparent reason.)

Some kids can't wait to grow up, others want to stay 4 forever, but they'll all have a ball at their fifth birthday before they launch into the world of school and beyond. These, then, are the days when you'll always be there when they skin a knee, know exactly what they had for lunch, and what they've been told about how people make babies. Your kid still needs you, but is quite happy to inform you sternly, "I'm not your baby any more. I'm a big kid now."

GOOD THINGS ABOUT LITTLE KIDS (AGES 3 TO 5)

* Now all those stain-removal ads make sense.

* Little kids enjoy being "grown up" and helping with things.

* Little kids tend to think you and their caregivers are brilliant.

* Little kids speak the unadulterated truth.

* Little kids have more stamina for outings.

* Little kids can learn the rules of simple games.

* Little kids want to understand about jokes.

* Little kids are open to suggestions.

* Little kids can be very determined to succeed and improve.

* Little kids, with help, can understand the "nothing has to be perfect" vibe so they don't feel crushed by "failures."

* Little kids have great big enthusiasms.

* Little kids are getting better at catching and throwing a ball, making some throwing games less of a complete shambles.

* Little kids are fun to watch when they're concentrating and learning.

* Little kids are more and more developing their own personality, whether it's shy, analytical, boisterous, all three—or something else.

* Little kids love the idea of having friends.

* Little kids can be introduced to more of the world and they love it.

* Older little kids can go to the bathroom by themselves.

* Little kids can get themselves a drink.

* Little kids can eavesdrop on your conversation and then repeat what you said in front of the wrong person, leading to social and family mayhem. Okay, maybe that's not such a good thing.

* Little kids can be good judges of character: they can often sum up for themselves when someone isn't sincere or seems scary.

* Little kids are often shy at first and then warm up: this is logical behavior. After all, we don't walk into a party and bellow "Hello, everyone! I'm ME and WHO ARE YOU?"—not unless we've had a few vodkas anyway.

* Little kids can invent or follow quite elaborate stories.

* Little kids are great inventors of theories and left-field solutions.

* Little kids are pleased by simple things.

* Little kids can dress themselves.

* Little kids will keep asking questions until they feel finally satisfied with the answer, which trains you to be more precise ("No, there are no bears near here," "No, there are no bears anywhere near here. They live a long way away," "No, bears cannot drive cars to come here," "No, there is very little chance of a bear coming through the mail. They're too big," "No, no bears will ever come here, not even for a visit. Not ever. Bears are not allowed to come here, and all the bears have heard it on the news.").

* Little kids want to be more independent, but they still need you very much as their kindly haven: which means that, even if they're rationed, you still get cuddles.

* Little kids have a longer attention span.

* You can have lovely conversations in quiet times such as after lights out and before the last kiss goodnight.

Little Kids and eating

You've probably worked out how to feed your kid what they need by now. If you have, please forgive a few extra hints, but kids can become exasperatingly conservative about what they'll eat.

clean hands

if you think they're not eating enough

Check out the tips given in the Toddlers and Eating chapter in *Part 2: Toddlers* for "fooling" fussy eaters. And if those don't work, what about trying bribery: "If you eat those three things, you can have cake, or fruit, or something else." Frankly I don't care that some "experts" say this is wrong, and that it encourages kids to think cake is yummier than broccoli. Wise up, professors, kids already know cake is yummier than broccoli. As long as you don't offer the bribe every night or in the same way and the vegetables get eaten, and sometimes the bribe is a nice piece of pineapple or melon and the piece of cake might be only a couple of bites, what's the worst that can happen? The professors get cross? Of course, it can't hurt to offer non-food bribes either. Try a star chart, stickers, little toys from the $1 shop, Dad's stupidest face, Mom's silliest dance.

More Info at the end of the Food chapter in *Part 5: Stuff* has recommendations for good family cookbooks.

Vitamin supplements

A vitamin supplement is not a long-term substitute for eating fresh, real food, which provides vitamins and minerals in a way that's better absorbed by the body, but could help if you're worried that your child's current intake is vitamin deficient. Give a mainstream commercial vitamin supplement specially formulated for toddlers or children (you can get them from drugstores and supermarkets). Read the label and follow instructions carefully.

This way you'll be reassured your child is getting some nutrients in. A kid who refuses all green and leafy things will at least be getting some folic acid, for example. A supplement that can be taken as a couple of drops is often better than a powdered one that masquerades as a milkshake because it doesn't fill the child up and is easily taken in a small amount of some other food or a sip of water, whereas if the kid doesn't finish the whole glass of the "milk drink" they won't get all of the supplement. Chewable tablets are also good (but be sure your kid cleans their teeth afterwards as they're very acidic).

If nothing works and your child doesn't seem healthy and energetic, ask your doctor to refer you to a child nutrition specialist.

> *"Sometimes a snack for him is meat and veggies and pasta. Sometimes it's a raw carrot. Other nights a bowl of Rice Crispies."*
> BROOKE

"I told my 3-year-old who wouldn't eat veggies to close his eyes so he couldn't see what was going in his mouth. He ate with his eyes closed for six months, but to this day he eats the veggies." MIRA

Tell your child the meal you have cooked is what Barney the Dinosaur (or other favorite character) eats. A FEW PARENTS

Don't let them eat with the TV on. SEVERAL PARENTS

"When he won't eat from his plate, I conveniently start 'cooking' with bits of cheese, raisins, chopped fruit, etc., and he eats standing up in the kitchen." EMMA

"My son would only eat peanut butter sandwiches and baby yogurts. The health nurse and the doctor . . . both said he'd grow out of it. He is now 8 and his favorite foods are still peanut butter sandwiches and baby yogurts." TRACEY

"All my kids hated veggies until they were 14 or 15 . . . The boys are now over six feet and around 180 pounds." MERONA

Miss Fiona's cunning disguises for healthy food

My clever cooking friend Miss Fiona has some suggestions for disguising foods for veggie-haters or protein-swervers.

★ Say "You can just have a fruit plate," then add cheese, sticks of sausage, slices of chicken breast, and so on to the plate.

★ Throw a lot of veggies into a frittata, or omelet, with cheese mixed in, then cut it into finger-food-sized slices. Serve warm or cold.

★ Put snowpeas and sticks of celery and carrot on a plate and add a bowl of hummus.

★ Apply the sausage roll principle that anything wrapped in pastry is acceptable—try a piece of sausage or hot dog, ground hamburger, or strips of fish or chicken, with veggies.

★ Say "You can just have a sand-wich," then put their dinner between two pieces of bread and squash it all together. You can do this even with bolognese sauce and cheese or veggies.

★ Try anything once. Miss Fiona says "Lots of little kids hate things with a fleshy or chewy texture and spit them out after a few chews. In desperation I made a steak spread for sandwiches and it worked."

a Packed Lunch

When your kid starts school, they will probably need to take a packed lunch unless your school cafeteria stocks pheasant under glass and Trifle Surprise and you have a school lunch budget equal to the for-eign debt of Bolivia. Most kids at day care need a packed lunch too. The following info and suggestions could be useful also for lunches at home.

A top-notch packed lunch has:

★ carbohydrate.
★ protein.
★ fruit.
★ veggies.
★ a drink.

If you can't fit it all in, don't stress. Say you don't put veggies in or you know your kid hasn't eaten them, just make sure there are veggies for the afternoon snack or dinner.

You can make up a packed lunch with one item from each of the lists below. Find out where the lunch will be stored: if there's air conditioning, it's safe to put in meats and dairy foods that would spoil at room temperature. Lunches can be kept cooler if you freeze the drink the night before and put it in the lunch box.

A lunch box your kid can easily open and close saves wasting

paper bags and prevents liquids from leaking into their bag or over their clothes. A name label on it will help it find its way home. Leftovers inside a lunch box qualify as hazardous waste by the end of the day.

Carbohydrate

Try:

- ★ a sandwich.
- ★ a muffin.
- ★ a roll.
- ★ risotto.
- ★ fried rice.
- ★ small, cooked pasta shapes.
- ★ pancakes.
- ★ rice cakes.

What isn't so good: a big slab of cake. It will fill your kid up without giving any of the vitamins and minerals they need. Fiberless white bread can contribute to constipation and also doesn't have much nutritional value.

Protein

Choose one of the following:

- ★ cheese as a wedge or stick or as a slice in a sandwich.
- ★ tuna in a salad or as a sandwich filling.

- ★ bean mix.
- ★ sliced sandwich meat.
- ★ nuts or a nut spread.
- ★ yogurt.

What isn't so good: skipping this part of the lunch–protein is a vital source of energy in the middle of the day. (Kids will still need red meat at one meal every two or three days, otherwise they'll need supplements of iron and vitamin B_{12}.)

Fruit

This might include:
- ★ an apple.
- ★ stone fruit (if your kid knows not to eat the pit).
- ★ grapes (in a plastic container).
- ★ a banana (with the peeling process started).
- ★ orange quarters or a mandarin.
- ★ dried fruit such as raisins.
- ★ ready-sliced fruit in non-sweetened syrup.

What isn't so good: fruit-flavored stuff instead of real fruit.

Veggies

Maybe:
- ★ sliced carrot and celery sticks.
- ★ salad in a sandwich.
- ★ baked veggies in a slice of frittata.
- ★ cooked veggies with pasta shapes.
- ★ veggie muffin.
- ★ cooked corn kernels in a plastic container.

What isn't so good: tomato sauce or a pickle posing as a vegetable serving—don't be conned into thinking either has any real nutritional value.

A drink

Your child might like:

* ★ a box of soy milk, with a straw.
* ★ water in a drink container.
* ★ juice and water in a drink container.
* ★ plain milk.
* ★ flavored milk, with no added sugar.

What isn't so good: milk in warm weather, juices or fizzy soft drinks with sugar (not good for teeth and have too many calories that don't provide nutrition), or caffeine (interferes with a child's concentration and ability to sleep).

MORE INFO

www.nutrition.gov

This website has lots of nutritional information for adults and children, including information on food and health issues involving kids as they grow.

www.eatright.org

The website of the American Dietetic Association has an extensive section on food and nutrition, with special information for parents and fact sheets on various issues and foods.

LiTTLe KiDS aND SLeePiNG

Maybe by now you're starting to catch up on the sleep lost during the baby and toddler days, although you might need some help with common little kids' sleep problems or with changing your routine.

I said, "Lights out"

TORCHO

giving up the afternoon time nap

Some kids keep the afternoon nap until they're 4 or older. If your kid is exhausted by 1 p.m. on the third or fourth day of having no afternoon sleep, let them have one. At this age kids are usually better at telling you (verbally or otherwise) when they're tired. The main thing to avoid is that late afternoon or early evening horror stretch of overtired and hysterical: you can try to be firm about a sleep or a quiet time earlier in the day if it is a problem. Likewise an afternoon nap might mean the kid doesn't want to go to bed until later and is still bouncing off the walls at 9 p.m. so this might be a feeling-your-way, transitional time (look up "afternoon nap" in the index).

Refusing to go to sleep

For help with getting your child to go to sleep see the Toddlers and Sleeping chapter in *Part 2: Toddlers*. Follow the same principles.

Bedtime routines

Little kids still associate certain things with going to sleep. Unless you want to keep doing it for months and maybe years, don't establish a bedtime routine where you stand on one leg with a pineapple on your head. If you've established a routine that's now causing problems, it's time to introduce two simpler elements while you phase out the pineapple headedness or whatever: perhaps phase in reading a simple story and exchanging a "Good night, I love you"—anything that suits you.

BeDWetTiNg

It's entirely predictable that kids will have a few accidents on the way to being fully competent at nighttime bathroom-using. But consistent bedwetting is a common problem that affects some kids into the primary school years. Don't punish your child: this is guaranteed to make the problem worse or go on for longer, and whether the cause is physical or psychological, it isn't their fault. Contributing factors can be family or child-care stress; huge drinks before bedtime (normal drinks shouldn't do it as most kids eventually learn to wake up when the need arises); or a physical problem.

See your doctor for a referral to a specialist to rule out a physical reason for bedwetting. Children's hospitals sometimes have special bedwetting programs, and some pediatricians and psychologists specialize in bedwetting. Again your doctor will be able to refer you. (See also More Info, which follows.)

Many parenting magazines have ads for "bedwetting systems," often involving alarms. Don't purchase anything before you see a bedwetting specialist.

more info

BEDWETTING

Medline

The US National Library of Medicine and National Institutes of Health has a ton of links to information on bedwetting.

www.nlm.nih.gov/medlineplus/toilettrainingandbedwetting.html

www.kidshealth.org/parent/general/sleep/enuresis.html

A philanthropic group set up this site, which has an explanatory section on bedwetting.

a POSSiBLe ROUTiNe fOR LiTTLe KiDS

Just like toddlers, little kids love a bit of a routine. I know it sounds screamingly dull to have a routine, but it means you can schedule in your own activities such as "Go to New York for shopping" and "Get Chef to do a cheese platter." All right. I'm lying. But the first intro I wrote for this chapter was quite tedious.

it's time for kindy!

it's saturday

fOLLOWiNG a PRESCHOOL OR CHiLD-CaRE-CENTER ROUTiNE

Child-care and preschool centers are terrific at having different set sessions throughout the day, and this gently readies kids for understanding how school will work, for following instructions and for anticipating what's next in the rhythm of the day. A weekly routine is gradually understood by most 3- to 5-year-olds—music on Thursdays, going to Grandma's every second Sunday in the morning, coming home just before dinner, and so on. But they'll still need reminders in the morning.

Bearing in mind that some preschools are just a few hours a week or some mornings only, it's always good to set a routine similar to theirs for the other weekdays. If there's preschool on Monday mornings but not Tuesday mornings, say, you can still stick to the preschool times on Tuesdays.

Your lifestyle may include a big nap in the afternoon and the kids in bed at 9 p.m. and up next morning at 9; or you may want to move the evening meal to as late as possible (say, 6:30 p.m.) so that everyone can eat together, making bedtime later too. Either of these bedtimes will be fine until your child hits child care, preschool, or school, when you'll need to rejig it, winding back slowly so that your kid gets enough sleep before they have to get up. (Most preschoolers and young schoolchildren still need to sleep 10 to 12 hours at nighttime.) It will be easier if you can keep as many aspects of the usual ritual as possible.

POSSiBLE LiTTLE KiD ROUTiNE

Here's a suggested routine you can fiddle with, or use to line the parakeet's cage.

Pre-7 a.m.   Wake up, amuse self quietly (a digital clock can help to display 7 a.m. in a child-friendly way).

7 Breakfast, discuss the day's plans.

7:30 Play and usual morning activities.

10 Morning snack.

10:30 Play: a physical activity, shopping, or a visit.

12 p.m. Lunch.

1 Quiet time or sleep for an hour or so (a quiet time usually won't last longer than an hour).

3 Afternoon snack.

3:30 Play: games, playing with friends, activities.

5:30 or 6 Dinner.

6 or 6:30 Bath.

6:30 or 7 Bed, stories, song.

7 or 7:30 Lights out.

Daylight Savings

Either keep the same time throughout the year so that the day starts at 6 a.m. during daylight savings and 7 a.m. normally or take a week or two before the time changes to adjust bedtime by a quarter of an hour every few days until you're at the new time.

Little Kids' Development (3 to 5)

Mental and physical development can vary widely between preschoolers. Some seem still like toddlers, others like school kids. Yet it's amazing how quickly they can change over a few months or even weeks. Child-care workers and preschool teachers can help you judge your child's level of development. Remember that a range of achievement exists—there's no race. If you're concerned, see your doctor.

Do allow for your kid's lifestyle: kids get better at the things they do often. If they never play catch, they won't be good at it.

3 to 4 years

Physical development (3 to 4 years)

Your little one:

- ★ can hop on one leg.
- ★ is learning better control over utensils, crayons, and paintbrushes.
- ★ with practice, can smoothly run, jump, climb, throw.
- ★ with practice, is improving at catching.
- ★ can pedal a trike confidently.
- ★ can walk up and down stairs in the adult way (but not in high heels).
- ★ has usually accomplished the toilet business, except often for nighttime.
- ★ can put on and take off clothes.
- ★ should have a full mouth of first teeth by now.
- ★ can do up and undo buttons and Velcro, but perhaps not buckles or shoelaces.
- ★ can use a kid's safety scissors.
- ★ can pour their own drink from a jug.
- ★ is learning to do rudimentary cooking (cookie cutting, peanut butter spreading, soft fruit slicing with a kid's knife).
- ★ is probably able to write their own first name and some other alphabet letters, to order.
- ★ can skip, sing, and program a computer at the same time (okay, I'm kidding).

Emotional and mental development (3 to 4 years)

Your little kid:

★ can be very indignant or furious if they can't get their own way. Many parents seem to think the tantrummy threes are worse than the so-called terrible twos.

★ understands cause and effect.

★ understands some opposites.

★ understands being given a choice and may compromise.

★ understands explanations that contain one or more concepts ("That river is very deep, and cold, and the water goes along very quickly").

★ is trying to do everything by themselves.

★ remembers a number of the words of some songs and books.

★ recognizes colors.

★ is able to use words to describe actions and emotions ("He's running away," "The puppy is frightened").

★ can make up stories and tell "fibs" and jokes.

★ recognizes letters and perhaps even simple written words if attention is drawn to them.

★ may count (up to 10 if encouraged) and begins to understand in a rudimentary way the purpose of numbers.

★ has a longer attention span for things they are interested in.

★ loves pretending ("You be the mad fairy and I'll be the baby frog").

★ can show compassion for others.

★ could be quite interested in the differences between boys and girls, and has a sense of their own gender and private parts.

★ might start drawing figuratively—that is, drawing stick figures or round faces with dots for ears, eyes, and mouth—and then regress to scribbles. This is normal and the figures will come back.

★ can learn songs and sing them with you or along with played music.

Communication development (3 to 4 years)

Your little kid:

★ is talking in sentences and can listen carefully to a response.

★ can adjust to requirements (we need to whisper, we're all joking, what would a rude person say?).

★ may ask the same questions over and over ("What would happen then?," "Why did that happen?," "Who was there?"). They are trying to analyze a situation, take it all in, look at it from different angles and understand the world around them—not being deliberately annoying.

★ understands much more, from eavesdropping on conversations, than you might think.

★ answers questions and can hold a conversation.

★ can anticipate things that are going to happen and talk about them.

★ may talk about or with an imaginary friend (this is not a problem).

What can you do?

Try simple jigsaws; sorting (all the blue washing in this pile, all the white washing in that pile); stringing big beads; painting; playdough; soccer; playing catch (start with a balloon and move up to firmer, but not hard or heavy, balls); soccer; swimming; climbing; sliding; swinging; bubble chasing. Perhaps introduce a bike with training wheels. (See More Info at the end of this chapter for a good book on preschool activities.)

Don't demand that your kid's drawings be "good": all drawings are interesting. What a drawing means to a little kid is the important thing—and that you show them you like it. Provide outlets for creativity such as collages and cutting as well as painting and drawing.

Let them get "dirty," with playdough, paint, clay, even mud that isn't compost or potting mix, and "wet," with a supervised hose or a wading pool—dressed in a bathing suit, old clothes, smock, rain coat and galoshes, or no clothes at all.

Read stories, make up stories, and get them to tell made-up stories. Also encourage your kid to make up songs and introduce them to different kinds of music. Take them to live performances or let them join in playing with friends and family. Be careful they don't watch music video shows on TV, which are full of discombobulating special effects, scary sights, and puzzling soft-porn imagery.

Little kids love to help with housework and do things for themselves: as they get closer to 4 years old give them some simple chores such as getting themselves dressed and setting the table.

If your child is at home with you each day, find opportunities for them to play with groups of other children: the kids will work out their own ways of introducing themselves and getting involved in imaginary stories, climbing, chatting, whatever takes their fancy; you can provide options. Allow children quiet play on their own as well as play with other children—all kids need time to themselves just to think things through. Talk with your kid about their day.

If you're sick of answering the sixty-seventh "Why?" question, getting them to call and ask a friend or relative is still a good option, and so is looking in a book or on the computer for the answer (preliminary research skills!). Try to be patient answering similar questions, or ask "Hmmm, what do you think would happen?"

Explain that some body parts are private (but not disgusting or shameful), and that most people don't show their private parts in public places and like to be alone in the bathroom or toilet, but it's okay with family—or whatever you're comfortable with. (See the Helping Kids Understand Grown-up Concepts chapter in *Part 4: Parenting*.)

Apologize to kids if you've been inconsistent or angry: this sets up the idea that apologizing is a good thing and lets them know nobody is expected to be perfect.

Encourage your child to express anger verbally and to ask for the situation to be fixed rather than hitting or yelling. Help them find the words to explain different feelings. "Grumpy" is different from "having hurt feelings." Like toddlers, kids this age who get frustrated and have tantrums can be asked to "use your words" to explain the situation: promise that you will try to sort things out when you've heard the words. This is a form of developing anger management and also helps them learn to negotiate.

Always try to explain the "why" of what you are doing or asking them to do.

Make sure that your kid understands you love them whatever and support them always: that when you are angry you still love them, and that if they do something you don't like you want their behavior to change but you still love them. Better to say you're disappointed with something that happened and that together you need to find a way to fix it so that it doesn't happen again than to say "I'm disappointed with you."

Be careful what you say in front of kids. They've been able to pick up things for a long time already, but now they can repeat what you've said about relatives or friends, which out of context (or in) can be embarrassing. "Aunt Betty, why do you sleep with anything that moves?" is a conversation best avoided.

4 to 5 years

All kids will continue to develop the ability to get a grip on complicated physical and mental skills over the next couple of years and then be able to build on those skills by practicing.

Physical development (4 to 5 years)
Your little kid:
- ★ is refining all their motor skills and physical capabilities and can skip, twirl, hop, and go backwards with skill and confidence.

★ is much better at balancing on one leg.

★ can "dribble" (run and kick) a soccer ball well with practice.

★ hits a ball well with a small, kid-sized bat.

★ can throw to quite a height and distance, and gets more accurate with practice.

★ can copy or follow very simple dance steps and instructions, but probably prefers a free-form, jumping-style dance.

★ probably can only ride a bike if it has training wheels, although they can ride a trike with great skill.

★ is getting themselves fruit or drinks and helping to cut veggies up (but not with a sharp knife).

★ can build complicated structures with blocks (not the Taj Mahal, but a bridge with a tower).

★ should be able to fasten some buckles, but probably not tie shoelaces.

★ is writing rudimentary alphabet letters, some little words and perhaps numbers, with encouragement.

★ draws figurative people more often, with more recognizable heads, features, perhaps arms and legs and hair all coming from the circle-face. At some point they'll add a torso.

★ can thread beads.

Emotional and mental development (4 to 5 years)

Your little kid:

★ can tell you in different ways they need a quiet time now and again.

★ gets very tired after learning and doing new things all day.

★ learns and follows the rules of simple games for one or more people.

★ follows the plots in a video or TV show that's age appropriate.

★ is able to argue with you or negotiate instead of having a tantrum.

- ★ but is still capable of huge tantrums when they realize what they can't do or control, despite all their new skills and desires.
- ★ tells you off for the things you tell them off for.
- ★ tells parents to stop arguing.
- ★ is developing a more acute sense of what's real and what's pretend.
- ★ speaks to new people after warming to them.
- ★ plays games well with other children.
- ★ can be bossy—or accept being bossed around by an older child.
- ★ may have reasonable recall of significant events from the last few months.
- ★ loves fantasy costumes and dress-ups—comic book heroes, fairies, whatever.
- ★ goes off happily to a familiar, good child-care arrangement (local, family, friends). May want to negotiate the pick-up time without really understanding the difference between 1 o'clock and 3 o'clock. Try "before the story," "just after lunch," or "when all the other mommies and daddies come."
- ★ knows how old they are and how old they'll be at the next birthday.
- ★ is enjoying lots of role-playing games, often playing animals, giants, or whatever they've picked up from books, other kids, or their own imagination.

Communication development (4 to 5 years)

Your little kid:
- ★ happily holds conversations.
- ★ should have a wide and ever-expanding vocabulary and use it rather than, say, pointing to what they want all the time.
- ★ their pronunciation should be easily understood by strangers as well as by family and caregivers.
- ★ is enthusiastic when explaining something of interest to them.

★ has improving grammar. Children listen to the way people normally put together a sentence, but still need a bit of help to deal with the variations in English ("I ranned to the back fence." "You ran all the way to the fence? Wow! That's great").

★ can get into a habit of treating you like a slave, rudely ordering you about without manners, if allowed—the "little prince" or "little princess" syndrome.

★ has a keen interest in what the rules are, often asking for confirmation or clarification, and may have a tendency to tell on other children.

What can you do?

You can provide opportunities for dressing-up and pretending with costumes; enjoying adventure playgrounds; learning to swim (teach special safety tips); hammering and building things; gluing crafts, with different fabrics; nature rambles; star gazing; musical instruments; dancing; different kinds of music; simple games such as dominoes, Chutes and Ladders, Go Fish; simple "jobs" such as choosing clothes or wiping the table; catching and bat-swinging games such as T-ball; throwing the ball for the dog; running games such as soccer dribbling; developing their throwing and bouncing ball skills; stretches; bike riding; paddling a canoe or kayak (all kids in any sort of craft must have a lifejacket on properly and at least one water-competent, alcohol-free adult assigned to accompany them and not to take their eyes off them); learning about skeletons and the bones and muscles that help the body move, and how food, drinks and sleep help to give us strength and energy.

With sports, remember it's not all about winning or training or the kid having to collect the tennis balls while you're having a hit with someone else. It's also a chance for family or one-on-one fun that the kid will love. The focus should always be on encouragement: "Oh, that one was a good shot! It nearly went in!" instead of "You missed" or even "You won that one!" Sports and games can be particularly frustrating when the kids playing are mismatched in age and size: the older ones get frustrated and so do the tykes. This is where taking turns can be important rather than pitting kids against each other.

Maybe try taking the training wheels off the bike in the next year or so. You'll need to help your kid develop the new balancing skills required.

Your little baby is so much bigger now but, even though they're really smart, they can't be expected to have the knowledge or dexterity of an older child: make sure toys and play equipment are still age appropriate (see the next chapter, Toys and Games for Little Kids and also the Being Active chapter in *Part 5: Stuff*).

Encourage your kid to use single and various colors, and to do shapes and objects in color. Limit activities that discourage creativity, such as copying, tracing, and coloring in an adult's drawing in a book, and encourage imaginative drawing and "writing." A drawing doesn't always have to "look like" or "be" something. It could be a feeling, a view, or the way rain might seem to a 4-year-old. Again, ask the child to tell you the story of the picture. Don't always say "What's this?"; say "Tell me about this lovely picture," "I love the way these colors go together" or "What's your favorite part?"

Make a shopping list together, go shopping, get your kid to hand over the money and collect the change and find the items, then cook something from the ingredients you bought. Shopping is fun and teaches all sorts of skills from visual recognition and verbal skills to measuring and counting (rudimentary math). But who cares? It's just fun at this age and makes them feel useful and important.

If people look to you often for a "translation" of your child's words, ask your doctor for a referral to a speech therapist. Clear speech is a big advantage in the first year of school.

Be careful how you praise your child and what for: if you only tell a girl she's pretty when she's all dressed up in ribbons and a frock, she gets the idea it's the finery that's beautiful, and that being strong or funny or clever isn't worth commenting on. If you tell a boy he's brave for not crying, he gets the idea that he should hide his true feelings (look up gender in the index).

Don't load up your kid with chores and expectations when they're starting preschool or kindergarten. Preschool and kindergarten take up a huge amount of physical and emotional energy. They will probably need some afternoons, or even days, off for a quiet time at home.

Kids this age get pleasure from being with their special adults and parents more than anything else: the simplest, cheapest, do-it-yourself activity enjoyed together can be memorable and delicious, even a cuddle and a chat or pouring sand from an old kettle in the sandpit—everyone loves a tea party.

MORE iNFO

Your Child at Play: Three to Five Years: Expand Your Child's Intelligence Through Conversation, Creativity, Letters, Words, and Numbers
by Marilyn Segal

I'd forget the "get ahead" connotations and just use the book as a resource for fun games and activities that match a child's development and growing awareness, capabilities, and interests. There's some great stuff about making friends, play that involves the senses, power dynamics, and communication skills.

toys and games for little kids

Your little one will probably be making up their own free-form pretend-time and other games. You may be onto this already, but you can get great ideas for games from books and activity days held at your local library.

ideas from parents

◎ Playdough ◎ sticking things such as their own paintings on the wall ◎ paint, crayons, pencils, felt-tip pens (throw out any that don't have the lid put back on—eventually there'll be none) ◎ large empty cardboard boxes for cars, houses, whatever ◎ imaginative play (pretending to be a mouse or a princess) ◎ a plastic tool set ◎ glitter on and in anything and everything ◎ cars ◎ dollies with their own beds, strollers, and so on ◎ snap-together blocks ◎ a magnetic screen or a homemade metal tray with magnet letters or pictures on it ◎ an old phone ◎ homemade musical instruments ◎ a tea set ◎ brooms and feather dusters (this can't last!) ◎ books ◎ age-related jigsaw puzzles ◎ dress-up clothes, including a fairy costume and wings ◎ blocks ◎ simple card games such as Go Fish ◎ a pack of cards ◎ dominoes ◎ easy board games such as Chutes and Ladders, with big squares on the board and large dice ◎ thrift-shop teddies ◎ magic wands ◎ plastic farm animals ◎ balls, bats, rigged up "goalposts" and low, big netball goals ◎ making jewelery from pasta, thread spools, big beads ◎ a doll's house and dolly "people" ◎ dinosaurs ◎ a keyboard or a guitar ◎ a flashlight with batteries—perhaps duct-taped in safely ◎ a toy medical kit ◎ pirate costumes ◎ toy animals ◎ old faithful teddy ◎ a superhero cape and dolls (when they're boys the manufacturers call them "action figures") ◎ a fire engine ◎ a cart to pull or push ◎ a magnetic drawing slate ◎ wood offcuts, a hammer and big nails (supervised) ◎ plastic jars with lids to screw on and off ◎ listening-to tapes ◎ own personal tape player with earphones ◎ transforming toys ◎ plastic sea creatures for the bath ◎ assorted kitchen flotsam such as old sieves, plastic measuring cups and squirters for the bath ◎ plastic jugs with food coloring in them and something to pour into and out of ◎ balloons ◎ puppets ◎ scissors for kids ◎ a pop-up tent ◎ a bucket and spade set ◎ wrapping presents and making cards ◎ a xylophone ◎ marbles (it's nice to have someone from the older generation to teach how to play) ◎ a spinning top ◎ chase ◎ hide-and-seek ◎ tag ◎ tree climbing ◎ sandcastle building ◎ hole digging ◎ nature rambles ◎ beachcombing ◎ cooking with an adult ◎ gardening with an adult ◎ "reading" alone ◎ drawing and painting ◎ cutting and pasting ◎ chatting on the phone or a pretend phone ◎ "writing" or dictating, and decorating letters and mailing them ◎ looking at kids' websites ◎ making cards and wrapping paper.

more info

Most kids' activities books are really for older children, who can do fiddlier stuff with their hands than little kids can, so look before you leap.

The Fantastic Rainy Day Book: Over 60 Step-by-step Projects to Paint, Build, Make, Bake, Sew and Grow
by Angela Wilkes, DK Publishing, 2001.
Has ideas for setting up a craft box and projects for doing inside. Many of the projects will be easier for older kids, but can be fun with a preschooler if you do them together.

www.childfun.com
Has ideas for kids' activities—you can ignore the mountain of advertising.

www.lionlamb.org
This website has info on non-violent games and toys and research on the effect on kids of violent play and TV, video, and computer violence. The organization was founded by a mom.

ready for school

This is it, the moment you've been waiting for or dreading or both: your little baby is off to school.

getting prepared

A year or two before your child is ready to start school check out the local schools to see which one best suits your kid. Once you've decided on a school and you've enrolled your child, find out what you and your child should expect. You'll both feel better prepared if you've checked with the school to see what's on offer and you've explained to your child concepts such as roll call, listening to a story at the library, show and tell, opening their lunch, sport, and art and music sessions with a different teacher. Playing school and practicing school skills months or weeks earlier is important.

Your school might have a program or orientation days for parents and beginners in the term before the new year starts.

The first year at some schools is part-time: don't assume you'll suddenly be able to work full-time. Kids are likely to be physically and mentally exhausted in the first few weeks as they take in all the new feelings, rules, and social arrangements, and toward the end of each term. Feel free to keep them home for "mental health days" or extra sleeps.

Apart from your being on call and possibly involved with school activities, school is usually over every day by 3:30 (or later in some areas), although many schools have before- and after-school programs.

when to start school

Kids usually start school before they turn 6. Many start preschool at 4 or 5 and kindergarten at 5 or 6. Reasons for this include recommendations from some authors that boys may benefit from starting school later; parents think their child will have an advantage if they start later; some kids are not socially or otherwise ready, especially if they turn 6 at the end rather than near the start of the school year; parents wanting to keep their child in long-hours child care for another year; and the preschool system in many places not preparing children for the more structured, longer school day experience. The best guide to when your child is ready will be the feedback from the experienced child-care staff. Ask for their assessment

READY-FOR-SCHOOL CHECKLIST

Your kid will need to:

* understand the concept of school and what will happen there, and be able to ask questions about it and have them answered.

* understand that you will come for them at the end of the day, and that going to school isn't just a one-day proposition— it's every day except weekends, although there are holidays.

* hear about the new experiences and new friends they will have, and that new friends might like to come home for afternoon snack—things your kid will see as positive about school.

* follow simple instructions from a teacher.

* be able to go to the toilet by themselves (will your boy need urinal practice?).

* have had a tour of the school to see the layout, find out where the toilets are (take them in to see and use the toilets) and meet their teacher.

* wear a uniform, or not— whichever is required.

* carry a school bag with a change of clothes, including socks and undies, a school lunch, and anything else required by the school.

* understand the difference between play lunch and lunch.

* be able to open their lunch box, unpack it, open their drink and reseal it if necessary, and undo cling wrap, foil, and paper bags (avoid plastic bags big enough for a head to get into); know where they might put the lunch box when they're eating; eat their lunch and have their drink; and

and also talk to the school about what will be required. There's no point holding a child to a boring repeat of a preschool year they don't need, or in rushing them to school before they're ready.

bring home the lunch box and drink bottle (look up packed lunch in the index).

✱ understand who they can talk to if they're worried or scared about anything.

✱ have you talk about how there will always be some teachers in the playground to go to if they need to tell an adult about something.

✱ know they can ask their teacher if they can call you at any time.

✱ know how to carry on or resolve a dispute with other children without violence.

✱ help you pack their school bag so they know what's in it, and be able to recognize their bag and their own clothes.

✱ have a clear name label on everything and practice recognizing their own name (because they can be asked at school to get their things when they're tired, in a hurry, or under pressure).

✱ have a little key ring, velvet material, or other comfort object sewn or safety-pinned into a pocket if they need a special reminder of home.

✱ be able to recite their name, address, and phone number.

4
PARENTING

IF YOU'RE READING *PART 4: PARENTING,*
YOU'RE PROBABLY INTERESTED IN . . .
EVERYTHING ELSE IN THE BOOK!

PARENTING PHILOSOPHY

Some people follow a general philosophy or even strict rules about parenting. Others religiously follow a guru, or combine a few theories, or muddle through without having a set of ready-made values and guidelines (motto: "Whatever . . ."). Any philosophy or system that puts the rules first instead of the

child and the parent is not much help.
Don't forget that you are the recognized
authority on your own child, even if, like
everyone else, you need help from time
to time.

CHOOSiNg aN aPPROaCH

A bunch of "parenting philosophies" are collected in this chapter so that you can see if anything takes your fancy. Some of the "philosophies" listed in this grab-bag of approaches and authorities are just descriptions of how many parents make decisions about their kids ("What would my mom have done?"); others are complex educational philosophies with their own handbooks and organizational network.

You'll already have some sort of a philosophy based on your own experiences and expectations, even if you don't have a name for it. Probably it's best to aim for being flexible and smart enough to question why you are doing things, whether they work and what might work better. There's no shame in saying "Jeez, I never expected to be up against this problem. I think I need a new solution." That's parenting.

The parenting theories outlined here are all different—so they can't all be exactly right for everyone. Some ideas from some approaches will work for some children. That's about the most scientific it gets, I reckon. You might find a method works well for your first child and just makes the second child look at you as if you've got to be *kidding*.

Plenty of books on parenting theory, especially the older and stricter ones, are by men who have never spent day after day looking after their own children, let alone anyone else's. Many parenting experts have co-written a book with their wives, who one suspects in the majority of cases did most if not all of the actual child business in the home; but on the other hand it's nice to see a shared approach and have a fresh, outside view. (Sometimes the wives get to share copyright, sometimes they don't.) I think you can often tell when a person has been a full-on parent by the useful extra details in their book.

Some theories are kind of scientific sounding and based on statistics and research; some are weirdly religious. At the outer edges of all of them lies inflexibility, putting the theory above results or a child's or parent's wellbeing, dangerous obsession and withdrawal from the real world. But most of them probably have some ideas you might find useful. If a guru or theory isn't working for you, don't blame yourself or your kid. Try another approach.

Of course lots of the books listed in the More Info sections of earlier chapters reflect various parenting philosophies too (see, for example, In the Beginning and Crying in *Part 1: Babies*). And so do those given in the More Info sections of the Dads and Teaching Kids How to Behave chapters coming up soon. Many of the books should be in your local library so you can give them a test run.

"My philosophy is common sense with a bit of luck." KEONA

THe RaiSiNg HaPPY CHiLDReN aPPRoaCH

Seems obvious as a concept, doesn't it? It's not a cohesive philosophy, with an organized group, but the priority of many parents, some of whom didn't have happy childhoods themselves and are seeking new ways of relating to their kids, with an eye to making them feel generally happy, safe, self-confident, and resilient. (It doesn't mean insisting that the kids look happy and grin like freaked-out chimps all day.) The assumption is that good behavior will follow.

At its best the happy children philosophy is a great thing to aim for and will minimize stress. At its worst, it could mean children grow up without knowledge of the real world and are shocked and ill-prepared for institutions and people who aren't motivated by kindness and patience. (Spike Milligan's son was appalled to find, in his late teens, that fairies weren't really writing him letters.) It's also important that kids feel secure about being able to express their natural feelings, including anger and sadness. Several books have the phrase "happy children" in their title. (See More Info at the end of this chapter for, well, frankly more info.)

> "If children know they are loved, then they are able to cope with most things life throws at them, so I always try to make home a happy and safe place and encourage them to confide in me without fear of reprisal. Communication lines must always be kept open." JUDI

> "I love being a mother. I've been quite ill the past two years and now I appreciate so much more. I love every day and have fun every day. I get down and get dirty with the boys and laugh and carry on and just have fun. I wouldn't swap this time for all the world."
> KARYN

> "One day he'll be 16 and answer 'Is there anything to eat?' when I say hello to him. I need all the cuddly baby memories I can get!"
> EMMA

attachment parenting

This philosophy is based on parental closeness with the baby and child—its basics
include breastfeeding, sleeping with your
baby, and carrying them in a sling most of the
time. Having one consistent caregiver rather
than several is emphasized. (In almost all
examples it seems to be the mom who is supposed to
do most of the attaching.) Discipline is non-physical
and separations are minimized. Parents are encouraged
to respond immediately to their child's wants. Attachment parenting advocates do not believe in leaving a
baby or a child to cry, even for very short times.

At its best, it's a warm and loving approach. At its most useless, it turns parenting into a world where the baby runs everyone
else ragged, an overtired baby is picked up instead of being helped
to a desperately needed sleep, the kid turns into a smug dictator,
and any problem with the child is blamed on the mother for not
being attached enough. (See More Info at the end of this chapter
for resources.)

> *"We know of wonderful mothers who do not [breastfeed] at night,
> but they are willing to get up and respond to their baby in the night,
> no matter how many times that might be."*
> ATTACHMENT PARENTING WEBSITE

using family role models

Some people rely very much on family advice or memories of how
somebody did things in their family. This person can be a mom,
mom-in-law, godparent, aunt, grandad, sister, or friend. The good

thing about this is that a solution is almost always on tap—"I'll just call Aunt Jean" or "I remember Aunty Jean used to . . ." The downside is that the solution might not work for your kid or might be hopelessly out of date: "Yes, just pop some leeches on him, dear, that'll deal with the diphtheria."

"[My philosophy is] anything my mother DIDN'T do." AMY

PeNeLOPe LeacH

Penelope Leach is a UK child psychologist whose bestselling book, *Your Baby and Child*, has lots of followers because it puts the child's needs first. It's one of those bibles many people swear by. Other people go a shade of mauve when they hear her name. Typical Leach quotes such as this one can really annoy parents: "If you take [the baby] around with you wherever you go, you can go almost anywhere you might want to go as a treat." Yes, Penelope, except a bar, a cinema, a theater, a club, a dance party, many schools, restaurants that ban babies, a row boat, a gym, or anywhere at all during the baby's "sacred" sleeptime. Not to mention Sub-Saharan Africa.

The best thing about Leach is you're never in any doubt as to where her moral compass is pointing—at the importance of children—even though *she* seems to be pointing at parents who aren't impossibly perfect. On the other hand you get enough judgmental guilts from everywhere else, why get it from a guidebook as well? (See More Info at the end of the In the Beginning chapter in *Part 1: Babies* for full details and review of Leach's handbook.)

"Penelope Leach seemed to make the most sense to me." ELENA

maximizing potential, accelerated learning, or hothousing

Many parents like to maximize their child's development by finding out which stages are coming up next and doing specific things to stimulate and encourage their child in that direction. Accelerated learning is the movement by parents to give their child an advantage by having them learn or accomplish things before most kids their age do.

According to many child-development experts, accelerated learning can lead to kids being bored at school, take the fun out of learning things, and result in no advantage in the long term. In other words children will be "ahead" when they're 4, but possibly stressed out and feeling no pleasure from "success," and when they're 6 will probably only be where they would have been anyway. Many parents who follow this approach start by teaching their baby reading and math and booking them into lots of classes and activities such as Gymboree, languages, and preschool math tutoring. (Just between you and me, it's insane to expect babies to learn to read and add.)

Unfortunately many of the parents who believe in this way of teaching children are persuaded by advertising that their kids need special advantages and are unaware of the research that shows children learn all the time, in great leaps and bounds, just from doing things that are fun, including chatting to themselves, tinkering, or making a cake. The upside of this is that knowing what development stage your child is at can help you introduce new games and fun activities. The downside is that everyone feels under pressure, and expectations of a genius child are almost always met with disappointment. There's a reason they call it "overachieving." (See More Info at the end of this chapter for resources.)

PareNts against "over-parenting"

This is a bit of a mixed bag, but the basic ideas can include: you don't need a guidebook to look after kids; parents should stop worrying so much about whether they are doing the right thing and whether their child is in danger; parents need to learn to trust their own judgment; and parents need to back off from pressuring their kids with lots of expectations, classes, and planned activities. This line can help an anxious parent relax, but ultimately parents themselves have to assess their own children's capacities and risks. And all parents need help sometimes. (See More Info at the end of this chapter for a book on this approach.)

"I'm the expert on my kids."   WENDY

triple p (positive parenting program)

This is a really great practical parent education program that has helped many parents around the world. It has been developed by Professor Matthew Sanders and the Parenting and Family Support Center at the University of Queensland in Australia, and is based on international research into child development and parental roles. At the basic level the program helps parents learn skills and strategies to deal with kids, and offers general help with kids' behavior as well as help with particular issues. At other levels the program can be used to help target specific behavioral problems or prevent or stop the abuse of kids at various ages. *Every Parent: A Positive Approach to Children's Behavior*, the essential book of the PPP, focuses on building a stable family foundation and nipping any behavioral problems in the bud, or even the seed.

The Center conducts training in the different levels of the program. There are videos, other handbooks, and work books to help parents learn the program. Triple P is also now operating in many other countries including the United States. (See More Info at the end of Teaching Kids How to Behave, a few chapters on, for contact and book details.)

active Listening or parent effectiveness training (Pet)

Active listening, or reflective listening, is now part of many parenting philosophies. Active listening and I-messages form the basis of a communication program called Parent Effectiveness Training. The system, developed by the psychologist Thomas Gordon, is also used in business and medical situations.

PET teaches a way to speak with and listen to children, deal with conflicts, and work on better relationships within a family. Active listening happens when a child says "There was a monster in the cupboard" and instead of saying "No there wasn't," you say "There was a monster in the cupboard? Tell me about it." An I-message is used to put the emphasis on the effect, not the wickedness, of an action: "I was hurt when you hit me" rather than "Hitting is naughty. Don't hit."

You may learn a positive way to communicate. Small children can respond well to not being judged—but still not care about or get the point of I-messages (which is that they need to change their behavior). Reflective or active listening can be encouraging for children but extremely boring for adults, and it isn't going to work in every situation. Sometimes a child will want you to suggest a solution, not just mirror their feelings back to them. Kids will sense that you're parroting a formula and may not feel supported. (See More Info at the end of this chapter for the relevant website.)

tHe New age, NatuRaL, oR "HiPPie" appRoacH

While it often seems a reaction against the harsh rules of a rigid religion or society, there are usually just as many rigid rules with this approach—just different ones, often involving what is acceptable to wear (only natural fibers), eat (various restricted diets), and play with (plastic is a no-no, merchandising is frightful). Generally these things will be embraced: breastfeeding, cloth diapers, recycling, organic food, herbal remedies, no rules for behavior. And these things rejected: disposable accoutrements and chemicals of any description, consumerism, 1950s-style repressive discipline, the bouffant.

At its most useful, the approach offers the central idea of treading lightly on the earth, which we can all benefit from and aspire to. At its least useful it involves turning away from the real world to home schooling and other isolationist activities, just like some strict religions. And children usually do love routines, clear rules, and behavioral boundaries, even though their parents may be over the whole idea.

fRugaL paReNtiNg

Everything is done proudly on the cheap: these people make their own diapers, sheets, clothes, and, in some cases, school education. The information is generally via websites and books, and it usually includes some good DIY recipes for things such as baby lotion and home-style games.

Of course, for many people doing things on the cheap is not so much a philosophical choice as a necessity. For example, some parents needing or wanting to be frugal sign up for drustore and supermarket "loyalty programs" (which may be confined to baby products). Loyalty programs "reward" members: they rack up points every time they buy and then they receive a discount coupon. (But if you join, make sure you're not paying higher prices to compensate for the discounts.)

The good side of frugal parenting is that you teach your child how to use their imagination and work for things; the downside is that you may turn into a penny-pinching miser even when you do have a spare dollar, and sadly you cannot make your child go to a fancy dress party as a nudist (no, really, you can't).

strict Religious groups

Some people look to a religious book such as the Bible or the Koran to frame their household values and rules. Those who follow the fundamentals of these religions place the father above the mother in a chain of command. Most emphasize strict rules of behaviour. Some Christian and Muslim groups prescribe the clothing for girl children as young as 4 or 5, which can include banning trousers and making wearing a headscarf compulsory, usually to indicate modesty, chastity, or sexual unavailability.

A subgroup of evangelical or fundamentalist Christians are those I'd call the spankers (see the Teaching Kids How to Behave chapter coming up).

A great deal of nuttery disguised as Christianity is contained in the work of the Babywise series of books, which promotes Parent Directed Feeding (PDF) and is backed by Growing Families International (GFI) and taught in churches in the US. *On Becoming Babywise* and *Babywise II*, for parents of "pretoddlers" aged 5 to 15 months, are slim books by Gary Ezzo, an evangelical Christian who has proclaimed himself a minister. His family runs the GFI, a group that intends to "capture the minds and hearts of the next generation and . . . to apply God's principles in parenting." There are two versions of each book: one for churches, which lists all the biblical references and talks about God (the Preparation for Parenting series), and the one sold in bookstores, which conceals the religious motivation for the parenting advice. Ezzo's wife is credited as a co-author on the church-based guides, and a pediatrician is credited on the "secular" ones. The books have been formally condemned by just about every baby doctor, lactation consultant, and psychologist in the known universe. Starvation, developmental delay, and psychological problems have resulted when parents followed the strict Babywise feeding schedules for a baby, which include refusing to give night feeds after a baby is 2 months old and an expectation of 9 hours' unbroken sleep for parents of very young babies.

> *"There is no such thing as an 'average' baby, nor is there such a thing as an 'average routine' that will work for everyone."*
> KATHLEEN AUERBACH

The "program" also includes the plainly wrong claim that breastfeeding a baby more than usual would decrease the milk supply (unless there's something the matter, the effect will be the opposite); and recommendations to leave a small baby crying for long periods of time, to leave babies in playpens a lot, to "swat" a baby over 6 months old for (heartbreakingly) "foolishness," and to spank with a "flexible instrument" after age 2. Children over 2 and a half who have a toileting accident are made to clean it up themselves as punishment. The philosophy says to avoid "emotionalism" in responding to a child's distress.

Mr. Ezzo's early opinions that contradicted research on sleeping positions to minimize SIDS have been removed without apology from later editions of the book.

People with these sorts of ideas have come before and will come again. They make a lot of money and get famous by claiming stupid things, which they say have the alleged backing of God, and by promising the impossible: that parents can be in control of everything, don't need to change their own life, and can bring up obedient children who will never become juvenile delinquents, if they use physically enforced rules.

The good thing about a strict religious upbringing is that everyone knows what the rules are. The worst thing is that many of the rules can be useless, and rejection by the family or group is often the price kids pay for independent thought or questioning. Children who are brought up to be passive are at greater risk in the real world.

MONTESSORI EDUCATION

This is a method of education opposed to the more rigid structures of most schools. It is based on the philosophy of Maria Montessori, a nineteenth-century Italian doctor and teacher who emphasized building the confidence and experiences of small children. Its philosophy is that the child should have opportunities to explore and express freedom of choice. Montessori schools use some specific equipment and teaching methods. Montessori's original tenets are interpreted as limiting television and computer use to older children, and encouraging creativity as a priority. (See More Info at the end of this chapter for the Montessori website.)

STEINER, OR WALDORF, EDUCATION

The Steiner, or Waldorf, schools follow a method of learning in kindergarten and school based on the teachings of the Austrian philosopher Rudolph Steiner, who founded his first school in 1919. The philosophy is heavy on guided creativity—all young students learn to knit and to play the recorder, are told which colors to draw with in the early years and sometimes restricted to only one color. For young children the emphasis is on imagination, art, and gardening rather than learning academic things. Television is effectively banned for preteen children. There is an emphasis on "natural" toys—a rocking horse rather than a toy car, homemade toys rather than manufactured ones.

Although individual schools interpret the Steiner philosophy somewhat differently, numbers, letters, colors, concepts of time, and facts about nature or science are believed to be best left undescribed until after a child is 5 years old. There are Waldorf schools throughout the country. (See More Info at the end of this chapter for the Waldorf website.)

Reggio Emilia Education

Reggio Emilia is a very brainy provincial city in Italy that spends 12 percent of its budget on education and services for preschoolers. The philosophy of its preschool education is helping kids do fun projects to extend their knowledge and to strengthen the relationships they have with other people and their environment. Kids' explorations are based on their own questions, and adults and teachers learn to recognize and encourage the different ways in which individual children learn and communicate: some kids are arty, others good with words; some express themselves with their face and body, others are musical and mathematical; some learn best by experimenting, others look at a visual "map" rather than listening to an explanation. Some mainstream preschool programs here are beginning to incorporate these ideas. (See the More Info section at the end of this chapter for websites.)

talking about your philosophy

Be careful when you speak to other parents that your chosen methods are not presented as the only way. One person's common sense is another's feral fascist load of waffle. (But probably best not to actually say THAT.)

> *"If Mom's happy, then everyone's happy, that's my motto."*
> **NICOLE**

> *"I just fly by the seat of me pants."* ALISON

> *"When I have low self-esteem regarding any aspect of raising my child, I think of people who have raised children successfully even when they were in much more difficult situations than me—young parents, single parents, people with disabilities."* BROOKE

> *"Shrug off the guilt and enjoy the kid."* FILIZ

more info

THE RAISING HAPPY CHILDREN APPROACH
Raising Happy Children: What Every Child Needs Their Parents to Know—From 0 to 7 Years
by Jan Parker and Jane Stimpson, Hodder and Stoughton, 2004.
A ripper. Really useful info and suggestions are delivered in short, relevant bits. The book starts with how to bond with your baby, shows how to talk with your young child so they keep talking to you, and how to talk about fears and bad things without either dismissing or being overwhelmed by them. It also gives practical advice on encouraging good behavior, how not to spank, tantrums, sibling rivalry, bullies, grief, blended families, and lots more.

Raising Happy Kids

by Michael Grose, HarperCollins, 2001.

Michael Grose delivers bite-sized, practical advice on helping kids develop self-esteem; how to talk to them about worrying issues; and how to keep home life as stress-free as possible, without letting the kids rule the joint.

ATTACHMENT PARENTING

The Attachment Parenting Book: A Commonsense Guide to Understanding and Nurturing Your Baby

by William Sears, MD, and Martha Sears, RN, Little, Brown, 2001.

The gurus of attachment parenting give their take on the kind and inclusive approach to discipline. *The Discipline Book: How to Have a Better-Behaved Child from Birth to Age Ten*, also by the Sears, is reviewed in More Info at the end of the Teaching Kids How to Behave chapter.

www.parentingweb.com/ap/ap_index.htm

A website that has articles about attachment parenting and its central tenets: co-sleeping, breastfeeding, and using slings.

www.pinky-mychild.com

This is Australian Pinky McKay's site, with a massive links page. Ms. McKay wrote the attachment-parenting-driven books *Parenting by Heart*, and *100 Ways to Calm the Crying* (for full details and review see More Info at the end of the Crying chapter in *Part 1: Babies*). It's a kind, light-hearted website with a chat room for parents and much reassuring business about being with babies, toddlers, and older children. She can send a monthly email newsletter with practical and calming ideas such as having a morning ritual as well as a bedtime one.

Other websites

These include www.naturalparenting.com, www.mothering.com, and www.sheilakitzinger.com.

MAXIMIZING POTENTIAL, ACCELERATED LEARNING, OR HOTHOUSING

Test Your Child: How to Discover and Enhance Your Child's True Potential
by Miriam Stoppard, DK Publishing, 1991.

This book's title is anxiety inducing for parents, but the book itself is full of really useful stuff such as what kids love doing at various ages with their minds and their bodies, their language, and their social interaction with family and other kids. Just try to ignore annoying headings such as "A Good Parent . . ."

Multimedia   There are *Baby Mozart* and *Baby Einstein* videos and lots of CDs, computer games, and videos supposed to stimulate your child's brain. Einstein himself didn't speak until he was 4 so do try to relax.

PARENTS AGAINST "OVER-PARENTING"

Paranoid Parenting: Why Ignoring the Experts May Be Best for Your Child
by Frank Furedi, Chicago Review Press, 2002.

The author says we all need to lighten up and stop trying to be the perfect parent who communicates in exactly the right way with their children all the time—sometimes we need to get the shopping done also.

ACTIVE LISTENING OR PARENT EFFECTIVENESS TRAINING (PET)

www.thomasgordon.com/family.asp
The website of the founder of Parent Effectiveness Training. This page is about parenting and families.

EDUCATION PHILOSOPHY WEBSITES

www.montessori.edu/
The official website of the Montessori organization.

www.awsna.org
The official website of Waldorf schools in North America.

ceep.crc.uiuc.edu/poptopics/reggio.html

The Clearinghouse on Early Education and Parenting has a links page to many Reggio Emilia related websites.

ecrp.uiuc.edu/v4n1/edwards.html

A comprehensive article on "Three Approaches from Europe: Waldorf, Montessori and Reggio Emilia," from an early childhood learning magazine.

UNPaiD WORK aND PaiD WORK

Some parents give up work outside the home, others work part-time or full-time. Some parents share both roles. And everyone is as busy as an ant at a picnic.

I'm going to miss you, darling!

PAY CHECK

This chapter isn't a blueprint for restructuring your life. It covers your options and what to consider in making a decision about who works where.

These choices are so individual that no one should ever presume to tell you which way to jump, or when or if you'll be ready to go "back" to work.

staying Home

As well as dealing with all the brand newness of being a parent, you might be coming to terms with another huge transition: the change from paid work "out there" to home work that's unpaid and under-valued. What mother has not made a huge effort to get dressed and out to a barbecue only to be asked "What do you do?" Her choice is simple. If she doesn't want to be snubbed under the Hill's Hoist, she should say "I'm a space shuttle pilot who strips in her spare time," not "I'm a stay-at-home-mom."

In a world where our work is supposed to define us, "I'm a stay-at-home mom" causes polite snorey noises in most new acquaintances. Even worse is having made all that effort, made it into Adultland, only to be stuck with another parent in the corner shouting about green poop over the Lenny Kravitz.

Although most of the people who make this transition are women, an increasing number of guys are "staying home" while their partner becomes the only breadwinner. And another big lot of parents are juggling, often with both parents doing part-time jobs, or one full-time, one part-time, and some child care thrown in. There's also a rapidly growing number of parents sharing custody, and sole parents (most of whom are women).

Unfortunately, many parents find it hard to see what it's like for somebody doing it differently. This is especially potent for

THE UPSIDE OF HOME WORK

* "Kids are only little for a short time. I want to be there."

* "I have given myself up to being at home for the time being so I don't need to worry about work, child care, or conflicts between work and home."

* "Watching and helping a baby develop into a child can be a wonderful and absorbing experience."

* "I've waited so long to have a baby, I want to immerse myself in the experience."

* "This is far more important than the job I had before."

* "My partner is earning more money than I could at the moment, and later it will be my turn again."

* "Apart from the housework, there's a lot of stuff to be organised and fixed around the house and garden that I've been meaning to do for years and can get done now."

* "It has forced me to slow down and see the world through the eyes of a child."

* "I decide what we do every day."

* "I know what my child is eating and what they are learning. I know them better than anybody."

* "I'm learning how to live on a budget."

* "I've made new friends among the parents at playgroup."

mothers because it feeds old-fashioned notions of what a "good" or "bad" mother is. Mothers who stay at home are often contemptuous of mothers who work, but secretly envious of their independence, money, and better dressed, seemingly more glamorous lives. Mothers who have another job often have to rush around breathlessly, feeling that they've failed as both paid worker and parent, and they envy what is seen as the calmer, one-job life

379

THE DOWNSIDE OF HOME WORK

* "I miss earning my own money."

* "I used to be respected and listened to; now people ignore me or their eyes glaze over because I'm 'just a mother'."

* "I used to be respected and listened to; now people say I'm doing something interesting and they wish they could do it too, but I can tell they are scornful of my decision to be 'just a father'."

* "Because I'm the person at home I do almost all the housework and it's boring."

* "I know the money is supposed to be 'ours', but it's hard to see it that way sometimes."

* "I feel trapped."

* "Sometimes I feel like a cross between a cow and Cinderella."

* "I feel bored and boring."

* "I miss the work I used to do."

* "I miss the social side of work."

* "Inevitably I have lost friends."

* "I only get to talk to kids or people who want to talk about kids."

* "I feel like my work is moving on without me, I'm missing the progress in the industry, and it will be harder to get back in."

* "I want to go back to work part-time (or full-time) but child care around here is too expensive, booked out, or not to a standard I'd like (or the older kids finish school at 3:30)."

of staying home (as if that's easy). The truth is, both situations have upsides and downsides.

Even those who seem to have the most in common probably don't. Consider the at-home mom with a wealthy partner, or even an independent income, who has her own car, a cleaner, unlimited babysitting, lots of splendid holidays, and a hairdresser who gives them a blowdry most days at 3 o'clock sharp. This person has very little in common with a stay-at-home mom who has to do all her washing and drying at a laundromat, who has to get a bus to the supermarket with the stroller, and who has no help from relatives. There is a huge gulf of experience between women who know they are making considerable financial and other sacrifices to stay at home and women who never expected to do anything else or have made a much more unambiguously pleasant "choice."

Being the Home CEO

Please don't read a book called *Sidetracked Home Executives: From Pigpen to Paradise*—it is full of awful stories from two American wives who wanted to be more organized, partly because they weren't getting their husband's breakfast or making enough effort to be pretty for him. (I've said it before: if a man can't make his own breakfast, you're better off living in separate zipcodes.) The women solve this problem by running their lives with the aid of a series of little white cards on which are filed chores and—yes, lordy—compliments they get on their housekeeping skills. Here is a quote from one of their husbands: "'I thought that if you loved me then I wouldn't have to go to work hungry and wearing wrinkled clothes. I figured if you really cared, you'd try harder to look as pretty as you were when I married you.'" You will be surprised to learn that this husband had the use of his own limbs, and that his wife did not explain that being the homemaker meant that she was to look after the home and the children, but not necessarily the breakfast needs of a grown man—and that doing a grown man's ironing and washing is not a responsibility but an act of generosity and kindness.

This is not to say that homemaking can't be a satisfying job—but it's hard to make it wholly satisfying otherwise I think you'd find very rich, powerful men would do it. There is an element of drudgery and sacrifice that has to be acknowledged, although you need to guard against going into that mad martyrdom where you want everyone to be grateful for your every polish (of course too far the other way and you'll feel like a doormat). Housework can have immediately satisfying results—the room does look neat and tidy—but those results are so easily and quickly turned into chaos that it's important not to lose yourself in the role.

Many books have lists (and lists of lists) to help you declutter the house (almost all books supposedly about home management are actually about decluttering), clean the house, spring-clean the house, throw a party, book a vacation. But you can make up your own. (See More Info at the end of this chapter for some useful books on housekeeping and handy-work.)

Basically to get really organized you are going to have to get a handle on:

★ household cleaning and maintenance.
★ whose money is whose and why.
★ household finances.
★ living within a budget.
★ balancing everyone else's needs and wants with your own.
★ making sure you're the home organizer and not a slave.

More importantly, in a household with two parents or two adults, the above list will need to always be open for discussion. It's a lot easier if everyone knows what their responsibilities and rights are and that these can be adjusted. To really understand each other, partners need to know what the other person is doing with their day and how it makes them feel. Otherwise you're not in the same boat together. You're in separate canoes, missing a paddle, and wondering how bad this metaphor can get.

One very stark example of how things can end up is the issue of family vacation. The home partner usually researches and books the vacation (and is therefore "responsible" for its success or otherwise); packs; washes, cleans, and sometimes cooks throughout the vacation; packs to come home; deals with everything that arose while the family was away; and gets everyone ready for school or work again. So who really had the vacation? (Of course even this may sound a wee bit like gorgeous luxury to a single parent.)

Don't forget to find out if you're eligible for any government assistance.

Don't be everyone's assistant

The world expects stay-at-home parents and people who work from home to always be available for them. It will be assumed you have time to burn. You will be approached for committees, car pools, helping other people's children learn to read, and looking after other kids. Of course you may enjoy doing these things, but other people shouldn't assume it's your duty to do them. Sometimes people will even ask you to run errands for them.

Guys at home

Guys who are unpaid, home-based parents may find the housekeeping and handy-work books in More Info at the end of this chapter helpful (and also the next chapter, Dads).

WHY PARENTS DON'T AUTOMATICALLY GO "BACK" TO WORK

There are a great many people who assume that at-home parents will go "back" to work when their kids start school. Anyone who's ever been asked why they haven't should photocopy the "'What Do You Do All Day?'" list coming up in a minute and silently hand the person a copy.

Parents of preschoolers often don't return to their previous full-time paid work because many preschools are part-time or morning or afternoon only, and at best finish by about 3 p.m. And many parents of primary school kids don't either because school ends at 3:30 or earlier. Some kids aren't suited to after care, especially in the early years when they're tired at the end of the preschool or school day. Most jobs don't give you the school holidays off.

"What do you do all day?"

Well, someone has to ◎ shop ◎ remove clothes stains ◎ wash the clothes ◎ dry the clothes ◎ fold the clothes ◎ iron the clothes ◎ distribute the clothes to drawers and closets ◎ do the financial planning ◎ clean the toilet ◎ do the floors ◎ plan a week's-worth of menus ◎ drive people in different directions and pick them up on time ◎ do the dusting ◎ wait for repair people ◎ wait for 45 minutes at the bank ◎ organize the bill paying ◎ be the family liaison person who arranges events and care rosters ◎ cook the meals ◎ do the dishes ◎ make the lunches ◎ help with homework ◎ play with the kids ◎ talk to them about their lives ◎ make the costumes ◎ talk to teachers about their kids' development, problems, and important breakthroughs ◎ plan everything ◎ clean the fridge ◎ bake for the fete ◎ fund-raise ◎ hassle the government about stuff it's doing wrong ◎ be on the PTA ◎ help with reading ◎ run community projects ◎ help the elderly neighbors ◎ look after ageing parents ◎ be there when a kid is sick ◎ be there on sports day ◎ help with the school concert ◎ be one of the people whose house kids go to until their parents come home from work ◎ do the spring-cleaning.

I could go on but my editor said sixteen pages would be too much to photocopy.

SOME TERMS OTHER THAN HOUSEWIFE/HOUSEHUSBAND

You might like to call yourself:

* homemaker.

* stay-at-home mom/dad.

* home executive.

* chief executive officer of (your address here).

* full-time mother/father/parent.

* part-time nanny, driver, cleaner, teacher, medical triage officer, retail consultant, stylist, home decorator, chef, events coordinator, project manager, company director, entertainment facilitator, arbitration expert, and so on.

JUggLiNg PaiD WORK aND UNPaiD WORK

Most parents are involved in part-time or full-time paid work, especially as their kids grow older. Well, unless they're independently wealthy and simply swan about their hobby trout farm or something. Many parents choose to work from home if they can.

If you work for a business, find out what policies your employer has on flexible and family-friendly work practices and hours. Ask your union about entitlements in this area. Your local employment office will have information and training opportunities for people wanting to re-enter the workforce.

Whether you do paid work full-time or part-time outside or from your home, much or all of the housework will probably be done by

THE UPSIDE OF PAID WORK

* It's, well, paid.

* It makes a nice contrast with the vacuuming.

* Looking after a baby or small children can be boring: having time away means you can go back to them refreshed.

* You're a better, more patient parent because you don't have to do it 24 hours a day.

* You don't feel so isolated from the world.

* You keep up with what's going on in your industry or somewhere in the outside world at least.

* Loving your job.

* There's only so much you can talk about with a toddler.

* For many people, it's a relief to get back to work.

* You usually have to change out of your sweats.

* If you're lucky, you can get part-time or flexible hours to maximize parent time.

THE DOWNSIDE OF PAID WORK

✱ Either you're feeling guilty about not being a good enough parent or you feel insecure about whether you're giving enough to work.

✱ Women especially who feel guilty about needing flexible work hours often do a lot more work than they're paid for.

✱ Kids don't run to a schedule.

✱ Kids don't want to be with anyone else when they're sick.

✱ Kids need "quantity time" with parents, not just "quality time" (short bursts of contact here and there). Make sure you can hang out together for an hour or two a day at least.

✱ Co-workers and bosses often don't understand what's needed when it comes to your family (like having to take off suddenly, or what it's like trying to concentrate after three nights of constantly broken sleep).

✱ There are not as many opportunities for food fights.

✱ It's much harder to balance life and get things done if you don't have a partner or somebody who shares custody with you. Or a housekeeper and a valet.

you too if you're a woman, statistically speaking. Have a look at the earlier Staying Home section because some of it will be relevant. To help yourself get organized see More Info coming up next.

The world of constant juggling and adjustment, of feeling guilty about home and guilty about work, is familiar to lots of us. Only you can judge whether you've bitten off more than you can chew, or whether spitting some out will make you feel better. Or if some element of mad scramble will be normal from now on.

moRe iNfo

HOUSEKEEPING AND HANDY-WORK

Home Comforts: The Art and Science of Keeping House
by Cheryl Mendelson, Scribner, 2002.

Even if you don't do everything (or anything!) this fabulous book
recommends, it's all here—from how to read laundry-care labels and the
best way to hang out the washing to preserving family records and how
long you can keep things in the fridge or freezer. A huge book that's great
for anyone who has to run or share the running of a household or is
moving out of home, and anyone who has argued about whether to wash
the glasses or the plates first.

The New Complete Do-It-Yourself Manual
Readers Digest, 1996.

No, I'm *not* saying this is a great time to renovate! But you're probably going
to have more time than money in the short term at least, and not be able to
splash out on tradespeople. (But please—no electrical work or other stunts
by yourself.) This book covers common household and garden jobs, with
illustrated instructions.

STAYING HOME

I don't like most of the books for stay-at-home parents that are available
because they seem to assume things such as you want to home school the
kids or you want dieting tips (!), or their main aim seems to be criticiz-
ing parents who work outside the home, part- or full-time, rather than
giving practical help or reassuring info for people who choose to be full-
time parents.

Staying Home: From Full-Time Professional to Full-Time Parent
by Darcie Sanders and Martha Bullen, Spencer and Waters, 2001.

Addressed to mothers and covers issues such as making the transition,
"creating a new self-image," your sex life, support groups, and making your

own future. The authors set four ground rules for your new life: know what you want your job to be; acknowledge your skills; validate yourself; and consider yourself a feminist.

www.athomemothers.com

A website with a magazine, info, and advice. Pretty much assumes you have a husband bringing in money but is otherwise very useful.

WOMEN'S LIVES

Wifework: What Marriage Really Means for Women
by Susan Maushart, Bloomsbury Publishing, 2003.

Ms. Maushart, now an Aussie, looks at the inequalities within many marriages and what can be done about them. This book could make you feel very cross about how much housework your partner isn't doing if you weren't a bit grumpy already. She tries to work out why women feel they have to do all the organizing while the guys get to play. She says because of the kids it's worth finding a way to make marriage succeed and be fairer.

The Price of Motherhood: Why the Most Important Job in the World Is Still the Least Valued
by Ann Crittenden, Metropolitan Books, 2001.

Feminist reporter turned feminist mom at home, Ann Crittenden, asks why conservative governments always bang on about being family friendly, but in fact full-time mothers are still not respected by society and politicians. She talks about the career sacrifices that are made, mostly by mothers, and the way mothers are perceived by others. She argues that if they "had more resources and more respect, everyone—including children—would be better off." And she explores why people say "motherhood is the most important job in the world" and then ignore any mothers in the room or refer to "mothers who don't work."

Reinventing Ourselves After Motherhood: How Former Career Women Refocus Their Personal and Professional Lives After the Birth of a Child
by Susan Lewis, Contemporary Books, 1999.

An essentially conservative book largely made up of anecdotes about women who choose to stay home and are happy with that decision, despite being shocked at what it entails and how nobody respects them any more. The book discusses important issues such as whose money, division of house-work, getting back to a career and volunteer work. It's more a sharing of feelings than a how-to book.

The Bitch in the House: 26 Women Tell the Truth About Sex, Solitude, Work, Motherhood, and Marriage
edited by Cathy Hanauer, Perennial, 2003.

This lively bestselling collection covers many things close to women's hearts: being cross about why men don't see the work that women do; the difference between being a girlfriend, a wife, and a mother; being sweet in the office and a gorgon at home; struggling to balance work and home; the theory of wanting a child versus the reality; having to look after your children and your parents; what motherhood can force you to give up and the emotional riches it bestows. The twenty-six speak about their different lives and make many honest observations that women are often scared to say out loud.

Piffle   The Amazon.com bookselling website lists *The Surrendered Wife: A Practical Guide to Finding Intimacy, Passion, and Peace with a Man*, by Laura Doyle, along with other useful titles such as *The Exemplary Husband: A Biblical Perspective* by Stuart Scott, *Liberated Through Submission* by P. B. Wilson and Bunny Wilson, *The Excellent Wife: A Biblical Perspective* by Martha Peace, *Men Are from Mars, Women Are from Venus* by what's-'is-name, and the gobsmack-ingly titled *You Can Be the Wife of a Happy Husband* by Darien B. Cooper. It's a book about how you should get yourself a husband and then do everything he tells you to do and never contradict him. Tremendously reassuring and useful if you are lost in the wilderness and you have a copy of this book, a bottle of lighter fluid, and a box of matches. Toast a marshmallow for me.

JUGGLING PAID WORK AND UNPAID WORK

The Working Mother's Guide to Life

by Linda Mason, Three Rivers Press, 2002.

Looks at child care, guilt, finding community support, getting organized, dealing with your employer, and creating a strong family culture.

www.homeworkingmom.com

About running a business from home.

DaDs

Yes, well, no more sex for you, and if you try

to do anything for the kid we'll roll our eyes

and laugh at you and make snide comments

about your hopelessness for the task, just to

make us feel more competent as mothers.

That's the worst-case scenario. Unless the

baby keeps vomiting down your neck.

No, really, it's all going to be marvelous.

Parenthood *is* marvelous—and boring and

complicated and hard and hilarious and silly

and guesswork and exhausting, and makes you proud and furious and bewildered and tired and more full of love than you thought possible.

This whole book is for dads as well as moms, but here's the men-only section.

good ways for men to be a real partner

One minute there's a bloated pregnant woman demanding that the baby come out, and the next minute she's an exhausted wreck saying she can't cope, her boobs don't work, she'll never be able to be a good mother and boo hoo hoo. Not much to be done, chaps, except pitch in and be true to the word "partner," emotionally and around the house. It can be tricky, especially in the early days with all the raging hormones and exhaustion and boobs akimbo but off limits.

Then you go back to work (we'll get to stay-at-home dads in a mo) and have a crying baby thrust at you every night after her long, hard day.

This is your chance to be a real hero. Listen, sympathize, don't try to solve everything immediately, do everything you can to reassure your partner that she'll work out the breastfeeding, and talk about being in it together and riding it through. This would be a good time to dip into any spare money for a weekly cleaner, even for just the first eight weeks. Get your relatives and friends to donate food and do shopping.

Women can feel trapped in a new role they can't get out of—"housewife," "milking machine," or "walking zombie." Without making it a competition, sympathize and say you feel trapped into being the main or only breadwinner for the next twenty years (or whatever your individual situation is).

Many dads love to have their kids for hours on end—they hang out for the prospect. And many understand that parenthood is a joint venture. Having a supportive partner in these early days can make all the difference for women between mild blues and thinking they're going mad. Mothers, especially those who are at home full-time, may need regular nights, mornings, or afternoons off at the weekend.

> *"It can be very overwhelming for dads too. We kept in close touch with family and friends, and the local mother-and-child health nurse for reassurance that we were doing the right thing. Sharing the home duties helps too."* SCOTT

> *"I pay someone to come on Sunday mornings and hubby and I go out for brunch (think of the cost as 'marriage insurance'). We tried going out to dinner but were falling asleep at the table by 9 p.m."* KATE

While recognizing common differences between men and women, there's no reason why men can't become as competent or even more competent at being a parent, if you don't count the boobs business. Moms don't have a monopoly on baby knowledge.

THINGS MEN OFTEN NEED TO KNOW

You probably have just as many parenting instincts as your partner. You'll both be learning new things all the time for the next few years. Talking honestly with other dads will show you that feeling scared or inadequate is not unique or strange.

The more you do things, the better you'll be at them. This includes diaper changing, bathing, getting clothes on and off a wriggler, and talking to your baby.

Anticipation is needed—try to think ahead about things that might happen and how to deal with them. You'll be better prepared. Don't wait until you're out of baby formula to buy the next lot, for example. Have baby acetaminophen in the cupboard. Get the kid a coat and hat before the first really cold days of winter. If you go to the supermarket for milk, get bananas and toilet paper too.

Stuff doesn't just "happen." It often happens because your partner has made it happen. Think about what wouldn't be done if she suddenly wasn't there. Not many dads do the planning stuff. Many or most dads wouldn't know how to make an appointment at their kid's hairdresser, find somewhere to take them for swimming lessons, tell a doctor their kid's habits and routine, or organize a birthday party, complete with invitations. But there are a lot more dads now who know how to do this stuff, and do this stuff, than ever before, and it would be helpful if you knew how—partly because sometimes you'll need to, and partly because it will get you many Brownie points and days off for golf or whatever it is you mysterious creatures do.

Write lists for yourself if that's a good way for you to get things right. Have notes about what needs to be in the baby bag at all times, and a list of essentials that have to be bought weekly or regularly at the supermarket.

Sometimes we women don't know you're afraid of the anger we turn on you if you get something "wrong": please don't stop doing things. So you dressed the baby in a stripy top and floral pants that don't match. Who cares? If your partner is horrified by this, find a couple of failsafe versions—that is, have on hand a few tops and pants that are the same color.

Women can often do six things at a time while planning another four in their head. Men often think and do only one thing at a time. Either develop the womanly ability or explain that you'll get the six things done but it may take a bit longer.

> *"My number one piece of advice for a new mother would be to ask the midwife in hospital to help your husband give the baby its first bath. After that, never suggest in any way that you are more competent or any better in any way at caring for the baby. If he is parenting from day one he will get good at it, and it's very sweet to see a daddy confidently nursing a little bub!"* JUNINE

Don't get squeezed out

If you're a stay-at-home dad for the day, week, or year, you have to do housework as well as look after the kid(s). In this arena I think you need to do the housework properly, even the bits you don't "see": think "dirty"—the bathroom needs to be done at least weekly, even if it doesn't seem as bad as the on the road ones.

If you don't know what needs doing, ask for a list, and for the tasks to be explained if necessary, as well as the standard of cleanliness needed for hygiene or family harmony purposes. This can help avoid the "What pile of dog poop under the carpet bigger than a bread box?" syndrome where some chaps seem to be legally blind in the presence of things many women think are obvious problems. (Of course, it's entirely possible that the sex roles may be reversed in this argument. I've just never heard of it.)

Don't take any crap, though, about small stuff such as the washed cutlery should be propped up to drain, not laid flat. Have a meeting on the separation of tasks and negotiate the standard to which they should be done.

Some men and women are happy to divide things sharply—women at home get to make all the decisions at home, men "out" at work get to do all that stuff. But if you want to be involved with your baby and kids, don't be shut out by any insecurity or arrogance that manifests itself as a woman saying she always knows best and you're incompetent because you're the man (even though you still have to take the garbage and the spiders out). If she thinks you're incompetent, ask her to teach you.

It's never just about housework. If, for instance, a woman feels that her central role is being a mother she might be devastated if her child runs to Daddy for comfort as well as Mommy. You'll probably need to talk about this.

Sometimes problems arise from a complicated psychological situation in which the woman thinks she's no longer good for anything else and needs to make you feel less competent on the home turf so she feels more competent. (In most families it's the woman who stays home with a young baby, and it's the woman who takes the biggest hits to her career or the other life opportunities she had before motherhood.) It would be most splendid for everyone to work through the situation tactfully and supportively (says Mrs. Authoresspants of Perfectville).

Very often the "mom always knows best" thing comes from generations of social conditioning and has developed because sometimes it has been the only control women have had in their lives. The best way for your partner to get over needing to be the Home CEO is for her to feel you're useful and reliable enough to take charge while she's out capering around somewhere.

Sometimes it drives women crazy when their partner asks them what to buy at the supermarket or how to wash something. We have to remember that you men want to do it right, that you don't want us to be mad at you for doing it wrong, and that if you weren't doing it we would have to get off our tushes and do it ourselves.

If you want to know more about how to do the housework properly or how to decipher those strange cleaning symbols on clothes labels, check out *Home Comforts*, a how-to book reviewed in More Info at the end of the previous chapter, Unpaid Work and Paid Work.

"We need to know not only that women can do what men can do, but also that men can do what women can do." GLORIA STEINEM, QUOTED BY CATHY YOUNG IN "MATERNAL CHAUVINISM IS A DAD'S GREATEST OBSTACLE TO PARENTAL PARITY," ON WWW.SALON.COM

THE SPECIAL USES OF GUYS

(Obviously the talents listed aren't exclusively male, but this whole section generalizes about things so shut up.)

* Guys can let moms know they're not in parenting alone, even if they're separated.

* Guys can be secretly smug because a baby usually says "Dadda" before "Momma."

* Guys are especially good at understanding the boisterousness of little boys.

* Many guys can perform the incredibly useful task of getting their girls interested in ball skills and sports.

* Guys can provide a fresh approach to settling kids—and at least provide a new target for them while Mom takes a breather.

* Guys don't have to be the strong disciplinarians, just present a united, agreed-upon front with moms.

* Guys can show kids that they enjoy being with them, which builds self-esteem.

* Guys can show boys it's okay to cry and do things like dress up.

* Guys can show girls how to climb, hammer, and do other traditional "guy things."

* Guys can be affectionate and available. So many modern men who had tough upbringings and cold relationships with their own fathers are bravely going a new way, determined to be loving and cuddly with boys and girls, and setting up a healthier and more rewarding future.

* A guy who is careful and kind to a child's mother is showing how to behave. Kids learn by example more than words.

Would you like to comb my moustache?

Guys and Babies

Most importantly you need to bond with the baby too, and this can take a while. The best way is to get to know your baby by spending time together, changing diapers, having quiet chats (you can go on about anything to a baby—they just like to hear you and see your face).

Don't let your partner, family members, in-laws, friends, or people in the street make you feel bad that you are learning how to look after a baby. If you do the wrong thing, that's just a step toward doing it the right way—or your way, which doesn't have to be how everyone else does it, as long as it is safe.

Looking after babies is too important and difficult and rewarding to leave it up to the women alone.

> "We find out what women have known for decades. You can't truly be a star at work if you're truly serious about being there for your kids as often as they need you. There will always be some hot-shot who's willing to give up more to get where you could go if not for what you need to do at home." STAY-AT-HOME WRITER–DAD, JONATHON KRONSTADT, IN "THE NEW DAD" ON WWW.SALON.COM

Guys and Sex

Many guys are astonished to find out how much parenthood gets in the way of a sex life. Keep talking about how you'd like things to change. Here are some reasons your partner may be uninterested in sex.

- ★ Her body has not been truly her "own" for a long time. Especially if she's breastfeeding, she may feel the pressure of too many demands.
- ★ She's tired all the time.
- ★ Her libido (sex drive) isn't what it used to be.
- ★ She doesn't want to get pregnant again.
- ★ She feels unattractive because of weight gain or loss, boob changes, or stretch marks.

What you can do

- ★ Keep talking about it.
- ★ Make her *feel* attractive as well as telling her. (Show it by your actions.)
- ★ Get help with housework.
- ★ Wear three condoms at once or do something else sensible about contraception—then everyone can relax.
- ★ Be patient.
- ★ Ask her what she wants.

MEN: AN INFURIATING CHECKLIST

- ✱ Bring in vast wage.

- ✱ Work flexible, part-time hours.

- ✱ Be fabulously artistic and amusingly unpredictable but also totally reliable.

- ✱ Be competent at all kid stuff but never usurp or contradict mother superiority.

- ✱ Make woman feel attractive and sexy.

- ✱ Be endlessly supportive.

- ✱ Talk.

- ✱ Shut up.

- ✱ Talk again.

- ✱ No, not about that.

- ✱ Oh, for heaven's SAKE.

DaDs WHO NeeD HeLP WitH DePReSSiON OR family ReLatiONSHiPS

Dads, like moms, can suffer parenting or postpartum depression. For help see the contacts listed in More Info at the end of the Feeling Overwhelmed or Depressed chapter in *Part 1: Babies*. Especially if your partner is depressed, you may need help too. There are special support groups for men to talk about their postpartum depression, dealing with their partner's problem, or family relationships (see More Info below).

> *"The answer to the question about housework makes my husband seem like a sexist layabout, but the reality is he's out of the house for 10 to 12 hours a day. Five days a week. He would dearly love to spend more time with our son, but by the time he gets home he's often asleep. Also I'm more than happy to do most of the housework as I'm the one at home. Before we had a baby we had a cleaner, so neither of us had to come home from work and clean the house, but we can't afford that luxury now. No matter what your views are on sexual politics, equality, etc., it's pretty hard not to start living a 1950s lifestyle if the parent at home is the woman and the 'working' parent is the man. And our son and I agree: he's a top Dad!"* KATE

moRe iNfo

STUFF FOR DADS

Babyhood

by Paul Reiser, Avon, New York, 1997.

Comedian Paul Reiser gives a stand-up-style account of becoming a dad.

400

The New Father: A Dad's Guide to the First Year
AND
The New Father: A Dad's Guide to the Toddler Years
by Armin Brott, Abbeville Press, New York, 1997.
A boxed set featuring advice from the "experts" and real dads on all sorts of
subjects including child development, changing relationships, and men's
feelings.

www.menstuff.org
A website about kids, child care, relationships, men's health, the kit,
the caboodle.

www.dads-uk.co.uk
An English website for dads, with articles, forums and links.

www.dadsanddaughters.org
A site about just what it says, with lots of hints and articles.

www.fathers.com
A store of articles and links covering many different topics and ways of
being a dad.

BOOKS ABOUT DADS FOR KIDS

What Dads Can't Do
by Douglas Wood, Simon and Schuster, 2000.
A gorgeous story about companionship between a small crocodiley creature
and a dad crocodiley creature. Dads and kids will get different frissons, and
share some, from this book.

My Dad
by Anthony Browne, Farrar, Sraus, and Giroux, 2001.
A greatly inventive kids' writer and illustrator looks at all sorts of dads and
their best points.

DADS WHO NEED HELP WITH DEPRESSION OR
FAMILY RELATIONSHIPS

Parent helplines and services are listed in More Info at the end of the second chapter, Your Support Team, in *Part 1: Babies*. See Relationships in Extra Resources at the end of the book.

COPING STRATEGIES FOR PARENTS

The following coping strategies are general ideas, and not all of them will work when your baby is very little. Keep some for later: only a fool would suggest you need a new hobby in the first few weeks or months! Everyone needs something different: one woman's exciting owl-shaped macramé project is another's sure road to screamy madness.

iDeas for Less stress

★ Sleep, meditate, or lie down and listen to soft music or read when the offspring is napping. Set yourself a bedtime and stick to it, even if the dishes still aren't done: there'll always be something to keep you up until 1 a.m., even if it is Jerry Springer.

★ Ask each visitor to fold ten things from the laundry basket, wipe down a surface, or make a cup of tea. Don't wait on them.

★ Make sure you eat well and don't skip meals. Never skip breakfast or have something silly like half a grapefruit.

★ Once a week you can try to cook big batches of things to freeze for the days ahead. Cut up raw veggies and put them in ziplock bags or plastic containers with tight-fitting lids. These can be kept in the fridge and the contents thrown in the steamer or microwave when needed each night.

★ Getting outside, moderate exercise, and chasing some sunshine (with UV protection) are factors that turn up all the time in studies and surveys about beating depression. If it's winter and you live up North, invest in a cold weather gear for everyone and get out amongst it.

★ Try exercising together as a family at a time when everyone is at home. Have the meal ready to heat up when you get back and go for a relaxing, debriefing walk. Or go with a friend.

★ Set very small goals and build up over months: today my special project is to shower, read a chapter of a book, go out for a drink with a pal without baby vomit on the back of my top, get away for a whole weekend, become president. Once-a-week activities such as a martial arts class, a craft group, or a walking club are also good to aim for— they're often more realistic than a daily routine early on. Once-a-month activities can include a reading group, a

gardening club, filling in the details in the baby book—
whatever takes your fancy.

★ Kid-free time is important for every full-time or part-time
caregiver of kids. If your partner won't pull their weight,
explain that you need them to do their share or you'll lose
your mind and get carted off and then they'll be stuck with
the lot.

★ Set yourself a regular session of your own time to do a class
or hobby or to go out and kick your heels up: your partner
or other babysitter will always know that's the time they're
needed. It could be a Friday night or a Monday morning.

★ If you don't have a relative or friend who can babysit for
you, find another parent who can swap babysitting duties
with you. You have permission to sleep, read a stupid magazine or a smart book, or go to a movie—don't do the
housework or any other work.

★ Pick a hobby that has a meditative aspect, a team sport,
a craft with a creative or intricate component—anything
where you have to think about nothing but what you're
doing for a while. Give your mind a holiday from hum-
drum stuff or worries.

★ Be careful of solitary, home-based crafts and pursuits that can
increase your isolation. You might love them or you might be
better off finding a hobby that involves making friends or
staying in touch with old ones. Have some friends you talk to
about children stuff and some other friends who aren't interested so you talk about different things.

★ If going out to dinner or a movie with your partner is too
hard or you're always too tired, try a Sunday brunch.

★ See a "cry-baby" film once a week. Some city and suburban
and country cinemas have daytime sessions for parents or
other caregivers that they can take their babies to and
nobody cares if a baby cries. This is harder if you have toddlers or preschoolers as well. And please be careful about

choosing the movie; babies can be very sensitive to fore-boding or loud music, unpleasant arguments and shouting, or your reactions to stressful emotions. *The Godfather Part III* is probably not a good idea. It's just more social to go out with other parents than to crouch in front of a video on your own.

★ Use the local paper, the library, the city paper, free child magazines, and your local health department to find out what services and baby- or child-friendly free entertainment are available to you.

★ Formal or informal weekend events with other people who have kids will at least give you some time to sit down while someone else takes a turn pushing the swings.

★ A parent who is at work all day can set aside special times for the baby or kids, including a wake-up welcome-to-the-day ritual (you and the kid fetch the paper you won't have time to read, go outside, and check the weather), and an evening routine that involves perhaps some quiet play or a bath or story before bed.

★ Plan what to do with any spare time at home: do you love to read, just lie on the couch with a twinkie and the TV guide, or learn to rumba? Try to get into another room, into the tool shed, or to the corner café away from the kids so you're out of sight, out of mind.

taking stock

If you feel like having a child is ruining your life, unruin it. What are you resenting? What is it you'd love to be doing? What do you miss most? Work out what it is and a way to do it again. (If it's being a submariner, it may have to wait. Is there something else you could try, at least on Saturday mornings and Thursday nights?)

Ask other people what they do to help themselves cope better or cheer themselves up (and see More Info below). And if you're having a really hard time and some stupid book (ahem) suggests all these perky, impossible ideas that make you want to throw up, why not burn it in the backyard in a 44-gallon drum?

more info

How to Keep Your C.O.O.L. with Your Kids
by Lou Makarowski, Perigee Books, 1996.
Makarowski, a psychologist and columnist, explains how various physical and mental exercises can help you relax, gain self control, and be a better parent.

a you-shaped family

Families, like baseball players, come in all different shapes and sizes. Here are some thoughts on big and little families, preparing an older kid for an alien invasion—a new baby in the family—the differences between girls and boys and approaches that can help when sisters and brothers fight.

family size

People who say things such as "She has no self-control" when a woman's eighth baby comes along, or "It's cruel to have only one child," are only showing their own ignorance. They have no idea why others do what they do: a person may have always wanted a big family, or there could be medical reasons why another child isn't possible. It doesn't matter. They should just shut right up.

There are many more families with only one child than ever before and far fewer with, say, twelve or more (hoorah for contraception). There are many different family set-ups now. Parents of "only children" are usually pretty conscious of giving their child opportunities to make friends and have special companions, including cousins. Only children will make their own friends and family groupings as they get older, just as we often have our kids call our close friends "Aunt" or "Uncle" even when there's no familial relationship—cousins in the next generation may have to be in inverted commas too. (See also More Info at the end of this chapter.)

Most of the websites I could find about big families were based on specific religious denominations, including some of those bizarre home-schooling cults. Other hints and books I came across were just generally about parenting, not about dealing with a big bunch. You're probably better off searching in other categories on the Internet such as organization and storage; frugal parenting; and recipes for large families or gatherings. I do know some people color-code their kids' stuff by asking each kid their favorite color and then buying their clothes and other items in that color. My guess is the kids would have to agree to make it work and keep agreeing for years (and what about the hand-me-downs?). I'm sure your best bet is to ask some moms (perhaps from an earlier generation) about dealing with a heap of kids.

MATCH THE KID WITH THE PARENT!
draw a line to match them up

A. SHOCKING OLD CYNIC

1. CRUISY BABY

B. CALM, SKINNY POET

2. ALERT, SPORTY GIRL

C. EXCITABLE BANK CLERK

3. ECCENTRIC, CHUBBY CAR-OBSESSED TODDLER

A. THAT'S RIGHT: IT COULD BE ANY OF THEM!

MINDING YOUR OWN BUSINESS

Don't say "I see you're having another baby" or ask "How pregnant are you?" before the person in question tells you they are pregnant. They may not be pregnant at all, and you and they will be hideously mortified.

Don't ask people "when" they're going to have children or "Are you going to have another one?" If they want you to know, they'll tell you.

Don't ask "Were you on IVF?" Likewise all variations on "Who's the father?"

Don't ask "Do you work?," "When are you going back to work?" or "What do you do at home all day?"

Birth order

Many people believe the position of children in the family determines their personality. I think this belief is too restrictive and only slightly more based on observation than horoscopes. But what would I know? I'm Sagittarius so I'm just jovial and tactless. (See More Info at the end of the chapter for resources on this subject.)

PREPARING a SMALL KID FOR a NEW BABY

Wait until the pregnancy is well advanced before you begin to prepare your child for a new arrival. Apart from the issue of making sure it's a viable pregnancy, time stretches out endlessly for kids and they'll find seven or eight months too long to wait.

★ Tell the child quietly and happily when only the immediate family is present, not when you tell anyone—or everyone—else and there's lots of carry-on and no time for reflection and questions.

- ★ Explain it in a way that helps them understand the baby will belong to them as well as you, using terms such as "your brother or sister" and "our baby." They'll need you to tell them a number of times.
- ★ Don't forget to explain that the baby will be coming to live with you—not just for a short visit.
- ★ Tell them that the baby will be bringing them a special present and follow through on the day of the birth with something whizzbang: the kid's idea of whizzbang, not yours—you might be thinking a scale model of a Tunisian royal palace while they're just desperate for a balloon.
- ★ Talk about what it will be like to have a baby around—how they cry quite a bit, need lots of attention, and sometimes drive everyone mad. And that all babies are like that and that's how they were. Talk about how you love a baby even when they're difficult and noisy.
- ★ Talk about how the baby won't be able to play games at first because it will be so little and will often want to sleep instead.
- ★ Describe what the baby might look like.
- ★ Talk to your older kid about when they were born and look at photos.
- ★ Get anything you need from your older kid for the baby, such as a car safety seat, months before the baby arrives if possible, and give them new "big kid" stuff so they don't associate the baby with things being taken away.
- ★ Give the kid important jobs such as helping you to buy things the baby will need or to get the nursery ready.
- ★ Explain that Mom will go into the hospital so the doctor will help the baby to be born, and that Mom isn't sick.
- ★ Explain to your child that Mom wants to give birth in private, and that a person your kid knows will take care of them during the birth. Plan and tell them about some special activities, such as a trip to the zoo, that they will be involved in while Mom is away or in her room at home.

Have a trial run or lots of discussion about what it might be like to find Nanna there in the morning and Mom and Dad gone to get the baby.

★ If you want a kid (over 7) at the birth, they will have to be very carefully briefed and have a grown-up minder assigned to them to explain what's happening or to go for a walk with them during any scary bits.

★ Get your older kid to draw pictures of where the baby is now, and what it will be like when the baby comes home, and discuss the drawings with them.

After the baby arrives

★ Teach your older kid to hold the baby gently on their knees, with an adult sitting next to them. Never leave an older child alone with the baby—toddlers and preschoolers may treat the baby as a doll because they're not old enough to understand yet.

★ Show the older kid how to gently stroke the baby and put their finger into the curled-up fist.

★ Be aware that your older kid may be only responding to ineluctable survival instincts that give a very good impression of being what we modern folk call "jealousy."

★ Make special times to be alone with your older kid and for them to have special times with other people without the baby.

★ Don't insist your older kid helps with the baby, but reward helpful behavior, and make it fun to help by, say, passing things to Mom.

★ Expect some possible regression—the older kid wanting to revert to diapers or thumb sucking. It's temporary.

★ Try very hard to keep your older kid to their routine: if it needs to change, run the new one in before the baby arrives so the association isn't made.

★ Remind your older kid that the baby needing so much care is a temporary situation: the baby will grow bigger quite soon.

★ Give toddlers or preschoolers special activities to do while you're breastfeeding—spraying water on a wooden floor and then wiping it with a towel, sorting red buttons into one jar and blue into another, or anything that will occupy them.

★ A toddler can have a dolly to breastfeed or bottlefeed while Mom feeds the real baby.

★ If you can't pick up your older kid because you have had a cesarean, get them to sit, stand, or kneel next to you on the couch or lie beside you on the bed for cuddles and one-on-one chats.

The Helping Kids Understand Grown-up Concepts chapter coming up soon has suggestions for answering small children's questions about where babies come from (and see also More Info at the end of this chapter for books about the arrival of a new baby that you might like to read to your older child).

if sisters and brothers fight

All sisters and brothers (and small friends) have disagreements, but some seem to have them all the time. Here are some approaches that might help.

★ Try to work out the reason for the fighting and how to avoid it.

★ Ask friends and relatives for hints.

★ Give your kids separate activities.

★ Try to unite them against a common enemy (not you!—maybe a puzzle that's tricky).

★ Get each of them to play with their own friends for a while.

am not

are so

★ Talk to each kid separately and get them to nominate the good points about each other.

★ Reward them for playing well together.

★ Take away disputed objects, but make sure one kid isn't always being disadvantaged.

★ Ask them for solutions in more rational moments, not in the heat of battle.

★ If the fighting is really making family life unpleasant, ask your doctor for a referral to a family psychologist: better to get independent help now than to live with this for fifteen or twenty years!

★ Protect kids from rough play, especially smaller and younger ones.

★ Don't saddle older kids with responsibilities that can cause resentment. A child under 12 can't be expected to look after another child and be fully responsible, for however short a time. Try instead to foster a sense that the older kid is protective, smart, and a helpful role model for their little sibling, and you're proud of them for that.

★ Make sure the older kid knows they can still have negative emotions, want a cuddle, and be Mom and Dad's little one too.

★ Try to establish boundaries of behavior and clear habits of resolution so that kids can start to sort disputes out for themselves ("Now it's your turn to say sorry").

★ Give kids their own, individual rights, and responsibilities. Discuss what these might be and make the decisions together.

★ Give yourself time to think about how you may be showing favoritism, even without realizing. I know a house where there are many photos of the first three children and virtually none of the fourth, who, even in adulthood, finds it deeply hurtful. Explain your methods so it's harder for kids to accuse you of favoritism.

★ Try to be thrilled with the achievements of all your kids, even if you've seen those milestones reached before and an older kid was better at them.

★ Maybe you can prove the "experts" wrong and not expect the best only from your first, not neglect your middle child, and not baby your youngest.

gender blender

Some parents are surprised to find that a 3-year-old boy in a sensitive household thunders around and plays swords at every available opportunity and reacts to seeing a toy by shaking it, whirling it about, and shouting "Raaaarghhh!!!!" Others wonder why a girl who's been quite interested in trucks decides, at 4, that she will never wear anything else but a "twirly dress with a prettiara." Many of us know a boy who liked make-up and wrapping himself in spangly fabric when he was 5 and is now an enormous, straight football player. We know girls who never wanted to wear a dress when they were little and still don't. In all the debate and research about nature versus nurture, and girls being quicker to learn most things, especially language and communication skills, and boys needing more space and tolerance of testosteroney behavior, we mustn't lose sight of the most important thing: all kids are individuals.

Each kid needs to be supported in whatever they're experimenting with. Each kid deserves a chance to play with both dolls and cars, to build up and knock down, to attend a tea party, and wear a pirate hat to attack the perimeter. Each kid deserves to be able to develop their skills and enjoy their favorite activities without being labeled, ridiculed, or pushed around. And praise shouldn't be rationed and given only for activities shared or approved of by parents or siblings.

Kids need to be allowed to have "phases," private loves and pursuits, and to enjoy things their parents think are dead boring or even odd.

Parents can ask themselves the following questions.

- ★ "When the boys take over the building-block corner at day care, why can't the girls have another building-block corner for themselves?"
- ★ "Would I let a girl run around the house screaming like that?"
- ★ "Did I really just tell my weeping boy to be a 'little man'?"
- ★ "How can a girl climb on the adventure playground in a long dress and those silly shoes?"
- ★ "I've worn only trousers since 1989, but if my little girl wants to wear a pink frock every day why should I stop her?"
- ★ "I don't mind my boys tumbling about, but should I draw the line at them pretending to have guns that kill each other?"
- ★ "How can I communicate with my son, and listen to him, in ways that don't include words?"
- ★ "So I've got a sensitive boy or a tomboy girl—why should that be seen as a problem?"

Ultimately, the response to all the palaver about gender is to be as clear-eyed as possible about the pressures that might be put on your kid by you or anyone else around them to change their natural inclinations. Are they being offered an opportunity to enjoy something or being pushed into a shape someone else wants them to be? The only way to get close to the answer is to know your child as well as you can, to accept them for whatever and whoever they are, and to respect what they choose to do when they've been offered a range of possibilities without judgment or criticism. (Unless they're biting the heads off frogs, in which case get them an agent.)

more info

Extra Resources at the end of the book has sections on Single, Sole and Shared-custody Parents, Gay Families and Teenage Moms.

ONLY CHILDREN

Parenting an Only Child: The Joys and Challenge of Raising Your One and Only
by Susan Newman Ph.D.
Newman reassures that being an only doesn't mean being lonely. Anecdotes, assumptions, and studies are examined.

www.onlychild.com
A website and newsletters about all sorts of issues concerning the one-child family.

BIRTH ORDER

Birth Order Blues: How Parents Can Help Their Children Meet the Challenges of Birth Order
by Meri Wallace, Owl Books, 1999.
Explains birth order issues and shows how to resolve these potential problems.

BOOKS FOR KIDS ABOUT PREPARING FOR A NEW BABY
Truelove
by Babette Cole, Dial Books, 2002.
Truelove the dog feels left out when the new baby arrives—but what a happy ending. A picture book with naughty cartoons and a modern approach.

Za-za's Baby Brother
by Lucy Cousins, Candlewick Press, 2003.
From the creator of the Maisy books. A zebra gets a new sibling.

My Little Brother

by Debi Gliori, Candlewick Press, 1995.

When the Teddy Bears Came

by Martin Waddell and Penny Dale, Candlewick Press, 1998.

Pretty standard straightforward stories for kids about a new baby arriving.

You'll Wake the Baby

by Catherine Jinks and Andrew McLean, Viking, 2000.

Two preschoolers try to play quietly and then the baby wakes up.

Waiting for Baby

by Trish Cooke, Walker Books, UK, 2000.

A little boy waits for the new baby, with a twist. Also good for families expecting twins and people who'd like a book with characters with darker skin than the usual book illustrations of Mr. and Mrs. Light-Pinke and family.

IF SISTERS AND BROTHERS FIGHT

Siblings Without Rivalry: How to Help Your Children Live Together So You Can Live Too

by Adele Faber and Elaine Mazlish, Avon Books, 1998.

Beyond Sibling Rivalry: How to Help Your Children Become Co-operative, Caring and Compassionate

Peter Goldenthal, Owl, US, 2000.

Two books (the first one by psychologists) for parents about sibling rivalry.

Rosie's Babies

by Martin Waddell and Penny Dale, Candlewick Press, UK, 1999.

A picture book for kids about sibling jealousy.

teaching kids How to Behave

Everyone gets into a tizz about "discipline." It combines all the elements of having children that are difficult: being grumpy when you're tired, not being in full control of your life, reacting in immature ways to situations—and that's just the parents.

A baby has been learning how to interact by observing for months. Somewhere along the line the parents start using the word no and the baby understands. The baby begins to learn about boundaries, and some time after—usually about the same age as they walk—they start trying to rule their world, and conflict can take over. Aarrgh! Not to mention, Aieeee!

WHat DisciPLiNe is

Unfortunately, when people talk about discipline they often think it just means punishment. The point of discipline is not to punish a child, but to teach them to behave with kindness and consideration, and understand the rules. That's why this chapter is called Teaching Kids How to Behave.

Try to think of yourself as the coach rather than as the punisher. It's impossible for a child to have the mental capacity to put themselves in *your* shoes, but you can, in every situation, try to imagine you are a child attempting to work out the right way to behave. And you know that nobody's perfect. You may as well set up an atmosphere in which, if you lose your temper or your child does, you can apologize and all's forgiven.

Here are some approaches you might find helpful.

★ Think of your child as your ally or apprentice, not the enemy.

★ Show your child the right way to behave.

★ Help your child learn when a behavior is wrong and why.

★ Recognize that your child may at first not understand or care why they're supposed to behave in a certain way, but establish a pattern of explaining why they must, even briefly, so it doesn't seem like a "no questions asked" boot camp.

★ Give your child choices of things that don't matter so much—a bit of apple or a bit of pear—but not whether or not they can have at the TV with a baseball bat.

★ Establish a small core of simple ground rules that are consistently observed, such as bedtime is 7 o'clock, no hitting, and you don't get what you ask for if you use a whiny voice—so the child isn't overwhelmed by trying to remember fifty-six rules.

★ Be clear that the aim is for your child to understand what are the right things to do, not that it's to humiliate them or make them feel inadequate or guilty when they do a wrong thing.

Above all set reasonable boundaries early on—these can start when your child is 1 or 2 and build through their preschool years.

WHY IS THE KID "BEHAVING BADLY"?

It's always useful to know why a child is "behaving badly." Reasons (and their solutions) can include the following.

★ **They're starting to get sick.** But they don't have the understanding to know what they're feeling or the words to explain. Check for an ear infection, fever, or other common causes of "bad behavior" that really mean they're not well.

BOUNDARIES FOR KIDS: SOME IDEAS

✱ We must be kind and gentle with people and animals.

✱ Kids must be in bed at bedtime (with perhaps half an hour to read or play in bed).

✱ We don't scream in this house.

✱ We use our words to fix a problem, not hitting or pushing.

✱ If we do the wrong thing or make a mistake, we say sorry.

✱ Parents are the bosses, but they let you choose some things.

✱ We need to say please and thank you.

✱ We need to say hello to people when we meet or they visit.

✱ We don't throw balls in the house.

✱ We don't throw our food or say it's yucky.

✱ We have to try a new food, but if we don't like it we don't have to eat it.

✱ When we get a drink or a piece of fruit, we ask if anyone else would like some.

✱ Kids don't go on the road without holding an adult's hand.

And

✱ Allowances will be made for a kid who is tired or otherwise having a hard time.

BOUNDARIES FOR PARENTS: SOME IDEAS

* Parents should speak to children with respect.

* Parents will decide not to hit.

* Parents need to say please and thank you.

* Parents will be consistent with rules and not confuse kids by varying their reactions to the same bad behavior (and will explain why if they do).

* If parents do the wrong thing or make a mistake, they say sorry.

* Parents will try not to yell.

* Parents will apologize if they have a tantrum or are rude.

* Parents are allowed to go into their room for quiet time.

* Parents must arrange time away or to be on their own to balance all the time they spend with kids.

* Parents will try not to throw their food or say it's yucky.

And

* Allowances will be made for a parent who is tired or otherwise having a hard time.

★ **They're tired.** Give them more fluids, introduce a nap or an earlier or stricter bedtime.

★ **They're hungry.** Produce a snack with protein and carbohydrates rather than a sugar base.

★ **They don't know what's expected.** Give short, clear explanations or instructions.

★ **They're grumpy about something.** Try a mood changer such as a nap, a bath, or a massage, or keep in the cupboard a standby activity that always cheers them, such as balloons or bubble-blowing solution (and see also the Bad-Mood Changers section later in this chapter).

★ **The kid is having a non-specific bad mood.** Explain that people do have bad moods or not feel very cheerful sometimes, but that doesn't mean they can be rude—or put the parakeet in the toilet. Suggest a choice of activities to snap out of it.

★ **They're bored with or understimulated by the general company or routine.** They may need a change of scenery or a new activity. Perhaps get them into a playgroup or child care, or have a relative or friend babysit for a while.

★ **They're testing the boundaries.** Be consistent with the rules and the consequences of breaking them.

★ **They want a show.** It's kind of interesting when Mom goes off like a firecracker. Stay calm, be consistent.

★ **They can't grasp the consequences of their actions.** Explain cause and effect—don't expect them to work this out by themselves or to necessarily remember after the first time.

★ **They don't seem to feel compassion or empathy.** This doesn't come naturally to all kids: explain that certain things will hurt feelings or cause pain to other kids, adults, babies, or animals. Don't try to explain too hard that a dolly doesn't feel hurt but a baby will—try to get the child to be kind to the dolly too because they can't really understand the difference. Kindness, like patience, is mainly taught by example.

★ **They don't know how else to react to a situation.** Explain how you can say "Oh, bother," like Pooh bear, or try again; that it doesn't matter if the tower falls down—you can build another one.

★ **Past annoying behavior has been rewarded.** A child without much language who can bang rudely on the door and shout "DOOR!!!!" and have it opened has worked out the magic formula. It's better for them to learn that the door isn't opened until a polite request is received at a lower decibel. Of course, you have to know they're capable of this. When babies are very little, a pat on the door and the word "Dodo!" can be met with "Yes, I'd love to open the door for you!" because you're interpreting their efforts to communicate.

★ **They want everything to go their way.** Acknowledge this and say you wish everyone could do whatever they wanted, but it doesn't always work like that. Don't be sucked into endless explanations of why not!

★ **Their usual routine has been disrupted.** Try to do something that gets you both back into at least one of your routines or a comfort zone.

★ **They know that a threat isn't always carried through.** Don't use threats you can't, won't, or shouldn't make good on.

★ **There is an underlying problem.** A trauma, a problem causing stress in the home or a worry, possibly even an overheard one, is causing your child to change their behavior. Deal with the family stress, getting professional help if needed: start with your GP.

★ **The explanations, concepts, and expectations you're giving are not age appropriate.** Find out what your kid is capable of at different ages. Try to think about a subject from their point of view. If they look confused they are confused. Answer questions about why a certain behavior isn't right and explain what's expected as well as what isn't acceptable.

★ **Things escalate too quickly.** The kid seems to go off like a rocket. Have you been accidentally setting an example of freaking out at the smallest things and making molehills into mountains and mountains into volcanoes? Do you say "OH, MY GOD!" at the slightest thing? Wind it back and watch the kid do the same.

★ **They ignore nagging.** Reminding your kid seventy-eight times a day to say thank you isn't as effective as holding onto a requested object until thank you is said, even if you have to remind them of the words.

- ★ **The kid is desperate for attention.** Even negative attention will show that you're interested in them. Give them lots of attention when they're not naughty.
- ★ **There's a vicious circle.** Everyone's tired and angry with each other. Your child feels humiliated or furious, you feel guilty or disappointed for hitting or shouting. Remind yourself that every new day is a fresh start as a parent and every hour can be too.
- ★ **You're both in a rut of reacting to each other in negative ways.** Try a mood breaker. You might even say "Okay, let's pretend to get up and start again. We'll even pretend to have breakfast." Kids over, say, 2 and a half sometimes love that sort of make-believe. Never tell yourself you've painted yourself into a corner so you have to keep hitting, shouting, or accepting bad behavior. Even old dogs can learn new tricks—they just need a ripper of an incentive. And having a calm relationship with your kid is a great incentive.
- ★ **The kid keeps forgetting the rules.** Write a list of the simple rules and routines such as bath, dinner, teeth cleaning, bedtime. This can be made into a chart with illustrations so the kid—even a non-reader—will get to know what's expected. Put the list down low on the fridge or noticeboard and perhaps award stickers or stars for completed tasks. Sometimes, even if your child won't take your word for it, they'll "listen to the chart," especially if they took part in compiling and decorating it.

You need fresh ideas

Sometimes the kid is "behaving badly" because you're caught in a generational vicious circle. You find yourself saying the things your parents said, which you hated, and hitting your children because that's what your parents did. It's the last thing you ever wanted, but it seems to be your instinct when you're stressed or angry—and who isn't, at least sometimes?

See More Info at the end of this chapter for help with learning new strategies to avoid repeating upsetting and useless patterns.

trying for patience, kindness, and consistency

It's not just crying babies who can make parents feel rage. Toddlers and preschoolers can be maddeningly rude, shouty, or difficult. But teaching kids how to behave requires patience, kindness, and consistency. And sometimes they're in short supply (I myself had a tantrum only this morning)—which is why the following always help.

★ Have a consistent, agreed-on set of rules that all parents and caregivers (including grandparents) know and follow: for example, the only TV allowed is between 3:30 and 4:30 p.m.; one candy each a day and it's before 5 p.m. If this isn't possible, make sure that older kids (getting on for 5 or more) at least understand there are different rules at Grandma's from at home, and behavior tolerated there won't be indulged at home.

★ Have a consistent approach to bad behavior. (One parent should not be the lone "disciplinarian" if there are two parents available).

★ Get as much help as you can.

★ Get away and do other things as much as you can to fortify yourself.

★ If you find your anger and resentment rising, give yourself time out. Put the kids in front of a video, go to another room and lie there, scream into a pillow, do relaxation techniques, read a chapter of a book—anything to get your frustration level down and reduce your fly-off-the-handleability. (It is so a word, shut up.)

★ Imagine your kid was your best friend and behaved the same way: your first reaction would not be to shout or say something rude.

★ Imagine you're in public or actually go somewhere public to react.

★ Take every opportunity to rest and enjoy your own pursuits—a happier person is usually a kinder, more patient person.

PARENTS WHO DON'T WANT TO HIT

I think not hitting a child is a fundamental break we can make with the past. It isn't about fashion, it's about progress and finding new ways. Kids used to bounce around in a car without seatbelts a generation ago and most of them survived: it doesn't mean kids without seatbelts is a good idea. I know people say "I got hit as a kid and I'm fine"—in fact I heard a homeless drunk say it in the playground park over the road just the other week—but I think it's a statement that needs further looking into. And anyone who has hit their children can learn new ways of dealing with their anger.

There are lots of people who were hit who wish they weren't; there are lots of people who know right from wrong who were never hit; and there are lots of people who were hit who can't tell you what the hitting taught them that another method couldn't have. Lots of us broke our arms when we were little or got badly sunburned. We're over it now, but it might have been better if it hadn't happened.

Arguments against hitting include:

★ it doesn't alter many kids' behavior—instead it teaches them that if someone is bigger, stronger, or believes they are right, hitting is okay.

★ it often results in them hitting other children, siblings, and animals when frustrated.

★ it punishes rather than teaches.

429

★ it makes kids wary of any of their own actions and words in case they're wrong or frowned upon and will result in physical pain.

★ it can escalate to abuse.

★ it might have long-term effects because children are vulnerable to being emotionally and physically damaged.

Many parents feel that hitting didn't fix the behavioral problem. Many parents recognize they hit not because the child was naughtier than usual but because the parent was at the end of their tether. Determined not to repeat their own past, they promise not to hit any more and then later find themselves doing it again, causing terrible feelings of guilt on their part and betrayal on the part of the child.

It seems to me that the urge to hit is very hard to break—firstly because it's a natural reaction we are born with to try to protect ourselves or get what we want (but we need to learn more sophisticated ways of behaving as we grow up otherwise we'd all be in the slammer), and secondly because most parents in the generations before us thought nothing of spanking and smacking their children or threatening to, just as they also thought nothing of kids being driven around without seatbelts. It's easy to say "I don't want to hit," but it takes some effort to learn new coping skills and new ways of disciplining.

It's only recently that alternatives to smacking have become widely known. I know some parents say they have found a quick, smart swat to the bottom has stopped their children behaving badly. And sometimes that's the important thing at that moment. But even if your child is doing something very dangerous, say, sticking a fork in an electrical outlet, it may be better to knock them out of the way or, if you have time, grab them quickly and remove them from harm's way rather than punish them. Perhaps the best outcome is to make the outlet safe with a snap-over cover, keep the forks out of reach, and explain why it's dangerous as soon as the child can understand.

The worst thing about smacking (apart from the fact it's a large person deliberately hurting a small one) is that at best it teaches the child "Don't do that because you will get a smack that hurts, shocks, or humiliates you." Instead kids can learn to stop doing something because "it hurts someone's feelings so they feel sad and don't want to play with you," "it's dangerous and could hurt you," "it makes a mess that you'll need to clean up," "it will break your toy and you won't be able to play with it any more," or "it will kill the plants and then the flowers won't grow." In this way kids learn more, eventually make more connections and develop a deeper understanding of what might be wrong, hurtful, or dangerous, and why.

Some parents say their hitting has no effect on behavior or causes hysteria, shame on both sides, and great guilt for the parent, who didn't want things to go this far. One depressing comment from a mom in the Kidwrangling Survey was "I hit him up to twelve times a day and it doesn't make any difference. I'm sure he'll catch on soon." Another wrote "Sometimes you feel like a broken record and you feel like you're smacking them all day but they will eventually learn." If it isn't working, you need to try something else. This chapter is for any parent who needs help with discipline that isn't working or who wants to find alternatives to smacking.

So many of the people who responded to the Kidwrangling Survey said they didn't like smacking—most often a slap on the hand or a swat to the bottom—but they still did it. One letter that made me sad said it had to "sting." Some of these parents said that a smack was effective; most did not. That's why I've put a lot of suggestions for alternatives to smacking in this chapter: not because people who smack are terrible (I'm sure the vast majority of parents have smacked at least once), but because so many parents want not to smack any more.

I think it's much harder to always be calm and consistent if you're a sole or single parent and don't have help in disciplining; if your partner wants to hit and you don't (or vice versa); or if you've got yourself into a rut where you keep "disciplining" but the kid's behavior isn't changing. You may need more support and babysitting help to let you have a break; couple counseling to work out a united front with the kid; or to start afresh with some new rules and methods you can be consistent with. (See More Info at the end of this chapter and Relationships in Extra Resources at the end of the book.)

It is illegal in some countries to hit a child with an object such as a kitchen implement or anything else. This is because objects can cause worse injuries than a hand, and some objects are heavy or dangerous. It is pretty much universally agreed that hitting a child repeatedly, hitting a child with a closed fist, "belting," or beating a child, or hitting a child on the face or genitals is child abuse. Others consider any striking, including slapping and spanking, to be abuse.

If you are at the end of your tether and feel you might hurt your child, see the family crisis contacts in More Info at the end of this chapter or call one of the parent helplines listed in More Info in Your Support Team, the second chapter of *Part 1: Babies*.

Smacking and religion

Although this will come as a surprise to many fundamentalist Christians, the phrase "Spare the rod and spoil the child" (in other words, if you don't use an instrument to hit your child, they will be spoiled) is not in the Bible and never has been. Most of the biblical approval for hitting children comes in Proverbs: Prov. 22:15, "Foolishness is bound in the heart of a child; but the rod of correction shall drive it far from him"; Prov. 23:13, "Withhold not correction from the child: for if thou beatest him with the rod, he shall not die"; Prov. 23:14, "Thou shalt beat him with the rod, and shalt deliver his soul from hell." (Incidentally the Bible also says it is okay to sell a daughter into slavery under certain circumstances, but this is illegal in most states.)

The majority of Christians of course do not interpret the biblical invocations as being about physical punishment, but rather about non-violent discipline.

"I always like to remind parents that the shepherds used the rod, for the most part, to guide their sheep, not whack them over the head."
DR. KEVIN LEMAN, CHRISTIAN WEBSITE SPANKING ADVISER

"I believe in the Christian principle—spare the rod and spoil the child." A MOM

SWeaRiNg

One of the problems with punishment is that a child doesn't always know the behavior is considered wrong. They learn so much by copying that if they see someone (it may not even be their parent) hurt their finger and say "Shit," they think that when you hurt yourself you're supposed to say "Shit." Kids usually don't start this stuff until they're 3 or 4 and expanding their vocabularies quickly. It's good that they're a bit older when they start repeating words because they can also understand a chat about "naughty words" or "swearwords." I reckon "dirty" and "potty mouth" are phrases best left out of it. Kids need to know that dirty just means getting dirt on themselves and not to confuse their own poop, or going to the toilet, with something wrong or naughty.

★ Don't swear yourself. (Damn hard, I know.)

★ Understand that kids don't know why words are "wrong," and before 5 is too young to explain great hulking swathes of sex and religion to them.

★ Explain that some people are offended by some words and that's why we don't use them. (We can talk about baby Jesus, but not say "Jesus" if we're cross because it hurts some people's feelings.)

★ Get a range of acceptable alternatives and practice them. Try something that amuses you—perhaps "lordy pants," "crikey," or "my giddy aunt."

★ If a kid has worked out that a word is shocking and repeats it for effect, get everyone to ignore it and pay attention to better behavior.

Washing their mouth out with soap is not a successful way to stop a child swearing: it makes a huge deal out of swearing, it can be dangerous to your child's health, and it's unfair when the child learns a new swearword and tries it out, not knowing it's a "bad" word. Think of all the new words they learn all the time. I mean, it's not as if you can hand them a list of words they're not allowed to say and ask them to memorize it.

WHiNiNG

Not really naughtiness or defiance, whining is a case of a kid thinking it's the best way to get what they want or to express many emotions. Some parents do anything to give the kid what they want because the whining tone is more irritating than an ad for a appliance store owned by someone whose first name is Crazy.

The consensus on this one is you should ignore whining tones and that sort of carry-on and explain that you will respond to a question asked in a "nice voice" or a "normal voice." This way a whining tone is never rewarded so it doesn't become the lever of choice. (Same thing goes for tantrums.) You'll have to follow up by really listening to the non-whiny. Kids may have to also be told that "pleeeeeeeeaaaase" does not work, and that asking sixty-seven times won't either. You must stick to this or you will be doomed to Endless Whining Hell. Distraction is often the answer to whining so think about learning to tap dance.

taNtRums

Tantrums, or hissy fits, can start before 2, last well past 3 years old and get worse in phases (especially with actors): tantrums are mainly a toddler's reaction to not getting their own way and part of their natural development towards independence. Having a tantrum is basically an immature reaction to a problem, which many adults themselves haven't yet grown out of. It's the best way a kid knows to express themselves about this thing that makes them feel so cross: you need to help them learn other means.

★ Tantrums should be ignored whenever possible.

★ A tantrum thrower who gets what they want learns that tantrums work.

★ Reward the non-tantrum thrower and behavior.

★ Try to avoid tantrum recipes: tired kid, bright supermarket with lots of temptations, having to get in the car and be somewhere IMMEDIATELY, a toddler not being given any choices at all—that sort of thing.

★ To ignore a tantie you may need some strategies: walk away; count to ten; do a meditation exercise; sing your favorite song to yourself, even if it's got a funny phrase in it such as "Climb Every Mountain!"; pop into the backyard for a moment. Use the Time Out technique described in the next section.

★ The post-tantrum thrower may be in need of a cuddle because they've freaked themselves out.

★ If the tantrum whips you into a frenzy or fury, try to remove yourself for 5 minutes, otherwise you'll end up losing control and smacking, or behaving in a very tantrum-like way yourself, which doesn't get across the message that tantrums are not acceptable.

> *"There are few actors who like seeing the audience walk out mid-performance and even the most thick-skinned toddler will tend to get the message."* CHRISTOPHER GREEN, *TODDLER TAMING*

time out

Different kid experts have different versions of Time Out. Parents who use Time Out differ about whether it is a cooling-off period or a punishment, but it's universally agreed by experts that it isn't meant to be used as a punishment. Unfortunately, the approach has been passed on by word of mouth among parents and morphed so that in some homes it has become a punishment along the lines of "Go into the boring laundry room for 5 minutes."

Time Out was devised as a way to quickly and decisively show a kid that their behavior isn't acceptable and won't be rewarded; to give the kid time to reflect on what they did and what the result was; and to give the parents time to cool off. One thing that helps reinforce this with kids who've hurt another child is that the other child gets lots of attention while they have Time Out. That wasn't what they wanted to happen at all!

A version of Time Out
The following version of Time Out is a cool-down period for everyone, not a punishment.

1 The kid does something totally defiant or unacceptable that they know is defiant or unacceptable. (That is, you don't give Time Out to a kid who accidentally spilled a drink. You give it to the kid who, after you say "If you keep your eyes looking at the milk, you can be careful not to spill it," looks you straight in the eye and deliberately pours their milk on the carpet or throws a screamy, kicking tantrum.)

2 The kid is told that their behavior is not acceptable, in a firm, not shouting way, and that it's now Time Out for them because of this behavior: "Go into your room for Time Out, please, and come back when you're ready to say sorry and behave properly again." The caregiver needs to be calm and very boring—and not turn on a fascinating display of their own.

3 The kid is escorted, herded, or carried firmly if necessary, or stalks off to the bedroom. (Some parents use the laundry room because they think it's more of a punishment since there are no toys there—but kids are so socialized they know that going to their room on their own is not a reward.) Quietly playing with toys is fine.

4 The length of Time Out is always kept pretty short. Suggestions vary, but include 30 seconds for kids less than 2 years old, with 1 minute per year of age after that; or until they are ready to say they're sorry or they'll be "better behaved."

5 Some moms cleverly say that after Time Out there needs to be a different activity from the one that caused the problem.

6 Sometimes Time Out needs to be followed shortly afterwards by a nap because tiredness is the actual cause of the behavior.

Popular Time Out locations:
- ★ the child's bedroom.
- ★ the (safety-overhauled) laundry room.
- ★ a special seat in the living room.
- ★ on the stairs (safely).
- ★ the back porch (in good weather).

Discipline ideas with a Hidden Downside

Although they may "work" to stop a child's behavior and so may seem successful to parents as methods of discipline, the following approaches can have more psychological impact than we realize.

It's very important not to crush the spirit of a child by making them feel they are a bad or terribly disappointing person. Humiliation can lead to real depression and sadness in a child. Make sure you get across that it's the behavior you want changed, not the person. It's better to say "My feelings were hurt when you said that. Let's think of a nicer thing you could say" than "I'm so disappointed in you. Get out of my sight."

Coldness or indifference in a parent is a much harsher punishment to a child than an adult may think. An icy stare or similar cold-shoulder treatments can create inner panic and fear and an unspoken, desolate sadness because they feel that they are not loved.

Saying "You're very, very bad" can make a child feel crushed and can have lasting effects on their self-esteem and confidence. Use something like "Let's try that again in a different way." If you separate being disappointed in them as a person from being disappointed in their behavior, they know that changing the behavior is a plus. But if you say you're disappointed in them as a person, all they can do is feel inadequate.

Shutting yourself in the bathroom or locking the kid outside the house can create a sense of panic in a child, especially if they have a temperament that makes this punishment very frightening.

ways to encourage and reward good behavior

"Yes"
Try to give kids lots of things to choose from and say yes as much as you can instead of saying no all the time. Put a positive spin on

things: say "Hey, come over here and splash in the sink with this squirty thing" instead of "Stop putting lipstick on the cat."

"Sorry"

I think that everyone in the family should be able to say a sincere sorry and have it accepted—but not if it's a stalling tactic before they do the same thing again, or a spat-out or shouted "SORRY!" in very unsorry tones. Parents as well as kids should be able to be genuinely sorry and say so. This helps kids to understand the concept of pain to others, and hurt feelings, and gives them one way of helping make the situation better. If apologies are just as sincerely accepted, this should cut down on grudges, sulking, seething, and revenge strikes.

Praise

Say:

- ★ "I'm so proud of you for saying/doing that."
- ★ "That was fantastic!"
- ★ "You tried so hard, it was wonderful."
- ★ "I love it when you do that."
- ★ "You are so good at that."
- ★ "You have lovely manners."
- ★ "What a great boy/girl."
- ★ "I really like doing this with you."
- ★ "Those colors are fabulous."
- ★ "What a splendid job."
- ★ "Daddy/Mommy/Grandma will be so happy to know you did that. Shall we tell them right away?"
- ★ "Good on you."

Body language—encouraging nods and smiles, eye contact, thumbs up, applause, handshakes— or stickers on a chart or on the hand can be good non-verbal things to add to what you've said.

SOLIDARITY

If you see a kid throwing a tantrum in a public place and their parent ignoring them, ignore them too and smile in a conspiratorial way with the parent before you move off without comment. Don't assume the adult is a terrible parent. You might be in the same supermarket aisle in their situation next week.

"Go easy on yourself. Everyone yells sometimes, everyone gets tired, and not everyone can react calmly when their child shows them how well peanut butter toast fits in the CD player." LATEEFAH

"When attempting to get numerous children, parcels, and the dreaded car keys in the bag, I tell my boys to stand with two hands on the car. If both hands are on the car, there's only so far they can step away from it. Also there is the psychological reward of looking at your kids lined up like gangsters." DIANNE

"I scream and shout and rant and rave and nobody listens. But when I'm calm, I get down to their little height and get them to look at me by speaking softly and telling them that 'You really scared Mommy when you opened the front door and ran up the road following the bottle truck.' My 4-year-old son listened to me and hasn't done it again." SOPHIE

"When it's 5 in the morning and you haven't tasted your coffee yet and your 3-year-old is having a tantrum because you cut the toast the way he liked it yesterday, it's difficult to be consistent in your discipline. I aim not to yell too much, provide consequences of actions, and just get through the day!" SARAH

"If my kids are alive at the end of the day, I've done my job."
COMEDIAN ROSEANNE BARR

"What works for one child will not necessarily work for another. Consistency, fairness, continuity, and perseverance. My son is no angel and even angels wear you down in the end . . . Treat them how you would expect to be treated yourself. Don't back down, once you've made a decision stick to it or they've got you pegged." KIRSTEIN

"Always praise when they're good." DEBBY

"Boring, long-winded lectures." PAMELA

"[When they're well behaved] they get a star sticker on a chart on the fridge. When they've collected a predetermined number of stars, a special treat is allowed: a sweet, a date with Mom or Dad, an extra bedtime story—this really works wonders. We have four children trying to earn as many stars as possible." TIFFANY

"We have two rules for our 19-month-old son. Don't touch the electrical outlets and don't touch the trash." HEI

"No performance will go on without an audience . . . [And] if they have hurt another child, they should help hold the washcloth or ice pack to understand the consequences. Yelling makes them yell back." WENDY

"She sits in the hallway with her back to the living room for 30 seconds—then my good girl returns. She would go hysterical if I closed the door of her room on her so this works well for both of us." JOANNE

"Give a clear choice: stop hitting your brother with the [toy] hammer or we will have to put it away." MARY

"Missing out on TV works every time. There is a no-hitting rule in our home." JENNY

"Time out and bribery!" RUTH

"Mostly discipline is what you do to encourage good behavior."
WILLIAM AND MARTHA SEARS, *THE DISCIPLINE BOOK*

"Removal of the object they are fighting over is always useful."
KAREN

"We always explain why we do things: he might not understand it yet, though. I think it's really important to discipline the behavior, not the child, if that makes sense. Let them know it's the behavior you find unacceptable, not the child." VANESSA

"If any of my boys threw a tantrum, it was often when we were in a shop and they wanted something and I said no. My advice is to walk away and pretend they aren't yours." DALE

"My husband barks orders and commands, which are promptly ignored." CUELBRA

"There's nothing worse than arguing with a 2-year-old when you're 30." HELEN

"As he got more logical he was entitled to tell us in the mornings he was a bit grumpy and then we would not expect too much of him."
SUSAN

"We have two Time Outs—one for them to go to their room and come out when they're ready to apologize; the other Time Out is when I'm so angry with them I need time to cool down: they are told to stay in their room until Mommy comes to talk to them. I've used changing rooms, baby rooms, even an elevator for Time Out—we rode up and down until my 3-year-old had screamed herself hoarse."
MAREE

"Do not argue with a child. A 4-year-old wants ten pieces of cake, but you know one piece is enough, so one piece it is."
TRISHA

"The happy chair. When a child does the wrong thing we give a warning; if it happens again we ask them in a calm voice to go and sit in the happy chair and think about their actions. We use a stove timer: 2 minutes for the 2-year-old, 10 minutes for the 8-year-old. After that we usually get a cuddle and a 'sorry.' Sometimes the children will take themselves there. When we're out, any chair can become the happy chair." GAYE

"Between her and the dog I say 'no' a lot: so my daughter knows not to dig up the garden and the dog knows not to throw food." NICKY

"I do as he demands." GREER

"I do explain how I expect something to be done, and that they need to listen carefully and maintain eye contact. I make sure kids know the rules and can repeat them back to me. Usually there's a warning and then there's thinking time in a corner, the laundry room, or near a wall. It's not punishment, but time to think about what they've done, how they can do it next time, or what not to do, and to apologize if necessary. It's very important to explain it's about what the child has done, not them personally, but the behavior we are fixing. I don't like using words like 'naughty'." CATHY

"It's important to distinguish between 'I want my own way' tantrums (which can be ignored) and more general meltdowns where everything gets on top of them and it spirals out of their control. With a meltdown there's usually an underlying problem like hunger, tiredness, boredom, or anxiety, and I just HAVE to stop whatever I'm doing to deal with that. The trick is to address the problem without rewarding the behaviour." KATE

Bad-mood Changers

These ideas have been suggested by parents who responded to the Kidwrangling Survey—they're worth a try for a kid who's woken up on the wrong side of the bed (or crib), to avert a tantrum, or to stop a bad situation getting worse:

* ★ a bath—even a kid reluctant at first usually winds down with toys, splashes, and homemade squirters in the bath (although some kids hate baths, in which case skip it).
* ★ safe water play of any sort—splash in the sink or bath and on hot days let them play with the hose.
* ★ food—often kids who are grumpy haven't had enough carbohydrates (try rice with veggie bits, mashed taters, even a sandwich, but not sugar).
* ★ water—a dehydrated child is a tired child.
* ★ magic glitter gel—glitter mixed in moisturizer to wipe on themselves.
* ★ take them outside—even bundled up and waterproofed.
* ★ a favorite video or book.
* ★ special toys put away for just this purpose.
* ★ a favorite music CD.
* ★ be funny or ask silly questions (underpants on head, shoes on ears, "Shall I eat this chair?").
* ★ create some favorite pictures and sounds to run on the computer.
* ★ have a cuddle and talk about what may be wrong.
* ★ promise a special made-up story at bedtime—and make sure you deliver.
* ★ sit or lie down for a quiet time, with or without a cuddle.
* ★ go out and look for birds, butterflies, orange cars.
* ★ a roll-around wrestle.
* ★ allow the kid to let off steam by going into the backyard or the park to yell and run around in a circle or all the way to the swings.

★ a weird rendition of a favorite song such as "Twinkle, Twinkle Little Star" sung opera-style.

★ "Appeal to their sympathies . . . once out at the mall I grabbed them and dashed for the public toilets. I was about to have an accident and they had to be quick! They forgot all about what they were making a fuss about because they had to save Mom from eternal public embarrassment!"

★ play with their dog.

★ feed the ducks.

★ hold them close and sing.

★ put on some music, pick up your kid, and dance.

★ a massage.

★ water the garden and pull out the weeds Mom points to.

★ allow them to rip something into pieces (give them the newspaper)—older babies and young toddlers love this.

★ dress-ups—even the parents.

★ housework—the kid feels needed, useful, and accomplished. Give them a feather duster, a sponge, or a dustpan and brush, or let them splash around in the sink "washing the dishes" (supply a towel for mopping up).

★ go to see what's happening at the neighbors' or the stores.

★ pretend to go to sleep on the floor.

★ ask what you can do to make them happy.

★ put most toys away and rotate them—too many are overwhelming. The new ones can appear, not as a reward for a tantrum, but when you sense boredom that could end up as a tantrum.

★ respect their mood—you're not nice all the time so why should they be?

★ see if they want to play on their own for a while, knowing that you're close by if they need you—you may have been "in their face" too much.

★ bring out the playdough.

★ grab the maracas and sing "I Go to Rio."

★ carry handbag-sized pencils, pads, and other activities and games to head off trouble when you're out.

★ a surprise chocolate frog.

★ sing a song with actions together ("Ipsy-wipsy Spider," "This Is the Way We Wash Our Hands on a Cold and Frosty Morning")—there's so much to concentrate on they'll forget the grumbles.

★ cook something easy together such as muffins.

★ a swing.

★ suggest they play quietly in their room until they're in a better mood—not as a punishment, but as a way for them to have a play and eventually decide to snap out of it.

★ talk to Grandad on the phone.

★ a tickle (although if a child is tired this could make them demented—always respect the rule that you stop tickling when a child asks you to).

★ water pistols in the bath.

★ separate two kids if they are fighting and give them different activities for a while.

★ talk in funny voices and accents, walk like a pompous person, or look frightened, as in exaggerated charades—kids are fascinated by emotions and body language because they're trying to learn them all the time.

★ go for a drive and talk about what you can see.

★ hide under the laundry in the laundry basket.

★ make a fort with blankets and chairs and throw in a cushion and a favorite toy.

★ make the Cookie of Joy or award the Magical Sticker of Smiley Boys—use your imagination.

★ check if they might be in a bad mood because you are—if you are, think what would make you feel better and suggest it (sex with a stranger in Trinidad is probably best left off the agenda at this point).

★ swap roles—you be the kid and they the parent—and see what words they give you and how they behave as you (it's a real insight).

★ make a puppet out of a toy and have it chat away with your child—kids over 2 and a half will happily chat to a toy with a silly voice even if you're sitting right next to it with your lips moving and your hand up its backside.

★ a cold shower if it's hot out.

★ make faces.

★ blow bubbles (for all ages—babies, toddlers, and preschoolers).

★ talk to them about how different emotions make us feel and what we can do about them—how everyone is sometimes mad, cross, confused, tired—and draw faces with your child of the different feelings. (Here's a tip: most of the time you only have to change the eyebrows!)

> *"My husband is really good at breaking a tantrum. He goes into the room and without looking at the child, starts to play with a toy. Eventually the child starts to watch and register that they're not receiving any attention, and slowly they start to join in. My husband never mentions the tantrum and just keeps playing. Things go back to normal and we can all move on."* TRISH

maNNeRS

Some people don't bother teaching their children manners, but that's a short cut to having a child who is disliked. There's a difference between using the right words—please, thank you, thanks for having me, and hello—and common courtesy, which means learning to wait your turn to speak, not pushing people out of the way to get where you want to go, and consideration for others.

Common courtesy is mainly taught by example and creates an environment in which everyone in the family says stuff such as 'Would you mind if I borrowed your glitter glue?," "Would anyone else like a guava mocktail while I'm in the kitchen?" and "Sorry, I didn't mean to whack you with a piece of lettuce." Children will learn that courtesy is a part of life (at least in your house—they may get a rude shock elsewhere).

It's obvious that a lot of parents don't think manners are important. I wish children could see that. At the very least, knowing how to use manners is a huge social advantage and an excellent manipulation tool—much better than whining. People adore a child with good manners and will give them lots of attention and unsolicited presents in shops and elsewhere just because they're so thrilled to meet one. A child will have an easier time of it if they learn that "lovely manners" will get them further in life than being a surly grasper (unless they go into business or politics).

Don't make a big fuss of bad manners, but reward the good.

The pleases and thank-yous are pretty much a matter of automatic speech—children usually learn to say them before they really understand that they are forms of politeness. The quickest way to reinforce these is not to hand over the goods until please has been said. The common, grating parental prompts include "What's the magic word?," "What do you say?" and "I can't hear you." Swore I'd never say them. Say them all. Hopeless.

Kids learning to actually share is a different matter and needs to be reinforced with talk of people "each having a turn": kids see that as fairer than the concept of "sharing"—both claiming ownership at the one time. Talk to your child about who owns what so they understand that they don't own everything in the world. (You don't need a full-scale explanation of the global economy, just a notion of your blocks, Mom's shoes, Aunt Sarah's car, Caitlin's hairclips.) Help your child understand that their toys will always come back to them: after all, you wouldn't let just anyone walk off with your TV. If there are some very special toys they don't want to share, agree to put them out of bounds to guests, and hidden away during visits.

General manners
General manners include:

- ★ saying please and thank you.
- ★ saying hello when introduced to someone or seeing an acquaintance and goodbye when leaving them (shy kids shouldn't be forced to do anything else in the way of conversation).
- ★ acknowledging guests but staying seated— young children shouldn't have to stand when adults enter the room because it is outdated, control freaky, apt to be misunderstood, and impossible for them to remember at an early age (also it goes against common sense as it's likely to result in drink or paint spills that are really not the kid's fault).

★ being kind and courteous to people and animals.

★ not teasing.

★ good sporting behavior—watch some sport together and explain who's doing the wrong thing (tantie-throwing or thuggish hockey players) and who's doing the right thing (players congratulating each other: hmm, you may have to demonstrate this yourself).

★ no screaming, especially in public places (that shrieky squeal of excitement can be misinterpreted by strangers as distress and is anyway very annoying and disruptive to others).

Interruptions

To avoid interruptions during conversations, on the phone or otherwise, try the following.

★ Give your kid something to do while you're talking.

★ If it's not a business call give them a turn, having asked the caller if they'd mind—this should not be longer than one quick exchange per call or it's too tedious for the caller unless they know them really well.

★ Tell your kid how long you need to be on the phone. For older toddlers set a timer for 5 minutes and for preschoolers 10 or 15 if it's an important call, and make sure you finish when you said you would. Give lots of rewarding praise for their long wait.

★ Put on a video if you simply have to talk for half an hour in a work snafu or family crisis.

★ Remember time is a lot slower for kids than adults—"in a minute" means something different to them.

★ Reward them for waiting their turn with a thank-you, great praise, a sticker, or a big cuddle.

Always assume your child can hear and understand your conversation even if they seem absorbed in something else.

Table manners

Children can grow up at home without learning any table manners because their family doesn't eat together at a table or has a lot of take-out, eaten with the fingers or just a spoon. As kids get older—between 3 and 5—they become good at feeding themselves and can start to learn a few table manners. Here are some basics.

★ Teach your kid how to set the table.

★ Take them to a café or restaurant and talk about how the table is set or where we place the cutlery.

★ Tell them that napkins—you can refer to these hilariously as adult lap bibs—go on the lap.

★ Let them practice putting forks on the left, knives and spoons on the right.

★ Show your kid how to use a knife and fork together (or chopsticks).

★ Explain how it's considered good manners to eat with the mouth closed; not to make loud chewing noises; not to spit food out; not to put too much in the mouth at one time; and that smearing banana on the waiter's hair is not okay (especially if the waiter is you).

★ Show your child how to put their knife and fork together on the plate as a sign that they are finished, and remind them to ask to be excused from the table.

★ Kids who can manage it should proudly be responsible for taking their own plates to the counter near the sink.

moRe iNfo

IF YOU FEEL OUT OF CONTROL

Childhelp USA

Childhelp USA has a hotline to help you deal with your child's behavioral problems and cope when you feel you are losing control. Counselors are available 24 hours a day and all calls are anonymous. On their website, you can find links to counseling and other programs and services.

1-800-4-A-CHILD

www.childhelpusa.org

HELP WITH LEARNING NEW STRATEGIES: THE TRIPLE P APPROACH

Positive Parenting Program (Triple P)

The PPP website will give you all the basics and lists all the available books, videos, classes, and training courses. To mail order their stuff by email, see the address above. To find out about classes, call the Head Office number given below.

Head Office 803-787-9944

email triplep@bellsouth.net

www.triplep-america.com

Every Parent: A Positive Approach to Children's Behavior

by Matthew Sanders, Addison Wesley, 1993.

This book's approach is based on programs at the Behavioral Family Intervention Program at the University of Queensland in Austrlia, now known as Triple P. Matthew Sanders is the professor of clinical psychology at the university. His book is full of extremely practical ideas to think about, such as the factors that influence a kid's behavior (among others the kid's personality, the family environment, "accidental rewards for misbehavior," good behavior going ignored, and instructions to kids being too complicated, not sufficiently detailed or not understandable for that age group). It outlines the things kids do that drive parents nuts (whining, tantrums, being a bad sport, or refusing to go to bed or eat everything).

452

The strategies for making a change have been developed from working with real families and real situations. This book covers all the common problems and takes you through clearly defined steps in response to each behavior, whether it's your child being cross about a new baby coming or throwing a tantrum in the supermarket. It provides a number of strategies such as reward charts, advice on how to set rules and have them observed, and ways for parents to teach kids how to behave better; and it sets out very clear, practical plans of action for Time Out and establishing a bedtime routine.

"Research shows that children who live in families where there is a lot of conflict and stress between the marriage partners have more emotional and behavioral problems than those raised in stable one-parent families. Serious marital problems should not be ignored. Conflict over parenting causes inconsistency, which in turn makes many behavior problems worse." PROFESSOR MATTHEW SANDERS

BOOKS ON OTHER "DISCIPLINE" APPROACHES

The Discipline Book: How to Have a Better-Behaved Child from Birth to Age Ten

by William Sears, MD, and Martha Sears, RN, Little, Brown, 1995.

A child-centered guide to creating a home where kids feel safe: for the early months this is based on the principles of attachment parenting, and later on recognizing the developmental stages of children and helping them become independent people who look to you for guidance, reassurance, and boundaries. It helps to identify the times and situations when bad behavior happens and how to avoid those "recipes." It presents many options for kids with different temperaments and varying needs, including kids with attention deficit disorder, hyperactivity, and severe timidity, but spanking is not one of them. The Sears's Time Out is a break so that the unacceptable behavior stops, the child reflects on their action, and the parent is able to calm down and avoid hitting or screaming. A lovely, useful book.

"Your discipline doesn't always have to make sense to the child. Sometimes all that is necessary is giving your child the message 'because this is what I want you to do': children expect us to be adults. That knowledge frees them to be children." WILLIAM AND MARTHA SEARS

1 2 3 Magic: Effective Discipline for Children 2–12

by Thomas Phelan, PhD, Parent Magic, 3rd ed., 2003.

While I think the strategy of saying "I'm going to count to three, and if I get to three it's Time Out for you" may work with some kids, it won't work with all of them. (Someone I know goes into a real panic, shouting "Don't count! Don't count!" because counting distracts her from thinking through the situation.) Also, although the book claims the strategy works for very young children, it seems geared to primary school kids and even teenagers. The thing I really don't like about this version of the 1-2-3 method is that Phelan says, "Think of yourself as a wild animal trainer": that is, there is no emphasis on why some behavior is unacceptable or on sitting down and explaining to kids why things need to be done a certain way. Even if a kid can't fully grasp your logic yet, they'll understand that you're being kind and patient and you respect them enough to try to help them learn. It also makes life so much more pleasant to explain something rather than just order people about. (Not that ordering people about can't be tremendously satisfying, come to think of it. I like nothing better than a good game of Shouty Rude Person, which we play at our house sometimes, with appropriate shock-horror from the person who isn't being Shouty Rude Person at the time.)

BOOKS FOR KIDS ON MANNERS

How Kind!

by Mary Murphy, Candlewick Press, 2004.

All the barnyard animals do each other favors.

Lady Lupin's Book of Etiquette
by Babette Cole, Peachtree Publishers, 2002.
This writer and illustrator, the queen of exultant cheekiness, gives her take on manners.

Miss Spider's Tea Party
by David Kirk, Scholastic, 1994.
A book about inviting people, being scared or shy, and a vision of a splendid, happy tea party with a beautifully set table.

HELPING KIDS UNDERSTAND GROWN-UP CONCEPTS

Grown-up concepts are things that need to be explained to little kids in language they understand, at a level of detail they can cope with. Usually, it's best to answer the questions they come up with simply rather than give encyclopedic lectures on subjects such as sex, death, fear, nudity, drug addiction, and why the Director of Immigration looks like a demented potato.

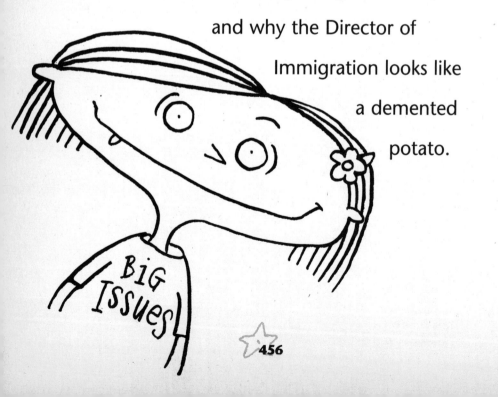

BIG Issues

Names for Bits and Bobs

Kids should be given names for things that will help them communicate with others. Words such as "poop" and "pee" are pretty universal, "tinkle" is less so, and "stepping on a frog" as a phrase meaning fart, as one kindergarten called it, is just plain nutty. The usual terms for genitals are "penis," "willie," "vagina," "bottom," and "private parts."

Bodily Functions

Sometimes we forget kids don't know what's happening to them. Unless they're really sick and uninterested, they may be reassured to know that vomiting means their body is trying to get rid of some food that had germs in it or the body is still waiting for the medicine to make their tummy better so it can do the right thing with food again; they feel hot and bothered because their body is trying to burn up the germs; they have a nasty rash but the ointment is going to go to work and start rubbing it out; or that having lots of naps is helping the body to fight the germs inside and make them strong again. You can explain simply that the body makes waste products, which we push out into the toilet and flush away.

Where Babies Come From

The arrival of a new baby sometimes prompts the question. A small child of, say, 2 and a half might be satisfied with "Mommy and Daddy made you" or "You grew in Mommy's tummy," and go off happily without any more questions for months or even years. But when the harder questions come, answer them specifically rather than explaining the whole palaver all at once. (See More Info at the end of this chapter for books that can help.)

Being in the Buff

Children under 5 don't associate themselves or others being in the nude with sex unless somebody makes that connection for them. You can tell little kids that some people don't like others being naked because they think it's rude but that it's okay at home or wherever applies to your family. (Do be prepared for the consequences of young children not knowing what's rude: yours may happily explain to a stranger all your nudey habits.)

When your child wants privacy in the bathroom or doesn't want to undress in front of others, respect this but be matter of fact about nudity and don't encourage them to feel ashamed of their body. Little kids can understand that some body parts are private. Obviously, you can't leave them in the bath on their own, and moms and dads must be allowed to inspect bottom areas for various sensible reasons. (I'm probably banging on about this too much, but some people do seem hung up on it.)

Masturbation

Some little kids, especially ones recently freed from diapers, might suddenly realize various bits of their body feel very good when they rub them. Some boys will have a stiffening of the penis on occasion. The less fuss made, the better. Masturbating children can be told that because the activity involves their private parts, it's a private activity they can do in their room. Any more elaborate "inappropriate" behavior is almost certainly the result of the child having seen something such as a tongue kiss or an adult TV show, and it's best to take a low-key approach to finding out the cause.

emotions

Kids understand different emotions and feelings from an early age. You can help them to give names to a wide range of feelings: a bit sad, really sad, full of dinner, furious, content, respected, upset in the tummy, confused, tired, worried, cross, happy, full of beans, excited, frightened, looking forward to something, missing someone, giggly. They can draw pictures of their feelings too, as expressions on faces or more abstractly.

Death

Kids at different ages and stages see death differently. They often need to talk it through and may ask the same questions over and over as they try to work it out in their heads. As with sex, keep pace with their questions and give them answers about what they're interested in rather than piling onto them everything you can think of. A counselor can recommend books suitable for your child's age (and see the books in More Info at the end of this chapter.)

The permanency of death is probably the hardest concept for children to grasp. But there are many related questions—"Did the baby die because I sometimes wanted them to go away?" "Where is Granny now?" "Will I die soon too?"—that can be discussed when the child feels ready to raise them in an environment that encourages talk, questions, and remembering the dead. Children will gradually develop their own theories and accept things in their own way, but it's very important for them to feel they can talk about death at any time. Books read together can help to prompt questions or answer them as they are raised by the child.

serious family situations

Children sometimes have to deal with their parents' separation, divorce, addiction or mental or physical illness, their own serious illness, and other difficult matters. The most important ideas to convey about unpleasant family situations or problems that are not fixable or immediately fixable are that they are not the child's fault; that some problems such as psychological ones can improve if tackled by parents and professionals together; and that the child is not alone—help is available and other kids go through these times too. Ask a bookshop for advice on specifically helpful books (and see More Info, which follows).

more info

ANSWERING KIDS' QUESTIONS

Talking with Children About Things that Matter
by Sheila Kitzinger and Celia Kitzinger, HarperCollins Publishers, 1989.
A thoughtful book on how to talk to kids about all sorts of subjects from war and the news to sexuality and morals.

Questions Children Ask and How to Answer Them
by Miriam Stoppard, DK Publishing, 1997.
Succinctly covers common topics kids need to know about but parents may find hard to discuss—separation, death, and much more.

www.fema.gov/kids
The website has articles on fires, floods, and how to talk to children about war, terrorism, uncertainty, and other traumas that may have befallen them, someone you or they know, or people elsewhere. The articles were compiled by emergency specialists and child psychologists.

BOOKS FOR KIDS ABOUT WHERE BABIES COME FROM

Mommy Laid an Egg!
by Babette Cole, Chronicle Books, 1993.

The older siblings explain to a shy mom and dad where babies really come from. For kids old enough to grasp the fundamental "facts of life." The pictures are funny, friendly cartoons, not scary diagrams. One to bring out when your child expresses interest in the nitty-gritty of how babies are made.

Let's Talk About Where Babies Come From
by Robie Harris, Walker Books, 1999.

A full-on, full-out cartoon-illustrated book that holds nothing back, from sperm, naked bodies, private parts, babies in the womb, how the baby gets food, genes, twins, and contraception. A great trigger for questions and one to keep for kids as they get older and understand more. Way too detailed, complex and advanced for toddlers and most little kids, but parents could use bits.

Where Did I Come From?
by Peter Mayle and Arthur Robbins, Citadel Trade, 2000.

The old, cartoon-filled classic you probably remember from the school library. Clear and fun.

BOOKS FOR KIDS ABOUT DEATH

I Miss You: A First Look at Death
by Pat Thomas, Barron's Educational Series, 2001.

For a child who knows somebody who has died. The book asks children to talk about their feelings and provides some possible ways to think about death. (A soul being a drop in the ocean and other concepts will be difficult for kids under 5.)

Badger's Parting Gifts
by Susan Varley, HarperTrophy, 1992.

Old Badger's time to die has come, but everyone remembers something Badger gave them, taught them, or showed them.

BOOKS FOR KIDS ABOUT SEPARATED PARENTS

Two Homes

by Claire Masurel, Candlewick Press, 2003.

A picture book about a little boy who has a room in separate houses and whose mommy and daddy still love him.

A New Room for William

by Sally Grindley and Carol Thompson, Candlewick Press, 2000.

When William moves into a new house, Mommy comes too, but Daddy has a new house of his own.

CHILD CARE AND PRESCHOOL

Only you can decide how many days of child care, if any, are okay for your kid and how much you can afford. Only you can decide whether being with your child 24 hours a day, 7 days a week, is good for you or them—or is going to turn you into a shrieking-mad harpy. Only you can decide whether your child needs or wants to be with other kids their age. Only you can decide whether partic-ular grandparents

paid less than some guy who runs H.B.O

I think I just pooed

are energetic, willing, and capable enough to provide a stimulating environment for a baby, a toddler, or a little kid all day or for several days in a row. Only you can decide who wants or needs to be at work, juggle part-time or full-time schedules, and all the rest of it.

waiting Lists

The first thing to say about child care is get from your local Child Care resource and Referral organization the details of child-care centers within reach and put your baby's name on the waiting lists NOW, even if they're 2 months old and you don't expect to want part-time care until they're 2 years old. No, I'm not kidding. Waiting lists for child-care centers can be several years long. Put your child's name down at a couple of different ones and take a good look at them when you're ready. If you move to another area, first thing you do before you sit down: put your child's name down in the new area. If their name comes up before you're ready you can always defer and stay at the head of the list.

So many parents are finding themselves without the child care or preschool they want and need because they didn't look ahead a few years. It's going that way that people thinking of having sex should probably call a child-care center first, just in case. (And while you're at it, put your name down for preschool or a kindergarten too—your local referral organization will have a list—because you won't want to miss out.)

so-called studies

Okay, I want you to prepare yourself. Train yourself now to chuck out any newspaper, turn off any radio, throw a boot at any TV examining the "child-care debate." Whatever decision you make about how to look after your child and have your child looked after, there will be people who disapprove and periodic "studies" reported that say you're turning your child into either an aggressive, attention-seeking prima donna or an antisocial throwback. Whatever kind of child care you use, you can find a study to "prove" it's making your child a more well-adjusted genius—and another that says your choice of child care is guaranteed to make your child stupid and confused for LIFE. It doesn't matter whether you have your child at home with you every day, you work full-time and have a nanny, you use part-time day care or full-time child-care center, or your parents look after the kid sometimes. It's important to realize that mothers can do no right and everything that can go wrong will be blamed on you, even if you have a husband with mutton-chop whiskers who makes all the decisions. Or some of your "decisions" didn't involve choices at all (there aren't many child-care centers in the middle of Nevada).

Of all the studies conducted by people in various countries on different kinds of child care, not one makes an assessment of what's best for an individual child: and in particular not one of them is about your child. They're usually studies of fewer than 300 kids—I've seen some reports with screaming headlines about how bad (or good) child care is based on a study in Finland of fewer than fifteen kids!

Take a front-page newspaper report not long ago (please), under the headline "Child Care Can Be Harmful: Study." Yes, the study of 212 kids from 12 different schools, by a university researcher, "found that children who are in child care for 4 to 5 days do not adjust to their first year of school as well as other children." The study says 3 days a week in child care is okay, but that kids who go to preschool (which basically is a form of child care and can add up to four or five days a week) "demonstrate higher levels of social skills and academic competence than those who don't." You may or may not be astonished to know that not a single child was spoken to as part of the survey. Their parents answered a questionnaire, and teachers rated the children on "social skills and academic competence": there were as many definitions as there were teachers asked. What a waste of time and money. *No* conclusions can be drawn from such a survey.

Ultimately, all this regular kerfuffly study releasing isn't helping us make up our minds about what's best for our own kids. That's going to take listening to our own conscience and knowing our own children and, frankly, experimenting until we get the balance right. Sit down and think and talk about what you'd like, and then see if you can make it happen. Stay flexible. The only way to work out what kind of child care is good for your kid is to work it out yourself, according to their needs, the needs of your family and what kind of good-quality child care is available, and by watching your child's progress and communicating honestly and openly with the caregivers you've thoroughly checked out. If you have access to a child-care center that is staffed by loving and cheerful, well-trained people, with a sensible ratio of staff to children, and your child is happy to go, the activities are varied and age appropriate and the other kids are mostly well adjusted and untroubled, you're already ahead of the game.

Commentators and debates

When people respond to media reports of child-care studies, there's always a flurry: talkback radio stuff, columns in the newspapers, and something on *Inside Edition*. What usually happens is that people line up according to what they've done with their own kids. The media get some moms who've stayed at home the whole time and say no child care is good, they get some moms who work full-time and say there's nothing bad about child care, and they make it look like the equivalent of a mothers' wrestling match in the ring. And the rest of the time they don't run enough stories on the quality or prohibitive expense of child care, or why men are hardly ever asked how they can work full- or part-time when their kids are little, or how decisions about child care can't be made on the basis of statistics.

Here's the big scandal of child care: governments that go on about family values and children being important don't fund child-care centers properly. There is almost always a crisis in child care because governments rarely put their money where their mouth is, private operators want to make a profit, and professional child-care workers leave their jobs because the pay is pathetic, given their responsibilities, level of training, and accomplishments—not to mention the fact that we put our children's lives in their hands.

We should stop judging and blaming parents who choose different ways from ours. I know parents who work full-time, parents who work part-time, and parents who have never worked outside the home. I know full-time at-home dads and dads who work part-time so they can spend more time with their kids. Everyone I know who is a parent who also works outside the home has taken hits to their career because they need to be available to their family, and they feel too busy, and too guilty, most or part of the time. Everyone I know who has stayed home wishes they could have their own money and misses grown-up stuff. But all of them are doing the best they can with the options they have and the choices they've made. The last thing we should be doing is fighting among ourselves.

CHiLD-CaRe OPtioNS

Child-care terms vary from state to state—for instance, in some places a preschool means a child-care center for kids aged 3 to 5, in others it means an educational program in the year before school starts or the first year of school. Costs also will vary: check with centers or government services about state-funded subsidies that are available to all families under a certain income.

Sadly people in remote or rural areas will have fewer options and may have to get a tad ingenious about kid-swapping clubs ("I'll have yours on Wednesday and you take mine on Thursday").

iNFoRMaL faMiLy aRRaNgeMeNTs

Many people use informal or formal arrangements with grandparents, either to give themselves a break here and there or so they can go to work. This can be great, but only if you have the right kind of grandparents. Looking after kids this young can also be an unfair strain on grandparents as they get older.

Some grandparents also have their own jobs or busy lives and don't offer more than an hour or two every few weeks, if anything at all. Others will have a child for an afternoon, but don't seem to have room in their life for overnight visits. Some kids go to their grandparents' house for days on end. There are grandparents who show little interest in babysitting grandchildren or few skills at all: this can change as the child gets to 4 or older and can use the toilet and becomes more engaging and conversational. Grandparents often like the idea of being grandparents, but confine seeing the kids to short visits, sending postcards, and little presents between times or turning up on birthdays or Christmas. Further complications include grandparents who have remarried someone with their own family commitments and grandparents who have short-term companions or ones you don't know well.

Sometimes grandparents want to look after the grandchildren but have forgotten how, or are unable to see important safety or nutritional points such as that a baby needs to be in a proper car restraint or a bag of candy just before going home to bed is not exactly an Einsteiny maneuver. It is impossible for some to properly stimulate the development of a toddler or preschooler for an extended time.

You'll just need to feel your way in making a decision, but a good indicator is whether a grandparent regularly offers to help and actually follows through. Another good indicator is a grandparent who seems stimulated by the encounters, rather than simply exhausted, and shows they want to really get to know their grandchildren.

Lots of people also have regular or irregular swaps with siblings—or friends—to give themselves a break. You'll need to make sure they know how to take care of *your* child.

"Home," or "family," day care

Local agencies inspect and license certain people to look after other people's kids in their own home. This can range from one morning a week to all afternoons or full-time, long-day care. Usually the caregiver can only have a maximum of, say, four kids, including their own, at any time. Children of differing ages often attend so a child is in a "family" situation, and the smaller group can suit some kids better. The care will probably be charged by the hour and is less expensive than child-care center rates. Your child will bond with one carer, although this can be a drawback if the caregiver is sick or replaced.

Child-care centers

A formal day-care center has professionally trained staff and complies with a huge range of government regulations related to everything from the kind of fencing and equipment needed to staff ratios and what to do with the poopey diapers. Local government agencies assesses the quality of each site as well as its adherence to the minimum standards set by law.

Do visit all the centers in your area. One person's popular and groovy center is another person's nightmare.

Some child-care centers are community run, others are profitable companies. Most are purpose-built or in a modified building and have large rooms, an outdoor play area, and lots of organized

GOOD POINTS ABOUT CHILD-CARE CENTERS

✱ Staff are usually dedicated beyond the call of duty and certainly their wages.

✱ Child care helps parents have a more balanced life.

✱ It helps full-time stay-at-home moms or dads have an essential break now and then, or once a week.

✱ It can allow a parent to be a better parent because they have breaks.

✱ It helps parents stay out of poverty as it allows them to take paid work.

✱ It comes closer to the sharing kind of child care in a community environment than does the isolation of one person at home with a child.

✱ Toddlers and preschoolers tend to adore the child-centered routine.

✱ Trained staff know lots of songs, games, and tricks for the right age group, and tend to have the energy to make giraffes from egg cartons.

✱ Staff can focus on the children as they don't have to perform other tasks during the day such as the washing and shopping.

✱ Kids get the opportunity to socialize with other kids of various ages—especially important in these days of smaller and one-child families.

✱ Many centers put on more staff than are required by regulations.

✱ Some centers are community run and the profits are directed back into facilities for children.

✱ Programs for optimum development have been prepared by professionals.

✱ A structured, kindly social environment can help children overcome shyness, aggression, and other social problems.

✱ Day care is a much better environment for a child than a home where they are not wanted or are resented.

✱ Good child care is good for kids.

BAD POINTS ABOUT CHILD-CARE CENTERS

✱ Long hours in a child-care center such as 8 a.m. to 6 p.m., five days a week, are generally regarded as not the best situation for a small child. A kid may, however, be better off there than in many home environments.

✱ Staff-to-children ratios are relatively good, but they can be better, and they should be standardized nationally.

✱ Good child-care workers leave because the pay is so outrageously crappy.

✱ It's a high-pressure job and some workers are better at it than others. You may not live near a center that can afford to be picky.

✱ Many centers are run for profit and governments don't put enough money into child care.

✱ A parent can come to rely on child care and get locked into a work schedule, and then it's harder for them to adjust when their child needs a break or fewer hours, or is sick or needs them.

✱ Child-care centers can have small grounds, and of course outings are problematical. A child at the same center for years, or doing very long hours, can be understimulated by the never-changing environment.

✱ Not enough men are attracted to the profession, and men who are child-care workers can be regarded with unfair suspicion ("Why would they want to do that?").

✱ The child care available to you may not match the personality and needs of your kid.

✱ Bad child care is bad for kids.

QUESTIONS TO ASK ABOUT A CHILD-CARE CENTER

Before you decide, visit the center more than once, if you like, and ask a caregiver and yourself these questions.

* What are the available hours, and which weeks are holidays?

* Who oversees the center: the local agency, a parent committee, a private for-profit company?

* Is the center affiliated with a religious group or based on a particular philosophy?

* Can I get involved in the management?

* Is the center accredited by the National Association for the Education of Young Children (NAEYC) or the National Association for Family Child Care (NAFCC) and for how many years has it been?

* May I inspect the premises? (Check that it looks clean but not weirdly clean.)

* Will my child be with kids of the same age and gender?

* Is the center's "preschool program" really an up-to-date, challenging curriculum geared to learning development, or tarted-up child care?

* Is there lots of space inside and outside?

* What's the vibe?

* Are there any kids off on their own, looking sad?

* Are the caregivers covered in cuddly kids or does the place seem a bit stand-offish?

* Are the kids outside wearing hats and sunscreen?

* What happens when a child cries?

* Do the staff speak respectfully to the children?

* Do the caregivers get down on the children's level or bring them up to theirs or do they always supervise from adult height?

* Are the kids absorbed in something and busy?

* Do the children look interested and happy?

* Do the staff seem to get on well together as adults?

* Is there a method to the madness or does it look like chaos and seat-of-the-pants stuff?

* Is it always like this? (Allow for reality—imagine if someone came to your place at a bad time.)

472

* Sit in the corner for a while, come back at different times, talk to the staff: is there a clear coordinator or director of the center, who is around to answer your queries and advise and support the staff?

* Who should I speak to if I have any worries?

* Is there someone always at the premises who has current first-aid qualifications?

* Who works or lives on site? Can I see or meet 'em all?

* What happens when a child is sick or needs emergency care?

* What do I have to bring? (Change of clothes, bottles, diapers, fruit?)

* What sort of meals do they serve? Are they cheap and nasty or is the center too obsessed about organic?

* Do the kids watch TV or videos and for how much of the day?

* Do the books, toys, and activities look interesting or like merchandising hand-me-downs?

* Is a wide range of toys available or are there strict rules such as no plastic toys and does the answer fit your philosophy?

* What activities and programs are available, and how do they encourage creativity, fun, and development?

* Can my child call me (if they're old enough) at any time?

* In the early days, if my child is overwhelmed or shy, is there a quiet-time space for them?

* What is the staff-to-child ratio in the room where my child will be?

* What discipline measures are used?

* What is the policy on bullying?

* Can I hang around a lot, when dropping off and picking up, to familiarize myself with the center and make my child feel secure?

After your child has been going to the center for a while, ask these questions:

* Is my child adjusting to being left?

* What does my child like doing?

* Who are their special friends?

* Is my child fine after I leave?

* Is there a day, morning, or afternoon when the mix of kids creates a nasty or a difficult dynamic for my child?

activities. Most also have a full- or part-time cook on site to provide meals. (Ask if the cook is considered part of the staff-to-child ratio: obviously it's better if they're not.)

Some centers have "family groupings"—rooms are occupied by children of different ages to simulate a family with different-aged children—but most take advantage of the fact that children at different stages of development want to be together and group activities can be tailored to their needs. Centers have to have special programs for each age. Many centers have a system where kids are with their own peers for some of the day and with all ages at free playtime in the afternoon, for example.

Some child-care centers will take babies from 6 weeks old; others may start at age 1. Some allow half-day attendance; most don't. Kids can be booked in from, say, 9 to 4, or longer or shorter hours, depending on the policy of the center. You may be charged for a whole day even if you only want care from 10 to 4 as you'll be keeping out someone who wants the longer day. Fees are sometimes calculated by the hour. Check with the center whether you're eligible for government help with them or whether they offer scholarships, discounts, or sliding fee scales. (See also More Info at the end of this chapter.)

a NaNNy

This is probably the most expensive form of child care because you're paying one person's wage, without any subsidies, and you need to organize tax for them and of course pay social security. Call the IRS and your state employer hotline, industrial relations department, or trades hall to find out your obligations with regard to state and federal taxes, disability insurance, medicare, social security, and the rest.

Some people share a nanny to look after a couple of kids, perhaps swapping between homes. Very few people can afford the money or space to have a live-in nanny.

The bonding and one-on-one care of a nanny is a huge bonus; the flip side is that the child can be very sad to be parted from them if the nanny wants to move on or you run out of money.

Hiring a nanny through an agency means it's easier to check their references, training, and work history. If a problem arises, you can take advice from the agency if you wish.

People who are employing a nanny through an agency as well as those who are employing them privately should observe the nanny with children, ask exhaustive questions, and personally check all references and educational qualifications such as nanny or child-care ones. (Less effusive references can be coded criticisms.) Most people prefer a nanny with child-care qualifications and a current first-aid certificate.

When you interview a nanny, make sure your baby or child is with you. Watch how the nanny interacts with them. It's a good sign if she (or he) is more interested in the child than in you: you want someone who sees the child as the first priority.

THE NANNY INTERVIEW

You need to sort out upfront, before the nanny starts, whether you expect them to do any housework or cooking aside from kid food. You should also make your expectations clear; for example, friends and other nannies can visit, but no taking the baby to the bar for a cold one.

If your instinct tells you it isn't working out, or the nanny seems to have a problem that will impinge on your life, don't hesitate to move on—the sooner the better, before bonding happens.

a BaBysitter

Before you leave your house in the care of a babysitter make sure all doors can be opened easily from the inside or that keys are always kept on the inside lock: it's important not to deadlock people inside the house. Give the babysitter a spare key in case they have to leave the house with the kids for any reason.

A bulletin board or a folder with plastic sleeves inside to keep essential info in is a good idea. You can even attach the folder to a nail on the wall or pin it on a bulletin board close enough to the phone for a number to be read while dialing. You might like to make some photocopies of the Info for Carergivers sheet coming up soon to use when you have a babysitter.

It may seem heavy but in Extra House Information on the info sheet you might want to record, for example, that "All rooms have smoke alarms. In case of fire, drop to the floor to avoid smoke and get the kids and yourself out the front or back door, whichever is nearest. Nothing else matters." And in the Special Instructions part, something like "Ari is allergic to peanuts."

A note about teenage babysitters

Sometimes it's convenient to have a neighborhood teenager or an older sibling take care of young ones. These babysitters should always have access to adult help, nearby or on the phone, as even the most

QUESTIONS FOR A CAREGIVER, NANNY, OR BABYSITTER

* What's your family situation?

* What are your child-care and first-aid qualifications?

* How do you feel about me working from home or popping in at any time?

* Why do you like children? (This often flushes out those who don't, and is subtly different from "What do you like about looking after children?")

* What are your strengths?

* Why did you leave your last three jobs?

* What are some of the things you do with a kid this age?

* Do you have a philosophy or approach to child care?

* What are your feelings on setting boundaries and discipline?

* What are the bad things about the job?

* What are the worst kind of parents to work for?

* The baby has been crying for an hour and nothing seems to work. What do you do?

* The baby vomits a feeding, feels very hot, falls asleep, and you can't wake them up. You can't contact the parents. What do you do? (Right answer: call an ambulance.)

* I ask you to do something a certain way and you think it's the wrong way. What do you do?

* How much notice do you want to give for vacations? And how much notice should we give for our vacations without you?

* Can my toddler or preschooler phone me to come home or to come and get them, or for a chat at any time? (Often kids feel more secure knowing they can bail out when they want to, and relax into enjoying the day.)

responsible teenager is still a teenager. It's not their fault, but teenagers do not have the brain capacity to understand every cause and effect, and they are usually inexperienced and inadequately briefed on what to do in a variety of emergencies.

info for caregivers

Kids' names and ages:
_____

Parents' full names:
_____

phone: _____ cell: _____
Our home address and phone number:
_____

We'll be at (address):
_____

phone: _____ mobile: _____
Emergency numbers—police/fire/ambulance: 911
Poison Control Center: 1-800-222-1222
Neighbor's name, address, and phone number:
_____

Back-up relative or special friend's name and phone number:
_____

Kids' doctor's name and phone number:
_____

Our children's painkiller is kept: _____
First-aid box is kept: _____
Flashlight is kept: _____
Diapers or pull-ons are kept: _____
Towels are kept: _____
Garbage bags are kept: _____
Cleaning stuff is kept: _____
Toilet rolls are kept: _____
Extra house information: _____
_____
_____

Kids' bedtime: _____
Usual bedtime ritual (including whether diaper necessary):
_____
_____
_____
_____

Any other needs: _____
_____
_____

Special instructions: _____
_____
_____
_____

© Kidwrangling: The Real Guide to Caring for Babies, Toddlers, and Little Kids

DROP-in Services

This service is particularly useful for parents who are usually at home with their kids, but need a brief break or to get to an appointment without kids. Drop-in Services are offered by many child care centers: some need prior notice; others will allow you to call that morning. Check with your local resource and referral organization for a list of centers offering occasional or part-time care. The fee is usually per session or by the hour, and they may have a minimum age limit.

PReSCHOOL OR HeadStart

Depending on your area, 3-year-old and 4-year-old preschool, Head Start, or an equivalent learning program will be available. These range from morning-only affairs, three-days-a-week arrangements, or every day from 9 until 3 to a variation of these. The more formal preschool education programs follow a set curriculum to make the most of children's development at this age and help to prepare kids for school. Many centers also have before and after child care.

Preschools are sometimes state run, but can be privately run, and in either case may be affiliated with or attached to a primary school for ease of transition. Your local resource and referral organization should have a list of options in your area—you may need to book years ahead.

It's now generally accepted that kids who've done a year or two of preschool will be better prepared for a transition to the first year of school.

settling into child care

If possible, especially in the first days and weeks, spend as much time as you can helping your child to settle and bond with the caregiver or caregivers or the nanny. It can be a delicate situation leaving a child you know will be happy 2 seconds after you leave, but meanwhile is weeping piteously and clinging to you for dear life. Some kids initially need to be "eased into the day," yet will end up hardly giving you a backward glance as they race to an activity ready for them on the kid-sized tables at child care or to hold Granny's hand and wave you off to work.

Never sneak away; always let your child know you are going and what time you'll come back (even if they don't quite "get" times). Check later with the center or caregiver to make sure any tears on your departure cleared up after you left, and that your child isn't showing signs of continuing separation anxiety or sadness throughout the day. Feel free to check up on their progress during the day even if they weren't upset when you left: you can tell your kid you called when they were happily playing in the sandpit, and they'll feel secure and become aware of the bridge between home and the child-care center, or between you at work and them at home. Depending on their age, your kid can understand they're allowed to call you at any time.

Make sure the caregiver or caregivers know they can talk to you openly about your child's feelings, demeanor, and development.

guilt about child care

Guilt about using child care is minimized if you can stay home with the child when they're sick or when they don't want to go: this can be very hard when you have other job commitments. (The juggling has begun!) The other way to minimize guilt is to try to look very dispassionately at your set-up and honestly assess whether your kid is happy and thriving after a few weeks of care. Don't make your decision based on other people's theories, what your mother thinks, a survey in Finland, or indeed the experiences of anyone else's children.

The real key to dealing with guilt is to make sure your child is having a happy, stimulated, social childhood, whatever child-care options or combination you choose. To do that, you have to spend enough time with your child to know them very well.

> *"It's Thursday afternoon and my son, Edward, is in child care so his mother can go to work. At least that's how most people would view our household arrangements. Edward is also in child care so that I, his father, can go to work. But few would consider that. Or that it might have been my decision to leave Edward in care, or that I decided to go to work rather than staying home with him. Nobody would bother to analyze my motives and my morality. Nobody would think I was selfish or a bad parent—because I am a father. But it's completely different when you're a working mother."* ANGUS HOLLAND, *REAL DADS*

Permission to relax

If your kid is in child care or with a babysitter, relative, or friend for a few hours—and it's not one of those times when you have to be at work or have to do housework, shopping, or part-time paid work—you are allowed to read a magazine, watch a video, or go to sleep. In fact this should often be compulsory. For sole parents and at-home parents who don't get weekends or any nights off, a bit of child care is a godsend.

Sometimes the parent who is the full-time carer has a little stumble on the first few days their child is in care: for some it's the first time they haven't had to be responsible and on 24-hour watch. Some women have told me they sleep all day long or even hit the bottle or other drugs, legal and otherwise, for the first day or so, straightening up by the time they need to pick up the kid. While this is understandable and in some ways tempting, if you do it for more than a day or two you'll need some professional help (start with your GP). Sleeping or other relaxing pursuits such as eating and having a bubble bath don't quite give you the same wipe-out, but oblivion isn't going to work when they ring and say your kid's been vomiting and needs to come home. Besides, wanting oblivion on a regular basis is usually a symptom of something that's going to have to be tackled.

more info

Child Care Aware

A government-sponsored database with links to finding child care, licensing requirements, information of child care subsidies, and more in your area.
1-800-424-2246
www.childcareaware.org

National Network for Childcare

Included helpful articles and resources for parents, including links to local resources.
www.nncc.org

Find Care Now

A private company (membership is free) that can help you locate quality caretakers (nannies, au pairs, centers, and so on). It includes many useful articles and tips on child care options.
www.findcarenow.com

HOW TO BE PERFECT

Being absolutely perfect at all times is utterly essential. Here's how.

a Day in the Life of a Perfect Mother

★ Get up before everyone else, wearing a peignoir (I don't know what it is either but I think it's see-through and has feathery bits) and prepare a nutritious cooked breakfast, with precisely balanced portions containing the five food groups, and the essential fatty acids, minerals, and vitamins—for everyone.

★ Practice yoga for one hour.

★ Learn how to spell Pilates.

★ Exercise strenuously for another hour.

★ Shampoo and style hair of all household guinea pigs.

★ Shampoo, dye, and style own hair, with something cheap from the supermarket, so it looks like it was done in a salon.

★ Cleanse, moisturize, tone. Neck cream, eye cream, elbow cream, foot cream, earlobe cream.

★ Foundation, powder, lipstick, mascara. Curl eyelashes, exercise pelvic-floor muscles, brush eyebrows, pluck nostril hair.

★ Brush teeth.

★ Floss.

★ Wake adorable children. Read them the original *Alice in Wonderland* and engage them in absorbing, quiet activities that develop their brain while providing wholesome, low-key fun.

★ Dress children in comfortable imported Italian separates.

★ Wake husband up (get husband if haven't got one) with firecracker sex, during which he is struck by uncanny resemblance of self to a young Michelle Pfeiffer, and save time by discussing the family financial situation during the afterglow.

★ Do hair and make-up again.

★ Dress quickly and deftly in very inexpensive clothes, designed and sewn by self, that look like designer-wear.

★ Reheat and serve breakfast.

★ Using a bar of antiseptic soap or a hard-bristled brush dipped in Pine-O-Cleen, scrub the poop off yesterday's diapers or the vomit from the crevice down back of couch.

★ Breastfeed a couple of children: yours if necessary.

★ Search organic vegetable garden for caterpillars and kill them by hand.

★ Air the home thoroughly and hang four loads of washing out, well spaced on lines, in a stiff, warm breeze.

★ Make some Christmas presents out of raffia, driftwood, and dried cannellini beans.

★ Give self manicure, including fake nails.

★ Put youngest offspring down for the morning nap, making sure they all go to sleep instantly, at the same time of day, for precisely an hour and a half.

★ Weed, mulch, harvest, converse with plants.

★ Mosaic the garage wall as an artistic role model for next generation.

★ Do dishes.

★ Buy or make presents for all husband's relatives, write and send cards, and keep up with all gossip and concerns of older generation.

★ Iron sheets, towels, and any lingerie bought this week.

★ Spend several hours' quality time with the children involving new activities, age appropriate for each child, that exercise all aspects of their physical, mental, and emotional development, and making each feel they have full attention of self.

★ Drive children to three or four different schools, child-care centers, relatives, and sporting fixtures.

★ Shop for items needed by different members of the family.

★ Attend Pilates class.

★ Surf Net.

★ Flirt with passing fireman.

★ Go to immensely fulfilling and undemanding part-time job that allows unlimited time off without warning for children's illnesses and other needs, and pays as much as the average full-time (male) wage.

★ Power nap.

- ★ Shop locally for cheap, fresh, in-season, biodynamic foods, as foods are not in peak condition by the end of the week if only shopping once, and will be own fault so must shop every day.
- ★ Read half of improving novel.
- ★ Listen to radio and read three daily newspapers to be well informed.
- ★ Discuss matters of state and global importance with friends who don't have children so as to keep in touch with the Other World.
- ★ Adjust push-up bra.
- ★ Exfoliate feet.
- ★ Clean up sick.
- ★ Morning snack: nutritious, quick to prepare but not at all fattening, such as a polystyrene cup of raffia, driftwood, and dried cannellini beans.
- ★ Browse homewear shops and buy throw-up-proof throws.
- ★ Update first-aid and foreign-language skills.
- ★ Wax legs.
- ★ Wax earlobes.
- ★ Inject poisons into forehead to pretend life hasn't caused facial lines.
- ★ Have a philosophical discussion with a 3-year-old about what's fair and what's not, and win on logic.
- ★ You Time: why not try a round of golf or learn a new skill such as electrical engineering?
- ★ Practice tinkling girlish laugh.
- ★ Test drive a new, attractive car that's practical for the whole family.
- ★ Lunch at small bistro; half carafe of wine.
- ★ Pick up brochures from travel agent.
- ★ Reading duty.
- ★ Purchase something for self: jewelery or perfume; or perhaps one-bedroom unit on Bermuda.

★ Pick up children—on time—from various schools, child-care centers, relatives, and sports fields.

★ Rearrange children, including extras, and deliver them to new set of locations.

★ Go out for drink with promisingly useful work colleague.

★ Pick up children in car and have meaningful dialogue with each individually, paying particular attention to bonding, nuances of unspoken feelings, opportunities for a learning experience (for you and for them), their own special ways of listening and learning, with eye to making important decisions that will determine their entire future.

★ Use a spatula, some home-grown produce, and some free-range cruelty-free chickens from your own slaughterhouse to fashion a nutritious and delicious meal that husband and children both enjoy, to later be served, according to the needs of family members, at half-hour intervals from 5 until 7:30 p.m.

★ Go out to see a new Hollywood film.

★ Bathe children, paying special attention to individual needs, water restrictions, and sibling fights involving pre-sharpened metal implements and sustained high-pitched shrieking.

★ Feed, water, and question guinea pigs.

★ Greet husband, on his return from work, dressed in cling wrap and a strategically placed mango.

★ Play mind-expanding games or listen to radio with children in their freshly pressed pyjamas as you do not have television but only home cinema system used for educational purposes.

★ Teach children to read.

★ And write.

★ Supervise homework.

★ Give husband hand relief in laundry.

★ Give children dinner.

★ Eat own dinner—a small sprauncelet of fileted reef fish with a julienne of fresh, seasonal vegetables and a coulis of curly endive.

★ Discuss the Congo situation, with particular reference to Bavarian history.

★ Get felt-tip pen stains off bathroom ceiling with white vinegar and cream of tartar.

★ Do cryptic crossword.

★ Feed and water livestock.

★ Repair CD player.

★ Put children to bed, each with different story.

★ Attend night classes in rowing.

★ Clean out school bags, catch up on handwritten correspondence.

★ Wax bikini line and attach raffia merkin.

★ Unpack and wash lunch boxes.

★ Moisturize neck.

★ Remember Bavaria no longer a country. Pore over atlas.

★ Sew name tags into each piece of clothing owned by off-spring, including hats, socks, velvet capes, and matching wands.

★ Accept phone calls from internationally recognized experts on child psychology.

★ Make set of queen-sized sheets with unbleached calico.

★ Check supplies of sun screen, peanut butter, clean towels, underpants, lunch boxes, children, garden implements, vases, soap, and hot-glue guns. Make shopping list for tomorrow.

★ Pay bills, balance checkbook, pay credit card on time, and compile tax records in three-ring binder.

★ Invite extended family to Christmas dinner.

★ Listen to relaxation tape.

★ Scrub grouting.

★ Go to bed.

★ Get up, make school lunches for tomorrow.
★ Go back to bed, stare at ceiling, ask unanswerable questions.
★ Close eyes.
★ Listen to a child somewhere audibly vomiting.
★ Pleasure self with dustpan and brush.

a Day in the Life of the Perfect father

★ Listen, I'll get right onto this list once I've emptied the compost bin.

5
stuff

Names and Paperwork

Some people have the first names all ready for a boy or a girl: some even know the gender and the name before the baby is born. Others um and er over names for weeks—even months—after the baby's born. I couldn't find any research on this at all,

just billions of books and websites full of
lists of baby names; nothing to help people
who seem unable to close their eyes and
jump with a name.

And once you've decided on a name, who
do you need to tell, what lists should your
baby be on and what other paperwork has
to be done?

CHOOSiNg a first Name

Some cultures give their newborn babies a cute name or "milk
name," which may be a diminutive of the formal name or a nickname: Carmelita instead of Carmel; Bird instead of George. In this
way, the formal name is in waiting. Some names—such as Reginald
or Lucretia—don't suit babies. But Reggie or Lulu might, until they
need the other one.

Although most hospitals say to come prepared with a name to
avoid paperwork nightmares later on, if you are undecided, don't
let family members or a bureaucratic official stampede you into naming your baby in the first week or two. Unless it is required by law
in your area, say firmly "No, *don't* put down 'Ferdie.' We'll let you
know when we have decided."

Part of the problem may be that you're waiting for the kid to
"look like" a certain name. This is no good: it actually works the

other way round. You give the baby a name and they start looking like it.

You may have some psychological trouble putting a name to the amazing thing that's happened in your life, represented by this little person. Explain to yourself you're not describing the whole head-spinning trip, just giving the kid a name. If you're still having trouble naming your baby after a few months, it's probably a good idea to have a chat with a counselor—not because you're crazy, but because at this stage of everyone's parenting life and lack of sleep, an independent eye on the situation is often a good idea. Your GP can recommend a psychologist. And don't be embarrassed. Your GP has seen people so much more confused or indecisive than you that you don't even figure on the scale.

If as a couple you can't agree, think about it for a while, then find three names you can each live with and do the hat thing. Promise that you'll go with the order they come out of the hat. If you pull Luke first, then Luke it is. You do have to be a responsible parent at this point and part of your job is to name the child. There is no wrong answer. Any decent name will become your child's own, and you'll love your kid and their name: eventually they're indistinguishable.

You can still use nicknames. Other kids in the future will bestow their own nicknames: you can't control what your child is called forever. ("Well, her name is Penelope. Nobody will be able to call her Penny.")

Don't saddle your kid with a name that usually belongs to the other gender: Chris goes both ways, but Fifi and Butch really don't. Leave the kid to make up their own cross-gender names in the future if they want to.

Stick with the name and keep using it—everyone will grow to accept it. All names seem okay, then weird, then okay again. Everyone has second thoughts and wonders if the name they have given is right. If you feel sure you've actually used the wrong name rather than just being unsure about it, change it—but only change once. You can't keep dickering around.

Your child may change their name when they grow up. I know one boy who was bored with his name, changed it at 3 to Huckle and took that into adulthood. Others have changed their New Age names to mainstream ones or vice versa. Most young kids, sometimes at about 4 years old, either insist that you use their formal name, not a diminutive or a nickname, or make up an imaginative one for themselves.

Last Names

Most babies are given the last name of their father, stemming from the days when a wife and children were seen to be owned by the man. Some are given the last name of their mother. Some get a double-barreled name, and some have their mother or father's last name as a middle name to avoid the hyphen. Some mothers use their first family name professionally and use their husband's or partner's name for anything to do with the child's world, such as school. Personally, I only ever use my partner's name if I am trying to hide my involvement in an off-shore diamond heist or otherwise behaving suspiciously, and my daughter has her dad's last name because, let's face it, who wants to have your mother's name when she's written books called *A Bun in the Oven* and *Kidwrangling*?

Registering a Name

Each state has a local registry of births, deaths, and marriages (how old-fashioned) that requires you to register your baby's name within a certain time (usually before you leave the hospital). Your hospital should prepare the form with your help and submit it for you. If you have a home birth, make sure someone is responsible for registering the birth. A birth certificate is official proof of your baby's date of birth and citizenship, and it is required to start school, obtain a driver's license, and apply for a passport. It may also be necesary for all sorts of other rights and benefits including marriage and social security. Usually, a child can be registered without a first name, then that name added later but you will have to submit extra forms and may have to pay fees. It's a good idea to go prepared with names. Each child, whether a twin, a triplet, or whatever, must have their own form.

All sorts of ludicrous details that are none of the state's business may be required on the birth certificate form, including the age, marital status, education level, and occupation of the parents, although most states will only collect vital statistics and names.

Usually the father's name will only be entered on a birth certificate if the mother is married (and the father doesn't deny parentage) or if both unmarried parents sign some kind of voluntary parental affidavit (varies by state) at the hospital and submit a notorized one later. Otherwise the father's name is simply left blank. Of course, if the father won't sign one and you need financial support,

PUTTING YOUR CHILD'S NAME "DOWN"

Putting their name down used to be only essential for people whose kiddliwinks were trotting off to the sort of private school that has a waiting list as long as the list of prefects who went on to join the Republican Party. These days—AND I'M ONLY GOING TO WARN YOU ONCE, MY FRIENDS (well, okay, the warning's also in the Child Care and Preschool chapter)—you need to put your child's name down for child care, preschool, or kindergarten and, in some cases, school WHEN THEY ARE BORN. I know some of you think this is mad and you'll ignore it. Just don't have a tantrum in three years' time when the kid has missed out on a place.

you'll have to file a paternity suit to get him to submit to DNA testing. Then his name can be added by court order.

OTHER PAPERWORK

Wills

You, or you and the baby's other parent if there is one handy, should agree on who is to have care of your child should anything happen to all available parents and put this down in a legal will or your wishes may not be followed. Consult your family lawyer or contact a community legal service (look in the government pages in the phonebook).

Health Insurance

You will need to add your baby's name to your insurance plan and pay the premium as soon as possible. Usually, you have to do this within thirty days. If your insurance is through your employer, they can help you with the forms. If you don't have insurance, check with your local health department or social services office to see what programs your child may qualify for: you may only have to fill out a couple forms for coverage.

Social Security

When you fill out the forms for the birth certificate in the hospital, there is usually a box you can check to automatically sign your child up for social security. Just check the box, and you'll get the new number and card in the mail in a few months. If you have a home birth or forget to apply for it while you are in the hospital, you can easily apply for it later by going to the local social security office. Applying for the number is voluntary, but your child will need it to open a bank account, qualify for medical coverage, and apply for government services. It's best if you can apply for the number before your child's first birthday, because after that, the process takes longer.

equipment

You're going to need some stuff.

A LOT OF STUFF.

CARRiage

shopping

safety standards

If you're buying new babies' or children's equipment, make sure each item has a Juvenile Products Manufacturer's Association (JPMA) Certified Seal. This seal means the product has been tested and meets the safety standards developed by the American Society for Testing and Materials (ASTM) and the US Consumer Product Safety Commission (CPSP).

It's usually best to shop at a section of a department store or a store that sells different brands of baby gear so that you can compare prices. Do your homework if you plan to buy second-hand stuff—you may be buying things that are unsafe, or superseded. And if you're acquiring something second-hand, get hold of and scrupulously follow the manufacturer's directions about construction and use. If there's no paperwork, contact the manufacturer and ask whether the gear conforms to the current safety standard and, if you can, purchase a manual. Remember, standards are regularly amended.

For some bizarre reason many safety standards are not enforced by law. Buyer beware!

SAFETY

Don't assume everything available for children is safe. The folks at Consumer Reports often find safety hazards when testing kids' equipment. For reports and reviews of specific equipment and for lots of essential info on what's a good deal, certified safe, and useful, read Consumer Reports or you can become a member and access articles and reviews on their website (see More Info at the end of this chapter).

See also the Home Safety chapter for info on general home safety (it's the next one).

Big Stuff

Buy, beg, borrow, or hunt down the following.

★ A large-capacity clothes washing machine. Bending down to a front loader is a pain—go for a top loader if you're buying new.

★ A clothes dryer: unless you live somewhere sunny and can get through a rainy season without one.

★ A car modern enough to have a safety belt designed to anchor your child seat securely. (If you're buying an older car, you may have to order parts from the manufacturer.)

You'll need a car with a back seat: kids up to the age of 12 can't be in the front if the car has airbags. You'll need a car with lap and shoulder belts. Children are much more at risk of serious injury in a car with old-fashioned lap belts. If you're buying a relatively new car, it will almost certainly have both belts and baby-seat anchor points, but it's worth checking. Ideally, buy a car with back doors to make it easier to get a baby and other kids in and out. Station wagons can be fitted with a cargo barrier so dogs and other heavy stuff don't fly in from the back in an accident, causing mayhem.

CHILDREN AND CAR AIRBAGS

Children under the age of 12 must not sit in the front seat of a car because the automatic deployment of an airbag can kill a child by breaking their neck. An airbag hitting an adult or a taller child in the chest will not have the same effect.

Basic Baby Equipment

Here's what you need.

★ A new baby car restraint. All child car seats manufactured today are required to meet federal safety standards. You can get ones that convert from a baby seat to a toddler and little kid seat. Don't buy a second-hand one. If one is given to you, make sure it's no more than a few years old, it's never been in an accident, it still has the original manufacturer's label, all straps are in original condition, and there's no Velcro involved (experts say the Velcro lasts for one baby's use only). Some baby seats are built to face backwards until the baby weighs about 20 pounds, after which it faces forwards until the kid's about 40 pounds. Then you're into toddler-seat territory (see below). Some adjustable baby and toddler booster seats will take you from birth to about 8 years.

★ A bed of some sort: you may want to skip the bassinet stage and go straight to a crib (look up cribs in the index for info on safety).

★ A baby bag: any big bag with a zip or fastenable top will do (see The Baby Bag section later in this chapter).

★ A changing table or an area that's set up with everything you need to change a diaper (look up changing table in the index for more info).

★ A carriage (some convert to a stroller): your carriage will need a wet-weather cover and a sunshade or an umbrella or, if you live in San Francisco, both on the same day. All carriages and strollers should have swivelly wheels for easy maneuvring. Your carriage or stroller should suit your lifestyle. If you walk to the shops a lot, get a sturdy one with a large metal shopping basket underneath. If you live in an upstairs, walk-up apartment, you'll need something that folds into a light, convenient package that can be hauled upstairs. A label should say JPMA Certified.

★ A stroller: you'll need a stroller that fully reclines until your baby has good sitty-up control, usually at about 6 months. See the details for a carriage, above, most of which are also relevant for strollers, including the safety certifications number. Some strollers have a small drinks tray that goes in front of the toddler. The expensive strollers are usually more comfortable for long walks or shopping. Strollers need to have a five-point safety harness so a toddler doesn't make a bold bid for freedom when you're halfway across at the light. Jogging strollers can be harder to get in and out of a car and may not fit easily or at all on public transportation, but they can be fantastically good for long walks or different terrains.

★ Bike gear: having a baby on a bike in a safety-standard approved seat, even with the regulation helmet on as well, is not necessarily safe. Think about what would happen if the bike was hit by a car or the rider lost control. Similar concerns also exist for bikes towing a baby trailer: even if the trailer has a flag on a flexible stick, it's much lower than anything drivers expect to see associated with a bike. Babies in these should wear a helmet and are still vulnerable to serious injury in such an unprotected and not very visible device. Riding in places where there are no cars is certainly a big head start for bicycle safety when it comes to babies and toddlers. Make sure your child bicycle seat meets the American Society for Testing and Materials (ASTM) standard for child carriers.

★ A highchair: you'll need a highchair with wide-apart, stable legs; a lockable tray so the baby can't whack it up and down on their fingers; and a harness that goes around the waist and over the shoulders, with a strap between the legs that goes up to the waist strap. If you always strap your baby in, as you do in the car, they'll assume that's the go and not fuss (fingers crossed). Always put the kid in the highchair yourself: don't let them climb in themselves. Don't leave the room when your baby is in the highchair. Kids are known to do sudden acrobatics you never thought possible—without a safety net. And they push against a table or another chair with their feet, which can tip their highchair over—usually backwards. Look for the JPMA Certification Seal.

★ A booster seat, which sits on an ordinary chair: toddlers graduate to these when they're good at climbing up and down. They are available at chain stores and baby shops and are usually made of hard, molded plastic: some come with anchoring straps so they can be attached to the chair. Some have a deeper seat on their other side for when the kid gets taller. Preschoolers often use booster seats because adult chairs are still way too big for them. Booster seats without straps are notorious for being involved in children's falls because they can move around and be halfway off an adult chair as a toddler starts to climb on or off, so if you buy one you'll need to supervise its use.

For other items you'll need see the info on baby clothes and first-aid kits in the Clothes and Health chapters a bit further on, and look up diapers in the index.

Equipment beyond the basics

You might want some of these.

★ A portable or folding crib for guests or traveling: these really do need to be absolutely up to the safety standard (JPMA certified), and the instructions for their special assembly and use strictly followed.

★ A baby monitor: these are one-way walkie-talkies so you can be at the other end of the house or outside in the garden (take your keys) and still hear if the baby cries. Most baby monitors have two channels—so if there's more than one or two babies with monitors in your street you may be tuning into the wrong baby. We listened to our neighbor's baby monitor for two days straight before we realized our baby appeared to be chatting to a builder about plans for the dining room.

wah wah erp!

baby monitor

★ Bouncy things: many safety experts say these are dodgy for babies and too much of a risk. A bouncer should always be used with a restraint. It should be placed on a safe surface where it can't travel

over the edge of the stairs, and never near a heater or a fire.
It should be abandoned as soon as the baby can roll. Babies
love to be reminded of womb-like feelings so enjoy baby
bouncers, or bouncing swings, and hammocks of any
description, but choose carefully and take notice of the
manufacturer's age and weight recommendations.

★ Those tenty things you can put up at the beach for a little
  shade: remember they can get hot inside—a bit of wet clothing or hat action can help.

★ A strap-on baby carrier: get one with the best back support
  you can—not just a scarfy thing that ties around you.

What not to get

These are downright dangerous or potentially dangerous.

★ Bumpers: these soft, padded sidey-bits that tie onto cribs
  stop the free flow of fresh air, and babies can also get their
  heads wedged underneath.

★ A baby walker: I can't understand why they're still sold—
  every safety mob between here and Neptune says they
  don't help kids learn to walk properly and cause a lot
  of accidents.

HEATING THE BED

For many reasons, including the danger of spilled drinks, pee, or
the blanket being left on or turned on when it shouldn't be, an electric
blanket is not suitable for babies or kids under 5.

A young baby cannot move away from a heat source when
they need to, and a hot-water bottle can cause overheating or even
slight burns. A hot-water bottle for a toddler or preschooler should be
avoided or filled with warm—never hot—water. It's best to regulate
bed heat with blankets (but not puffy bedding such as a duvet for
babies).

★ Bunk beds: these are not suitable for children younger than, say, 7. They're a common cause of broken limbs from falls. It's no good telling the kids not to go up the ladder or horse around. That's what kids do. If you do buy them, they should be certified to meet the mandatory and voluntary safety standards set by the CPSC and the ASTM.

Basic Toddler Equipment

The following items are essentials.

★ Stair guards: you can get expandable safety standard barriers from baby shops. Have them fitted by someone good at it. Look for the JPMA Certification Seal.

★ A child's car booster seat: a baby usually goes into a toddler booster seat when they weigh about 40 pounds. Ideally, a toddler booster seat for a car needs to have a full back, some semblance of sides, and a strap to adjust the height of the car's own belt so that it goes across the kid's chest, not their head or neck. A booster seat is usually hard, molded polystyrene, with a washable cloth cover. Those old plastic, potty-like seats are no longer considered a safe option. (An older child shouldn't discard their booster seat until they're tall enough for their knees to bend at the front edge of the car seat when their back and bottom are against the back of the car seat, the seatbelt goes across their chest, not neck. This is usually not until they're about 8 or older.

★ A toddler bag: stash in it the stuff listed in The Toddler Bag section later in the chapter.

★ Socks with raised plastic bumps on the bottom: these will stop your toddler slipping over.

carting it all around

If you use a car, you'll want to keep a stash of useful kid stuff in it. The Travel Near and Far chapter further on has lists that should give you some ideas.

The baby bag

You don't have to have a wildly flash, celebrity-endorsed designer bag. You need one that stuff can't fall out of—so it needs to zip up somehow. Men: you may want a small backpack or courier-style bag so it's not too girly. Women: you may want to get a handbag with a long strap that you can wear across your body so your hands are free. The time for a clutch purse or a lone wallet may be gone for several years to come unless you fancy the look of duct tape. Backpacks are also excellent because they leave your hands free. Keys can be attached somewhere to the bag with a clip so you never lose 'em.

> "I buy a poacher's waistcoat with plenty of pockets for bottles and rice cakes and tiny boxes of raisins. I do not look like a poacher . . . I look like the Unabomber. But I can't get away with a handbag."
>
> IAN SANSOM, *THE TRUTH ABOUT BABIES*

Things to keep stocked in the baby bag:
* diapers.
* baby wipes.
* plastic bags tied in a knot for safety.
* a waterproof roll-out changing pad, plus soft cloth diapers for laying over it or to use instead of it.

★ packets of formula milk powder if you're bottlefeeding (see the Bottles chapter in *Part 1: Babies* for the full info).

★ a spare baby blanket or a muslin wrap.

★ a bib or two or three or four . . .

★ a change or two of clothes.

★ baby toys or rattles.

Things to put in at the last minute:

★ medicines, with childproof caps, and inhaler if necessary.

★ sterilized bottles of sterilized water if you're bottlefeeding.

★ sunscreen lotion and a sunhat.

★ a sweater and a warm hat.

★ snacks.

★ a bottle of water for you (and one for the baby, depending on their age).

★ a pacifier or other comfort item.

The toddler bag

It's always good to have a bag on an outing. Things you could include in it:

★ pull-ups if the toddler is just starting to use the toilet or finding a toilet could be impossible, or diapers if your toddler's still using them.

★ baby wipes.

★ plastic bags tied in a knot for safety.

★ a change of clothes.

★ toddler toys or games.

★ portable CD or tape player, with safe, kid-friendly earphones (from, say, age 2 and a half)—a luxury item.

★ a paperback picture book.

Things to put in at the last minute:

★ medicines, with childproof caps, and inhaler if necessary.

★ sunscreen lotion and a sunhat.

- ★ a sweater and a warm hat.
- ★ snacks.
- ★ a bottle of water for you and the toddler.
- ★ a comfort item.

The little kid bag

Now that your kid is finished with bottles and doesn't need diapers (or as many diapers), you can stop lugging around a mammoth duffel bag full of mysterious accoutrements. But it's always worth having these in your bag (or car):

- ★ medicines, with childproof caps, and an inhaler if necessary.
- ★ wet wipes.
- ★ plastic bags tied in a knot.
- ★ an easy change of clothes or at least a top.
- ★ crayons and paper and small, absorbing toys.
- ★ a bottle of unopened still water.
- ★ the kitchen sink.
- ★ a wad of cash.
- ★ a bar of chocolate.
- ★ a small inflatable craft of some description.
- ★ a spare pants suit made from caravan upholstery.

more info

Juvenille Products Manufacturers Association

Its website features easy-to-use links to current safety standards (established by the American Society for Testing & Materials [ASTM]) and tips for buying all types of children's products. To become JPMA Certified, a product must be tested by an independent testing facility for compliance with the specific ASTM standards. If a product passes the tests, JPMA allows the manufacturer to label it with the JPMA Certified Seal.

www.jpma.org

US Consumer Product Safety Commission (CPSC)

Website has latest consumer product recalls. You can also sign up for automatic email notices when a new recall has been issued and they have a toll-free hotline. Report all injuries caused by unsafe products to this commission.

www.cpsc.gov/

Safer Child

Comprehensive links to authoritative, reliable sites for info on just about any safety topic you can think of.

www.saferchild.org

Consumer Reports Best Baby Products, 8th Edition

by Editors of Consumer Reports, Sandra Gordon, Consumer Reports, 2004. From the leading consumer information source. It lists all sorts of recommendations, based on independent tests that take into account safety, design, durability, and price. It also contains equipment checklists, ratings on car seats, play yards, travel systems, and carriers, a list of recent recalls, and a shopping guide.

The Girlfriends' Guide to Baby Gear: What to Buy, What to Borrow, and What to Blow Off!

by Vicki Iovine, Peg Rosen, Perigee Books, 2003. Part of the famous Girlfriends's Guide series. Real life advice from moms about what's good, what's essential, and what's all hype.

Home safety

As I said in my book on pregnancy, *A Bun in the Oven*, the only way to childproof a house is to never let a kid into it, but you can try to make it safer. The more mobile a baby gets, the more dangerous the house becomes. There's a wide age range for milestones: your baby could be an early roller, your toddler could be an early climber. The most common causes of death and injury in little kids (oh, this isn't at all cheerful) are falls; poisonings; car and pedestrian accidents, often in their own driveways;

HELMUT

drowning, even in diaper buckets; choking; suffocation; burns; and electrical accidents. The good news is you worry less once you've made everything as safe as you can. (As safe as, well, houses.)

Basic Home Safety

The checklist that follows will give you an idea of where to start, although the hints are probably more useful for city folk (not much point only being worried about a puddle when you also have a dam). You might also like to check out the Safety Standards section in the previous Equipment chapter for info on safety standards and the First Aid section in the later Health chapter.

★ There should be a working smoke alarm or several (in most states landlords are required by law to provide these). Change the batteries each time you switch to or from daylight savings time.

★ Make sure your fuse box is fitted with a safety switch that will automatically turn off the power if someone is getting an electric shock. (If you are renting, the landlord is probably legally bound to provide this.)

★ Use electrical outlet covers (from a hardware store or the safety section of other stores).

★ It's expensive but "they" say all kitchens should have an extinguisher that covers every kind of fire and which you know how to use.

★ Get a tamper-proof poison cabinet and first-aid kit, and reorganize cupboards so that the following are on higher ground, safely out of reach: poisons, cleaning agents, medicines, alcohol, cigarettes, matches, lighters, batteries, pesticides, plastic bags, mothballs and camphor, soaps and shampoos, cosmetics, essential oils, and sharp things such as needles and scissors.

★ Store dishwasher tablets and powders high up in a safe cupboard, with other strong caustic products such as bleaches and cleaning solutions that can burn a baby or kid's throat and stomach. Only put detergents in just before you turn on the dishwasher and make sure a baby or kid can't get at the dishwasher.

★ Anything that will fit into a film canister is a choking hazard for kids up to an average-sized 3-year-old.

★ The thermostat of your hot-water heater should be set at 120 to 125 degrees Farenheit. At this temperature a child would have to hold a hand, say, under the water for 1.5 to 2 minutes to cause a serious burn. At 150 degrees burning will take just over a second.

★ Tie knots in all plastic bags and lock and get rid of old fridges, trunks, and other suffocation hazards.

★ Put safety locks (from hardware shops and the safety sections in other stores) on all drawers and cupboards with anything sharp, heavy, or pointy in them. (This probably leaves you with only saucepans and old Tupperware accessible.)

★ Plate-glass and other windows can be replaced with "safety glass," which breaks into non-cutting pebbles, or covered with an invisible film that will hold shards together. Look in the Yellow Pages for a glazier.

★ Make sure there is a pool fence, with a self-latching, self-locking gate at your place and the places of neighbors, relatives, and friends—anyone who has a fenceable pool or pond. Pool fences, pool covers, and filtration and reticulation systems should meet all ASTM performance standards.

Your baby might walk before 12 months and crawl way before that. And children virtually never cry out and often don't make a splash when they fall in or get into trouble. All it takes to drown is a couple of minutes, and parents of toddlers know how many times they suddenly realize their child isn't where they thought they were.

★ All other sources of water, including ponds, dams, buckets, water features, toilets, and recurrent puddles, need to be considered—kids can drown in a couple of inches of water. (Don't have a false sense of security about any young kid who has had swimming lessons: they are just as likely as the other kids to sink to the bottom because they do not have a water survival instinct and often forget to swim. No child or adult is drown-proof, no matter what their experience and capabilities.)

★ All play should be supervised: children's hospitals see many casualties each year caused by backyard trampolines and other common childhood play equipment, especially those involving wheels.

★ Make it as hard as possible for a non-scheduled wander to roads, rivers, and other neighborhood hazards. Often older children and adults leave doors and gates open no matter how many times they're reminded.

You might also like to read the Kitchen Safety section in the later Food chapter; see the index. Your local health department should have standard-issue safety pamphlets; children's hospitals are also good resources and some sell safety products as well (see More Info at the end of this chapter).

THE FREEZING GAME

It's a great idea to play a fun, special game with your kid as soon as they're old enough to "stop" or "freeze." Sometimes give rewards, and spring the game on them every now and again. You can say "STOP!" in all sorts of safe situations—such as randomly in the park or yard and before driveways when you're on a footpath (you can never rely on them to remember to always stop here).

This way, when your child is running somewhere dangerous, such as into the path of a car, you can say "STOP!" and they will automatically stop—perhaps just long enough for you to get to them or for the car to miss them. Otherwise, if it's out of the blue and they're frightened, they might run across a driveway into danger. And sometimes you really need them to be still—especially in the case of a growling dog, a spider, or a snake on the trail. And watch out for those jugular-jumping crabs! (Heh, heh.)

Doing a "safety sweep" through the house

Pretend you're an inquisitive baby or toddler. Get on the floor and look around the room: is there anything irresistibly dangly, such as a tablecloth or an iron or a cord that looks like it needs pulling? A slippery rug that could be skated on (not to mention Ming vases and other valuables that could be knocked over)? A sharp coffee-table corner at eye level? Something high up that looks tempting that a chair could be pushed near? (Pianos and couches make great ladders. So do ladders.)

Are there drycleaning bags hanging over clothes in the closet? Plastic bags or sharp things in kitchen drawers? Bottles and sprays of cleaning products that are temptingly accessible? A dodgy fire guard that could be squeezed around? A hair dryer near a sink filled with water? A maniac in the wood shed?

TOYS

All toys sold here should meet a safety standard and be age appropriate. Most are labeled with an international safety standard (ISO) that is acceptable to the United States. (The local standards are less used on toys.) A few toys slip through without being inspected for safety standards compliance and some that initially meet a standard are sold and then recalled as a problem is found because of injuries to children. Keep in mind also that some toys safe for older children can be dangerous for smaller children.

aNimaLS

I do not refer here to unmentionable exes, but the pet variety. Many animals and children do not mix. There are more and more diseases being passed on by "exotic" animals to humans, and even some traditional pets, including caged birds, can spread disease too. The list of unsuitable pets for health, safety, or conservation reasons is quite long and includes poisonous snakes or other creatures; anything with large jaws and a genetic history of guarding or attacking (that is, many breeds of dogs); crossbred dogs; native or other wild animals; animals that are easily harmed, even by a well-intentioned small person. Also elephants. And Crazy Ants.

All children should be taught not to pat animals that they are not familiar with, whether or not a person says sweetly "Oh, he never bites" or "She's harmless."

It is not within the intellectual powers of a child under 5 to take responsibility for the feeding, grooming, and other care of animals, although they can help with these things under supervision. Before buying a pet for the family, research the species or breed at the library or on the Internet (and see More Info at the end of this chapter).

Dogs

This is shocking, but thousands of Americans, mostly children under the age of 5, are bitten by dogs each year: many are disfigured or disabled, and a very small number are killed. (Only the patients treated in hospital, not those attended to by a GP, are included in the statistics.) Most dog bites happen in private homes. The common biters are German shepherds, rottweilers, blue heelers, dobermans, pit bulls, and kelpies, but any dog, even small dogs and lifelong docile dogs, can and do bite or attack. Labradors and golden retrievers always feature high on the lists of dogs who have savaged or bitten a child—not because they are bred to be vicious or cranky, but because the very opposite is true. People assume these dogs (and many other family favorites) are safe and leave them alone with children.

Older babies, toddlers, and preschoolers can all get into a tussle with a dog over food (either animal or human food) or accidentally or deliberately torment an animal by poking or intimidating them. No dog is a rational being that makes decisions. A dog has inbred responses to certain situations: even if later they "know" they shouldn't have bitten, they will bite in some situations. Even one bite can severely disfigure or damage a child.

Putting a face near a dog is considered a challenge by most dogs. And a child's face is very much at the height of the face of many dogs, especially when the child does things such as hugging them. The majority of bites to kids under 5 are to the face, with hands and arms the next most likely parts. Because children are smaller than adults, the bite or injury is usually more serious and needs hospitalization more often. Another point to remember is the bigger the jaws, the more damage that can be done before a dog is pulled away, even if there has been only one bite. Have a look at the head of your baby or child and the jaws of your pet or another dog and draw your own conclusions.

Sometimes people say their child is so used to being with dogs that the kid thinks they are one, but the pack mentality of dogs makes this situation very, very dangerous. When the kid arrives in

the family after the dog, the dog usually considers the child lower in the pack hierarchy. This is a recipe for disaster, especially if the child is in the habit of wandering around with food, gets between the dog and its food, or tries to take something from the dog such as a stick or a bone. Trainable animals such as dogs must be taught to recognize all members of the family as superior animals in the pack. If possible have the child first and get the dog as a puppy when your child is old enough to be a "top dog." A puppy can be "socialized" to accept small children and other dogs. But regardless of training or temperament, dogs—and cats, and all other animals—should never be left alone with a child or baby.

Some dogs off leash will attack a child who is running or on a bicycle, or for no apparent reason. Some dogs, even accidentally, can knock down or badly frighten a child. If you take your child to areas where dogs are off leash, you are relying on every dog being firmly under the voice control of their owners.

Many books and children's hospital sites carry information about choosing, caring for, and dealing with a dog (see More Info at the end of this chapter). But watch out for ancient books that give old-fashioned training methods ("Beat the animal regularly and cheerfully").

WHAT TO TEACH CHILDREN ABOUT DOGS

If you have a toddler, start with the simplest info listed below and add more info as needed or as the child gets older.

* Never go near a dog you don't know.

* Never touch or go near a dog that is eating or sleeping.

* If an adult is with you and says it's okay, approach a dog with the back of your hand held down flat for it to sniff.

* Don't bend down and put your face in front of the dog's face.

* Pat a dog gently and calmly.

* You don't have to pat a dog because someone tells you to: it's okay to be scared and to stay away.

* Don't talk loudly or in a high-pitched or excited voice, or wriggle about when you're patting a dog.

* The warning signs of a bite or an attack include raised hackles, growling, lips drawn back, and ears down.

* Stand still if a dog approaches and don't look it in the eye or go down to its level.

* Move away from dogs that are fighting: never try to stop them.

* Never touch dog (or any other animal) poop: it's yucky and has germs in it.

* Always wash your hands after patting a dog.

Cats

Cat poop is a known cause of toxoplasmosis, which can cause damage to a fetus when it infects a pregnant woman. Pregnant women, or women who might be pregnant, should be gloved and meticulous when disposing of cat litter, should garden with gloves on, and keep other people's cats away from their garden.

Children too should not come in contact with cat poop because even though the cat may be healthy it can carry diseases and parasites. As with dogs, kids need to be told they must wash their hands after they've touched a cat because cats have germs and lick their bottoms. Cat fur (and the hair of some other animals) can cause an allergic reaction.

more info

BASIC HOME SAFETY

Unintentional injuries are the leading cause of death in children between the ages of 1 and 21 in the United States. There are a variety of organizations that provide helpful information about how you can make your home and child safer.

National Safety Council

Its website features links to a home safety checklist and how to baby proof your home. There are also downloadable fact sheets.
www.nsc.org

Keep Kids Healthy

Website with lots of helpful links and articles.
www.keepkidshealthy.com/welcome/safety.html

The American Red Cross

American Red Cross first aid, CPR, Child and Infant CPR classes teach you emergency situation skills that can potentially save a life.
www.redcross.org

ANIMALS

Each breed of animal will have its own fanciers' club or organization. You can use a computer search engine to find them; for example, type in "border collie". Always supervise your kid if they are searching the internet for a certain breed or for subjects such as "pets", "kittens", and "dogs". Unfortunately, nasty porn sites sometimes pop up when least expected.

The Humane Society of the United States

Has sections dedicated to pet care, preventing animal bites, and teaching your children about how to avoid getting bit (including downloadable coloring activities), and how to select the right pet for your family.
www.hsus.org

Pets 911

Pets 911 consists of both a web site (www.Pets911.com) and a toll-free, automated hotline (1-888-PETS-911) that allows pet lovers to access local information simply by providing their zip code. You can scan through pictures of adoptable pets posted by some 950 animal shelters and adoption groups, and search by breed and other characteristics. You can search tens of thousands of lost-and-found pet listings from all areas of the United States. You can also find nearby emergency veterinary hospitals, pet-friendly apartments, and more.

About-Dogs.com

Info on dog breeds, how to choose the breed that is suitable to your personal and environmental circumstances, pet care, obedience training, and so on. Includes a Dog Questionaire designed to help you select the dog breed appropriate for you.
www.about-dogs.com/choosing_a_dog_questionnaire.htm

CLOTHES

Really expensive imported kids' clothes that cost more than yours are a waste of time and money as children grow out of them so quickly. Many of them are ludicrously impractical and more for the sort of person who likes to dress a child as a little adult, which is always kind of creepy. They are often made of child-

unfriendly fabrics such as leather and require drycleaning, hand washing, or an on-call staff of cashmere-laundering valets. Some catalogs for children's clothes look more like very dubious kiddie-porn, what with their lipstick and bikini tops for people who won't have breasts for another twelve years. I don't know why I'm mentioning this, it's just that it gives me the whim-whams.

saving money on clothes

Generally, most of the expensive sturdy brands of clothes (not the frou-frou brands) are better made and longer lasting, although price is no guarantee. Some designers now are making clothes with let-downable hems and arms so they last longer.

Sensible gear such as undershirts, undies, T-shirts, and skivvies are best bought at inexpensive department stores, especially during sales. Boys' departments are often cheaper for no good reason except that a plain onesie is cheaper than one with a fairy on it. You can buy a girl the cheaper boys' trousers since at this age they don't know the difference. Discount outlets and thrift-shops are great sources but do keep an eye out for shoddy clothes—"cheap" means expensive if they fall apart in the second wash.

You can shop at sales if you plan ahead and buy clothes out of season and squirrel away bargains for use in a year or so, although you need to predict what size your child will be next summer or winter. I bought a size 9 dress on sale for my daughter when she was 6 months old but I think I was technically demented at the time from lack of sleep—in fact I can't think what I was doing out of the house.

It's always useful to hook up with someone with kids a little older than yours so you can get their hand-me-downs, and to find someone to hand yours on to, unless you're saving them for another baby.

Once kids get to the toddler and preschool stage they're a lot harder on clothes than babies are and don't grow out of them so quickly so there'll probably be fewer inherited or handed on, or they'll look a little shabbier than the baby hand-me-downs.

Parenting magazines, especially freebies, often have ads for clothes-swapping shops and sales outlets for kids' stuff. Shopping on e-bay can yield interesting bargains.

Being able to sew really comes in handy for children's clothes. Fabric shops always have details of nearby sewing classes.

fOR a BaBy

Try to grab baby clothes from thrift shops, friends, or at sales. You need lots of each item because, although babies don't run around getting dirty, they can have quite surprisingly explosive poops and vomits, and you can't always be at the washing machine. Don't dress babies in unnatural fabrics: a polyester–cotton blend and polar fleece are as unnatural as you want to go. Nylon is definitely a no-no: partly for comfort and "breathability" reasons—nylon can be hot and itchy—but also because children's clothes must be as fire-resistant as possible. Make sure all baby clothes are machine wash-able and, unless you live in perpetual sunshine, will go in the dryer. Clothes with stretch and a soft feel are best, which is why "broken in" second-hand clothes are great—it's such a strange new world outside the womb that most babies are extremely disgruntled by being changed.

Babies need six to ten undershirts. Some come in wool, but this can irritate a baby's skin and lead to overheating even in cold areas as babies are usually inside in nasty weather. You'll need cotton for the tropics and summer.

Tiny babies could have three or four cotton nighties so it's eas-ier to change their diapers without fuss. After a couple of weeks to a month those little all-in-one suits are good, but make sure they're always a bit bigger than your baby as babies grow quickly.

Expensive flouncy outfits should be left to the relatives and friends to buy: they're such a hassle for babies at this age, who throw up on them anyway.

You'll need three to ten bibs, depending on how dribbly your baby is—once babies start to teethe they seem to dribble a lot. Towelling bibs are good; plastic-backed ones can become a bit humid underneath. Tea towels and cloth diapers make excellent substitutes (and are good for wiping up spills as well).

Winter or northern babies will need warm clothes and a warm polar fleece or wooly hat, extra layers, and bootees. But if you live in the South and even if your child will never need a good warm coat, they will definitely need a sunhat (and baby sunscreen lotion) wherever they live. Get a sunhat that really does shade the face and neck. Babies sometimes become fascinated by a hat on their head. If everyone else in the group wears one, and the baby is given something else interesting to distract them, hat-staying-on may be more achievable. Ideally, go for hats such as soft cotton ones without nylon-sewn labels so they're not itchy or uncomfortable.

furry hat

Sunhat

Shoes should be fitted at a children's shoe shop or department store. Kids don't need a proper pair until they're walking steadily outside, and even then they should go barefooted often for their development.

You'll work out the rest as you go along.

BABIES' CLOTHES SIZES

0 to 3 months = up to 10 lbs   9 months = 14 to 16 lbs
6 months = 11 to 14 lbs   12 months = 21 to 24 lbs

fOR a tODDLeR OR a LittLe kiD

Clothes get dirty now that the kid is on the move so you'll need lots of tough outfits. They should be easy to get out of for using the toilet and so that the child can start to dress themselves. Long skirts or dresses on a girl will restrict her ability to learn physical skills such as climbing ladders or running.

It's nearly always good to buy the next size up so your kid's clothes will be comfy and not too tight, and they can wear them a bit longer.

KIDS' CLOTHES SIZES

Children's sizes are basically related to ages from 1 to 14, although some clothes such as raincoats, and all clothes from some brands, are just labeled "S," "M," and "L" for small, medium, and large—you'll have to ask for sales help. And some European clothes have sizes such as "116." Ask for help or move to Milan, darling.

Brands vary a lot with their sizes: some are generous and some are not. A kid aged 2 may be into a "Size 3" regardless of whether the kid is small, average, or big for their age.

You can store sales and thrift-store bargains in bags or boxes marked "Size 2T," "Size 3T," and so on.

Pacifiers and Thumbs

Man, those little creatures like to suck. It calms them and they make cute noises like Maggie Simpson. But enough about businessmen with cigars.

Some people are very stern about pacifiers (and some of the sternest end up using them). Some want to use a pacifier but the baby spits it every time. Others never feel the need. Some parents prefer their kids to suck their thumb and then realize that there can be serious teeth misalignment, resulting in eating or speech problems. Other people say Praise Be the Pacifier and the Thumb for yea, verily, a parent gets a better night's sleep. Pacifiers and thumbs (or fingers) are certainly not newfangled ideas: both have been used for generations.

Pacifiers

Good points about pacifiers
- ★ Most babies love them.
- ★ They will temporarily soothe an upset baby unless they're hungry or have a shockingly irritating diaper.
- ★ They can help solve a sleep problem.

The trouble with pacifiers
- ★ Using them in the first month or so can confuse a baby learning to suck from the nipple in the right way.
- ★ They cost money.
- ★ They deteriorate.
- ★ They get lost.
- ★ You usually need a few to rotate.
- ★ If a baby can't replace their own pacifier, they'll cry until you come and do it about ninety-four times in the night. (This is a very good moment to give it up: one or two nights of fussing and it's over, otherwise it's weeks of getting up those ninety-four times to pop the pacifier in again.)
- ★ Pacifiers are addictive.
- ★ When the kid has a cold and they want to suck on their pacifier, they can't breathe.

★ They can "buck" and misalign teeth, especially the longer they're used.

★ If used a lot, they deprive a baby of time to learn to feel with their mouth, speak, and sing.

★ They need to be sterilized.

Using pacifiers

Don't use pacifiers:

★ to shut a child up instead of trying to find out what's wrong.

★ unless they're going to sleep.

★ if the child always spits it out.

Pacifiers need to be:

★ for the right age—see your pharmacist.

★ sterilized regularly (after your kid gets bigger and you see what else goes into their mouth you probably won't be quite as rigorous with sterilizing—but, still, sticking it in your own mouth is amazingly NOT, technically, sterilizing).

★ checked regularly for nicks, cuts, tears, and any other damage—throw out any damaged ones.

★ rotated—always have a few spares and one or two in the baby or toddler bag or your handbag in a clean container with a lid.

Getting rid of the pacifier

Here's some advice from parents who responded to the Kidwrangling Survey. You'll need to match a suggestion to the personality and sensitivity of your kid or gently experiment.

★ Either give the pacifier up when the baby is young enough to not be able to put it in themselves, or wait until the child can participate in the decision to stop, so it's not traumatic.

★ Don't try to do it when a new baby comes along and needs a pacifier.

- ★ Leave it out for Santa, the Easter Bunny, or the Pacifier Fairy to take. Something appropriate will be left in its place—a present and maybe some sparkles.
- ★ Give it up on an important birthday: explain that the Birthday Pacifier Fairy will come.
- ★ Mail it to a newer little baby who needs a pacifier.
- ★ Don't tell the child it's wrong to like the pacifier, just that older kids don't have pacifier and they should let you know when they're old enough not to have one. Older siblings, cousins, or friends can help by saying they don't use one now, but they mustn't ridicule the little one: get them to just set a non-critical, matter-of-fact example, maybe even saying they missed theirs for a few minutes on the first night they didn't have it, but then they forgot about it.
- ★ Say "You're a big girl now" or "You're such a big boy," and have a discussion about getting older, then ask them if they're ready to give the pacifier up themselves. (Some children will just announce that in that case they most certainly are not big, thank you.)
- ★ A ceremonial throwing in the trash is good—but you must be firm and not go backwards by admitting you can buy new ones at the drugstore.
- ★ Pretend you've left the pacifier at home, at the vacation place, or at a friend's, or that it's lost. Be very sympathetic but positive about not having a pacifier any more.
- ★ Safety-pin the pacifier to a teddy or dolly who needs it more than they do that night and the next, and then teddy or dolly can lose their pacifier.
- ★ Cut the pacifier using down strictly to only sleeptimes in the crib, then to only nighttime, and then go cold turkey.
- ★ Introduce another aspect to the sleep ritual (such as a special sleep toy) before you take the pacifier away.
- ★ Let the child choose when to swap their pacifier for a new toy they really want: then it's their decision.

★ Get up early together and give the pacifier to the garbage crew: you can watch them go away in the big truck and then have a special breakfast to celebrate getting older.

★ Cut down to one or two pacifier, then "accidentally" drop the last one in the toilet.

★ Plant the pacifier in the garden to see if a pacifier tree grows.

★ Pierce the pacifier—a large hole means it won't be satisfying any more (but make sure bits can't break off and become a choking hazard).

I have to say a lot of kids will see through any ruses. For the sort of child who's likely to say "Well, why don't we buy one with my credit card on the Internet?" the direct bribery approach is best.

This was the worst suggestion I've EVER heard: "The Pacifier Monster took it away." It almost made *me* cry.

Many parents said to let the child go until they decide—which they sometimes do to save embarrassment on sleep-overs.

BLaNKieS aND OtHeR comfoRt items

Remember Linus in the Peanuts cartoon strip, always carrying around his security blanket? Kids who suck their thumbs, and some who don't, often have little bits of fabric (velvet, sheepskin, or a silky material are favorites) or a soft toy to stroke while they're sucking—part of the comfort ritual. It's always a good idea to rotate a few pieces so they don't get too filthy and there's one on the go while another's in the wash. And keep a spare in the baby bag in case one is flung out the window of the car.

It's usually tough for everyone to give up a comfort object and a pacifier or thumb sucking at the same time. You will probably need to have a program of cutting down, then eliminating, the comfort object, following some of the suggestions for getting rid of a pacifier, before you can start tackling the thumb sucking. (I know a grown woman who still sucks her thumb and rubs a piece of fabric—but not when she's on a first date.)

†HUmB SuCKiNg

Thumb (or, less commonly, finger) sucking is certainly cheaper than buying pacifier, but you can't throw away a thumb and know the habit has stopped, and it's more likely to cause buck or misaligned teeth. This situation is obviously more serious when permanent teeth come in (at 6 or 7 years of age). Most parents use a gradual, conscious cutting down and rewards system for stopping the thumb sucking. Daytime stopping is largely a matter of keeping the hands busy and nighttime will need some new comfort rituals or objects.

Apart from gently taking the thumb out if it creeps in when the kid's asleep, many people suggest something bitter tasting on it to break the habit before adult teeth come in, with an extra-special reward given when the habit stops. This is a bit too much like a punishment rather than an encouragement and support: it's probably best to give it a miss and skip straight to help, reassurance, and a bribe.

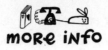

moRe iNfo

Helping the Thumb-Sucking Child

by Rosemarie Van Norman, Avery Publishing, 1999.

Ms. Van Norman is a "certified oral myologist" and basically works with kids to help them stop sucking their thumb. She explains how thumb sucking can damage teeth and speech, and suggests gentle ways to phase it out.

teeth

Some kids are even born with weeny teeth, but the majority have their first couple start to come through between about the age of 6 and 10 months. They usually get the teeth at the front first, often at the bottom, and then the rest are "filled in" over the following months. These first ones are some- times called "milk teeth." You can ask your dentist for a chart if you

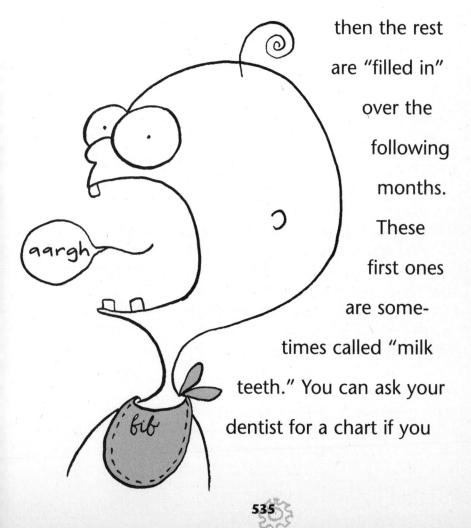

aargh

bib

want to know the usual order, and what a lateral incisor is.

Generally, a kid has enough teeth for a good chew by the time they're 1 year to 18 months old, and all their teeth by the time they're 2 and a half to 3: the full mouth is about twenty teeth. (Eventually, with the second, or permanent, teeth, the kid will probably have thirty-two.)

WHat aRe tHe symptoms of teetHing?

Sometimes a baby rubs their gum, cries, or is cranky from the pain of the teeth coming through. The following symptoms are not recognized as teething related by baby experts but are often attributed to it by parents: drooling, red cheeks, a runny nose, fever, diaper rash, sleep disturbance. The gum will often look red, then you'll see a bit of white poking through and suddenly there's a whole tooth. Each tooth that comes through may cause the baby to be cross and feel pain or they may hardly notice.

What can you do?
Explain soothingly to your baby what's happening: even if they can't grasp everything they will feel reassured. Give them lots of cuddles and perhaps rub their gum gently with your finger. Giving babies

frozen things or ice to bite on can be too harsh and freeze the tissues in the mouth. Mostly kids want to chew on something, whether it's really cold or not, which is why zweibacks (like tiny, hard breadsticks) are popular: check that any you buy are sugar and salt free. Give them teething rings from the drugstore that can be refrigerated (but don't freeze them). Sucking on a pacifier also often helps the pain. This can be a good time to start your baby learning to sip from a spouty cup because babies find biting on the spout, like biting on a zweiback, gives them some relief.

Teething gel, which is supposed to numb the gum, is not recommended by a lot of doctors because it gets sucked off quickly. You can give a baby painkiller if the pain seems really bad.

Prepare to have the usual sleep routine dickered with as your baby deals with the new feelings of pain and soreness. They can find it hard to resettle themselves on the nights when a tooth is about to appear.

Looking after teeth

The main thing is not to give any sweetened drinks or undiluted fruit juice (it's very acidic so dilute it 1:1 with water), or to let babies or older kids suck on bottles of milk or juice for ages, particularly at night. All these things almost guarantee decay and, in the worst-case scenario, the unhappy prospect of a general anesthetic and the pulling out of lots of milk teeth before kids get their permanent ones. It's best to give a bottle of milk before bed, then clean their teeth. Any daytime drag-around drinks or nighttime sips should be water. Breastfed babies can also have their teeth wiped or brushed after the last feed of the day. Avoid sweetened medicines, but if you have one prescribed with sugar give it before teeth-cleaning time. Make dessert

New!

Sticky Lumpy Things

very BAD for teeth

and treats a "sometimes" thing, not an everyday or always-after-dinner thing.

Some kids genetically have "strong teeth" or ones that are shaped better to avoid decay, but they will still need to take care of them; others may have to work harder to get the same protection with cleaning. When the teeth arrive, take the kid to the dentist once or twice a year.

Cleaning teeth

Kids are supposed to have their teeth brushed twice a day—it's most convenient after breakfast and after dinner. For the very early baby days dentists recommend using a soft cloth—but if your baby has a strong gag reflex you'll have to be careful. See if your pharmacist can find you a tiny brush. There are baby and toddler toothbrushes and toddler toothpastes. Ask your dentist or pharmacist what's appropriate for your kid in the way of fluoride: it will vary depending on the fluoride they're already getting from the water supply.

bad, BAD toothbrush

At first you can do the teeth cleaning, making sure you get to every surface. When your child is a toddler, and if you can afford it, introduce a battery-operated toothbrush—the kid can do more themselves and get more surfaces done properly before you give a final once-over. Babies and kids should only have a tiny amount of toothpaste for each cleaning. It's usually described as no more than the size of a pea (your guess is as good as mine as peas vary in size—the ones under my mattress do anyway): ask your dentist. Put a mirror where the kid can see it—it will guarantee more time spent cleaning the teeth. Kids aren't able to clean their own teeth thoroughly until they're about 10.

TEETH ON THE MOVE

Some teeth may naturally grow in odd spaces or at different angles: check with a pediatric dentist if you're concerned. Little teeth are sometimes moved by pacifier or thumb sucking. In some cases this makes a difference to chewing or speech. The teeth will often travel back slowly to the right position if the habit is broken (do this gently—see the previous chapter, Pacifiers and Thumbs).

going to the Dentist

Explain why we need to visit the dentist (because they help us look after our teeth, not so we can enjoy the blindingly painful razzle-dazzle of root canal work). Practice at home or at child care, especially opening the mouth and letting someone look inside, being on a big chair that goes up and down (pretend or visit someone with one of those TV-watching recliners the size of an aircraft carrier and shine a light in). Take your kid with you a couple of times when you visit your dentist—just for cheery check-ups, not to any sessions where actual work or drilling is done. They can lie on your lap and let the dentist look in their mouth at the end of the visit as practice.

You can tell your kid just before you take them or that morning so there's no time for some idiot to scare them about the dentist. Don't ever use the dentist as a threat ("You can't have any candy because you'll get holes in your teeth and the dentist will have to drill your teeth and it hurts"). If your kid is apprehensive, find a dentist who specializes in children and has a drawcard such as a fish tank in the waiting room or special things to look at in the surgery, and plan to come back a couple of times if your kid refuses to open their mouth. (See More Info at the end of the later Reading chapter for a kids' book about going to the dentist.)

Your dentist will probably have all manner of pamphlets, free toothbrushes, and other paraphernalia tucked away in the cupboard.

LateR: LOSiNg teetH

The milk teeth begin to drop out when kids are about 6 years old. Check with other parents to see what the going rate is with the Tooth Fairy. If a baby tooth is knocked out, don't worry about replacing it, but see a dentist as soon as you can to check that it's all out and there are no complications. When your child is older, get a fitted mouth guard for sports.

moRe iNfo

www.adha.org/kidstuff
The kids' page of the American Dental Hygienists' Association explains the difference between incisors and cuspids, and more besides.

food

You might be an expert whizzer in the kitchen already, able to conjure up a family supper from some stale cumin, a parsnip, and half a can of mackerel. Or you might be serving a toddler truffle-oil bavarois of nutkin fern imported directly from a family-run vineyard in Sardinia. On the other hand you might be shocked—*shocked*—to find that not all food comes from Café Splat or, after adding

boiling water, from a polystyrene cup. Even if you're a gourmet dinner-party cook, you might have no idea how to feed a family with those pesky nutrient thingies. This chapter aims to soothe you as effectively as half a package of cookies.

cooking for your baby and toddler

Most people start off having to learn everything about feeding babies and toddlers and so they begin with lots of books, worry about it all the time, compare notes with other parents, freeze little ice cubes of color-coordinated puréed things, and then a few months later find the kid is eating whatever the grown-up department is having that night and the books are propping up the wobbly end of the kitchen table.

It's in your interest to introduce a wide range of food to your baby and toddler from the get-go, but there's never any guarantee this will result in a child who will eat everything (even tripe-flavored spinach sticks). Lots of babies love all they're given and then gradually get sterner about the whole caper. (You may be interested in the earlier chapters on eating in the babies, toddlers, and little kids parts of the book.)

Do ask your GP or pediatrician for the latest nutritional guidelines. Lots of grandparents and older books recommend using honey to sweeten things, but dentists and some nutritionists disagree with this—it must be awfully rare, but honey *can* be a cause of botulism in babies—so remember that "expert" advice changes over time, especially in this area. (Which is another reason not to worry too much: I mean, if they don't know what they're doing, why should you?)

Beware of child-centered cookbooks that are full of pictures of children's food shaped into fishes with carroty fins, and boats with tuna flags—you know the sort of thing. And these kinds of books are always full of recipes that take too much time. Plus, frankly, they're written by aliens.

carrot rocket

"I told my 3-year-old daughter that mung bean shoots were called mung bean candies. She loves them." AHEM, ANONYMOUS AUTHOR

DRINKS

Commercial fizzy drinks, colas, lemonades, and other flavored drinks that come with bubbles in cans and bottles are a bit of a disaster for little kids. Along with undiluted fruit juices, they're the largest cause of tooth decay and a big contributor to children being over a healthy weight. They have also been implicated in other health issues, which is hardly surprising when you find out there is the equivalent of several teaspoons of sugar in most of them. Drinks with caffeine (including colas) shouldn't be given to children because their little bodies aren't ready for the chemicals.

So avoid fizzy drinks whenever you can—if your kid doesn't have them as a habit, they won't ask for them all the time unless they're watching TV ads for them. Milk, water, and fresh fruit juice diluted 1:1 with water are much better for kids than expensive soft drinks.

Fizzy drinks for special occasions can be the non-sugar versions. Kids won't know the difference!

If a toddler or little kid has constant access to water in, say, a little pop-up-top bottle that can be taken on travels and left on the table or the floor during playtimes, or from a filter system or a cold tap, they should be getting enough fluids on a self-serve basis. Refill commercial water bottles with tap water so the kid is getting fluoride—it's a lot cheaper too! Milk and other drinks can also be offered through the day. (Ovaltine and similar drinks are a good source of iron: check the labels for what else is in there.) If a child is constipated, drinking more water will help.

cooking for the family

Many moms (and some dads) come from the full-time workforce to full-time or part-time parenthood and house executeering (I don't know what that means but clearly the word "housewifery" is out of the question). People are sometimes amazed to find that cooking becomes fun—or at least one of the more creative and rewarding parts of homemaking life. You may find you have time for experiments and waiting for things to rise, cook, or marinate—at least once in a while. And in all but the most alarming cases, you get to eat your mistakes.

Of course, you may still hate cooking, but even so the next few years are going to be a lot more pleasant if you learn ways to get it done efficiently. From now on money will probably be tighter than usual, unless you've just cracked onto Prince Harry, so eating in may be your only option most of the time.

My cooking skills rivaled those of an enraged marmoset before I was pregnant. With the help of some books I am now approaching snappy chimp status. These books, listed in More Info at the end of this chapter, are basic cooking bibles, with some multicultural influences, for beginners. You can take up others whenever you're ready: Asian food guru Charmaine Solomon, Moroccan mavens Greg and Lucy Malouf, Lebanese mama Abla Amad, Madhur Jaffrey for Indian, early Jill Dupleix for modern Aussie with nostalgic tweaks, Jamie Oliver's first books for 1990s Pommy chutzpah cooking and pervy nostalgia.

food allergies and intolerances

Many children have allergies or intolerances to various foods, which can include milk, wheat, peanuts, strawberries, and oranges. Allergies are relatively rare and many children grow out of them or turn out to have been misdiagnosed. An allergy is a reaction by the immune system against something, such as a food, that most people don't have a problem with. Children usually don't grow out of an allergy that causes a violent reaction. You'll probably start with suspicions and instincts or the food allergy will suddenly become obvious because of a reaction.

Food intolerances arise when the body is unable to process a certain kind of food because of, say, enzymes not working properly to break down the sugar (lactose) in milk (this intolerance is often avoided by having kids use soy milk, yogurt, and other lactose-free stuff). Some babies are unable to process the lactose in breast milk and need to go on a soy-based formula or alternate breast and bottle for a period recommended by their GP—but this is rare and usually temporary.

Your doctor will help you isolate an allergy or intolerance. It's very important to have your suspicions professionally confirmed. Support groups on the Internet and specialized books can help you manage any lasting problem. Unfortunately, some people are airy-fairy and dismissive of allergies and may try to give your children the wrong food in the belief that you or your child is just fussy—you will need to explain the allergy and what's required calmly and firmly to the child as well as to others looking after your kid or running a party.

Children should not be given peanuts until they are over 4 years old (some people say 5), and then watched carefully for a reaction. Any violent reaction that involves breathing difficulties means you need to call an ambulance immediately—that's ana- phylactic shock. Other substances that can cause anaphylactic shock include eggs and shellfish (and latex on skin contact).

See More Info at the end of this chapter for books on the effects of food, and cooking for children with allergies and food intolerances.

"My kid screamed and was in pain for the first 18 months of his life. We were told he had really bad gas and colic. Finally, my doctor suggested we try the find-the-allergy diet. He's now great unless he eats something on the no-go list, when he gets stomach cramps, diarrhea, cries a lot, and often gets hyper and uncontrollable." AN

vegetarian and vegan kids

Many vegetarian parents allow their young children to eat meat, and many vegan parents give their kids meat, dairy products, and eggs because they see this as the best way for their kids to grow and develop in the early years. Many will seek out organic meats, free- range eggs, and other products that are aligned to their philosophy. Rather than impose their beliefs, these parents are usually content to allow their kids to make up their own mind later about whether or when to become a vegetarian or a vegan, which is most likely to happen in the teenage years.

Any form of vegetarian or vegan diet you are on during pregnancy and breastfeeding, or you are giving your baby or children, needs to be okayed by an independent nutritionist who knows your individ- ual needs. A pediatric nutritionist or a dietician at your nearest chil- dren's hospital or community health center will help you make sure you're meeting the special needs of babies and kids.

Vegetarian kids

Vegetarian children have very special needs. Because vegetarian food is high in fiber, kids often feel full before they've had enough nutrients and calories. This can mean that they're smaller than they would otherwise be and don't fulfill their growth and brain potential. They need energy-dense foods as well, such as dairy products, fruit, chopped nuts (but not peanuts before 4), seeds, avocado, protein such as eggs, and soy products. They will also need special care to get iron, calcium, fat, and nutrients such as B_{12} and zinc. See More Info at the end of this chapter for recipe books for vegetarians.

Should kids be vegans?

Of all the children whose families insist its members follow strict dietary rules, vegan kids are the most at risk of damage or deficiency. Avoid any vegan websites and books that simply apply the principles of adult veganism to children as this is dangerous. Many vegan websites have suggested diets for pregnant and lactating women and for babies and kids, but don't forget to check these with an independent nutritionist who can adjust them to you and your child's special needs.

If you are very committed to being a vegan, you will need to take great care during your pregnancy and entire period of breastfeeding to ensure that your intake of various nutrients is enough for your baby to thrive. Babies who aren't breastfed *must* be given a commercial baby milk formula based on cow or soy milk, not soy milk, rice milk, or some combination you mix yourself.

Vegans need to address the very real risk of a vitamin B_{12} deficiency in a fetus or a breastfed baby, and in vegan children. A B_{12} deficiency causes serious damage to mental and neural development. It's probably safest for pregnant and breastfeeding vegans to take a daily supplement that contains B_{12} as any B_{12} stores are rapidly used up. Although many vegan writings on diet suggest that B_{12} is in many foods, this is not always the case. Vitamin B_{12}-fortified soy milk is a good source, but other often-recommended foods such as mushrooms don't always contain absorbable B$_{12}$. Make sure you are getting the recommended daily dose for you and your baby.

Children on a vegan diet who appear well ("His height and weight are okay according to the charts, and he's happy") can in fact be deficient in iron, vitamins, calcium, and calories, and not be as tall or as heavy as they would be otherwise. Vegan babies, toddlers, and children who fill up on bran, grains, and other high-fiber items will feel full but are not growing to their full potential, physically and mentally. To be honest, even among committed vegans themselves, only a minuscule minority of people advocate veganism for babies and small children, and I could find very little detailed information about how to achieve optimum health for them on such a diet, even on vegan websites.

"UNDERWEIGHT" AND "OVERWEIGHT" KIDS

Babies need those roly-poly thighs and "rolls": they are not too fat. Many toddlers grow into a rangier shape, losing their "baby fat," while others maintain that cute sticky-out tummy. Remember that genetically your child may not be like you, your partner, or any of your other children. They may resemble Great-Uncle Feargal and be just the shape they are meant to be. One of the greatest and most useful gifts you can give your child is to lead by example and help them maintain a healthy body image. Try not to use terms or voice tones that carry a sense of disapproval or judgment to describe your body, their body, or anyone else's. If you say "I'm so fat" or "He's so scrawny," your kid will learn to think badly of themselves, whatever they look like.

Underweight kids, especially babies, need their problem corrected quickly so they can continue to thrive. See your doctor right away if your child is losing weight—kids in the under-5 age group should not consistently lose weight unless they are above their healthy weight. Some will not have a buffer zone of adorable extra chub and observable weight loss is often a sign of illness. Having said that, try not to panic about it—kids will go up and down a little all the time and you don't need to weigh them. Just know them well so you'll notice a big change. (Toddlers who are fussy eaters can go for days on a cheese stick and glasses of milk. I think they secretly do it to mock us.) If you are really worried, make sure you are referred to a child nutritionist specialist.

Children should not be fed too much fast or junk food (as opposed to fresh, home-cooked food) because it can be very filling, with few nutrients, and it is too salty, which can damage the kidneys. Kids who are above their average weight need to continue to eat a filling, nutritious diet and, most importantly, exercise each day. The diagnosis of "overweight" must not be made by a relative or parent who thinks everyone should look "thin," but by a pediatrician. Kids who are in a healthy weight range should never be deprived of full-fat foods. (Low-fat foods are almost always for adults, unless prescribed by a pediatric dietician.) It can be hard to change a whole family's habits, but a nutritionist can help you. Ask your GP for a referral to find out what your child needs and the easiest way to achieve it.

See also the Being Active chapter coming up soon.

COOKING WITH KIDS

A lot of recipe writers don't seem to understand that cooking for kids and cooking with kids are entirely different kettles of mashed fish. Most cookbooks supposedly teaching kids to cook are exclusively devoted to totally crap, sugary things. I like making a chocolate cake too, but not every day. Sometimes cooking something savory is an extremely useful way to amuse the tots *and* get some dinner at the end. The world has enough toffee apples: one recipe is too many. And making anything with toffee can be one of the fastest ways to get from your kitchen to a children's hospital—all that boiling, sticky stuff.

Here's a classic example of a recipe that sounds kid friendly but isn't: certain pizzas. Some require you to cook the dough base at a very high temperature before the toppings can go on—another easy way for kids to burn themselves. So you have to leave enough preparation time for the base and tray to cool down completely before the kids start chucking on the toppings and the mozzarella. By that stage it's 10 p.m. and you've drunk the vanilla essence and sent everyone to bed with a ginger snap and a mushroom.

Better to either make pizza bases in advance and freeze them or get ready-made ones from the supermarket (good lord, that can't be right!) so the kids can get stuck into the fun part straight away. I know making dough can be fun too, it's just not for everyone.

Cookbooks for kids

Simple recipes from your own books are best. Most cookbooks for kids, no matter how groovy looking, are nothing but fudge, sludge, and pudge. When kids get a bit older, they might be interested in the books given in More Info at the end of this chapter.

Good things to cook with kids

You might like to try making:

- ★ cookies and gingerbread folk—kids can cut the shapes with cookie cutters or a blunt baby knife.
- ★ muffins—measure, sift, pour, stir, spoon.
- ★ sandwiches—butter, fill, and squash down.
- ★ pancakes—you fry and they sprinkle on lemon and sugar, savory bits, or fruit, then roll.
- ★ smoothies—kids can cut up soft fruit with a blunt knife and chuck the chunks into the blender, pour in the milk and a dollop of yogurt, and break in the eggs (but kids should never operate the blender, and some small children will

want to be under the bed with fingers in ears during the jooshing bit anyway).

★ pizza—the kids add the decoration to a cooked, cooled pizza base or a ready-made one.

★ mashed, squished, and extremely distressed potatoes.

You could also let kids:

★ "help" to measure or pour while you work—rattly sounding things such as uncooked rice, barley, or dried chickpeas can be satisfying poured into or ferried from a cold saucepan to a bowl and back. Don't let them do this if spills bother you or it will be stressful for everyone.

★ plant and pick things in the garden.

★ help work out shopping lists and look for items in the supermarket.

★ help with meal preparation—pod peas, unwrap corn cobs, tear lettuce into bits, and so on.

Aprons

Plastic aprons can be very hot and, obviously, not absorbent, but they're good for kids to wear if you're making anything with flour because the claggy mess is easier to wipe off than clean up for the washing machine. Cotton aprons are good too, but will need to withstand lots of washes. Aprons that just go round the waist as a fronty sort of skirt look good in Doris Day movies but are otherwise, much like many of Doris's roles, decorative rather than useful.

Safe spots for kids

Kids can start being involved when very young by doing something fun and tactile with food on their highchair tray. After that safe spots need to be found for them, such as a highchair stationed at the kitchen counter but away from anything hot, or at a nearby kitchen table.

kitCHeN safety

As well as generally making your house safe, you'll need to look hard at the safety of your kitchen, particularly once your kid is able to walk and climb and is ready to enjoy "helping" you to cook and wash up (see the Home Safety chapter for what to do with sharp knives and poisonous cleaning liquids and powders).

Teach kids from the earliest age about stove tops and ovens being hot. But don't expect small children to remember this applies every time—they've seen you touch or clean a cold cook top and oven. They also can't necessarily make the connection that somebody else's stove might sometimes be hot too. Perhaps you can institute a rule that kids have to have their hands behind their back when looking at the hotplates or through the glass door of the oven, or when a cake mixer is going, for example. Balance this taboo with lots of things they *can* touch, pour, stir, and measure.

Don't let children near a coffee maker (or any other heating appliance with those child-height easy-push taps!), a kettle, or some other stay-hot device, and be vigilant when anything is on the stove. And make sure there are no dangling electric cords. Most children's scalds are from hot liquids such as tea, coffee, and water, and usually on the hands, or on the face and chest when they pull a container down on themselves. Crawlers and toddlers are at special risk.

If you have a really inquisitive toddler and a dangerously designed kitchen, try cooking during their sleeptime and serving something cold or warmed up in a microwave oven (we'll get to the dangers of microwaves) in the evening when you can't be as vigilant because of everything else going on.

THINGS KIDS SHOULDN'T DO IN THE KITCHEN
(UNTIL THEY'RE WELL TRAINED, SUPERVISED, AND AT LEAST 8)

* Stir hot things.

* Go near the stove top.

* Put things into or take things out of the oven.

* Operate any electrical appliance, including the toaster.

* Taste things without direct permission (it could be chile powder).

The stove top

Always turn saucepan and frying-pan handles away from the front of the stove so they can't be grabbed or knocked. Avoid cooking that's likely to cause burns or a fire. Why risk frying things in oil? French fries can be made in the oven on trays brushed with oil. If your kitchen is badly designed or your child is really into everything, check out safety guards for stove tops, which are available at children's hospital safety shops. These prevent toddlers from pulling things down on themselves.

If you are cooking on the stove top and have to leave the kitchen, turn off the hotplate. It's better to be delayed than on fire. (What a splendid motto.)

Ovens

A microwave oven will heat random bits of the food to scalding temperature, yet often leave the container cool to the touch, so anything cooked, or warmed in a microwave must be thoroughly stirred, rested, cooled, and tested before being given to children. Don't put glass bottles in a microwave: they can break. Some microwave ovens heat more strongly and more quickly than others so be careful with unfamiliar ones.

If your ordinary oven is hot to the touch when it's on, try to rig up some sort of barrier, such as a bit of a playpen, so that the oven is out of bounds then. With food cooked in either kind of oven, be careful when taking lids off as steam can burn severely.

Water

Kids love splashing about in the sink and this can sometimes incidentally even be helpful with the washing up. Start the little ones on a low stool or a chair in front of a sink full of plastic things and lots of suds, and don't worry about splashes unless they're slippery. Always stay in the room with them when water is involved. If children visit or live in your house, make sure the hot-water service has been adjusted so the maximum possible temperature is 125 degrees Fahrenheit so that it takes longer for the water to burn. (Schools and child-care centres are usually required to have their water set to 120 degrees.)

more info

COOKING FOR YOUR BABY AND TODDLER

Super Baby Food
by Ruth Yaron, F.J. Roberts Publishing, 1998.
This is one of the best-selling baby food cookbooks on the market. A hefty volume, *Super Baby Food* explains how easy it is to make baby food at home. Covers the usual ground-busy parents, healthy food, avoid stuff in jars. The author also details nutritional data, feeding schedules, and cooking techniques. All vegetarian.

Simply Natural Baby Food: Easy Recipes for Delicious Meals Your Infant and Toddler Will Love
by Cathe Olson, Goco Pub, 2003.
Emphasizes fresh, natural food choices for your little ones. Includes recipes for breakfasts, lunches, dinners, snacks, desserts, breakfasts, and beverages.

www.organicconsumers.org

The website for the Organic Consumers Association can help you find organic food and products in your area.

COOKING FOR THE FAMILY

The Cook's Companion

by Stephanie Alexander, Viking, Aust., 2002.

The must-have Australian classic. If you only have one cookbook, it has to be this 'un. Encyclopedic and expensive and big enough to bring down an elephant. Ask friends or family to form a cartel so you can get it for a birthday or Christmas. It really does have everything you'll need to know about kitchen equipment and techniques, unique and essential information about what to look for when buying and how to store foods (tomatoes don't go in the fridge? Who knew?), different ways of cooking the same ingredients, which foods go well with other foods if you like to make things up as you go along and ferzillions of precise recipes if you don't, solid old-fashioned cooking, Christmas specials, multicultural recipes, and various fripperies.

Because it's arranged by ingredient, you can buy foods in season when it's cheaper and always find recipes for what to do with them. Beginners can feel clever straight away by starting with standard roast chook and banana muffins (yes, that's two separate recipes) and work up from there. With baking especially it's better to weigh ingredients precisely each time: but if you're always frantic and don't mind slightly dodgy results, you can translate weights into cup measures and jot them down in the book. (Real cooks are horrified by this: it isn't perfect, but neither are we.)

How to Eat: The Pleasures and Principles of Good Food

by Nigella Lawson, Wiley, 2002.

This is another basic book, with lots of ideas and info on techniques, and handy headings for parents about feeding babies and small children, cooking in advance, quick food, and cooking for one or two. Written in a chatty but dignified style.

How to Be a Domestic Goddess: Baking and the Art of Comfort Cooking
by Nigella Lawson, Hyperion, 2001.

Excellent tongue-in-cheek title and a book full of baking recipes and ideas including a fabulous kids' section. Important asides come from experience: here is someone who cooks with as well as for children, and for the school fête—someone who knows that one batch of cupcakes can give you superparent status instantly. Full of comfort food in the way of loaves, puddings, and cakes: great things to make with kids on a Sunday morning when you each have an apron on and it's raining.

Off the Shelf: Cooking from the Pantry
by Donna Hay, Morrow Cookbooks, 2001.

Modern International easy-cooking philosophy, working with everyday items such as canned tomatoes, beans, tuna, rice, noodles. Life will never look like these pictures, unless you take a glass or six of cooking sherry.

FOOD ALLERGIES AND INTOLERANCES

Fed Up: Understanding How Food Affects Your Child and What You Can Do About It
by Sue Dengate, Random House, Aust., 2003.

A comprehensive book about how food additives (chemicals) and different foods themselves (natural chemicals) can affect kids. Sue Dengate includes a list of "Failsafe foods" to try to see if your child's symptoms improve. "Failsafe" stands for Free of Additives and Low In Salicyclates, Amines, and Flavor Enhancers. Remember, though, that any diagnosis you make yourself should be rechecked by a specialist and that thankfully some intolerances are short term.

What's to Eat? The Milk-Free, Egg-Free, Nut-Free Food Allergy Cookbook
by Linda Marienhoff Coss, Plumtree, 2000.

Recipes for people who can't have wheat, eggs, and other common allergy-causing foods. Contains lots of good suggestions for replacement ingredients.

The Failsafe Cookbook: Reducing Food Chemicals for Calm, Happy Families

by Sue Dengate, Random House, Aust., 2003.

Many—not all—children suspected of having attention deficit disorder (ADD) have benefited from a change of diet. Sue Dengate's lists of what to avoid will help people who need to scrutinize labels when shopping.

www.fedupwithfoodadditives.info

Author Sue Dengate's website helps parents with newsletters and updates on food additives and their effects, and by displaying a recommended diet for children whose behavior and health may be affected by additives—but don't forget it's important to get a professional diagnosis and recommendations on your child's individual problem. There are links to lists of suspect additives; support groups; petitions; fact sheets; and info on lobby groups.

American Academy of Allergy, Asthma, and Immunology

Its website is easy to use and has a multitude of links including articles, fast facts, links, video Q&As, best practices, patient support groups, free educational materials, and a just-for-kids corner. Includes a searchable allergy database and physician referral directory.
www.aaaai.org/patients/resources/

www.fankids.org/FANKid/kidindex.html

A food and allergy news website for kids that includes a discussion board "clubhouse" and tips for dealing with allergies

www.foodallergy.org

Has lots of useful info about many kinds of allergies and their effects, how to cope with them, recent relevant research, strategies for school and social life, food alerts, and allergy-free recipes, including a milk-free, egg-free cake.

allergies.about.com

It's a central site providing links to sites on different allergies, cross-referenced with other common problems such as asthma: includes dust mites, mold, peanuts, cats, lactose, and many more. (The prayer link isn't for people allergic to prayers. It's for people who think prayer might help.)

VEGETARIAN KIDS

New Vegetarian Baby: An Entirely New, Updated Edition of the Classic Guide to Raising Your Baby on the Healthiest Possible Diet
by Sharon K. Yntema and Christine H. Beard, McBooks Press, 2000.
The Vegetarian Child
by Sharon K. Yntema, McBooks Press, US, 1995.

The book on babies now includes advice to vegans as well, but at the time of writing the book on the vegetarian child was still in its original edition and didn't. These handbooks explain what children need and their eating habits, and examine the cultures that, usually by necessity, have diets based on vegetarianism. A must for parents who need to know about nutritional values for children on a restricted diet, and who want to be well informed for their children's sake and to help ward off disapproval.

vegetarian.about.com

This is a website with lots of links to recipes, info, and articles, including vegan and vegetarian stuff relevant to babies, toddlers, older kids, and family meals. (And please consider the links to fruitarianism websites as entertainment value only. Fruitarians believe that cooking food makes it toxic. They want you to stop murdering lettuces and celery and only eat fruit because picking it doesn't kill the tree or vine. While this means they can eat nuts, I can only suggest this also means they're eating their relatives, part of the wider nut family.)

COOKING WITH KIDS

The Children's Step by Step Cookbook
by Angela Wilkes, DK Publishing, 2001.

Lots of big, useful photos and, refreshingly, a really packed list of recipes—including snacky bits, eggy things, "toasty treats," main meals, "fruit Frisbees," and ways to keep fresh food interesting. Bear in mind the recipes are really designed for older children, but you can make them together and kids will like to see the photos of other kids doing the business and be thrilled when they do some steps by themselves. Can also be used as a fun picture book for younger kids—they can see pictures of utensils and food and talk about them. Vegetarians are so not going to enjoy the name-that-meat page.

How to Teach Kids to Cook
by Gabriel Gaté, Allen and Unwin, Aust., 2002.

A kid's cookbook based on Aussie food and sensibilities, with many good ideas and child-friendly tips. It has lots of real food, not just cakey things: it would be perfect except that the recipe type size is really annoyingly weeny and all squished up. The book is sponsored by the Canned Food Information service: substitute fresh ingredients for the canned ones if possible.

Health

When people used to tell me that they couldn't come to work because their kid was sick, I thought that was nice of them to stay home with their kid. I imagined a cherub sitting up in bed in a pair of freshly ironed pajamas, quietly doing a jigsaw puzzle on a tray, with a box of tissues, and a small posy of pansies in a short, bulbous vase on the bedside table.

For some reason, I didn't imagine a kid projectile vomiting over twenty-four surfaces just after you'd put

Say 'Aaarrgh!'

new sheets on the bed; the shock of feeling your child's forehead and it almost burning your fingers; the effect of three nights of randomly broken sleep on a parent trying to make smart decisions about health care; the listless misery of a child who doesn't understand why they feel bad; the fundamental need of a sick child to have their parent in sight at all times. I was, quite frankly, not even in the vicinity of a clue.

Kids get sick. It doesn't mean they're unhealthy or sickly; it's how they build up their immune system. And kids have accidents. So this chapter will tell you about injuries and first-aid kit essentials as well as about lots of common complaints and their treatment.

fiRSt aiD

Going to a first-aid course and regularly practicing is the only way to be proficient at stuff such as resuscitation. The American Heart Association, the Red Cross, the National Safety Council, and local hospitals, police and fire departments, and community education centers have courses specific to children as well as general lessons. These sometimes can even be run as a one-time class at a playgroup, child-care center, or school at a minimal charge if there are several participants. See the More Info section at the end of this chapter for contact details.

You should know how to:

★ revive a child.

★ treat a broken bone until you get to a doctor or the ambulance comes.

★ get a child away from an electrical charge without being injured or knocked out yourself.

★ recognize when you can move an injured child and when you shouldn't.

★ recognize and treat clinical shock.

First-aid kit

Keep a first-aid kit anywhere the child often goes—home, car, grandparents' house, and so on—and always out of their reach. Safety experts recommend you store your home first-aid kit 4.5 feet off the ground in a locked cupboard but I don't know anyone who has such a thing. Just be as safe as you can—perhaps a plastic tool box with a child lock, on top of a high cupboard so adults need to stand on a chair to reach it, and there's no way a child can climb up. Make sure any medicines that need to be in the fridge are safely out of toddler or kid reach. Strictly observe dosages, use-by dates, and doctor's instructions on the label.

A home first-aid kit should include the following.

★ **Painkiller:** buy age-appropriate acetaminophen or ibuprofen, which are also used to bring down a fever (but see the Fever

medicine dropper

and High Temperature section later in this chapter). Kids may have a preference for the taste of one or the other (see Giving Medicines later in this chapter). Children under 12 shouldn't be given aspirin or soluble aspirin because of a slight chance of developing a serious illness called Reye's syndrome. Annoyingly children's painkiller medication is sometimes in heavy, dark brown glass bottles or has a label all the way round—so it's always good to have a spare because you can't tell if they're nearly empty. There are some acetaminophen tablets that are to be put up a baby's bottom so they work faster: frankly I wouldn't bother unless your doctor recommends them for a specific reason, such as they'll otherwise be vomited up.

★ **A medicine measuring cup, dropper, and no-needle syringe:** for giving medicine.
★ **Cotton balls or squares:** these are good for cleaning cuts or infected skin because they can be thrown away afterward.
★ **Antiseptic cream or liquid:** lightly apply it to a cleaned cut or sore.
★ **Sterile adhesive strips:** use these for minor cuts and sores.
★ **Sterile gauze dressings:** these are useful for larger cuts and sore areas.
★ **Bandages:** you can wrap one firmly around, say, a big cut, and fasten.
★ **Waterproof tape:** to keep on bandages or eye patches.
★ **Optional thermometer:** many doctors now say decisions about whether to give acetaminophen, or to go to the doctor, shouldn't rely on the level of temperature but on other symptoms (see the Fever and High Temperature section a few pages on). If you decide to keep a thermometer the American Academy of Pediatrics (AAP) now advises parents to avoid glass mercury thermometers because of concerns of exposure to

mercury should the thermometer break. Of the other options, digital thermometers are the most reliable; forehead strips the least so. Ear thermometers tend to give falsely low readings in young kids, so the AAP does not recommend them for kids under 3.

★ **Saline solution and an eyebath:** these are useful for washing eyes or getting something out of an eye.

★ **A wheat pack or a hot-water bottle:** these can be used warm, not hot, for sore ears or tummies.

★ **An ice pack:** these should always be wrapped in a tea towel or other fabric before being applied to bumps and bruises.

You might like to keep handy an illustrated first-aid book (see More Info at the end of this chapter). A steam vapourizer to place in your child's room at night to keep down sniffles and coughs is also useful.

POISON CONTROL CENTER
Phone 1-800-222-1222

Put their number in your home first-aid kit, car first-aid kit, and on the wall under your other emergency numbers.

This toll-free number will put you in touch with the Poison Control Center in your state. If your child has collapsed or is not breathing, call 911. Poison experts at the Poison Control Centrer are on call 24 hours a day, every day of the year. Keep the container of the swallowed substance with you so you can tell them exactly what the chemical is and in what concentration. The unfamiliar or horrid taste will probably have deterred the child from taking more than a mouthful so stay calm even if you're frightened.

Ipecac syrup was used in the past to induce vomiting. It's now considered likely to do more harm than good. Don't do anything such as trying to induce vomiting unless advised by the Poison Control Center.

CHOOSING a DOCTOR

You'll need to find a good local doctor, usually called a GP (general practitioner), which can save you lots of worry. Ideally, you'll be wanting a doctor who specializes in kids or lives in an area where there are lots of kids—they'll know what's "going around." See the second chapter, Your Support Team, in *Part 1: Babies* for info on how to choose one.

There is nothing wrong with going to another GP for a second opinion or insisting on a referral to a specialist.

> *"I recommend that dads take the children to the doctor. The medical profession treat a sick child and the dad totally differently than if a woman presents with a sick child."* CHRIS, "HOUSEHUSBAND"

WHEN TO CALL AN AMBULANCE WITH AN INJURY
Call the general emergency number: 911.
Call an ambulance if your child has:

* been unconscious or is unconscious.

* a convulsion (a fit).

* can't breathe or stopped breathing and needed or needs resuscitation.

* a suspected injured neck or back (don't move the patient).

* a serious head injury.

* a suspected broken bone—support it with your arm and hand or a pillow and keep the patient still until the ambulance arrives.

* had an electric shock.

* gone into clinical shock after a trauma (usually caused by bleeding or a burn)—a quiet child, perhaps with staring or glazed eyes, is probably in shock.

* anaphylactic allergic shock—very rare and usually triggered by an insect sting, a drug, or a food.

"Always have baby acetaminophen in the fridge." ANONYMOUS

iNJURieS

When to see a doctor with an injury

See a doctor right away if your child has:

- ★ concussion. Signs and symptoms following a head bang or injury include amnesia, headaches, floppiness, tiredness, difficulty concentrating (hospital policy before discharging a patient after a bad knock to the head is usually to watch them carefully for a few hours—a doctor may get you to do the same).
- ★ a severe cut or a deep wound.
- ★ something inserted into an eye, ear, or other body opening.
- ★ a blistered burn larger than a pea.

Small injuries: DIY

The best remedies for minor accidents are antiseptic cream and perhaps an adhesive strip (for small cuts and very small burns), ice packs (for small bumps and bruises), sympathy, and kissing it better.

"Acknowledge that it does hurt instead of jollying them out of it. Be truthful: 'Oh, darling, I know it's really hurting a lot now, but it will start getting better and it will stop soon.'" JILL

BURNS aND ScaLDS

These first-aid steps for scalds and burns are based on the advice given by the Child Safety Center at the Royal Children's Hospital, in Australia. Move quickly and get through the list as fast as possible.

1 If there is a scald, whip off any wet clothing, because the heat of the liquid can continue to burn, and any clothing around a burn unless the material is sticking to skin.

2 Immediately run cold water over the area. Use the nearest cold tap. Keep the burn area under running water for at least 20 minutes or until the ambulance arrives. This will help alleviate pain and stop the area burning deeper, and applies to all scalds and burns. Keep the child warm.

3 Call an ambulance as soon as the burn or scald is under running water or get someone else to if * the burn area is bigger than the child's palm (about 1 percent of their body area) * a serious burn is on the face, head, hands, feet, or genitals * the burn area is whitish and not hurting (signs of charring and nerve damage) * the child is quiet despite a bad burn * the burn was caused over some time (for example, a hand on a heater wasn't taken away immediately) * you are really worried and the GP's office is closed or you can't leave the house quickly because you're, say, looking after a bunch of kids or your other child or baby is asleep.

Follow the instructions the emergency services give you over the phone while you wait for the paramedics to arrive.

4 Cover the area with a clean, dry gauze bandage or a cotton or non-fluffy cloth, such as a non-flannel pillowcase or a flat kitchen towel, not a towel: you don't want threads or fluff sticking to the wound. Don't use ice on the burn or put the child in a chilled bath. Don't put butter, oils, or anything else on the burn—these will only have to be removed by paramedics, doctors, or nurses, often painfully, so they can see the wound, and they don't have any beneficial effect.

5 Take the child to the hospital or your nearest doctor. You'll need medical advice for anything more than a very small scald.

CHOKiN9

Choking risks include long, stringy things such as bacon rind, soft pliable foods such as a marshmallow, hard candies, and any object such as a shell or a whole nut that can act like a stopper, as well as a bit of food or small pieces of a Barbie doll. Choking kids can always do with three hefty blows in the middle of the back between the shoulder blades. If that doesn't dislodge the object, try to remove it gently with your fingers. Turning the baby or small child upside down can also work. You can take a class through the Red Cross to learn the Heimlich maneuver.

If the object doesn't come out, encourage the child to be calm and call 911. Follow the instructions the emergency services gives you over the phone while you're waiting for the paramedics to arrive.

THE IMMUNE SYSTEM

The immune system recognizes and repels many viruses and bacteria you've had before, preventing you from getting sick again. Having an immune system in good shape helps kids recover more quickly. But even the best immune system won't stop all germs or prevent all illnesses.

Good immune system boosters:

* breastfeeding.

* fresh air.

* exercise.

* enough protein and carbohydrates.

* being calm and happy.

---

getting sick

The first six to twelve months of major contact with other kids (siblings or kids at child care or preschool) means it's germ free-for-all. This is one of the reasons it's so hard for a parent to work outside the home during the child's early years, even if it's part-time. Luckily, very few of the things kids are developing immunity against are going to kill them, especially in the U.S. where we have almost universal immunization and our hospital staff are all generally wonderful (even though our politicians don't give nearly enough money to hospitals, the filthy swine). Kids usually get sick suddenly, although after a while you might be able to recognize when they're "fighting off something."

When a kid gets sick their immune system works to develop antibodies to provide future protection. Healthy kids under 5 can pick up a minor viral infection, which they fight off without treatment, every couple of months (a head cold, being quiet, and "off-color"—meaning pale—or an unidentified rash might be clues). As well as that there are minor sniffles and assorted "tummy bugs" that kids tend to pick up and get rid of over a day or so here and there.

If your kid has a chronic or very serious illness, make sure you get all the medical opinions you can and insist on seeing a specialist with the widest possible experience in the area, usually at your nearest major children's hospital. Inquire about any and all services available to you, from accommodation for rural visitors to support groups, tax breaks, and equipment sharing.

What causes illnesses?

Childhood illnesses are usually caused by viruses and bacteria, which are both germs. Viruses are "bugs" that need to live and multiply in cells to survive, so they live in us and reproduce themselves by being passed on to other people, who then get sick and pass them on, and so it goes. Bacteria are little organisms that can live and grow independently (such as germs on a toilet seat), with the side effect of infecting people.

When are illnesses contagious?

Illnesses are most contagious when the germs are multiplying the fastest. This often happens when you first "catch a bug," before any symptoms appear, and in the first few days of symptoms. Sneezing and diarrhea are really efficient ways of spreading the germs, so while these symptoms continue, whatever the stage of the illness, the bug is probably still contagious. It usually takes three to five days for the incubation of a common cold, meaning from catching it to the end of symptoms. Despite the fact that parents often say "It's not contagious any more," they're often just guessing.

Should kids go back to playgroup, child care, or preschool?

Child-care centers usually say kids with a stomach bug should be kept home until 24 hours after their last vomit or bout of diarrhea.

Kids should be kept home from group care while they continue to have symptoms of an illness and until they're feeling bouncy again—not only because the bug is still contagious, although that's

---

WHEN TO CALL AN AMBULANCE WITH AN ILLNESS
Call 911.

Call an ambulance if your child:

✱ has a convulsion (a fit).

✱ has difficulty with or stops breathing.

✱ can't be roused.

✱ has fever, repeated vomiting, a stiff neck, and their eyes are sensitive to light (the symptoms of meningitis, a brain inflammation). You need to get your child to a hospital *right away* so call an ambulance if you're too stressed to drive safely.

✱ is miserable, has fever and a stiff neck, their eyes are sensitive to light, and they have a spotty rash that starts as red but turns purple and doesn't fade when you press it (the symptoms of meningoccocal disease).

a big issue, especially with more serious illnesses, but because kids with symptoms are almost always below par or even miserable. It's harder for them to get one-on-one care in a child-care center, even though I know staff do their very best. It isn't fair to the child, and they want to be at home with a parent. Many parents who work outside the home eat up their own sick-day allowance (if they have one) looking after their kids.

When to see a doctor about an illness

Keep the phone number of an extended-hours clinic near the phone, or see if your hospital has an "advice nurse" you can call. My Cousin Suze, the paramedic, says "as well as getting better quickly, kids can often deteriorate quickly." She says parents need to keep a careful eye on a sick kid: "It's always suspicious if a child is quieter than usual. It's generally better to have a screaming one than a quiet one."

See or contact a doctor in any of the following situations:

★ Your kid has been in contact with an infectious disease that they haven't been immunized against.

★ Fever is accompanied by worrying symptoms such as misery, listlessness, repeated vomiting, or an inexplicable rash (see also When to Call an Ambulance with an Illness opposite).

★ You're worried because your child is "not themselves," too quiet, uninterested in anything, or "floppy."

You know your child best so take your own uneasy feelings seriously. All parents have these: some call them "instincts" and act on them, others mistrust them and are unsure whether they're worrying unnecessarily, but they're the same feelings so start calling yours instincts. The only way to check them out is to take your child to a doctor. Even if nothing is revealed, keep on trusting your instincts—you may need to try another doctor or the kid may have just beaten a bug.

★ Your child develops wheezing.

★ There's unexplained crying that isn't helped by the usual methods, especially in kids who can't tell you what's wrong.

Sometimes the only symptom of a kid's illness is listlessness, whining, and a pressing need to be right next to Mom or Dad, or at least in the same room. A nurse I know always tested her post-toddler-age children by asking them to jump three times—if they couldn't, she knew they were really sick and not faking it. Kids under 5 are not likely to fake being sick unless it's learned behavior (they can often suddenly say they have a sore back if you have one, for example, and will learn from you how to react to hurts and pains).

For books on recognizing and dealing with illnesses see More Info at the end of this chapter. You'll find some illustrated books on anatomy for kids and about going to a doctor or a hospital listed in More Info at the end of the later chapter called Reading.

When to go to the emergency room with an illness

If you're very worried about your kid and you can't go to your local doctor because it's late at night or a weekend, you may need to go to the nearest emergency room. Please be aware, though, that these are only for true emergencies, and that you may have to wait many hours in a brightly lit area and then see an overworked doctor or nurse. So if you are anxious about, but not freaked out by, your child's symptoms, a good alternative to the almost certain hell of waiting in the ER can be to call your doctor's answering service for a recommendation. Some doctors have a nurse triage–service that will help. It's a good idea to find out from your doctor what to do in an after-hours emergency before one occurs.

Looking after a sickie

- ★ Sick babies can be carried in a sling or wheeled about with you in a carrigage or stroller.
- ★ With a toddler or little kid, help the patient camp out in the room you're working in. Make up a nummy bed on the couch with special toy friends and settle the patient in for the day so they're not isolated; or move an armchair into

their bedroom with some reading, the phone, or work you can do there. If disgusting vomiting or pooping is not a possibility, the parental bed can be a good haven.

★ Sick kids often sleep a lot as a natural defense or because of the sedative effect of medicines such as painkillers or cough suppressants. Don't use painkillers to sedate: it's not good for kids to have too many painkillers (see the Fever and High Temperature section later in this chapter).

★ Don't insist on games or activities—sometimes kids are too sick to do anything but lie about.

★ Read them a favorite book or two or play favorite sleepy-time or relaxing music.

★ Don't let them veg out for ages in front of TV or new videos. The younger the child, the more it can addle their brain when they're sick—too many new sights and concepts to take in. Tried and true, quieter, old favorite videos can be useful.

★ Offer simple food and healthy favorites. Old-fashioned comfort food such as custard or mashed potatoes can be good, depending on the illness. An upset stomach means a very restricted diet (we'll get to that), and kids with stuffed-up noses can't taste anything. Sore mouths and throats often mean food rejection.

★ Don't forget to change the sheets after an illness to freshen up, and get some outside air into the room during an illness if possible and definitely after.

★ You want to be able to be as sympathetic as possible without making being sick a great adventure preferable to being up or going to child care or preschool.

★ If you've had to cancel work or something else important to be at home, make sure you plot against the illness in partnership with your kid ("I can't wait to go to the park! Let's go as soon as you're better!") rather than resenting your child for being sick ("I hope you're better tomorrow because I missed some important things at work today").

★ Put your kid in a tepid bath if the weather is horribly hot, or a warm one can be relaxing if it's cold. If your child doesn't want one, try a "sponge" bath. The patient can try a dry wash of teddy first.

★ Reality check: you may have to re-establish your child's sleeping routine after an illness.

"Forget commitment, housework, and cooking—cuddles, cuddles, cuddles." ANN

"Take them seriously about their illness. If you are seen to be concerned they can worry less themselves, and should recover sooner." ROBERTO

Giving medicines

Most children's medicines come as a liquid that can be sucked up into a dropper or syringe (without the needle bit, obviously) and squirted into the child's mouth; or it can be given on a spoon or in a tiny measuring cup. The dropper, spoon, or measuring cup may come with the medicine or you can buy them separately at the pharmacy.

It's always handy to teach your kid how to take medicine from a dropper as soon as possible. Try to make it a game.

In cases of full-on, arched-back rebellion, when taking the medicine immediately is imperative, hold the child's nose so they have to open their mouth, squirt it in, and then hold the mouth closed until it's swallowed. This is of course an absolutely last resort and can usually be avoided by reassurance or sneakiness.

If you have to disguise medicine in a mouthful of something, use a tiny amount of breast or formula milk for a baby or food such as ice-cream for older kids. It's no good putting medicine in a glass of juice because they'll only drink 56.78 percent of the juice and then you'll have no idea how much of it was medicine. Unfortunately, pharmaceutical companies seem to insist on over-flavoring

PAINKILLERS: ACETAMINOPHEN AND IBUPROFEN

* Buy baby or toddler acetaminophen or ibuprofen (you'll see there are major brand names for both) and have it on hand. As well as dulling or removing pain, acetaminophen is commonly used for bringing down a temperature, although both will do this (but see the section Fever and High Temperature later in the chapter). Ibuprofen shouldn't be given to a kid with a history of tummy ulcers or another serious tummy trouble.

* Acetaminophen isn't designed to be used all day every day, for several days in a row, without medical supervision: a whacking great acetaminophen overdose can cause permanent kidney shutdown. Long-term use or longer-than-recommended doses of ibuprofen cause tummy upsets and bleeding. That's why those bottles have childproof caps. Both should be kept out of reach and locked away.

* Don't ever exceed the dose—more will not kill pain quicker or more efficiently. The recommended dose should do it within 20 minutes. If it doesn't, you'll be needing medical advice.

* If you do accidentally give too much medicine, don't panic. Call the Poison Control Center immediately (1-800-222-1222) and let them know how much you've given. It's almost certainly fine—it's more likely that you would harm your child by giving consistently too-high doses or for too long a time.

* Aspirin or soluble aspirin shouldn't be given to kids as in rare cases it can contribute to Reye's syndrome, a liver failure and brain inflammation leading to convulsions and coma with a high death rate (10 to 25 percent).

See More Info at the end of this chapter for more on acetaminophen.

and coloring children's medicines, which is guaranteed to make any baby or fussy toddler deeply suspicious.

Some parents have success with bribery—you take your medicine, you get a sticker or a star on a chart.

Never leave a bottle of medicine where kids can reach it.

"Try putting your baby's medicine into an upturned nipple and let them suck it like it was on a bottle." SAMANTHA

"My kids will take medicine off the 'magic spoon' (we got it out of the kids' pain reliever package)." SOLI

Natural therapies

Many people see a herbal or naturopathic practitioner—yours should understand when it's necessary to have a medical diagnosis before natural treatments. Just treating symptoms might allow an underlying cause to go unnoticed. Natural therapies are good for minor ailments when the cause is indisputable. Your practitioner should be both qualified and experienced in children's remedies, and the cause of the ailment should be fully medically established. Herbalists should be told about any medications the child is on, and doctors told of any herbal remedies the kid is taking as well. Sensible herbalists will not recommend their remedies alone for serious illnesses or injuries.

Mindful of the long list of powerful and complicated aromatherapy essential oils, small children should probably only be given drops of eucalyptus oil on their hanky or pillow (to combat the sniffles) or drops of lavender oil in their bath for relaxation. Don't use aromatherapy candles or burners for children, and never leave these (or anything else with an unprotected flame) untended in a room that a child is in.

When you get sick as well

This is when you find out who your real friends and actually helpful relatives are. Many people want to stay away when there is illness in the home. It can be especially daunting, even frightening, when you are a sole parent and have been literally laid out by something really serious. Don't be afraid to ask friends and family for help, insisting if necessary.

Caregiver fatigue

I never used to understand what people meant when they said that having an ill child was difficult. Now I understand it can mean hours and hours of grinding exhaustion and sacrifice, the kind of worry that makes you realize you never really had a worry before, and the total inability to do anything at all apart from tend to the patient, get them to and from the doctor, and wash mega tons of sickie bed linen, jammies, and towels. Most children who are sick wake up a lot, distressed, and even if *they* go straight back to sleep *you* might lie awake until the next "alarm." If you have a partner, try to alternate the sleepless nights. One partner can wear earplugs or sleep in the furthest room when it's not their turn on shift.

If your child is in care or preschool, use the first few days they're well and back there to get some sleep during the day. Otherwise, see if you can get help from a friend or relative so that you catch up on your sleep. The more tired (or the sicker) you are, the harder it is to have good judgment and stay patient.

The common illnesses and conditions given in the following sections of the chapter are in no particular order except that they start with the more temporary and common ones and end with the more long-term conditions.

fever and High temperature

We are all so attuned to the idea that fevers are scary, it can be a horrible shock to pick up your baby or toddler and realize they're "burning up." It's comforting to know that most fevers are a friend: they have a sensible purpose—it's the body's way of "burning off" germs. Your kid's immune system is doing its job.

One of the quickest ways to see if a baby has a fever is to put the back of your hand against their tummy (their forehead and extremities may have been in a cold wind or near a heater and are not as close to the body's core temperature). If it feels very hot, there's probably a fever.

A febrile convulsion

It's rare, but a rapid rise in temperature can cause a "febrile convulsion," or fit, which causes the eyes to roll back and the baby or kid to shake and jerk. A fit is scary but usually takes only a few minutes and has no lasting effects, and doesn't cause brain damage or death. (A tendency to have fits sometimes runs in the family.) Call an ambulance if you're freaked out (let's face it, who wouldn't be?) but it'll probably all be over before they get to your place, with no harm done except to your nerves.

Doctors say it's likely that the rate of the temperature rise causes a fit rather than a magic high number such as 104 degrees Fahrenheit. So by the time you know your kid has a high temperature, if they haven't had a fit they're probably not going to. Remember: the vast majority of kids never have a febrile convulsion and those who do are not harmed by it.

Ways to treat a fever
- ★ If your baby or child has a convulsion, call 911.
- ★ Don't keep the kid too bundled up, and don't use ice or anything else sudden to "bring down" a temperature.

★ If the kid is in pain or miserable, give them a dose of aceta-minophen, according to the label. If they're jaunty, let the fever fight the illness.

★ See a doctor if your kid has other worrying symptoms, such as being "not themselves," cranky, listless, confused, off their food, or having a rash, repeated vomiting, or breathing changes. You'll probably want to take a baby under 6 months to the doctor if you feel they have a high temperature to rule out anything worrying.

★ If you're frightened by the high temperature or it's 4 a.m. and you're feeling exhausted, you can use a dose of aceta-minophen to bring down the fever and see a doctor the next day.

The American Academy of Pediatrics recommends that a baby under 3 months with a fever of 100.4 degrees or higher, an infant between 3 to 6 months with a temperature of 101 degrees or higher, or a child over 6 months with a temperature of 104 degrees or higher should be seen as soon as possible by a doctor.

Stomach Bugs

"When they say they have a tummy ache and turn a shade of green they ARE going to vomit." TRACEY

We're talking here about an upset tummy—the vomiting and diarrhea associated with a short-term bug rather than something longer-term such as a tummy parasite, or the one-off vomiting caused by stress, coughing, or getting a chunk of apple caught in the throat. The throwing up is often very upsetting for a baby or kid, especially if it wakes them or they don't know what's happening.

Generally, vomiting plus diarrhea plus fever means you need to see your doctor, although it's almost certainly a short-term bout.

SIGNS OF DEHYDRATION

✷ The baby or kid has repeated runny poops over the course of 24 hours.

✷ Their skin feels dry and papery or cold and clammy and is paler than usual.

✷ The skin on a baby's fontanelle looks sunken.

✷ The kid has a dry mouth, lips, and tongue.

✷ The face and eyes look sunken.

✷ The baby or kid has a spaced-out, glazed look.

✷ There's less pee than usual or fewer wet diapers.

✷ The pee is darker colored than usual (this is sometimes hard to see when the child is wearing a diaper).

✷ The kid's breath is foul.

The main danger, to babies in particular, is dehydration if they're too sick to keep down or keep drinking fluids. This can happen quite quickly to babies: 24 hours of vomiting and diarrhea can be enough. If you can't rehydrate them, they need to go to hospital to be sedated and go on a nice drip of fluids and mineral salts for a day or so. Scary for you, but standard procedure.

Stomach bugs are caused by a virus picked up anywhere really, but often in a place where there's a concentration of other kids; by bacteria, perhaps in contaminated food (food poisoning); or, in rare cases, by a rather violent allergic reaction. Symptoms are usually most full-on for the first 24 hours, and the diarrhea often lasts longer than the vomiting. There may be only throwing up or only diarrhea.

A viral case usually comes on suddenly: the kid complains of feeling nauseated or goes quiet, then suddenly vomits. It may be accompanied by other charming features such as runny poop and sniffly cold symptoms. This is the most common, catching kind.

A bacterial stomach bug such as food poisoning usually comes on within about 12 to 48 hours of contact. The food involved can be anything from a tiny bit of old milk not jooshed out of an otherwise clean formula bottle to something that touched a surface contaminated by raw chicken. Tummy cramps and explosive poop usually come first, followed by vomiting. It normally lasts two to three days.

Treatment for stomach bugs

There's not much in the way of medication you can give for a stomach bug—usually you have to ride it out by doing the following:

★ Help your baby or child and be with them while they are vomiting, then clean up as soon as you can.

★ Give them reassurance and cuddles. Throwing up is an unpleasant experience and they need comforting and soothing.

★ Rest your child's tummy from rich foods (see What Not to Feed a Kid with a Stomach Bug further on). Do this for a day—more if it seems to be still upset.

★ Rehydration is the important issue. Give your kid lots of fluids. Basically keep offering the breast, bottle, or cup as often as you can to babies. Keep a drink next to a child who is old enough to help themselves and also offer it to them often.

You can get an electrolyte solution from the pharmacy (you may need a prescription for some, others can be bought in bottles or packets over the counter). It needs to be appropriate for your child's age and weight and contain the right mineral salts as well as fluids. Some can even be frozen as Popsicles to make them more attractive to kids.

This is what you need, not lemonade. Remember that some drugstores will home deliver.

★ Keep cross-infection to a minimum by washing all utensils, sick bowls, towels, and jammies in hot, soapy water.

★ Always take a child to the doctor if you're worried or there are any signs of dehydration.

BABIES UNDER 6 MONTHS WITH A STOMACH BUG

★ Off to the doctor with you, just to make sure it's all okay: ask for advice about rehydrating.

★ If the baby is breastfed, keep offering the breast regularly.

★ If the baby is formula-fed, ask your doctor whether you should try a special rehydration formula for their age from the pharmacy in their bottle for a day, then their own formula at half-strength for a day, before going back to normal. Some babies come good suddenly and can probably go straight back onto their formula.

OLDER BABIES WITH A STOMACH BUG

★ See your doctor if the vomiting and diarrhea last longer than 24 hours or if you're worried.

★ The baby should go back on breast or formula milk as soon as possible.

TODDLERS AND PRESCHOOLERS WITH A STOMACH BUG

★ Keep giving plain water and clear fruit juice diluted 1:1 with water or rehydration fluids or Popsicles from the drugstore.

★ Never assume a toddler or a preschooler knows what's going on. Explain why you're offering different foods and drinks, why you're going to the doctor, why it's good to stay quietly at home.

★ A kid old enough to understand (but who may have forgotten what throwing up is) should be reassured that the situation will end soon, that they have a germ that is making their tummy have a tantrum, and that you're trying to fix it as fast as you can but sometimes it may take until tomorrow (anything longer is virtually incomprehensible).

★ If a toddler or a preschooler with a bug wants to eat, feed them bland things and don't worry too much—they will be getting a few nutrients even if they throw up everything soon after (see What to Feed a Kid with a Stomach Bug, which follows).

★ See your doctor if the vomiting and diarrhea last longer than 48 hours.

WHAT TO FEED A KID WITH A STOMACH BUG   Don't force feed—start food when your child is ready. Try:

★ plain cooked rice and pasta.
★ rice pudding.
★ fingers of dry toast and bread.
★ plain dry crackers, with reduced salt.
★ oatmeal made with water.
★ mashed potatoes.
★ puréed, mashed, or sieved frozen blueberries and raspberries or little bits of fresh fruit.
★ plain soy milk.
★ grated or paper-thin apple slices.
★ stewed pear.
★ banana.
★ mashed carrot or zucchini.
★ apple sauce or jello.
★ finely chopped steamed chicken breast.
★ plain homemade chicken soup.

WHAT NOT TO FEED A KID WITH A STOMACH BUG

★ Only plain water for longer than 24 hours: the body needs more nutrients than that.

PRACTICAL TIPS FOR LIVING WITH THE VOMITS

Sick bowl
Protect yourself and bedding from sudden vomits by teaching your child as soon as possible to use a sick bowl. Make sure you have a couple of non-metal sick bowls or buckets (who wants to see their reflection at that point?) and plenty of layers of towels to avoid getting vomit on the bed or furniture. The towels will have to be washed in very hot water and an antibacterial washing powder such as a diaper one. The bowl the child uses will have to be disinfected with boiling water at intervals too, with the spare kept in circulation in case there's a need while the other one's being washed.

Stripping the bed
When a kid throws up in bed, it's all hands on deck. This is why you never throw out old, threadbare towels—keep all the towels you can.

Soothe the kid thoroughly first, then completely clean them with a nice warm washcloth and a soap substitute, paying special attention to their face, hands, and hair. Rinse off the soap substitute, wrap your darling in a clean towel and prop them in a corner or on a beanbag where they can't fall over (but never leave a baby on a beanbag while you go into another room). Dress them in loose clothes that you'll be able to get off easily if they're sick again. Don't assume they won't vomit again or that there's "nothing left to come up": protect the immediate area.

★ Full-strength fruit juice or full-strength lemonade because both are too sugary and can stimulate diarrhea—water it down to at least 1:1.
★ Flat soda or sugar dissolved in water—it's much better to get a rehydration formula from the drugstore.
★ Bottled electrolyte and sports drinks: they're for adults.
★ Spicy, acidic, or rich foods, chocolate, junk foods, sweets, cake, and other sugary things: these can make the diarrhea worse.

Strip the bed of all the sheets and any bedding with vomit on it and soak up any extra vomit with old or used towels. Clean any vomit-touched surfaces with antibacterial spray (or similar) and another towel. Explain that you're taking all the bedding, jammies, towels, and vomity stuffed animals to the laundry, or leave everything in a pile to take away later.

Come back; have a cuddle and remake the bed: if you don't have a waterproof mattress protector use a couple of layers of old towels. Make up a top sheet with a bath towel that folds back to protect the top layer of sheet, duvet or bedspread. Have the sick bowl ready next to the bed before the child gets back in. Prop an older child up with pillows and make sure the only toys that stay are washable. (We've had to have Pinky re-upholstered twice and it's quite undignified.) Explain that the vomiting might happen again but it might not, and what's causing it. Offer them a drink of water. Reassuringly tuck them in and send them off to sleep.

To do the laundry, rinse off anything chunky, do a short but adequately cleansing washing-machine load with antibacterial powder in hot water.

If you're unlucky, do it all again.

Of course, if there are two adults divvying up the actions just described it will work even better.

★ Salty things: these can increase dehydration.
★ Anti-diarrhea medicines unless your doctor prescribed them specifically for this bout of illness (these medicines are rarely given and hardly ever to babies).
★ Milk and other dairy food because they're too fatty—soy milk can replace cow's milk until the child is better.

Sniffles and Colds

Home remedies

★ A steam vaporizer can be bought from a drugstore. You fill it with water and it keeps pushing steam into the child's room at night—this helps keep the airways open and greatly reduces a stuffed nose and coughing. Some people put eucalyptus drops in but that's not necessary for it to work effectively.

★ A vapor rub (from the drugstore) on the chest for toddlers and preschoolers may help clear the schnozz.

★ Add a few drops of eucalyptus oil to the bath.

★ Eucalyptus drops on the pillow, underneath the pillow case, might help too.

★ Elevate the head of the bed with a few Yellow Pages volumes—the mucus will drain down.

★ Books or music on a tape can be soothing.

Coughs

★ A wheezy cough: this could indicate asthma and should always be checked by a doctor.

★ A cough that ends in a heaving sound (a "whoop") as the baby or child tries to take in air: this should also always be checked by a doctor.

★ A croupy cough (one with lots of rattly phlegm in the chest): this can often be suddenly improved by placing a steam vaporizer in the bedroom at night.

Pharmacy shelves are chocked full of expensive cold, cough, and sniffle remedies for kids, but doctors are dubious about their effect on illness. A honey and lemon drink could well be just as good. Remember that children's cough medicines must be literally made for children—never use a smaller dose of an adult cough mixture—and that most have quite a strong sedative as well as a cough suppressant in them. So generally they are most helpful at night to let a kid get some sleep (and you too) if that's what's become necessary.

Babies under 1 year mustn't have off-the-shelf decongestant cough mixtures: these must be prescribed for them by a doctor.

"Moms tend to see changes in a condition where dads see variations from the normal state. Listen and act on both concerns."
GRAHAM

ear PROBLems

Lots of babies and small kids get ear trouble, usually after a cold or other virus. Although unusual in a tiny baby under a couple of months old, after that it can be a battle, with some kids having constant problems for years. Most kids will have at least one ear infection before school starts. The three main types of ear condition are given below. (If you want to have your child's hearing tested, see the contact given in More Info at the end of this chapter.)

Outer ear infection
This is often caused by "picking something up at the pool." You can see the ear is red, with maybe a discharge—older kids may say it feels blocked or sore. It may go away by itself but should be seen by your doctor and may need antibiotics or steroid medicines.

Middle ear infection
Inside everyone's ear is a thing called a eustachian tube that drains any fluid from the middle ear, which is protected from the outside world by the eardrum. In kids under about 3,

the tube is often rather horizontal before developing a downward angle so fluid can drain away. If the fluid doesn't drain and sits there, it can get very infected and yucky and can eventually burst out of the eardrum, causing sudden pain (or it can cause "glue" ear—the third type of ear condition listed).

The symptoms are usually bad earache and a lack of interest in food (because it hurts to swallow). Unfortunately, a little baby or toddler may not be able to understand and articulate the pain or show you where it is. The early signs may be listlessness, tears, and deafness that might be obvious or not.

The first treatment is pain relief—usually the label dosage of acetaminophen for the correct age. If the yuck has burst through the eardrum, the pain of the pressure will be released and the drum will probably heal nicely by itself (not that you'd want this to happen repeatedly). Antibiotics can be used to clear up the infection behind the ear, but the problem is likely to recur until (or if) the tube starts draining properly.

EARS

* See a doctor if there is ear pain, redness, pulling at an ear associated with pain (not the typical baby "What's this thing on my head I've just discovered?" behavior), perceived or suspected hearing trouble, or a discharge from the ear.

* If you need to give ear drops, have your child lie down with their head sideways on your lap and let gravity help you. Say it won't hurt (if that's true) but might feel wet or tickly while the drops are draining into the ear.

* Don't push anything, even a cotton swab, into a baby's or a kid's ear. Clean the bit you can reach with a face washcloth.

Glue ear

The ear becomes blocked when fluid can't drain away or doesn't burst through the eardrum, but it's not necessarily infected. There's no pain, but there is significant partial to total hearing loss. Quite often someone else notices it first—a child-care worker or a relative. Kids can get very good at lip reading and finding other ways around their deafness. Parents often first realize when a child has their back to them and doesn't respond to questions, or keeps asking for the music or TV to be turned up.

In persistent cases or where the alternative is a partial or complete deafness in one or both ears that would lead to learning and social difficulties, the kid may have to have an operation under general anesthetic to insert "grommets." These are little eyelets holding open holes in the eardrum so that the fluid can drain out. Kids can swim with grommets in, but not dive or jump in the pool or ocean waves in case water pounds into their inner ear. After a few months grommets drop out of the ear naturally and the drum heals itself.

Incidentally, those candle things that people burn outside a kid's ear that are supposed to draw out a blockage are completely useless. Even if a candle could draw out material from an ear, there's an eardrum in the way, making it impossible. Natural remedy ear drops should only be used when your doctor is certain the eardrum has not been perforated.

CHickeN POX

Chicken pox usually starts with a fever, listlessness, loss of appetite, and a rash, which are followed by the tell-tale spots, usually ten days to three weeks after catching the virus. It is when the spots erupt that it's contagious, but sometimes the early ones are hard to see. The spots keep appearing for a few days and they all go through a process of becoming blistered, then itchy, before finally drying up.

Scratching them may cause a tiny scar. It is very contagious until the last sore has dried up.

Chicken pox is not usually life threatening, but it is very miserable and irritating for most kids—some get nasty sores inside their mouths, down their throat, and on their genitals.

There's now a vaccination against chicken pox that provides 99 percent protection against a severe case and 80 percent against getting it at all.

A few advances have been made in chicken pox treatment. Nothing "cures" it—it has to run its course—but a special bath oil (ask your pharmacist) will help cut down the irritation of the itchy sores. Rather than the traditional calamine lotion, many pharmacists and doctors now recommend a cooling, less drying gel to put on the spots.

TOO MUCH SUN

Because running around in the fresh air and sunshine is one of the bonuses of being a kid—especially in the south—we have to find a happy medium between toasting our children and making them move slowly in the shade dressed in head-to-toe bee-keeping outfits.

You probably already know the US has a high skin cancer incidence and that the more times you're sunburned, the more chance you have of developing cancers. (Some people are now developing aggressive skin cancers in their twenties and thirties.) The main risk factor for later cancers is getting burned a lot when you're a kid.

Time in the sun

It's ultraviolet radiation (UV rays) that are the problem. UV rays are most intense between 10 a.m. and 4 p.m: basically the hours when the sun is highest in the sky, especially between April and September when the UV levels get very high. Kids should be indoors, in the shade, or very well protected during these times. It can take as little as 15 minutes to get sunburned, depending on the time of year and lots of other factors. The American Cancer Society recommends that babies and children be kept out of the sun as much as possible, especially between 10 a.m. and 4 p.m. In some parts of the country, these recommendations can apply all year round: check with your local American Cancer Society office for specific directions (see More Info at the end of this chapter).

Weather

UV rays themselves don't feel hot so sunburn is very common on days when people don't expect it. Cloudy days? Yes, you can be burned on cloudy days. And on cool days with sun and on windy days that feel cool. And at the snow where there's lots of intensifying reflection. The biggest factors are time of year and time spent outdoors. Even if you're making sure your kid is only at the beach in the early morning or later afternoon, you should still slap sunscreen on them.

Skin type and sun care

While fair-skinned blondies and darling freckly red heads are most in danger from sunburn, kids with olive or dark skin do get sunburn and can get skin cancer too. A tan or freckles are evidence of sun damage—of the skin trying to protect itself. A tan does not protect kids against further damage or cancer.

Sun care for babies

Sunburn for a baby can be very serious, causing blisters and rapid dehydration. They shouldn't be exposed to direct sun, as in suntanning. They'll get plenty of vitamin D and sunshine without being directly exposed. Babies lying on a blanket in the park or at the beach should be in the dark, sharp-edged shadow cast by trees, those pop-up tenty things, or under an umbrella. They will still need to be protected from reflected or "scattered" UV rays by being covered up (see the info about clothes and sun further on). Sunscreen alone should not be relied on to protect a baby, even in the shade. Try only to use sunscreen on your baby to protect those little bits that can't be protected any other way.

A baby in direct sun must always be covered up, have infant sunscreen on, and wear a hat that shades their face and neck. If they are being wheeled around, they must have serious shade covering. Remember UV rays can get through mesh netting.

Sun care for toddlers and little kids

All the above stuff about babies applies, but they should use a toddler sunscreen.

Sun protection

SUNSCREEN   This should be broad spectrum (which means it absorbs both kinds of relevant UV rays); sun protection factor 30 (usually labeled as SPF 30+), which provides the most protection, especially for infants and toddlers; and water resistant. No sunscreen can offer 100 percent protection.

You can test a little bit of sunscreen on the back of your kid's hand to see if it causes a rash. If it does, talk to your pharmacist about a replacement: rashes are usually a reaction to perfumes or preservatives rather than the sun protection part. Remember that a thick layer of sunscreen lotion will make a kid hotter: it's better to cover large areas of skin with loose protective clothing.

Sunscreen should be applied about 20 minutes before going outdoors (there's a complicated chemical reason that will put you to sleep) and should be reapplied at least every 2 hours. Some people burn within that time even with sunscreen on. And it should be applied more often than that if it is likely to have been wiped, washed, or sweated off. Apparently sunscreen, particularly as a spray, is usually not applied thickly enough or rubbed in sufficiently, although nobody seems to be able to explain exactly how much you should put on kids. And it's recommended that if your child (or you) are in the sun for 2 hours, more protection, from hats and clothing, will be needed as well.

Sunscreen ingredients cost about the same so if you pay more, it's for perfume, moisturizer, or a brand name. Check the use-by date and don't apply the sunscreen beyond it.

SUNHATS   These should be legionnaire-style (like a baseball cap with a flap at the back and sides) or broad-brimmed (the recommended brim size is 3 to 4 inches). They should not be mesh or have holes in them that let sun through. A lot of UV rays are reflected from below by water, sand, or concrete.

SUN CLOTHES   Kids in the sun between April and September should be dressed in loose clothes that cover as much of the body as possible. If you hold a fabric up to the light and the light passes through, UV rays will too. Tags showing UPF (ultraviolet protection factor) 50+ have the most sun protection. Most cotton has about UPF 20+. All fabrics have less UV protection when they're wet. I'm starting to think we should live underground.

SUNGLASSES   Intense sunlight can make babies and toddlers squint, get cranky, and even long term lead to the development of cataracts as the eyes try to protect themselves. Shade your baby's eyes by not having them in the direct sun. Look for sunglasses for your toddler: they need to block out at least 98 percent of all UVA and UVB rays (check the tag). Groovy toy sunglasses will probably offer no protection. Wrap-around styles will protect the eyes from sun coming in at the sides. Some toddlers and preschoolers won't have anything to do with them, but others when told they look cool may wear them proudly.

SUN ON WHEELS   Most baby and car shops sell screens you can stick on a car window to shade a baby or toddler. You can get stick-on ones that will peel off later if your toddler pulls off the more temporary ones held on with little suction cups. Carriages and strollers should have a shade roof. Drape a solid cloth over the carriage or stroller to get complete protection if you can't get into the shade, but make sure the baby is cool and well ventilated. A soaked, then wrung-out muslin wrap can be very cooling draped over a carriage top, but not on the kid's skin.

LEADING BY EXAMPLE   Little kids won't be bothered about sun-care issues if you don't have a hat and sunscreen on. They love to do what older kids and adults do.

Head Lice

Lice is the plural of louse (as in lousy); they're the little critters that can invade a child's hair, lay eggs (called nits), which are "glued" onto the base of hairs with icky, lousy secretions. The first sign of nits or lice is usually your child scratching their head, or an alert from playgroup, child care, or preschool. The itchiness is caused by the lice— euwwwww!—sucking tiny amounts of blood from the scalp. You will, on close inspection, probably be able to see the tiny, yellowy white eggs, like dandruff, on the hair shaft near the scalp and maybe some little browny grey lice disporting themselves. If an egg is one quarter of an inch or more away from the scalp it's either dead or hatched. The live eggs are down nearer the scalp.

Don't be embarrassed and don't make your kid feel like they've got something appalling. All kids get lice and will continue to. It has nothing to do with personal hygiene. Lice can't jump and they can't live on pets. Chemical companies say lice can live for up to a week without their human host; natural treatment advocates say lice rarely survive this for more than a day or so.

A louse can lay several eggs a day. Eggs hatch in about a week, and within a week the babies are laying their own eggs. This is no time to feel the kinship of motherhood. It's time to kill, kill, kill.

Lice-killing stuff

Get from the drugstore these 3 things:

1 a fine-toothed metal, not plastic, lice comb—the placcy one is a bit bendier and so not as efficient.

2 lice-killing lotion—depending on your philosophy either the full-on poisonous chemical stuff or the natural poisonous stuff (usually tea-tree-oil based).

3 conditioner—the gloopier the better and the more gaudily colored so the eggs are visible against it. The CDC says not to use conditioner 1 to 2 days before using a lice-killing lotion and don't rewash hair for 1 to 2 days after.

The usual chemical ingredient in prescription treatments is malathion, an organophosphate pesticide solution used in high concentrations on farms and in mass mosquito spraying—but at a concentration of only .5 percent in prescription lice lotions.

Other classes of poison used to slay the evil lice menace are the chemicals permethrin and pyrethrin, and eucalyptus and tea-tree (melaleuca) oils, all at precise dilutions and combinations. These are available over the counter at drugstores. This is not a DIY situation: never try making lice-killing stuff from chemicals or oils yourself—remember they are killing creatures so you need some chemical expertise about formulas. Tea-tree oil shouldn't be used by pregnant women in its full-on incarnation. To kill lice my Nanna used to put her three girls through the sheep dip in the 1950s (full of now-banned chemicals at eye-popping concentrations) and they've survived. Mind you, they're all completely mad. But Mom says their hair was very shiny.

Ask a pharmacist, not a shop assistant, for info when you buy lice products. Also read the fine print (which can be virtually unreadable), especially on the chemical treatments, in the pharmacy before you buy; it may tell you that the treatment is not suitable for children under a certain age. Babies and very small children shouldn't be treated with strong chemicals: the CDC recommends not treating children under 2 with these chemicals, instead lice should be removed by hand.

Some people don't use any lotion except conditioner, which makes it easier to get to the eggs, preferring to comb out all lice and eggs and squash them rather than use chemical or natural killing agents.

How to get the lice out

Babies are usually pretty easy to inspect for eggs and lice, which you can remove yourself, because they have less hair.

It's important not to use lice-killing treatment unless someone is definitely infested: this can only be decided after a thorough inspection. Follow the instructions on the label. It's essential not to get any of this stuff in eyes or mouth.

Do not put a kid in front of a heater or use a hair dryer. The chemical lotion may be flammable. (Gawd.)

Rub conditioner or a lice-killing lotion gently but thoroughly through the kid's hair. Sit the child on your lap on a towel and comb their hair meticulously with the metal lice comb. Get out all the dead lice and drag out all the eggs. This can take a very long time. Older children can be kept amused by pretending you are a family of chimps. (Do not go so far as to eat the lice. Please.) Wash your hands and wash the towel in hot water.

Wash all the bedclothes, fluffy toys, and clothes the child has been using in hot water. Woolen sweaters and other things that will shrink in hot water can be treated with an anti-lice soaking solution available at the drugstore.

And that's it. Check again in a few days and repeat the treatment in a week if the critters come back. Keep the lice lotion safely out of reach and keep an eye on the use-by date. If swallowed, call the Poison Control Center immediately at 1-800-222-1222.

See More Info at the end of this chapter for resources.

Hiccups

Hiccups are quite common in babies and nothing to worry about. Painless hiccups that go on for a while in toddlers and children are also not a problem. Don't try to give the kid a fright. And don't give them an adult preparation such as an antacid.

But if your child seems unable to stop and is affected by the hiccups, try getting them to:

- ★ hold their breath—you may need to show them how.
- ★ drink upside down—again you may need to show them.
- ★ drink from a cup while you put your fingers gently in their outer ears.
- ★ breathe in and out of a paper bag—for 1 minute only.

eczema

Itchy, dry skin can develop a red rash and flaking known as eczema, which can affect babies and kids. It's more common in kids who have allergies, and sometimes pet fur or a certain food can make it worse. Most kids grow out of it before they start school.

Moisturizing creams to help with red, dry skin are sold in supermarkets and drugstores, but check which ones can be used on a baby's or an older kid's face and hands (in other words the bits most likely to be sensitive or that can easily transfer cream to the mouth). You may need to apply moisturizing cream to your child before and after they go swimming, after baths and hand washing, and perhaps morning and night or whenever it's needed. See your doctor if the dry skin becomes rashy and doesn't respond.

Like bad diaper rash, if the eczema rash breaks the skin, or the skin is scratched, it can become infected: see your pharmacist or doctor for info about a therapeutic cream or antibiotics.

Babies usually get eczema on the face, especially the cheeks and around the mouth. Factors that make eczema worse include wetness, such as in high-dribble places, heat, and dryness. Avoid woolen clothes or hats, "non-breathing" unnatural fabrics, and soap and detergents, which dry the skin. Keep the car and stroller as cool as possible with shade devices. We often take off one layer for while we're in the car: don't forget to do this for your baby or kid as well.

Car and home heaters can be very drying, particularly those that blow hot air. Better for you all to put a sweater on than to turn the heater up. There's not much you can do in a windy, drying, harsh environment or a humid, sticky one, but try to adjust for the weather as much as you can. Duvets can be too hot (and mustn't be used for babies anyway): try using a combination of cotton blankets and woolen ones (away from the skin) or, in the case of babies, a cotton sleeping suit (like a sleeping bag with arms, available at baby clothes shops and department-store baby sections). Washing-machine detergents can be too harsh: it's best to use gentler wool or hand-washing mixes. Chemically treated water, such as swimming-pool water, can also be very drying.

Baths should be tepid (but not cool or chilly) and short and a soap substitute used. Two to three baths a week will do.

For extra help see More Info at the end of this chapter.

asтHma

Asthma is caused by the little tubes in the lungs being squeezed or inflamed so it's harder to get big, full breaths in and out. The mildest symptom is usually wheezing, stepping up to asthma attacks or "respiratory distress," which in very severe cases results in the child not being able to breathe at all. The United States has one of the highest childhood asthma rates in the world.

Not all wheezing is asthma: it can be caused by bronchitis or another virus, so it's important to get a proper diagnosis. Other causes of wheezing include the kid swallowing something while nobody noticed, which has got stuck in a tube; an infection in a baby under 1 year old (bronchiolitis); and smaller airways than normal.

It's not known why some people get asthma and others don't, but the incidence is rising and known trigger factors include a smoker in the house, having allergies, the house-dust mite in dust, pollen, mold, and pet fur. It's held that breastfed babies are statistically more likely to grow up asthma free, but many children who were breastfed for years have asthma and many formula-fed children don't. So whatever you do, don't blame yourself for your child's illness. Your nearest asthma organization can give you a checklist so you can rejig your home to avoid triggers and can keep you in touch with the latest research results and treatments (see More Info at the end of this chapter).

Asthma is not so much cured as managed or controlled so that it has as little effect on someone's life as possible. The main medications used are liquid medicines and inhalers—some are preventative and some are used for an asthma attack. Asthma doesn't mean a kid should stop being outdoors and playing. Kids can be taught to exercise in ways that don't trigger it.

A child who suddenly has an asthma attack should be taken to a doctor or hospital right away, where they can be treated and you can be given a plan for managing any further attacks. Shortness of breath or an obvious asthma episode mustn't be ignored as a severe attack can cut off breathing entirely.

Current medical thinking is that preventative steps and medication are much better ways of managing asthma than intermittently having to use heavier drugs to treat severe attacks. Specialized slow-breathing techniques have helped some people.

Part of the trauma of an asthma attack for a kid is the panic that goes on around them. Let the professionals do their job, while you concentrate on keeping your kid calm.

Your kid's babysitter, child-care center, or preschool needs to be told about your kid's asthma status and about any regular or emergency treatment or procedures. The center's or preschool's fridge can hold a spare inhaler, with instructions attached, if necessary. Consult your doctor about any instructions these places should be given, provide them in clear writing, talk through the action plan with two or three staff members (a regular may later be away at a crucial time), and keep copies for babysitters, relatives, and friends.

Spare inhalers should be kept in your toddler bag; your handbag; at the homes of grandparents and close friends and at other regularly visited houses; the car glove box (check that the inhaler won't be affected by heat); the travel first-aid kit; and anywhere else sensible.

MANAGEMENT OF ASTHMA

1 Take asthma medications as directed.

2 Monitor the asthma.

3 Stay active and healthy.

4 Identify and avoid triggers such as allergens whenever possible (but most kid asthma is triggered by unavoidable viruses).

5 Be able to recognize early warning signs and be prepared with a written asthma action plan to refer to.

6 Visit the doctor regularly.

autism spectrum disorders, including asperger's syndrome

Autism is often referred to as the autism spectrum because it covers many levels of related disorders, including a subgroup called Asperger's syndrome. Autism is diagnosed much more commonly than in the past. Basically it is believed to be caused by problems in the brain that have some kind of genetic basis (boys are more likely to have autism and so is the twin of a child with autism).

Autism and its variation Asperger's syndrome should be diagnosed by a specialist. Because medical services and special programs have long waiting lists and because great improvement commonly occurs when treatment is begun early, don't hesitate to see your doctor the minute you feel any unease about your baby's or child's development, and a specialist if that's needed.

If autism is diagnosed, aggressively seek special programs that can help your child. Hassle your local representatives if necessary. Symptoms of autism and Asperger's syndrome are most often seen from 18 months onwards, although many parents say they saw earlier signs but did not then have the information to be suspicious. (See More Info at the end of this chapter for resources.)

It's probably needless to say, but many development problems have nothing to do with autism and are in the normal range.

Why is the autism rate rising?

The area of autism is still under intense study, there are lots of theories, and variations of the syndrome are being described more thoroughly and applied as a diagnosis more than ever before. Several groups have been set up here and in the UK by parents who believe their child's autism was caused by the MMR (measles, mumps, rubella) injection, although mainstream autism organizations and the vast majority of doctors believe there is no connection. As the Immunization chapter explains, no link has been shown.

SOME SYMPTOMS ASSOCIATED WITH AUTISM DISORDERS

A child:

* has a delay in speech development.

* is unwilling to make eye contact.

* doesn't like to be cuddled.

* seems detached.

* has rages caused by frustration.

* has repetitive, obsessive movements or pursuits.

* does not engage in imaginative play.

* is anxious if there's a change to routines or something expected.

* has difficulty communicating or conversing.

People with autism rarely understand jokes, feelings, body language, or how to behave in many social situations.

Doctors say that the rise in cases is explained by the fact that autism syndrome is now usually viewed as a spectrum—a diagnosis of autism or Asperger's syndrome is made where in the past a child with mild autistic symptoms or Asperger's syndrome would just have been described as "difficult," "different," "retarded," or simply "not good with people."

Meanwhile in the computer-industry-dominated Silicon Valley area of California, there has been a very sharp rise in the number of autism-type cases, and especially of Asperger's syndrome. It is thought by some in the field that the "intermarriage" of people affectionately known as computer geeks, many of whom had variations of Asperger's syndrome, has led to the passing on of other variations to their children.

attentioN Deficit HyPeRactivity DisORDeR (aDHD)

Attention deficit hyperactivity disorder (ADHD), sometimes called attention deficit disorder (ADD) is a clinical diagnosis that has been given to the sort of kid who bounces off the walls. The commonly recognized symptoms include:

- ★ a short or no attention span.
- ★ fidgeting.
- ★ being "hyperactive"—always on the move.
- ★ aggressive behavior.
- ★ boredom.

It's not a diagnosis that should ever be made by a parent, a teacher, or a GP as commonly happens. There is a fierce debate in medical circles about whether ADHD is a real medical disorder or a name given to a wide range of behaviors that are not necessarily medical at all. There is also much dispute about whether children diagnosed with ADHD should be given the strong brain-chemistry-affecting drugs associated with the medical treatment of ADHD, the long-term effects of which are unknown.

Many people believe that ADHD can be used as a convenient label for kids who have short attention spans, or who are easily bored and often disruptive in class, or who have psychological problems, and are more controllable when drugged. There is some evidence of this. Some areas, for example, have a vastly higher rates of both diagnosis and drug treatment than other areas, and this has led to accusations of a disturbing over-diagnosis of ADHD.

Some of the symptoms of what might seem like ADHD at first glance can actually be treated with family counseling, behavior strategies, diet changes, or even a change of school or parenting philosophy. Many of the symptoms, unless absolutely out of control, are the sorts of outer-edge-of-normal, rambunctious behavior shown by intelligent children—often boys. In very severe cases diagnosed as ADHD some doctors say there are neurological (brain) differences. (See More Info, which follows, for resources.)

ADHD must be diagnosed by a pediatric specialist and should only be treated with drugs as a last resort.

more info

FIRST AID

Johns Hopkins Children's Center: First Aid for Children Fast
Allen Walker, DK Publishing, rev. ed., 2002.
Lots of pictures and step-by-step first-aid info, including what to have in a fully stocked first-aid kit and tips for sprucing up safety in your home and life.

Red Cross
The international humanitarian mob we all look to in a crisis. They offer first aid and child/infant CPR classes throughout the country.
www.redcross.org

COMMON CHILDHOOD ILLNESS AND CONDITIONS

None of the following handy reference books and websites should be considered a substitute for individual, face-to-face medical diagnosis and advice. As with all books that involve medical information, get the latest edition. Don't forget to check these at your local library of they are too expensive for your budget.

Mayo Clinic Family Health Book, third edition
by the Mayo Clinic, HarperResource, 2003.
A great basic home health book. Contains descriptions of the body and how all of its parts function and information on diagnosis and treatment of common illnesses and injuries.

**American Academy of Pediatrics Guide to Your Child's Symptoms:
The Official, Complete Home Reference, Birth Through Adolescence**
by Donald Schiff, Steven P. Shelov, and the American Academy of Pediatrics,
Villard Books, 1997.
Basic advice from the American Academy of Pediatrics on identifying illnesses, rashes, and other medical problems. Contains everything from limp-
ing and sniffles to whooping cough and muscular dystrophy.

www.kidshealth.org
A website established by a philanthropic foundation, which has info on common ailments, kids' feelings, and a preventative lifestyle. There's a glossary of
medical terms and stuff for kids with disabilities. The advantage is that all
health problems are explained at a kid's level—it may help you explain
things to your little one (and yourself!).

www.keepkidshealthy.com
Lots of info, forums, and articles on many common kids' health problems.

MedlinePlus Health Information of the National Library of Medicine
This is an excellent website with links to authoritative resources on over
650 topics, conditions, and diseases. Interactive tutorials, extensive information on prescription and non-prescription medications, medical dictionary,
physician and hospital directories, health information in Spanish, and latest
health news articles.
www.medlineplus.gov

ACETAMINOPHEN AND IBUPROFEN
Kids Meds
Its website is sponsored by the American Pharmaceutical Association Foundation and features calculators for acetaminophen and ibuprofen. Also has free
"info-sheets," links to Poison Control Centers, and a Pediatric Pharmacist
Online service.
www.kidsmeds.org/calculators.ccml

EAR PROBLEMS

National Institute on Deafness and Other Communication Disorders (one of the National Institutes of Health)

Information for parents about ear infections. Answers to FAQs such as what is an ear infection, what causes it, what happens in the ear when its infected, will it cause deafness, how to be sure you're giving medications properly, and more.

www.nidcd.nih.gov/health/hearing/otitismedia.asp

TOO MUCH SUN

Skin Cancer Foundation

The Skin Cancer Foundation publishes an illustrated bookmark and other literature about skin cancers and also provides information via its website.

1-800-754-6490

www.skincancer.org

American Cancer Society

The American Cancer Society publishes an excellent booklet, "What You Should Know About Melanoma," which can be requested by phone or online. They also provide an online "Melanoma Resource Center" with information about all aspects of melanoma.

1-800-ACS-2345

www.sunprotection.org

An exceptionally user-friendly educational site for children and families.

HEAD LICE

The Centers for Disease Control (CDC) & the National Center for Infectious Diseases, Division of Parasitic Diseases

Lots of good public health info on lice.

www.cdc.gov/ncidod/dpd/parasites/headlice

www.headlice.org

A non-profit website based on an anti-pesticide approach to lice control, with lots of handy info on alternatives including mayonnaise. The site carries some product advertising.

ECZEMA

National Eczema Association for Science and Education

Features information and lots of advice and hints on controlling the condition and connections to support groups.

www.nationaleczema.org

www.undermyskin.com

The website includes an illustrated children's book about eczema available in PDF. You can view the book all at once or chapter by chapter.

ASTHMA

www.epa.gov/asthma

Features an article about how to clear your home of asthma triggers, an asthma fact sheet and FAQs, asthma quiz, and downloadable *Dusty The Asthma Goldfish and His Asthma Triggers Funbook* for kids. They also sponsor a national toll-free asthma hotline:

1-800-315-8056

www.noattacks.org

Articles about asthma, asthma triggers, and how to prevent attack.

AUTISM SPECTRUM DISORDERS, INCLUDING ASPERGER'S SYNDROME

Autism Society of America

Maintains a good website with information about autism, facts, downloadable brochures, a searchable database to help you locate local organizations that provide parents with advocacy, training, and information on their children's educational rights.

www.autism-society.org/

National Alliance for Autism Research
Has these links for parents to a number of sites on autism.
www.naar.org

www.exploringautism.org
Educational site focusing on genetics of autism sponsored by Center for Human Genetics at Duke University Medical Center and Department of Psychiatry at Tufts New England Medical Center. This site also offers French and Spanish translations.

www.talkautism.org
Resource for the autism community to share knowledge, information, and assistance.

www.asperger.org
Website of the Asperger Syndrome Coalition of the US, a national nonprofit organization committed to providing up-to-date and comprehensive information on Asperger Syndrome and related conditions.

The OASIS Guide to Asperger Syndrome: Advice, Support, Insight, and Inspiration
by Patricia Romanowski Bashe, Barbara L. Kirby, Crown, 2001.
Explores pervasive developmental disorders, including autism, but focusing mainly on Asperger Syndrome. The authors are both mothers of children with Aspergers and they offer a good balance between practical information and personal perspective.

Behavioral Intervention for Young Children With Autism: A Manual for Parents and Professionals
by Catherine Maurice, Gina Green, and Stephen C. Luce, Pro-ED, 1996.
Includes a FAQ section and case studeis. Focuses on research-proven methods of treatment and behavioral interventions for kids with autism. It is also useful for child-care centers and schools to help them cope with the difficulties involved in meeting the needs of children with autism.

Asperger's Syndrome: A Guide for Parents and Professionals
by Tony Attwood, Taylor & Francis Group, 1997.
"By a Brisbane clinical psychologist."

Asperger's Syndrome, the Universe and Everything
by Kenneth Hall, Taylor and Francis Group, 2001.
"Fascinating book by a 10-year-old Irish both with Asperger's syndrome. Suitable for children and adults."

www.wired.com/wired/archive/9.12/aspergers.html
The Silicon Valley gene theory is explored in a *Wired* magazine article, "The Geek Syndrome."

ATTENTION DEFICIT HYPERACTIVITY DISORDER (ADHD)

Different Kids: Growing Up with Attention Deficit Disorder
by Sue Dengate, Random House, Aust., 1996.
A well-regarded Australian book. See the full details and reviews in More Info at the end of the Food chapter of other books by Sue Dengate and her website, in which she investigates how different foods and additives can affect behavior. You will still need medical help to get a diagnosis of ADHD however.

ADD/ADHD Behavior-Change Resource Kit : Ready-to-Use Strategies & Activities for Helping Children with Attention Deficit Disorder
by Grad L. Flick, Jossey-Bass, 2002.
Explains ADHD behavior, diagnosis, and treatment options and offers parents and teachers different behavioral strategies.

National Resource Center (NRC) on ADHD
A national clearinghouse dedicated to the evidence-based science and treatment of ADHD. The website is very helpful.
www.help4adhd.org

www.attentiondeficitdisorder.ws
A website of links to all things ADHD.

Being active

Unfortunately, almost every book about kids

has pages and pages on what to feed them

and pages and pages on what development

stages they're supposed to be at, and almost nothing about appropriate exercise for toddlers and little kids.

Exercise is a crucial part of preventing kids from developing an unhealthy body. Exercise in this context just means being active. An added bonus: kids sleep better when they're physically tired.

Kids in the past were outside a lot more and stood, walked, and played more, using up energy. Now they tend to play indoors and to eat more calorie-rich food than kids used to twenty years ago, yet do less exercise. Some of the reasons for this include parents themselves not getting outside or exercising as much, kids watching more TV and backyards becoming smaller or non-existent.

All health professionals stress that unless the whole family is willing to get involved in a more healthy and active life, it's almost impossible to help a TV-addicted kid this young learn to enjoy pottering about the garden, climbing trees, playing sports, and having other outdoor fun.

exercise that's good for kids

Dr. Elizabeth Waters, director of research and public health at the Center for Community Child Health in Melbourne, says people can get too uptight and formal about exercise for little kids: "The best thing for parents to do is get out there with their kids and make walking and playing in the park part of normal life . . . The worst thing is to put kids through their paces at clubs or organizations where it isn't family fun and natural play together." (I just love it when an expert says something sensible like "Oh, just go outside and play and talk and do stuff that makes you laugh.") Dr. Waters suggests that parents aim to have a chat and a activity with their kids every day, but not to freak out if they miss a day here and there. Dads and other guys can often get special joy from passing on important ball and balancing skills.

★ Babies who can't walk can roll balls and move to music.
★ Toddlers can do fun stretches, kick a ball, and start to learn to catch (try a balloon first and work up to soft balls).

★ Little kids can throw a large, light ball with two hands (throwing with one hand began the first time they dropped something on the floor).

★ Kids who can run can start doing obstacle games and soccer.

Exercise doesn't need to be structured. But to keep it interesting, and to develop different muscle groups and skills, choose one or two age-appropriate activities from the list Good Exercise Stuff to Do with Kids (next page) to concentrate on each day.

Instead of taking an adult angle and saying kids must exercise for a certain time each day, be guided by your kid: how long are they interested in this exercise or game? When they sit or lie down, get cranky, yawn, or want to do something else, that's the time to stop. Have another go later or the next day. It's important to remind everyone that it's all about fun and experience, not setting goals: anything that isn't fun is guaranteed to fail.

Keeping exercise varied will give a kid a chance to find out what they like and what they're good at. Training or concentrating on one sport is not good for young children: it is too restrictive mentally and physically and can lead to injury and underdevelopment in other physical areas. I heard recently of some parents who encourage their 3-year-olds to do laps of a pool equivalent to swimming a half mile: I would like to slap them. That kind of "achievement" is not applicable to toddlers. "The notion of winning doesn't need to emerge at this age," says Dr. Waters. (Or at least until they're 32, if you ask me.)

info on being active

★ Local agencies and libraries often have information about hidden opportunities in your area. You might find that even in the inner city, there's a ramshackle adventure playground with lots of things to fall off and climb under. These and some other adventure playgrounds can be more

GOOD EXERCISE STUFF TO DO WITH KIDS

* Ball throwing and catching.

* Riding a trike, a bike, or other wheelie device.

* Running with paper streamers.

* Exploring the garden or park, and perhaps having a picnic.

* Doing exercises in the garden or park.

* Flying a kite.

* Balancing.

* Doing "acrobatics" (somersaults and cartwheels) on the lawn.

* Mucking around at the adventure playground.

* Going to the local swimming pool.

* Walking to the shop (take the stroller for sudden fades).

* Playing variations of soccer, football, tennis, handball, baseball, or basketball.

* Playing monkey-in-the-middle.

* Playing in the sandbox.

* Going on a nature hike or treasure hunt to collect things (find a red leaf, a pinecone, a bent stick).

* Making patterns in sand or dirt with a rake, shells, stones, or sticks.

* Dancing.

* Playing chase.

* Running through the sprinkler (but not when there's a drought).

* Jumping in puddles, wearing galoshes.

* Pottering in the garden, doing some weeding, planting, and picking.

* Running around with the dog (but always supervised).

* "Painting" the fence with water.

* Sweeping the paths.

* Climbing trees or other things.

* Decorating trees.

* Playing hide and seek.

614

dangerous than the pristine, rounded, almost guaranteed no-injury, plastic-molded climbing equipment made only for the youngest children. (A child of 3 on a monkey bars will need to be very closely helped, for example.) But if you're prepared to take a few risks, and supervise properly, they can be so much fun for kids.

★ Toy libraries may have activity equipment such as balls, trikes, and mats to roll on.

★ Parenting magazines and newspapers often have ads for kids' physical activity programs, frequently held during school holidays. These are usually for older kids so be careful.

Toddler gyms

Movement-based groups such as these can be fun for kids and can be a sort of parents' group as well. They are held in many areas and can be for babies aged 1 month up to preschoolers. A trained coordinator uses songs, bubbles, climbing equipment, exercise mats— all sorts of things—to develop coordination, muscles and physical capabilities. Movement programs aim to promote intellectual development also, which makes sense. But rather than thinking of them as "hothousing" or "training" your child to "get ahead," it's much nicer to think of them as good fun and good for children.

An organized, gym-style program will not suit many children, especially the ones who don't like being regimented, and equipment that must all be used and in a certain way can curb creativity. Sometimes a program is held in too small a space, which can be restrictive for kids who need to explore. Gym-style routines shouldn't be a replacement for kids just having active fun with their family and friends. You can make a DIY physical-fun session: see More Info below.

moRe iNfo

Moving to Learn: Making the Connection Between Movement, Music, Learning and Play (Birth to 3 Years)
by Robyn Crowe and Gill Connell, book and music CD set, Caxton Press, NZ, 2002.
This Aussie–Kiwi collaboration between two early-childhood professionals presents all sorts of info and ideas for fun physical activities. Ideal for parents, playgroups, and child-care centers. US orders can be placed on their website at www.movingtolearn.com.

GARDENING

Kid's Gardening: A Kid's Guide to Messing Around in the Dirt
by Kevin Raftery, Kim Gilbert, and Jim M'Guinness,
Simple starter ideas and crafty projects for toddlers, preschoolers, and older kids. Includes a shovel and seeds.

Roots, Shoots, Buckets & Boots: Gardening Together with Children
by Sharon Lovejoy, Workman, 1999.
Full of creative and fun gardening activities for kids. Everything from a "pizza garden" to "sunflower house".

TODDLER GYMS

Gymboree Play and Music
More than 530 locations where parents and caregivers participate in fun play, music, and art classes with their children.
www.playmusic.com

YMCA
Offers affordable toddler tumbling classes, swimming classes, day camps, and more.
www.ymca.net

immunization

In developing countries parents who can see the effects of crippling and fatal diseases around them eagerly attend government and charity clinics for their kids to be immunized. In the developed world, where many of these diseases have been shown the door, parents are often more worried about the real and rumored side effects of the vaccinations themselves. Only about 80 percent of Americans have their kids fully immunized.

This has gotta be worth a candy bar!

immunization overview

The United States has a list of recommended vaccinations for all kids, called the immunization schedule. Basically by the age of 5 a child should be protected from measles, mumps, rubella, diphtheria, tetanus, whooping cough, polio, a bacteria called Hib (*Haemophilus influenzae* type b) that used to be the most common cause of meningitis among other things, hepatitis B, meningoccocal bacteria, and now even chicken pox. No doubt other vaccines will go into the mix in the future.

The immunization (also known interchangeably as vaccination) programs have two aims: to protect individual children from these "old-fashioned" diseases; and, in some cases, to have a public health campaign to eradicate a disease altogether. It isn't compulsory to have the vaccinations, but it is urged by all doctors and the vaccines are provided free by the government for kids on Medicaid, the uninsured, and the underinsured (although you may have to pay a small administration fee). Your child can receive vaccinations at a private doctors office, private clinic, hospital, public health clinic, community health clinic, and in some states at some schools.

The World Health Organisation (WHO) says that almost 3 million people a year are alive because they've been vaccinated against diseases. It's a calculation based on the pre-vaccination death rates of various diseases.

There are some way heated debates about vaccinations. At the extremes there are doctors who say it isn't worth discussing the fact that a relatively tiny number of kids are damaged by vaccines because it's far fewer than those who would have died from the diseases if there had been no vaccinations; and at the other end there are some nutty anti-vaccinators who say extremely dodgy stuff, often on their websites, including this: "Children who were breastfed and are well looked after have an immune system which will protect them against diseases." (This, frankly, is a big fat fib.)

Parents don't always look at the big picture and I think doctors need to understand this. We are usually more worried about what effect a vaccine might have on our individual tiny person than thrilled to participate in a disease-eradication public health program. When doctors say there's less than a one-in-a-million chance of a serious vaccination reaction such as inflammation of the brain, they should remember we're all worried that our baby might be that one in a million. (For the vast majority of parents, it gets easier by the second lot of scheduled shots because the first ones caused no problems at all.)

Parents with legitimate questions can be treated like rabid twits by both sides. On the one hand the "information" given them in anti-vaccination books and on websites is most often a shocking mix of lies, twisted statistics, and accusations. On the other hand, a few worried parents have been bullied by doctors instead of being given information respectfully. (Time to find another doctor if that's the case: the majority will talk to you sensibly about concerns.)

Most people have already made up their mind about what they think of vaccines by the time they have children. Some get whatever's on the schedule, no questions asked. Others vehemently oppose vaccinations and won't be swayed by any facts presented. The following is really for people who want more info before closing their eyes, crossing their fingers, and jumping (a time-honored, metaphorical parent-decision-making technique).

Despite the claims of many anti-vaccine lobbyists, the dedicated medical staff who immunize children are, hey, *probably not* part of some bizarre, worldwide, shifty-eyed conspiracy to make money for drug companies, and *probably not* brainwashed, robotic devotees of weird science. And it seems equally evident that sadly a very, very small number of individual children among millions may be harmed by a vaccine. In a perfect world each child's reactions would be perfectly predictable, each child with a medical predisposition would have obvious symptoms, and each vaccine dose would be individually tailored to the levels of immunity in each child without needing blood to be taken with yet another injection. Ultimately, parents will have to weigh up the tiny statistical risk for their child against the protection from diseases.

CURRENT US immunization schedule

The current schedule will change in the future as new vaccines are added or even dropped as a disease is eradicated. The following schedule operated at July 2004:

- ★ **birth to 2 months**—hepatitis B (dose 1 of 3).
- ★ **1 to 4 months**—hepatitis B (dose 2 of 3).
- ★ **2 months**—DTaP (diphtheria, tetanus, whooping cough) (dose 1 of 5), Hib (dose 1 of 4), polio (dose 1 of 4), pneumococcal (dose 1 of 4).
- ★ **4 months**—DTaP (dose 2 of 5), Hib (dose 2 of 4), polio (dose 2 of 4), and pneumococcal (dose 2 of 4).
- ★ **6 months**—DTaP (dose 3 of 5), Hib (dose 3 of 4), and pneumococcal (dose 3 of 4).
- ★ **6 to 24 months**—flu shots recommended.
- ★ **12 to 15 months**—Hib (dose 4 of 4), pneumococcal (dose 4 of 4), MMR (measles, mumps, and rubella) (dose 1 of 2).
- ★ **12 to 18 months**—chickenpox.
- ★ **15 to 18 months**—DTaP (dose 4 of 5).
- ★ **2 to 5 years**—pneumococcal polysaccharide.
- ★ **4 to 6 years**—DTaP (dose 5 of 5), polio (dose 4 of 4), and MMR (dose 2 of 2).

See also the table Diseases and Their Vaccinations coming up soon in this chapter.

Newborn immunization

Some parents who don't consider their child at risk of hepatitis B are not going with a first injection at birth, but waiting until the vaccines given at 2 months old or later. If you're one of those, you will need to be absolutely certain that you don't have it—most people with hep B don't know they have it—to avoid the risk of your baby getting it without your knowing. Of course, babies who are at risk (ask your doctor about this) really need the injection as early as possible. Parents who delay the hepatitis B injection after the birth will have to assess the risks of this.

How Does a Vaccine Work?

Vaccines against bacterial disease usually contain a form of the bacteria or toxin that causes the disease it will protect against. A tiny bit of, let's say, Hib bacteria has been treated so it can't actually cause the disease itself but prompts the body to produce antibodies—protection against the disease. In some cases, an inactive component of the bacteria (for example, its sugar coating) is mixed with a protein known to help it produce the required reaction in a young body.

A vaccine might also contain a preservative and barely detectable traces of formaldehyde, used to kill the contagious bit of

---

KEEPING A RECORD

Many child-care centers, preschools, schools, and even colleges require a copy of a child's official record of immunizations.

It's always a good idea to keep this important info in an easy to find place. Your child may need the info through their adult life and for their own kids.

The CDC has an interactive scheduler that can help you keep track of when your child will need each vaccine and when they are received. (See More Info at the end of this chapter.)

Text continues after the following Diseases and Their Vaccinations table

DISEASES AND THEIR VACCINATIONS

Disease	Symptoms and effects	How it can be spread
Hepatitis B	A virus that causes fever; nausea; tiredness; dark pee; yellowy skin; liver damage, and, in 25 percent of cases, liver cancer in midlife (babies usually don't show symptoms when they are infected but develop liver damage in four or five decades).	In adults, usually by unprotected sex or sharing a syringe, razor, tattoo needle, or even a toothbrush with a carrier; in children, being born to, or breastfed by a carrier, (very rarely) stepping on a syringe, or possibly wound-to-wound contact.
Haemophilus influenzae type b (Hib)	Not actually anything to do with flu virus but a bacteria. Can cause meningitis (inflammation of the brain), swelling in the throat that can suffocate, pneumonia, joint and tissue infection, and death. A severe problem for the under-fives.	Coughs, sneezes, contact with bacteria on hand or hanky.
Diphtheria	A growth in the throat can lead to suffocation. Rarer effects include paralysis and death in 7 percent of cases.	Sneezes, coughs, contact with bacteria on hand or hanky.
Chickenpox	Rash, itchiness, fever, and tiredness. Can lead to scarring, sever skin infections, pneumonia, brain damage, shingles, and death.	Person to person through the air or by contact with fluid from chickenpox blisters.
Tetanus	Muscle spasms; breathing problems; convulsions; the nervous system shuts down; and, if untreated, often leads to death.	A common microorganism in dirt and manure, which will produce a toxin if it gets into a deep cut or puncture wound.

Possible side effects of the vaccine	Why we need the vaccine	Alternative to the vaccine that would guarantee safety from infection
Rarely, low-grade fever, sore arm at injection site; allergic reaction, very rare.	Increasing rate of children born to hep B carriers becoming infected themselves: one in three of these children will develop serious liver disease. The vaccine is on the schedule because public health authorities say hep B is one of the preventable causes of cancer.	None. If a person knows they've come in contact with hep B, they can have an injection within three days that might prevent them getting it.
Low-grade fever, sore injection site (the thigh in babies up to age 1, and the arm for older kids because the muscle is bigger then), nausea, joint pain.	Before the vaccine was introduced, Hib disease was the leading cause of bacterial meningitis in children under 5. About 20,000 children got the disease in the US every year, and about 1,000 people died.	None.
See whooping cough (next page).	Thanks to immunization programs, the disease is virtually eradicated in many Western countries.	None.
Soreness or swelling where the shot was given, a mild rash, or fever. Rarely seizures.	About 12,000 people are hospitalized each year due to chickenpox, and around 100 people die from it annually.	None.
See whooping cough below.	Tetanus is rare in the US now and almost exclusively strikes older, under-vaccinated people. The death rate of patients is about 10 percent. About 800,000 babies a year in developing countries die each year because of low or no vaccination.	None. Unimmunized people should have a tetanus immunoglobin injection and vaccine as soon as possible after a wound. There's a long list of possible side effects of the immunoglobin jab (see your doctor) so better to be vaccinated.

DISEASES AND THEIR VACCINATIONS *continued*

Disease	Symptoms and effects	How it can be spread
Whooping cough (pertussis)	Distressing coughing fits and inability to draw breath until spasm ends, when desperate intake of breath causes "whooping" sound—the coughing can continue for months; more rarely, convulsions and coma; often fatal in babies under 1 year old and a death rate in under-twos of one in 200; survivors may have permanent lung or brain damage.	Coughs, sneezes. The bacteria is highly contagious—three vaccine doses by the age of 6 months are needed to give high protection to a baby.
Poliomyelitis (infant paralysis)	Fever, vomiting, muscle stiffness, nerve damage; 5 percent who get it will die from their breathing muscles being paralyzed and half of the survivors will have permanent crippling of the legs.	A virus spread by saliva and poop (for example, due to a diaper-changing hygiene problem).
Pneumococcal	High fever, cough with mucus, shaking chills, breathlessness, and chest pain. Can lead to bacterial meningitis, pneumonia, deafness, brain damage, and death.	Cough, sneezes, or close contact.

Possible side effects of the vaccine	Why we need the vaccine	Alternative to the vaccine that would guarantee safety from infection
Within 1 to 3 days of the shot, mild side effects might include fever; redness, soreness, or swelling where the shot was given; tiredness or fussiness. Vomiting is a less common side effect. Rare problems include seizure, non-stop crying, or a high fever. Allergic reactions are extremely rare.	Because it's so contagious, whooping cough epidemics still occur every three or four years and some vaccinated children will still get it, with much reduced effects. Unvaccinated babies under 2 months old are at greatest risk but the vaccine doesn't usually work before then. In countries where the vaccine isn't used, whooping cough is still a major cause of death in children.	None.
There's a chance of getting a sore spot where the shot was given. Allergic reactions are rare. In the US, the shot is now recommended over the oral vaccine to avoid the extremely rare chance of contracting the disease from the vaccination.	Polio was a major health crisis, daily infections causing public panic before the introduction of a vaccine. In 1916 a polio epidemic killed 6,000 people and paralyzed over 27,000. Hospitals had to set aside special wards for all the children with paralyzed legs trying to recover. Some did, some didn't. No wild polio has been reported in the US in over 20 years.	None.
Redness, tenderness, or soreness where shot was given, fever, fusiness, loss of appetite.	Pneumococcal is the leading cause of severe pneumonia in children, and causes more than 1 million children deaths annually worldwide.	Once contracted, the infection is usually treated with antibiotics. However, because antibiotic resistance is increasing worldwide, treatment is not always effective.

DISEASES AND THEIR VACCINATIONS *continued*

Disease	Symptoms and effects	How it can be spread
Measles	High fever, cough, conjunctivitis, feeling miserable, irritability, exhaustion, a red rash usually begins on the face after a week. One in twenty-five previously healthy kids with measles gets pneumonia; one in 2000 gets encephalitis (inflammation of the brain): of those with encephalitis 10 percent will die and up to 40 percent will have brain damage.	Sneezes, coughs, or other contact. Astonishingly contagious virus, active for four days before and after the first appearance of the rash.
Mumps	Fever, headache, big puffed-out cheeks caused by infection of salivary glands. Rarer side effects include deafness; swollen testicles in post-puberty males, which in a few cases causes infertility, brain inflammation in one out of 200 kids.	Sneezes, coughs.
Rubella (German measles)	Swollen glands, joint pains, a two- to three-day rash on the head and neck. It's easily recovered from, but if transmitted to a pregnant woman in the first eight to ten weeks there's a 90 percent chance of severe birth defects, including blindness, deafness, mental retardation; the risk continues to twenty weeks of pregnancy.	Very contagious: coughs and sneezes.

Possible side effects of the vaccine	Why we need the vaccine	Alternative to the vaccine that would guarantee safety from infection
Sore arm; in 10 percent of children a mild fever and non-catchy rash five to twelve days after the injection. Up to one in a million children may develop encephalitis. A case of measles itself is much more likely to cause encephalitis.	Measles used to be a common childhood disease in the US, and continues to kill millions of people worldwide.	None. The MMR (measles, mumps, rubella) vaccine given within 72 hours of contact, or an immunoglobin injection given within seven days, may or may not prevent or modify the disease.
Low-grade fever, which is related to the measles component, and in about 1 percent of cases slight facial swelling.	Nearly all kids in the US had mumps before the vaccine made it very rare.	None.
Slight fever and sore arm are the most common; some women develop transient joint pain.	Before immunization, it was a very common cause of deafness.	None. Women need to be immunized up to one month before getting pregnant, if they have not already been vaccinated.

Sources include: CDC National Immunization Program; National Institute of Allergy and Infectious Diseases; Australian Immunisation Handbook, *7th edn, Commonwealth Government, Aust., 2001;* A Field Guide to Germs; *Australian federal Department of Health; Dr. Jenny Royle and Dr. Nigel Curtis, Royal Children's Hospital, Melbourne.*

the bacteria or virus in the lab. Some vaccines that protect against viruses are "live" but have been altered so that they are a very weak form of the virus. They produce immunity but don't cause the disease. Initially, a vaccine is tested on laboratory animals, then larger animals, then finally on human volunteers. Results are reported, published, and checked by government licensors.

getting an immunization

If you have a lot of questions you'd like answered, it's probably best to go to your doctor or health clinic. They should ask you some questions to make sure the vaccine is safe for your child and your family, and that there are no previous illnesses or allergic conditions that mean your child should see an immunization specialist at your local children's hospital.

After the injection, hang around with your baby or little kid for 15 minutes to ensure there is no anaphylactic shock (see the section Reactions later in this chapter).

If your kid is quite sick and has a fever, it's probably best to postpone the immunization in case it's harder to spot any side effects of the vaccination. If your kid has sneezes, sniffles, or an ordinary old cold it's almost always fine to go ahead with the immunization, but ask if you're worried.

> *"The oldest inhabitants recollected no period at all at which measles had been so prevalent, or so fatal to infant existence; and many were the mournful [funeral] processions . . ."* CHARLES DICKENS, OLIVER TWIST, 1837

How to help a child on injection day
Babies usually just look momentarily horrified and accusing when they get their injections, and cry briefly until they're cuddled and distracted, perhaps by a breastfeed or bottlefeed. Older kids usually are stoical or cry a little and they too forget the pain moments later,

actual size

especially when cunningly distracted. You may be surprised to see how slender and quick the disposable needle is these days.

Have on hand tissues for tears, two special treats for an older baby or small child, a comforting toy or other item. The following things should help with toddlers and little kids.

★ There is usually no point in describing the scene to a kid or building up anticipation (which is likely to be fearful)—but be guided by your specialist knowledge of your toddler or preschooler. Jennifer Irwin, an immunization nurse, says "Think about how much preparation your child needs before any new experience. Sometimes it is good to have a story or two a day or so before or perhaps some play with a toy medical kit to prepare." You can ask your playgroup or child-care center to have a group chat about it.

★ You can use a pretend or toy syringe to give injections to a teddy or dolly, but it's probably not a good idea to "train" kids to pick up real-looking syringes.

★ At the actual time be matter of fact about having an injection; don't build it up to be important or scary.

★ Never say "Don't cry."

★ Explain (even if it's been explained before) that the nurse or doctor is going to put some very special medicine inside them to stop them from getting bad sicknesses, and that the nurse or doctor is going to use a needle and it will only take a second.

★ If asked, don't pretend that it won't hurt. Say it might sting for a short time but you'll have a special surprise treat ready for them straight afterwards.

★ You will be asked to hold the kid firmly to help them be very still. Try to make this feel cuddly rather than restraining.

★ Distraction is the key. Most kids prefer to look away, but some like to watch: either is fine. Some like a cartoon adhesive strip over the injection spot.

★ Immediately afterward ask the kid to make a choice between, say, a sticker or a jelly bean: a choice of treats is very distracting and will usually stop any crying.

★ Praise them for sitting still during the injection and having it. Make a fuss of them.

★ You can press on the injection site afterwards to dull the stinging, but don't massage it.

★ If the injection site is red and sore afterwards, a cool pack can be held gently on it and a usual dose of baby or child acetaminophen (see label) could be given.

★ Toddlers and preschoolers will appreciate a "debriefing" so have a chat about why they had the injection and how they're protected against special sicknesses now. Keep up the praise.

★ The site of the injection may be sore to the touch for a few days. This is because injection into soft tissues can cause low-level bruising.

★ Ask your doctor or nurse for any side effects you should keep an eye out for and what to do if they appear.

Teddy's had 27 injections

Reactions

Most children show no reaction at all, apart from being a bit affronted and up for a major bribe straight after the injection. Breast or bottle milk or drinks can also be comforting. If there is a fever a trip to your doctor is a good idea: it might not be the immunization that is causing the high temperature. (Young children pick up new infections often but usually fight them off.) Don't give acetaminophen to bring a fever down, but only if your kid is in pain or miserable. A sudden high fever can cause a brief fit (look up convulsion in the index). Fever does not cause brain damage. If there is a convulsion, call 911 immediately: it's best to be safe.

In extremely exceptional cases, vaccination can cause anaphylactic shock, an immediate allergic reaction. Because babies and small children rarely faint after an injection, a loss of consciousness should be assumed to be anaphylaxis—a life-threatening emergency because it can cause throat swelling leading to suffocation. If it's going to happen, it will almost certainly do so within 10 to 20 minutes of the injection. Treatment is usually a swift adrenaline injection, possibly extra oxygen, and always a trip to hospital for observation. (A nurse giving 100 immunizations a week for fifty-two weeks a year would see one of these reactions once every 200 years. And she'd be very wrinkly by then too.)

If your child has had a reaction such as fever to an injection, talk about it with your doctor, call the immunization clinic at your local children's hospital for a chat, and maybe schedule the next injections at their clinic where they're specialized at this sort of thing. In the rare event your child has a serious reaction to a vaccine, the federal government has started a program to help you pay for their care. (See More Info at the end of the chapter for contact numbers.)

arguments about immunization

Additives

The argument against the MMR (measles, mumps, rubella) injection used to be that mercury in the injection was causing health problems. Despite the claims of most anti-vaccination books and websites, Americans can be assured their MMR jab and now almost all other childhood vaccines are free of mercury. If you're concerned about mercury, talk to your doctor or nurse to see if they can order mercury-free brands, but unfortunately, you may have to pay extra if they don't automatically stock them.)

If you're worried, ask your doctor to get out the list of ingredients from the packet and take you through them. If there is anything in the mix that bothers you, talk about ordering another brand if that's possible.

There may be a tiny amount of pork gelatin in one brand of MMR vaccine. If a family has a religious objection to pork products, an alternative is available.

Autism and vaccines: no proven link

Various anti-vaccine activists have accused various vaccines of causing various things, including autism, in the past. Now, largely because of publicity over a controversial piece of research in England, the triple MMR (measles, mumps, rubella) injection has been accused of causing autism and intestinal problems there.

Basically, it's the vast majority of the doctors and immunology scientists in the world versus a handful of doctors and many parents of sick children who say they are worried about various aspects of the MMR, which range from mercury additives to opposition to the idea of giving three vaccines in one injection (preferring three injections spaced over time) or a theory that the measles vaccine alone is causing problems.

Dr. Nigel Curtis, a pediatrician specializing in immunization, says he understands why parents might blame an illness or condition on immunization when it is not actually the culprit. Like other doctors, he points out that most kids who get autism do have the MMR injection—and most kids who don't have autism have it too.

"On any given day there are hundreds of babies having their MMR jab or preschoolers having the booster. That means any cold, cough, fever, or dribble could be mistakenly blamed on the MMR even though it is probably not associated at all. One child in the line here the other day had a fit just before his injection. If it had been 5 minutes after, it would have been blamed on the injection. There is no connection between MMR and autism except that parents usually first notice signs of autism around the same age as the MMR injection is given," he says.

No study or doctor can prove that vaccines don't cause autism in a tiny number of cases, say, one in a million, because that's impossible to prove. But it is also true to say that absolutely no link between autism and MMR has ever been proved despite exhaustive checks of all the relevant research going back decades, and new studies following up kids in many countries who have had the MMR vaccination (see More Info at the end of this chapter).

For info on other theories of why the autism rate may be rising, see the section on autism in the Health chapter.

Usual reasons for opposing immunization

Religious reasons   Many people who oppose vaccination do so from a religious point of view: some Christians because of their idio-syncratic interpretation of the Bible.

It isn't natural   If you look at it that way, neither are tampons, anesthetics, airplanes, or men without beards. But they can all be quite useful on occasion.

The diseases don't exist any more   Yes they do. Whooping cough cases are in most children's hospitals at any given time; measles and many other diseases are just an incoming plane away. In 1999, six-teen people who went to the movies in Melbourne one night and walked past a cinema usher who had caught measles overseas caught it themselves—it's that contagious.

Vaccines don't work   Vaccines have been remarkably successful in reducing or eradicating diseases, but a very few vaccinated peo-ple can still contract a less virulent form of some of the diseases such as whooping cough and chicken pox. The medical establishment has always acknowledged this.

It is too much of a challenge to the child's immune system to give so many vaccinations, especially triple whammies
Millions of children have taken the vaccine "load" without incident or injury. A very small number of children may have had a prob-lem, but this is not provable. Some doctors say kids could take thou-sands of vaccines without a problem, and that's not provable either because it's a stupid and unnecessary suggestion. Doctors should just admit that they're offering a vast improvement on the past, when

your child ran a much, much higher risk of pain, suffering, damage and death from preventable and rampant childhood diseases. As my Grandma used to say "You pays your money and you takes your chances."

There are alternatives, such as breastfeeding and organic food Several anti-vaccination lobbyists claim that you can protect your child from childhood diseases by breastfeeding and giving your child love, fresh air, and organic food. This is a cruel and stupid lie that encourages some parents to think their dangerously sick or dying child wasn't given enough love, fresh air, unsightly carrots, or breast milk when it has nothing to do with any of that. Some of the vaccine-preventable diseases are so wildly catching that an infected person walking into a room full of unimmunized people is likely to infect 90 percent of them, regardless of whether they were or are breastfed or how healthy they are. It is true that all those things will help build a better immune system. But that won't stop you from getting a very infectious disease.

There are homeopathic and herbal "alternatives" to vaccination These have been discredited by responsible herbalists and by all large homeopathy associations. No homeopathic "vaccines" against childhood diseases have been scientifically tested: they cannot protect against diseases such as whooping cough or measles.

Childhood diseases are mostly trivial, just requiring a couple of days in bed Oh, poop (see the Diseases and Their Vaccinations table earlier in this chapter). Whooping cough still kills children in the US. Measles still kills hundreds of thousands of kids worldwide. It is certainly not true that childhood diseases are trivial for everyone, especially among children who are already at risk, such as babies in remote areas of the world, and whom we also want to protect.

Pro-vaccination contacts

Your local health clinic or your doctor will have all the official info on your immunization schedule and can provide pamphlets and info about individual vaccines and the diseases they protect against.

Most pro-vaccination books are heavy-going medical bricks that are only understandable to people in cardigans covered by white coats who use words such as "histocompatibility antigen specificities" in their lunch hour, and the books concentrate on the wider issue of public health rather than helping you to make an individual decision (for the more accessible books and publications see More Info at the end of this chapter).

Anti-vaccination contacts

I totally understand the parents of autistic children wanting more research done on vaccines. I tried to find an anti-vaccination book or website that seems perfectly sober and reasonable. God knows I tried. But to be brutally candid, I only found nutty ones. This is one of the reasons why the writings are almost always self-published—big publishing houses and magazines won't touch them. Most of the authors fervently claimed that immunization doesn't prevent disease—which is demonstrably not true. Almost all books, websites, and articles in "alternative" magazines quote the same handful of self-described "researchers" or "experts."

You should be aware that some self-described "independent" vaccination network websites are actually anti-vaccination websites, and that many anti-vaccination websites and books repeat as facts claims that have been disproved, such as that vaccines cause sudden infant death syndrome or cancer and germs do not cause disease, or are unprovable. Most give lots of statistics, often obviously quoting from each other rather than primary sources, but on further investigation the statistics are selectively used or plain wrongly interpreted. They have said immunization causes (variously) shaken baby syndrome, asthma, attention deficit disorder—in fact anything that has statistically risen since the introduction of vaccination, including (there is a whole book on the theory) criminal behavior. Sometimes it seems a bit like saying that because a lot more bicycles have been manufactured since the Tasmanian tiger was killed there must be a link.

more info

National Immunization Hotline

This hotline is staffed with live, trained specialists between 8:00 a.m. and 11:00 p.m. EST. They can give you the most up-to-date immunization info, send you free publications, and give you referrals to many resources including local clinics and programs.

1-800-232-2522
1-800-232-0233 (Spanish)
1-800-243-7889 (TTY Service)

A Field Guide to Germs

by Wayne Biddle, Doubleday, 2002.

An entertaining, almost fun history of diseases and germs, with sections on polio, diphtheria, whooping cough, measles, mumps, rubella, and hepatitis so you can see what you are protecting your kids from and how many people used to die from them before immunization. Plus, entertaining stuff on the plague, rabies, and other disgusting matters to keep slightly older children saying "Euwwww!" for hours.

Vaccination: The Facts, the Fears, the Future

by Gordon Ada and David Isaacs, Allen and Unwin, Aust., 2001.

These two Australian medical authors answer lots of your questions. A little or a lot of scientific knowledge is needed once you start wading through precisely how vaccines work. More relevant to parents making the decision whether or not to immunize, they answer specific questions such as what is the effect on the immune system of a child, and the future of immunization (somewhere in the world they're already working on vaccines you can eat instead of inject: HURRY UP!).

Centers for Disease Control
The website for reliable info on immunization in the US. Everything from an interactive scheduler to a national hotline, from downloadable brochures to a 94-page booklet for parents.
1-800-799-7062
www.cdc.gov

www.childrensvaccine.org
To find out what's happening in developing countries see the website of the worldwide vaccine program. It explains the case for child immunization and its history and looks at the arguments of the anti-vaccination activists.

www.polioeradication.org
This is the website of Global Polio Eradication Partners (comprising WHO, Rotary International, the Centers for Disease Control and Prevention and UNICEF). The organization was set up to try to wipe polio out worldwide, with the help of massive vaccination campaigns run by volunteers in the developing world. The website has fact sheets and answers to the most frequently asked questions about polio, as well as moving photographs, important stories, and hornswoggling statistics.

www.skeptics.com.au/journal/anti-immune.htm
The article "Anti-immunisation Scare: The Inconvenient Facts" takes on some of the many misleading statements by the anti-vaccination lobby.

www.thelancet.com
The *Lancet* medical journal's website has information on specific issues and worries about vaccination such as those about the measles, mumps and rubella jab and autism controversy. Click on and then search "MMR vaccine." Some of the info is very "medical" and in researcher language, but much of it is not so mystifying. You can also search for other vaccination information.

MULTIPLES

More and more twins, triplets, and other multiples are being born in developed countries due to better nutrition and health care, and there's a suspicion that women who have their babies from their late thirties onwards tend to have twins more often than younger moms. Some twins and triplets are due to the IVF process (because fertility drugs increase egg production and more than one egg is implanted in the womb to get the best chance of a pregnancy).

HOW PEOPLE REACT

Luckily, when you have multiple babies, and especially if you already have older children or a toddler, you are too tired to shout at people who say silly things to you. Don't forget the golden rule of parenthood: while it's interesting to hear what people say, some of them are no more intelligent than a trout, although most mean well. Here are some comments you've probably already heard and some handy replies.

"Oh, my God!" "Yes, thanks, we'll put you down for an hour of housework and bringing over dinner every Thursday, shall we?"

"You'll go mad." "Well, I've had lots of practice."

"You're kidding." "Yes, I love a jolly good joke about a multiple birth—oh how we laughed."

"Are there twins in the family?" "There are now!"

"Were you on IVF?" "I have no idea. I must ask my husband." (Even if husband fictitious.) Or "Were you?"

"They must be a handful." "No, I hardly notice they're around the house really."

"Are they identical?" "I'm not sure. I've never looked."

"Wow, double (or triple) trouble!" "So they tell me [*stifled yawn*]."

"How much time are you taking off work?" "I'm not sure yet." Or "Oh, a couple of hours, I expect."

"Well, I see you are eating (have eaten) for three!" "Come over here and let me strike you on the nose with a rolled-up newspaper." (Some people put on lots of weight with twins, others don't.)

your feelings and fears

There are fears and issues around having more than one baby at once, just as there are about having one. A pregnancy with multiples is likely to involve more exhaustion, more hormones running around your system, often a greater weight gain, and worries about whether your babies might come early, be underweight, or need special medical care.

Because you will have an extra dose of pregnancy hormones that "turn off" after the birth, and you face the possibly daunting task of being mom to twins or more, you may be likely to go through a period of feeling depressed or freaked out. You'd be mad if you didn't feel at least a bit apprehensive about how you'll manage everything. (See Feeling Overwhelmed or Depressed in *Part 1: Babies* if that's how you feel.)

Here are some things to remember:

★ Lots of people have had twins or more and managed it really well.

★ None of them tried to do it without help: don't try to be a martyr and go it alone. There are people you can talk to and places you can go to, from phone counselors to local organizations, if it all gets too much (see More Info at the end of the second chapter, Your Support Team).

★ If you are loving and kind to your babies, it doesn't matter if the washing isn't done—but ask a friend to do it anyway.

★ It doesn't matter if everything is not perfect. In fact, it doesn't matter if NOTHING is perfect!

team effort

Ideally, parents of twins, and especially of more babies, will initially have a project manager: a sister, mom, close friend, or partner who can take at least a month or two off work and set in place rosters for

REASONS TO BE CHEERFUL

✱ That weird fashion of dressing twins in exactly the same clothes has long gone.

✱ Fingers crossed, multiples will play together so you can get things done.

✱ You may have produced a whole family all at once, like an efficiency expert. (Oh, try to look like you did it on purpose.)

✱ You have a ready-made excuse not to do anything else, such as bring a plate to a family do (try to make this last until the babies leave home).

✱ You're not alone. There are parents like you and support groups everywhere.

✱ Each child will gradually have their own special interests, ideas and possessions, but in the meantime, they can share equipment and toys (although one mom informed me this honeymoon period ended at six weeks).

✱ Most people will be cluey enough to refer to your children by their individual names rather than "the twins" each time.

helpers and food bringers and do other sensible things such as answer telephones, organize meals, and keep visitors away unless they're actually assisting the process of settling the newies into the home.

People often don't offer to help because they don't know what to do: assign tasks based on capability and ability to learn rather than waiting for people to work out what to do. This makes them feel needed and wanted instead of all at sea.

Ask for help from strangers as well as family and friends. "Here, feed this baby with a bottle while I do the other one" said a mother of twins to my friend once in a public place: he was thrilled. People are almost always happy to help with strollers and hold doors open as long as you let them know you won't bite and you actually want the help.

If it's at all possible, get someone to pay for a house cleaner for at least a while. If it isn't, try a roster of friends and family.

See the contacts in More Info at the end of this chapter for support and help. (If you come across the term "super twins" it means a multiple birth with more than two babies.)

> *"If you have twins get a hands-free telephone that clips onto your clothes, and a headset that allows you two hands so you can chat while doing things. Always tape a good TV show to watch while feeding because it makes you feel like you're doing something for yourself at the same time, and can take your mind off your worries."*
> JENNIFER

stuff to keep in mind

The first eighteen months are likely to be really intensive. Apart from finding time for feeding, changing, and washing (and that's just the grown-ups), you'll be getting to know two new people with different personalities.

Some twins fight and will need to be separated or distracted; some will always want to hang out together. Some may benefit from being in separate rooms at their child-care center or preschool; others will want to be together.

feeding

This is probably the biggest early issue for moms (and dads) of twins. Boobs, bottles, or a mix of both? Don't make a decision before you have the babies and then stick to it no matter what. The most important thing is to change if you need to. And use all the help with feeding you can get.

Feeding one baby while the other cries is very difficult emotionally as is not being able to spend one-on-one feeding time with each baby. But if you have other one-on-ones with them, don't stress about feeding times being sacred for this. Better to have two happy, fed babies to play with afterwards. Some moms use expressed breast milk in bottles for one baby during the day and breastfeed that twin at night. For ideas on how to breastfeed two (or more!) as a routine, get in touch with La Leche League. It has special booklets available and other resources for the multiple feeder—that's you, my multi-skilled goddess of plenty (contact details are given in More Info at the end of the Bosoms chapter in *Part 1: Babies*). Or talk to some moms who've breastfed two armfuls—you can find them through La Leche League (see More Info below).

moRe iNfo

TWINS

Twins: A Practical and Emotional Guide to Parenting Twins
by Katrina Bowman and Louise Ryan, Allen and Unwin, Aust., 2002.
This Australian book is a good resource for parents of twins. It acknowledges their range of feelings—euphoria, fear, shock, regret, relief, and joy. Some expectant parents have found it reinforced the idea of having twins as frightening and intimidating, so perhaps don't read it all at once like a novel, but look up bits as you need them.

It's written by two moms of twins, including one who was on IVF treatments. They give their honest assessments of the feelings and fears involved and the practicalities, from finding out and pregnancy right through to after the birth and the equipment you'll need, plus lots of quotes from other mums, info for dads, contacts, and sections on breastfeeding, bottlefeeding, the early weeks and all the nuts and bolts of sleeping. It's the only book I've seen that has a parent-centered, sensible, and understanding section on having a preterm baby. It also has a glossary of terms used by doctors, nurses, and other baby industry folk.

www.nomotc.org
This is the website of the National Organization of Mothers of Twins Club. Clubs meet monthly to discuss the care and development of multiple birth children. Local groups also offer clothing and equipment exchanges.

www.twinsmagazine.com
An online magazine.

www.potatonet.org
For parents of twins, triplets, and more. Chat rooms, merchandise, other links, and stuff for dads as well as moms.

TRIPLETS AND MORE

Raising Multiple Birth Children: A Parent's Survival Guide
by William Laut, Kristin Benit, and Sheila Laut, Chandler House Press, 1999. Parents of triplets offer advice on raising twins, triplets, quads, and more.

www.mostonline.org
For parents of triplets, quads and more, the Mothers of Supertwins international website is a non-profit outfit. It has sections including "Breast Leakage Inhibitor System" (lordy) and relevant resources, support volunteers, and books on the subject.

www.tqq.com
The website of the triplets, quads, and quints association of Canada: another non-profit mob.

ReaDiNg

Here's the main reason to read to your baby, toddler or little kid: they LOVE it. It sparks all sorts of questions and stories and drawings, and at bedtime it can calm them and prime them for sleep. You and your kid will find there are so many lovely books to be borrowed from the library, swapped, or even bought. It's a ready-made bonding activity wrapped up in educational phoofery. My mother read to me as a child and now I make up words and can't even string a sentence . . . what?

a Head start

Educational experts say that kids who are read stories a lot or as a daily ritual get a huuuuge start in learning to read. You don't actually have to try to teach them to read; just read to them and show them words and letters if they're interested. The main thing is to get them thinking books are fab.

If your kid loves stories and sees learning to read as an entry to a whole lot of absorbing stories and experiences, and you reinforce that every night you can, then you're doing them a big favor. Just set yourself up comfortably so they can see the words and pictures, and away you go.

Part of the fun in reading to your child is rediscovering childhood favorites as well as discovering new ones together. I remember *Eloise, Pippi Longstocking,* and *The Cat in the Hat.* I remember Enid Blyton's *Magic Faraway Tree.*

You can start reading *your* favorite books to your 4-year-old even if they're technically about older children. Just be guided by what your child maintains interest in. Reading a book without pictures can work well for some toddlers and little kids because they use their imagination for the visuals.

Reading aloud

You can start showing your baby a book in their first few months. Reading to a baby, a toddler, or an older kid is a shared, interactive experience. Find a comfy spot where you can both see the words and pictures. If you point to words as you read them, talk about what's happening in the pictures and pause often for questions and chat then your kid is learning as well as having fun. Eventually, they will recognize the words of stories and pull you up if you say a wrong word or miss a page, and one day they'll start recognizing the sound of letters. You're not teaching them how to read—school will do that. You're teaching them to love reading. Everything else will follow.

Don't be afraid to be a ham acting it up when reading: an adventure can be "acted out" with put-on voices, gestures, and amazed eye contact with the kid. A relaxing nighttime book can be read in a sleep-encouraging way.

good books

Good books are not necessarily the serious ones with "important" or obvious messages: they are those that kids love and request again and again, those they're enraptured by. Kids love all sorts of books: ones with rhymes, ones that are familiar, ones that have repetition, ones with a surprise, ones that pop up or have flaps you lift. Sometimes the simplest of stories has that special appeal. A list of books for specific occasions, such as going to hospital or being frightened of monsters, as well as popular classics is given in More Info at the end of this chapter. Be prepared to be disappointed by books that are produced as merchandise to tie in with TV shows: they're usually just thrown-together rehashes of shows and often badly written.

The big-issue books

Many books aimed at primary school children are about heavy issues, but I don't think books about bear baiting and refugee horrors are suitable for kids under 5, or maybe even under 10, depending on the book and the kid. Obviously, as children grow older and can ask questions and understand more complicated concepts, these sorts of books may be a good way to get into serious subjects with them.

And of course, children under 5 do have sadness and confusion in their lives. It is difficult sometimes to recognize what a troubled child is going through. If a kid is having a challenging life, books can be a wonderful escape or a safe place to "go." They can help them make sense of what's happening to them and may make them feel less alone. But introducing distressing concepts when a kid can't process their feelings may only distress and burden rather than enlighten them. Trauma, major challenges, or the death of someone close is best dealt with by parents working with professionals; this process might include the use of books that stimulate conversation and understanding (see More Info at the end of the Helping Kids Understand Grown-up Concepts chapter in *Part 4: Parenting*).

WEiRDy OLD NOTiONS

Beware of some of the stuff in the classics. (Often old copies have been handed down in the family or found in thrift-stores.) You may have to change some sentences on the run, depending on your child's age and sensibilities. For some kids, the Australian classic *Snugglepot and Cuddlepie*'s big bad Banksia men are damned frightening, especially if there's a banksia tree outside the bedroom window. Some children will be devastated by Chapter 2 of *Blinky Bill* when Blinky's father is shot. *The Magic Pudding* has some fabulous drawings and fun expressions (we just love saying "puddin" a lot) but requires a great deal of explaining as life and language have changed so much since it was written. Kerosene is no longer a common household item, and punching someone on the snout is fairly out of fashion as a conversation starter.

Some of Beatrix Potter is now virtually incomprehensible without detailed explanation. When Mrs. Tiggy-winkle (who seems to have some sort of obsessive compulsive disorder) "goffers" an apron , I am unable to explain what she's doing except it's something to do with ironing an apron. When it comes to "dicky fronts" and "pocket handkins" (an unsanitary object for carrying snot around in the pocket before tissues were invented to make parents feel guilty about the environment), I give up. But if a 4-year-old loves it, then what the hey, goffer away.

FINDING GOOD BOOKS FOR KIDS

Your friendly local librarian (or children's specialist in a bookshop) can help you choose books that are appropriate for your kid's age. (Books need to be age appropriate because otherwise you run the risk of boring your kid or reading them stuff that goes over their head.) If you have kids of different ages, ask about stories that will appeal to all of them so you can have an all-in-together reading session sometimes.

Librarians often have inventive and sensible recommendations for kids' reading, and organize read-aloud story times and other activities that even tiny children can enjoy. You can borrow books and have a never-ending supply of new ones, as well as your for-keeps favorites at home. Librarians know a lot of useful things: just ask 'em. May I also recommend that if your local government wants to restrict the hours of your local library, or close it, that you get very loud indeed.

Queensland author Melissa Lucashenko has alerted me to the 1967 Puffin edition of a Doctor Dolittle book, which has the following lines: "'This is all very well,' said the Doctor, 'but it isn't so easy to make a black man white.' 'I don't know anything about that,' said Polynesia impatiently, 'But you MUST turn this coon white. He'll do anything for you if you change his color.'"

Some of it is worse. And don't start me on the lack of decent female characters in most of the older books, or the kleptomaniacal gypsies in Enid Blyton's Noddy series. You'll have to make executive parental decisions as you go.

Some fairytales are absolutely bloodcurdling and are not good bedtime reading: the real Rapunzel story involves baby abduction, deliberate blinding, deep despair, psychological torture, and imprisonment. Just the thing for an impressionable tyke. Toddlers are probably better off with simple stories and interesting pictures to look at so they can learn to love reading and look forward to story time.

more info

These books are just to whet your appetite, not a comprehensive list.

BOOKS FOR PARENTS ABOUT KIDS' READING

Reading Magic: Why Reading Aloud to Our Children Will Change Their Lives Forever
by Mem Fox, Harvest Books, 2001.
Mem Fox is a children's author (*Possum Magic* is the biggie) and an authority on literacy. This book is her take on why and how you should read to young children. She recommends reading aloud for at least 15 minutes a night, or three picture books a night, to give your kid a big head start in learning to read and enjoy stories.

The Reading Bug: And How You Can Help Your Child to Catch It
by Paul Jennings, Penguin, 2004.
Mr. Jennings tells parents, caregivers, and teachers about his methods of helping a kid learn to love reading. It's mainly relevant to kids over 5, but has suggestions for good books for kids under 5 as well.

BOARD BOOKS FOR BABIES

Bibs and Boots, Happy and Sad, Crashing and Splashing, and **Bumping and Bouncing** (also available as a boxed set)
by Alison Lester, Kestrel Press, 1989.
Fun words and lovely drawings.

BOOKS FOR BEDTIME

Good Night!

by Claire Masurel, Chronicle Books, 1995.

A board book for very young children about the ritual of getting everything ready for bed.

Goodnight, Moon *(first published 1947)*

by Margaret Wise Brown, HarperCollins.

A classic that's one of those deceptively simple books that has adults wondering what kids see in it. A beautiful, calming, sleepytime book.

Good Night, Fairies

by Kathleen Hague, Chronicle Books, 2002.

All the wonderful things that fairies do at night when kids go to bed. Old-fashioned illustrations.

Guess How Much I Love You

by Sam McBratney and Anita Jeram, Candlewick Press, 1996.

A classic before-bedtime book about a little rabbit whose dad loves him to the moon and back.

BOOKS ON NIGHT SCARES AND MONSTERS

Where the Wild Things Are *(first published 1963)*

by Maurice Sendak, HarperCollins, 2003.

Max sails away and hangs out with the monsters.

Don't Look Under the Bed!

by Angelika Glitz and Imke Sonnichsen, Franklin Watts, 2001.

Tom's mom is scared of what's under Tom's bed but he knows what's really going on.

We're Going on a Bear Hunt

by Michael Rosen and Helen Oxbury, Little Simon, 1997.

A traditional repeating story about a family who encounter a bear and run all the way back home to be safe in bed.

A BOOK ON SEPARATION ANXIETY

Owl Babies

by Martin Waddell, Candlewick Press, 1992.

The mommy owl goes out hunting for food—but she always comes back to her three children.

A BOOK ON GOING TO THE DENTIST

Harry and the Dinosaurs Say "Raahh!"

by Ian Whybrow and Adrian Reynolds, Random House Books for Young Readers, 2004.

A boy and his dinosaurs go to the dentist and open wide.

BOOKS ON GOING TO HOSPITAL OR THE DOCTOR

Children's hospital bookshops have a wide selection.

Curious George Goes to the Hospital

by Margaret Rey, H.A. and Rey, Houghton Mifflin Company, 1976.

Curious George eats a puzzle piece and has to have an operation, which isn't as bad as he thought it would be.

Dr. Dog

by Babette Cole, Dragonfly Books, 1997.

Oh, what a disgusting family Dr. Dog has to treat—farting and all.

I Don't Want to Go to Hospital

by Tony Ross, Ipicture Books, 2001.

Not strong on detail about what might happen in hospital—it has only one picture of actually being in the hospital—but gets over the message that people are nice to you there. Probably best for when a child is just going for a one-time visit.

BOOKS ON ANATOMY

The Human Body

by Fiona Payne, Dorling Kindersley, 1995.

A picture book that will allow little kids and older kids to examine how their body works, and includes "cool facts" type stuff.

Amazing Pop-up Pull-out Body in a Book

by David Hancock, Dorling Kindersley, UK, 1997.

A book and 3D poster showing how the bits work and what they do. You can hang the poster on the wall and tickle the spleeny bits.

A BOOK ABOUT HOW STUFF WORKS

The New Way Things Work

by David Macaulay with Neil Ardley, Houghton Mifflin, 1998.

A huge, fun book that explains everything from levers and floating to radio and computers. A kid's first reference book and a science book for toddlers, preschoolers, and primary and secondary school kids.

BOOKS WITH GIRL CHARACTERS

Eloise *(first published 1955)*

by Kay Thompson and Hilary Knight, Simon and Schuster.

A 6-year-old girl lives in the Plaza Hotel in New York with her nanny, turtle, pug, and pigeon. And room service.

Pippi Longstocking *(first published 1950)*

by Astrid Lingren, Puffin, UK, 2000.

Pippi lives alone inside her home while her dad is away at sea. She's terrifically strong and has a treasure chest full of gold coins to spend. Her horse lives on the porch.

Stella Queen of the Snow and **Stella Fairy of the Forest**
by Marie-Louise Gay, Douglas & McIntyre, 2000.
Stella is brave and adventurous and answers her little brother's questions
about life as he tags along.

The Terrible Underpants and **Wanda-Linda Goes Berserk**
Hyperion Books for Children, 2003 and Viking Children's Books, 2003.
(Yes, all right, both these Wanda-Linda books were written by me, now
that you mention it.)
Sort of about self-esteem and tantrums, respectively, but also about
appalling underwear, a sensitive hairy-nosed wombat, and the always
appalled Mrs. Kafoops.

Olivia
by Ian Falconer, Simon & Schuster Children's, 2000.
A tale of an energetic little pig who sings, dances, builds, paints, and
explores.

BOOKS ON WILDLIFE AND THE ENVIRONMENT

Earth Watch, Animal Watch, Food Watch, and **Ocean Watch**
Dorling Kindersley, 2001.
A series of big hardback picture books for kids called Planet Ark, made up of
books about the environment, wildlife, and a sustainable future.

The Waterhole
by Graeme Base, Harry N. Abrams, 2001.
How a drought affects a waterhole—and all the creatures who depend on it.

The Lorax *(first published 1971)*
by Dr. Seuss, Random House.
A wonderful classic. What happens if all the truffula trees are cut down?

A BOOK ON POLITICS

Yertle the Turtle and Other Stories *(first published 1958)*
by Dr. Seuss, Random House.

Yertle wants to be king of the heap, but a turtle on the bottom says ordinary turtles shouldn't have to suffer because of the turtle on the top.

BOOKS OF FIRST PEOPLE'S STORIES

Big Rain Coming
by Katrina Germein and Bronwyn Bancroft, Clarion Books, 2000.

A BOOK ON NUMBERS

My First Number Book
by Marie Heinst, Dorling Kindersley, 1992.

Presents numbers and rudimentary maths concepts such as pairs, groups, addition and subtraction, with lots of pictures. For preschoolers.

BOOKS ON THE ALPHABET

Many beautiful picture books are based on the alphabet, including these two.

Alison and Aldo
by Alison Lester, Houghton Mifflin Company, 1998.

Animalia
by Graeme Base, Harry N. Abrams, 1987.

A BOOK ON READING

My First Phonics Book
Dorling Kindersley, 1999.

All about letters, sounds, and words, with big pictures. May be one for later.

BOOKS OF RHYMES

"The Owl and the Pussycat" and anything else by Edward Lear for children.

Mother Goose
illustrated by Willy Pogany, SeaStar Books, 2000.
Beautifully illustrated reissued classic with Three Blind Mice, Jack and Jill, Old Mother Hubbard and that vicious and bewildered old bag who lived in a shoe.

OLD AND NEW CLASSICS

All these books, like the classics already given, are continually reprinted, sometimes by a number of publishers.

The Cat in the Hat (first published 1957), Green Eggs and Ham (1960), One Fish, Two Fish, Red Fish, Blue Fish (1960) and many more
by Dr. Seuss, Random House.
Terrific characters, stories, word play, and illustrations. Theodor Guisel (Dr. Seuss) was as close to a genius as most of us would allow.

Winnie-the-Pooh (first published 1926) and the other Winnie-the-Pooh books
by A. A. Milne, with illustrations by E. H. Shepard.
Read about the characters of the 100-acre wood including Piglet, Tigger, Eeyore, Christopher Robin, and Winnie-the-Pooh.

The Giving Tree
by Shel Silverstein, HarperCollins, 1986.
A sweet tale about the gift of giving.

Maisy books
by Lucy Cousins, Candlewick Press.
Brightly painted illustrations and very simple scenarios. The books about Maisy the mouse have led to lovely marketing spin-offs including a pop-up Maisy house and a Maisy wardrobe book.

Curious George *(first published 1942)*
by Margret and Hans Rey, Houghton Mifflin.
A monkey keeps getting into trouble when he investigates things that look interesting. Get the originals—the "new" stories by someone else are not as charming.

The Tale of Peter Rabbit *(first published 1900)*
by Beatrix Potter.
Peter Rabbit and Beatrix Potter's other books are old-fashioned English story-books based on the imagined lives of country creatures.

The Very Hungry Caterpillar *(first published 1970)*
by Eric Carle, Philomel Books.
Like his other books such as *The Very Quiet Cricket* and *The Very Busy Spider*, this is a big favorite with toddlers. Their good gimmicks variously include caterpillar holes in the pages and an electronic cricket noise.

Hairy Maclary from Donaldson's Dairy and other Hairy Maclary books
by Lynley Dodd, Tricycle Press, 2001.
Author Lynley Dodd's books have irresistible rhymes and simple neighbor-hood-pet stories.

OTHER BOOKS

You'll find books for kids on other subjects listed in the More Info sections of chapters such as toilet training in the Using the Toilet chapter in *Part 2: Toddlers*; and dads in Dads, a new baby in the family and sibling rivalry in A You-Shaped Family, manners in Teaching Kids How to Behave and sex, death and family separation in Helping Kids Understand Grown-Up Concepts in *Part 4: Parenting*.

tv, videos, and films

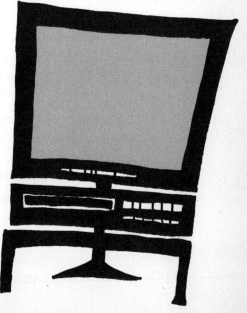

Watching TV and videos affects each kid in a different way. Some become slack-jawed zombies. Others jump about and follow all the instructions of a perky presenter ("Put your hands on your head," "Pretend you're an umbrella," "Mail Mommy's purse to this address").

Kids who are scared by what they see might scream and cry or they might watch silently, feeling confused and frightened on the inside. One toddler's family-fun video could be the source of a preschooler's three-night run of baroque nightmares.

So—what's going on? And what should go off?

tv PROGRams foR LittLe ONes

The Federal Communications Commission (FCC) currently requires every broadcaster to air at least 3 hours of educational shows aimed at children each week. These programs must "serve the educational and informational needs" of kids 16 and under, and be at least 30 minutes in length, and must be aired in a regularly scheduled time slot sometime between 7 a.m. and 10 p.m.

Ratings recommendations

The US TV ratings work with a V-chip. The V-chip is built into most newer TV sets and electronically reads television ratings and allows parents to block programs that are unsuitable for their kids. All TV programs are rated by the FCC. A TV Y rating means this program is appropriate for all ages. The themes and elements of these programs are specifically designed for very young children. TV 7 means the program is directed at children aged 7 and up. These programs require the developmental skill to distinguish between make-believe and reality; there may be some mild fantasy or comedic violence. A rating of TV Y7 FV designates programs that fantasy violence is more intense than in a program rated TV 7. Programs that aren't made specifically for children, but which are suitable for all ages are rated TV G. These contain little or no violence, no offensive language, and little or no sexual discussion or situations. TV PG means parental guidance is suggested. These shows may contain moderate violence, some sexual situations, infrequent strong language, or suggestive dialogue. TV 14 strongly cautions parents that the material is probably unsuitable for kids under 14 and TV MA means the program is specifically designed to be viewed by adults and contains graphic violence, explicit sexual activity, or crude language.

A G or PG rating is not a guarantee that there will be no violence or adult concepts in a TV show or film. (And it is no guarantee the show isn't a parade of piffle either.) Lots of kids under 5 love the character, but the latest movie version of *Spiderman*, now on video and DVD, is too violent and puzzling for them. Despite the fact that many parents think PG means a child of any age can see a film if they are accompanied by an adult, it's not that simple. It means a 12-year-old might love it while seeing it with a parent, but it's way too terrifying for a 5-year-old. Even some G films might be frightening or mystifying for the under-fives. And something that a friend's 3-year-old loves might send your 4-year-old into hysterics or inward turmoil. Unfortunately, it's a matter of trial and error, and knowing the sensibilities of your own child.

You can always make your own video tapes from bits of favorite TV shows that you think are suitable for your kid, but make sure you watch them first. Even nature documentaries can have graphic sex scenes or over-the-top violence.

Try to always be in the same room when your kid is watching TV so you can help explain something or turn off the TV. You never know what's going to be confusing or confronting. Even an incident in *Bananas in Pyjamas* can be shocking or worrying for a child who is too young or otherwise not ready to see the full horror of teddy bears—avert your gaze now if you are sensitive—falling off bicycles. Things that look as if they should be for kids are sometimes deceptive: the hilarious Canadian animated *Angela Anaconda*, starring cute cut-out children, is aimed at 10-year-olds up to adults.

Preschoolers are probably the latest group of kids to be noticed by the entertainment world—now that they're starting to influence what their parents buy, they're a marketing target.

Good points about TV shows, videos, and DVDs

* ★ A parent can get a few things done while the box is on.
* ★ TV, videos, and DVDs can be a good reward or a mood changer.
* ★ They are relatively cheap (especially if you tape programs).
* ★ You can tape foolproof stuff that avoids the ads and unpleasant surprises.
* ★ They can be beautiful and educational.
* ★ They're another means of story telling apart from books and yarns.
* ★ They can be the best way for kids to see things, such as deep-sea jellyfish or lions in the wild, that they'd never see in real life.
* ★ You can watch and talk about them together.
* ★ Your child's reactions will tell you a lot about their temperament and personality.

Bad points about TV shows, videos, and DVDs

* ★ When watching TV, videos, and DVDs a kid isn't doing anything creative.
* ★ You can't choose what's on TV.
* ★ There's not enough quality TV programming for kids under 5.
* ★ On TV there could be a violent news flash, disturbing ads, or an unscheduled program that worries them.
* ★ The TV ads are designed to make your kids whine for things that aren't good for them or you can't afford.
* ★ The TV ads are deliberately and carefully designed to make your kids feel bad and inadequate if they don't have the stuff being advertised.
* ★ A lot of TV shows are geared toward selling matching merchandise.
* ★ A TV show could come on that bombards their brain with information or concepts they can't process yet.
* ★ TV, videos, and DVDs can over-stimulate and overexcite kids.

★ They can turn children into zombies who don't use their brain.

★ A lot of kids' animation is ugly and cheap.

★ A lot of videos and DVDs are annoying to adults.

★ Rented videos for children are often worn-out or bad-quality.

★ Some TV programs for kids aren't useful for their development, they just fill in time.

★ Seeing violence over and over desensitizes kids so that they come to think violence is normal and okay.

kids' favorites

Here are some of the perennial TV and video favorites of toddlers and little kids (and see More Info at the end of this chapter for some matching websites). I haven't included feature or animated films because none are specifically made for the under-fives: they are all made for a wider audience and parents will have to judge for themselves whether they're suitable.

The Wiggles

Conventional wisdom has it that the Wiggles have a perfect provenance for a kids' act—they were former members of a pop group who met at teachers' college. The Wiggles are four grown-up singing men with seemingly pointless "friends" who seem to contribute very little other than turning up. These include Wags the Dog, Dorothy the Dinosaur, Henry the Octopus (all people in animal suits), the puzzlingly spooky officer Beadle, who looks like a cross between an English bobby, something out of *A Clockwork Orange,* and a dancer specializing in mime who doesn't have anything much to actually do, and the most entertaining character, a buffoonish, fally-down pirate called Captain Feathersword.

The Wiggles' main attractions include catchy songs and the fact that each member wears a signature colored shirt. Some of their old

663

videos are particularly lame, such as a series of Captain Feathersword snippets held together by unconvincing links by the four (one of whom seemed to be on vacation). Their most recent releases have the highest production values and much better direction, presumably because they've been able to put money back into them. Always good-natured and inclusive, with irresistible tunes, they are a humungous hit and tend to appeal to the 2- to 4-year-old set.

Apart from live shows there's merchandise, including song cassettes, toys, and clothes as well as the videos.

Sesame Street

The Children's Television Workshop, which makes *Sesame Street*, was originally formed as a charity but now makes a profit from sales of videos, song CDs, toys, and heaps of licensed products, which is put back into productions. *Sesame Street* stars mostly male characters: Big Bird, Elmo, Bert and Ernie, Oscar the Grouch, Baby Bear, and Snuffleupagus. It emphasises community harmony and preschool learning of the alphabet and numbers. A lot of money is spent on this series and the production values are high. TV episodes run on PBS and the videos can be bought from stores or rented from local video stores.

Elmo is especially popular with the 3- to 4-year-olds. Babies and young toddlers will find most of it mystifying or even disturbing. Older kids will be totally transfixed by the way *Sesame Street* creates its own world.

Teletubbies

These strange burbly creatures (grown-up people in big diaper-bottomed, toddler-shaped suits) with rudimentary toddlery speech patterns ("e-oh" instead of "hello"), live in an odd pad, with a vacuum cleaner called Nu Nu, surrounded by green fields, dull, drizzly weather, and wild bunnies (that would be England). There are repeated live-action sequences of real children doing various activities that supposedly are screened on the tummies of one of the seemingly genderless Teletubbies, whose names are Tinky Winky (dressed in purple), Dipsy (green), La La (yellow), and Po (red and the littlest).

The series is made for the under-threes but can be screened as the equivalent of comfort food for a year or so after that. Bizarre and baffling for adults and older children, who regard it with scorn, the show clearly speaks very directly to toddlers, especially those aged 2 to 3. The worst thing that happens is that the tubby custard machine malfunctions, as does the tubby toast device.

This BBC series is shown here on PBS and videos are also available. The recorded sound cassettes are shockin': you really need visuals for the *Teletubbies* to work. Merchandise also includes dolls and other toys.

Hi-5

This very popular Australian show is now on cable channels in the US. It's about a gang of warm, super-polite Aussie twenty-somethings (two guys, three girls, "And together, we're Hi-5!") who cheerfully (and, it seems, tirelessly) sing, dance, tell stories, and look as if they've been dressed by a hippie mum with a sewing machine and a direct chute from the fabric remnant shop. Each member of the *Hi-5* team focuses on a different aspect of child development through play, movement, stories, and music. *Hi-5* is a cut above a lot of commercial TV and is now making inroads into older kids' viewing. The material is always educational or at least interesting to older toddlers and little kids, and it often gets them dancing and acting out stories in front of the TV. This is another program you don't have to worry about in terms of grown-up, confronting or inexplicable concepts—unless you count some of the outfits.

Merchandise includes videos, CDs, clothes, toys and books. Each video has a different theme, including summer, dreams, and animals.

OTHER SHOWS MADE FOR LITTLE KIDS

The inclusion of a show on the following list isn't necessarily a recommendation: it just means it's aimed at little kids. Most of the shows are cartoons or "stop" animations—objects are photographed, moved slightly, then photographed again. These shows are often 10 to 15 minutes long and "linked" or simply run one after another. ◎ *Angelina Ballerina* ◎ *Arthur* ◎ *Babar* ◎ *Bananas in Pyjamas* ◎ *Barney* ◎ *Bear in the Big Blue House* ◎ *Bob the Builder* ◎ *Brambly Hedge* ◎ *Busy Buses* ◎ *Dora the Explorer* ◎ *Kipper* ◎ *Madeline* ◎ *Maisy* ◎ *Miffy and Friends* ◎ *Noddy* ◎ *Pingu* ◎ *Postman Pat* ◎ *Reading Rainbow* ◎ *Roly-Poly Olie* ◎ *Sponge Bob Squarepants* ◎ *Thomas the Tank Engine* ◎ *Titch* ◎ *The World of Peter Rabbit*.

Fads

Shows come and go. Years ago there was *Power Rangers*, then *Pokemon*, and at the moment *Bob the Builder* is big. Most of them will stay as long as they have the power to sell toys and clothes.

THINGS THAT MIGHT REALLY ANNOY PARENTS

✱ The cloying voice of Lulu the teddy bear on *Bananas in Pyjamas*.

✱ The endless whining of Fizz in *Tweenies*.

✱ Barney, a disgustingly twee giant purple dinosaur.

✱ TV stations that break into children's programs with scarifying news flashes.

✱ A favorite TV show being taken off the schedule without notice.

SHOWS WITH "POSITIVE" GIRLS

Girl characters in shows for preschoolers do tend to be whiners. Books are a better source of feisty girls (see the Reading chapter). Most shows made for children of this age have male heroes, although Bob the Builder's receptionist, Wendy, has started doing some building (not that there's anything wrong with answering phones); the Madeline books have been made into a cartoon series; and in the *Maisy* cartoons Maisy has a girly name although, more to the point, is a mouse. You may prefer to avoid *Thomas the Tank Engine*, in which all the engines are men and the carriages female. The male *Bananas in Pyjamas* are the stars, the faffy female teddy bears very much the also-rans . . . well, second bananas. Kids under five are probably too young to recognize the obvious exclusion of girl characters, especially from the exciting bits, but because it is so prevalent I wouldn't be surprised if it had a subconscious effect on them.

HOW MUCH WATCHING A SCREEN IS TOO MUCH?

According to statistics, the more TV a kid watches, the more likely they are to be above a healthy weight, unfit, and falling behind at school. Surveys routinely suggest that children of all ages are watching up to 7 hours a day and that many of them even have a television set in their bedroom, which they can watch unsupervised.

You can tailor the TV and video rules in your house to suit yourself. Basically, a baby shouldn't be watching any TV at all because they won't understand it. From about 18 months they can be fascinated by something like the *Teletubbies* for, say, half an hour, every second day. By 3 or 4 they could watch a video or show that lasts for 40 minutes to an hour. Some older preschoolers will enjoy watching a whole feature film or video.

You may like to let your child watch TV or videos for a set time each day, only every other day, once a week, or on special occasions, depending on your own feelings. Some parents are happy with once a week, others are happy for little kids to watch for hours each day. Anything more than an hour every few days for little kids is probably taking too much creative time away from them.

Whether watching TV is mentally healthy or not depends not only on the number of hours, but what is on. A lot of kids will watch anything, even Thud and Sherisse or whatever their names are on *The Bold and the Beautiful*. You look at kids in front of the TV and realize their brain has been sucked into the world of the screen—sometimes you have to speak to them loudly three times before they hear you. (But if your child is always asking you to turn the volume up a few notches higher than needed, get their ears tested. And if they're always a nose away from the screen, get their eyes tested.)

Don't forget to factor in computer use when considering how much time your kid spends staring at a screen.

ViOLeNce

TV cartoons or shows with violence are not suitable for kids under 5 because they can't distinguish pretend from reality, and some will try to act out what they have seen—either on TV or in their own home. At this age kids are very much "monkey see, monkey do." They shouldn't be watching or listening to the news either because it's simply too distressing or puzzling. They can't understand and process facts such as "The war is a long way away and won't happen here."

Many studies and guesstimates have shown that the average child watching their several hours of TV a day will "see" thousands of murders and violent acts by the time they reach their teens. It is generally agreed that this has a desensitizing effect and may cause depression, but there is disagreement about the extent to which it could make a child consistently behave violently in childhood or adulthood.

> "Violence on television does lead to aggressive behavior by [some] children and teenagers who watch the programs . . . Not all children become aggressive of course . . . The research question has moved from asking whether or not there is an effect, to seeking explanations for the effect."
> TELEVISION AND BEHAVIOR REPORT, NATIONAL INSTITUTE OF MENTAL HEALTH

aDVeRTiSiNg

One of the best things you'll ever do for your kid (well, all right, it's actually so they don't nag you) is to keep them away from advertising and teach them what advertising is when they're old enough to understand. After about age 10 kids can feel superior when they recognize marketing techniques: "They're trying to make it look like if I buy that food I'll have more fun." You'll need to watch ads with your kid and explain why the ads try to make them feel they're not worthy if they don't have the products—and why they don't need the products. The under-fives have no way of comprehending that ads on TV are different from the shows they watch: ads aimed at this age group are truly preying on their innocence. The best way to subvert ads is not to watch them.

> "The average young person says they have to ask nine times before their parents give in and let them have what they want. Eleven percent of 12–13-year-olds admit to asking their parents more than fifty times for products they've seen advertised."
> REPORT OF A 2002 US SURVEY OF 750 KIDS AGED 12 TO 17

"It's estimated the average American child sees more than 20,000 commercials every year—that works out to at least 55 commercials per day." AMERICAN ACADEMY OF PEDIATRICS, "TELEVISION AND THE FAMILY" FACT SHEET

KiDS' ViDEOS aND DVDS

A lot of parents prefer their kids to watch videos or DVDs rather than TV because there are no unexpected news breaks or ads to teach them to nag for something, and they're often neatly divided into sections, which is a cheap way for TV producers to bang out a video using three TV episodes, but also a way for parents to find a logical break to turn off. Longer, narrative videos, and DVDs, such as the film-length versions of *The Little Mermaid*, *Milo and Otis*, and *The Lady and the Tramp*, captivate some 3- to 5-year-olds but terrify others. Videos and DVDs of films are usually about an hour and a half or longer, and the stories usually involve something scary, something sad and a triumphant happy ending.

It is not possible for a child under 5 to understand what is or isn't real or to understand that any death—on video or in real life—is permanent. Often young children watching a video or a DVD with older brothers, sisters, or friends become frightened or confused even though the others are enjoying it. Unfortunately for older kids, a group video or DVD needs to be at the lowest common denominator, not the highest (which is not usually how the pecking order works). Shorter, episodic videos and DVDs are better for littlies, especially those under 4.

If a child shows signs of being distressed or frightened by a video (or TV), stop the tape and discuss what is distressing about the subject. (Worries and fears may surface after the video has finished—that night or in the days to come.) Don't try to get the child "used to it"—this may happen, but the fear will still be there. Put the tape away until you feel your child is ready for it, then try again.

670

You can now borrow videos from most local libraries and you can swap videos with friends. Many of those you rent from local video stores are clapped-out tapes. Always complain about this—it's unfair that shops take money for worn tapes just because it's kids who'll be watching. If you want to buy your own videos you'll find them at stores everywhere or you can shop online.

fiLMS

Taking kids under 5 to a cinema can be a very hit-and-miss affair—especially for a birthday party because someone will spill something, someone else will wet their pants, one will scream, another will be transfixed and refuse to leave, and a few will run away in terror. It's always worth explaining beforehand what the cinema experience will be like as it can be overwhelming for little ones, and picking a dead-cert movie with no frightening scenes can be impossible before you've seen it. Wait until your child is really interested or you're sure they'll enjoy it, talk about it a lot, and maybe call into a cinema and have a look around but not stay for the film the first time. Some kids may be ready at 3, others at 6 or 7.

RaDiO

In old days, radio used to run shows for children, which was great for those in isolated areas particularly, who had, little other available entertainment tailored for them. Unfortunately, commercial radio, as far as I can tell, never bothers with this anymore.

COMPLAINTS ABOUT TV SHOWS

You can complain directly to a TV station about a show that you think is classified wrongly or oversteps any boundaries or you can file a complaint with the FCC directly. For indecency and profanity complaints, context is key, so be sure to include specifically what was said (not just a general topic), the date and time of the broadcast, and the call sign of the station involved (see More Info, which follows).

MORE INFO

TV PROGRAMS FOR PRESCHOOLERS

Public Broadcasting Service (PBS)

The PBS website has a complete list of programs, information, and supplementary reading.

www.pbs.org

KIDS' FAVORITES

www.nickjr.com

The kids page of Nickelodeon.

www.thewiggles.com

The official website of the Wiggles.

www.sesamestreet.com

The *Sesame Street* website is extensive and has interactive activities for kids.

www.teletubbies.com

The official *Teletubbies* website has links to the production company, the BBC and PBS, all of which have interactive bits, sound bites, and info for parents and caregivers of preschoolers.

ADVERTISING

www.newdream.org/kids

Shows you how to identify what the commercial world is trying to do to you and how you can free your family from the sell, sell, buy, buy mentality.

aRt aNd music

Yes, you can have your very own arts festival. Just make sure the audience is wearing wipe-down vinyl. Here are a few ideas for arty fun.

aRt

Kids can start drawing from the time they can hold an implement in their hand. At first they need large colored crayons or pencils: crayons are good because they don't have to be sharpened and are easy to hold with little fingers. Buy ones made specifically for kids: these will be labeled non-toxic. Pay a bit extra for quality brands and the brightest colors—they will be less breakable and will last longer.

You can make up non-toxic poster paint at home from bought powder or buy thick paint in tubes or plastic bottles, which will last longer and be runnier if you add a little water. Mix some interesting colors for kids. Having lots of white available is always a good idea because you can make much brighter, more kid-friendly colors by squirting it into the darker colors usually sold. Kids will combine colors until there's a yucky brown so to prevent this happening too quickly, and the paint drying up between sessions, only make up small amounts at a time.

From the age of about 2 and a half children find a chalk-board easel a great idea (one you can clip paper to for painting on is ideal). Rolls of paper can be useful for large paintings or for drawing the outline of your child on to give them a start painting a big, life-sized figure for fun. A long piece of paper is also good for them to make footprints or a mural on. Washing lines make good drying racks for paintings.

Help your child to grasp the crayon or brush so that they get the most control they can for their age, and praise all efforts. As well as using crayons, pencils, and paints on scrap paper, kids can draw with chalk on safe footpaths or concrete areas; with a stick in packed dirt or wet sand; with water on footpaths, sheds or brick walls; or even with paint on walls or sheds if you're murally minded.

Older babies and young toddlers will make scribbles and dots, little kids will do impressions of feelings, figures to represent people, and so on (see the earlier Development chapters if you want to pinpoint stages). You don't need to teach your child to draw "properly" and they don't have to draw recognizable items. Don't insist on your idea of what kids draw. You can suggest, but allow them to lead the way. Let them enjoy the colors, lines, and shapes, and don't worry whether it's anything recognizable: this will come. Children of all ages use drawing to express their feelings and situation, and draw what they're obsessed with at the time. You may get weeks of rocket ships and then a slug, both of which look like tumbleweeds. Encourage them to talk about the drawing and remember to praise different things: "I love those bright colors," "What's this interesting thing over here?," "Tell me about your painting." Not always "That looks like a person" or "You're good at drawing cars." Display their drawings and paintings around the house or in a special place. Don't demand that drawings be "good": all drawings are interesting.

Kids of almost any age can help to make birthday cards and wrapping paper. Display their works prominently on a wall or pegged to a piece of string rigged up inside.

Take your kid to an art gallery and explain what that's all about. Keep your eye out for opportunities to point out other art forms, at sculpture parks or public spaces, and old or modern buildings.

An art box could have all or some of the materials listed in Art Box Supplies, which follows, depending on the age and capabilities of your child and whether they have access to it or you get it down from somewhere safe and supervise the contents carefully. Adjust your art supplies to suit all ages of kids in the house—for example, no plastic bags and no long string or ribbons for unsupervised kids.

"My daughter loves cutting up the paper and sticking pieces onto pages without any particular method to the madness. She loves it when I join in but is happiest doing it side by side rather than trying to divvy up the cutting and the sticking. I used to try and help her cut around particular objects but I decided in the end that she was trying to do that herself anyway and was happiest with the result if it was her own work even if she missed the object she was trying to cut out all together. A lot of the time she is happiest watching and then copying rather than having me try and manipulate her hands/scissors/whatever for her. I step in with a helping hand when she wants it but I have to fight back the temptation sometimes to take over." CAROLINE

ART BOX SUPPLIES

* A smock for each kid—and one for a visitor.

* Paintbrushes—fat ones with short handles are best.

* Poster paints–white, red, blue, yellow, and black are a good start for mixing.

* Big colored crayons.

* Big colored pencils and a corresponding pencil sharpener.

* Maybe felt-tip pens (although it's usually hard to wash out the marks and toddlers and many preschoolers will inevitably leave lids off and mangle tips by pressing hard).

* Little sponge shapes or potatoes for printing with paint. (Well, okay, don't leave potatoes in the art box.)

* A glue pot with a brush, or a pop-up glue stick.

* Sticky tape—the wider the better (and be careful that a dispenser doesn't have a nasty sharp edge).

* Oil pastels (can be messy but have intense colors).

* Colored chalk.

* Scissors made for children's use.

* Keeping safety in mind, a collection of pieces of felt, Popsicle sticks, pipe cleaners, tubs of glitter, fabrics, snippets of string and ribbons, wrapping-paper scraps, cut-out magazine pictures, dried seed pods, and autumn leaves, cardboard tubes, egg cartons, streamers, bought feathers, buttons, and craft items saved from going out with the trash or bought in a craft shop. These can be used for collage or construction projects.

music

A baby starts making music with their cooing and their rattle, and it's all fun from there on.

Make tapes of music you like that's suitable for children and listen to them together. Point out when a different instrument is used or talk about who is singing at different stages of a song.

Don't restrict music to the "made for children" variety—but be careful of adult concepts in the lyrics that will need to be explained. Music that works on two levels is good. A small girl I know loves Dave Graney and the Coral Snakes songs such as "Feelin' Kinda Sporty" and "I Held the Cool Breeze," without understanding the finer nuances of some of the lyrics but also without being disturbed by any of them. That sort of compromise is much easier for parents who've heard their 900th Wiggles song for the day (see More Info at the end of this chapter).

Take your child to see free performances of classical and other music, but avoid frightening moments that might put them off, such as a sudden introduction to angry-sounding thrash metal that hurts their ears. Kids' ears will be damaged by rock-concert or bar-band level noise. Festival performances held outside or performances specially for kids (ask your local library or community center what's coming up) are best. Have family and friends singalongs or play and sing to videos and recordings at home so it's sometimes a passive experience and sometimes an interactive one. Compilation CDs or singalong tapes for the car are good and kids can help choose what goes on.

The point of "making music" is participation—and fun. Young children are rarely capable of playing complex music such as tunes or mastering the harmonica. The kid shaking, banging, and blowing on something can be their own music, or you can join in. Or you can get them to "accompany" music. You or your musical friends or relatives can teach your child some skills and give them a few hints when the kid is a toddler or preschooler, but "untrained" fun is good too.

What you add to your box of musical instruments will depend on the age and capabilities of your child and whether they can get

MUSIC BOX SUPPLIES

* Plastic containers filled with dried beans to shake (make sure the lid is secure) or shop-bought maracas.

* Drums—you could supply saucepans and large, empty plastic yogurt containers.

* Wooden clap sticks.

* Bells.

* Whistles.

* A stringed implement of some description (depending on the

kid's age and destructive tendencies).

* A xylophone.

* Cymbals (saucepan lids are good).

* Triangles (although these can be annoying because the various bits always get separated, and they don't ding properly without the little string holding them up or the dinging wand).

* Tooting things.

at it freely or you keep it somewhere safe and supervise the use of its contents closely when you bring it out. Don't give a child an expensive musical instrument and expect them not to break it: they're not old enough to have the mental or physical capacity to be responsible for fragile things.

Dance

Dancing with your kid can start when you hold them as a baby and progress until you're teaching a preschooler elementary "choreography." Buy or borrow music videos and recordings with join-in ideas for small children. Some kids mightn't want to join in or follow movements and dances: let them sit it out if they like.

You'll see how presenters on TV shows such as *Sesame Street* and *Hi-5* show kids how to copy a dance. Kids can also be encouraged to do their own free-form dancing. Little kids from age 4, say, may enjoy a non-competitive or non-performance-pressure dance group (or music group).

more info

Apart from music you already like and may have on CDs or tapes or have compiled for travel, the following music for kids is bearable for adults. And anything by Raffi (American) or Paul Jamieson (Australian) is usually loved by kids.

World Playground
A collection of songs for kids and families released by Putumayo World Music. Includes a Pitjantjatjara version of "Waltzing Matilda" ("Nyanpi Matilda") and some catchy tunes kids love to sing from Africa, the Caribbean and elsewhere, including "Three Little Birds," "Mardi Gras Mambo," and

"Just Keep Goin' On." Other kids' CDs are available. The website is www.putumayo.com.

Rocket Ship Beach, Family Dance, and Night Time
by Dan Zanes and friends, released by Festival Five Records.
Three CDs by a bunch of cool singers and musicians, including Rosanne Cash, Lou Reed, the Wonderland String Band and Rankin' Don ("Father Goose"), get together to create a family-friendly sound with lots of interesting instruments and songs such as "Rock Island Line," "Polly Wolly Doodle," "So Long, It's Been Good to Know Ya," "Keep on the Sunny Side," and "Skip to My Lou."

www.sfskids.org
The groovy San Francisco Orchestra site introduces kids to instruments, notes, and concepts such as rhythm, pitch, and harmony.

Travel Near and Far

This chapter is called "Travel" because going away from home with a baby or kids is hardly ever a vacation, unless you're packing several support staff with experience in child care, catering, and massage technique as well as the wet wipes. Quite often a "vacation" means harder work for a parent or caregiver: having to pack a gerzillion things and cook on a campfire with a stick; having to get a child to sleep in an unfamiliar, sun-drenched room, in a different time zone from home,

wheeeeeee!

CUBA

in a house where people think a rousing, screechy game before bedtime is a good idea; or having to stay in a cabin without a fridge or a motel with no place to heat up a bottle. While some Americans don't do lengthy plane trips overseas, even traveling within the US can mean a flight of several hours or a long stretch in the car. Going outside your usual routine and familiar life can be fun—but there's a reason why they invented the phrase "comfort zone" so in this chapter there are a few handy hints to make things go more smoothly.

If you don't have school-age children, make the most of the time you still have to go away somewhere quiet and cheaper when it isn't a school vacation.

traveling with a baby

Although some people claim you can take babies anywhere and everywhere because they just lie about passively, this is piffle. Many babies love routine and don't like it being broken. You too will be out of your natural habitat and often in situations where your baby crying or being fussy makes you anxious because it may bother other people (on the airplane, in a restaurant, or wherever you're staying).

I think traveling comfortably with a baby depends on the baby and on the parents. If you're laid-back, easygoing, and don't have to do anything but take each moment as it comes, it will probably be fine. (Especially if you're an independently wealthy hippie.)

The best kind of trip with your baby is one when you have doting, helpful relatives at the other end. The worst kind is when the baby is sick or otherwise unhappy, you're unhappy, there's nobody to help you, you don't understand the language, the general hygiene isn't up to scratch, and the fish is off.

Very small babies will be exposed to new germs in places such as air-conditioned planes, trains, and hotels so it may be wise to wait until their immune system has kicked in a little more.

Avoid places overseas that need lots of vaccinations as your child may not be able to have all of them yet (and don't go anywhere without the right vaccinations). This isn't the time to indulge your fondest wish to explore the Congo.

Carrying food for a baby can be tricky. Fruit or veg mixes are probably best because they don't need refrigeration. Or you might want to pack some commercial baby foods.

The following checklist and the two tick lists on the next double page will help you to get organized. Obviously, the check lists will need to be adjusted depending on whether you're planning a weekend at Gran's round the corner or a three-week touring holiday in the Balkans. Some of the items in the Cargo to Take for a Baby When Traveling one you could also arrange to have waiting at your destination when you arrive. Make your own check lists or photocopy the two provided, striking out what doesn't apply and adding your own essentials.

CHECKLIST BEFORE LEAVING WITH A BABY

* When booking accommodations, make sure they're not anti-baby or child: some places are dangerous and some don't allow children to stay.

* If you're bottlefeeding, get your baby used to drinking room-temperature or cool formula in case you can't heat bottles during the journey.

* Leave your doctor's phone number, your insurance details, your credit card numbers, and any other vital information with a reliable friend or relly.

* If at all possible, line up relatives, friends, or reliable babysitters at the other end to pick you up or hold the baby.

* Pack a baby bag to be carried as hand luggage at all times. A small backpack is easiest to carry when traveling because it leaves your arms free when you're on the move.

* Pack a case or large bag for your baby and a separate one, or separate compartment in the bag, for yourself.

Traveling with a Toddler or a Little Kid

So you want to take a toddler on a vacation? Get someone to lash you to a chair until the feeling passes. Why you want to travel with a toddler is not really important. Either you have temporarily lost your mind or you don't have a choice. It'll be hard, it'll be tough, and if you want to make it out alive, you'll need a duffle bag packed with efficiency and foresight (but not bananas).

CARGO TO TAKE FOR A BABY WHEN TRAVELING
(and usually bring home)

Item	Packed to go	Packed to come home
packed bag or case of baby clothes	☐	☐
baby bag as hand luggage (see next check list)	☐	☐
baby seat for car travel	☐	☐
carriage or stroller	☐	☐
black-out material for baby's window (from fabric store), masking tape, or other fastening	☐	☐
travel crib and bedding	☐	☐
baby monitor	☐	☐
night-light	☐	☐
highchair	☐	☐
bottle sterilizer	☐	☐
plastic spoons and bowls	☐	☐
disposable diapers	☐	☐
baby wipes	☐	☐
deodorized plastic diaper bags	☐	☐
bath soap or substitute, diaper-rash cream, washcloths	☐	☐
special toys and books	☐	☐
clothes _____	☐	☐
_____	☐	☐
_____	☐	☐
_____	☐	☐
_____	☐	☐
extras _____	☐	☐
_____	☐	☐
_____	☐	☐
_____	☐	☐
_____	☐	☐
_____	☐	☐

© *Kidwrangling: The Real Guide to Caring for Babies, Toddlers, and Little Kids*

THINGS TO PACK IN THE BABY TRAVEL BAG
(hand luggage)

Item	Packed to go	Packed to come home
two baby blankets or muslin wraps	☐	☐
breastfeeding paraphernalia for you (bottled water, nipple cream, nipple shields)	☐	☐
formula bottles of sterilized water and powdered-formula packets to last trip plus any delay	☐	☐
deodorized plastic bags for dirty diapers, sticky clothes, rubbish	☐	☐
changes of clothes	☐	☐
disposable diapers	☐	☐
baby wipes	☐	☐
diaper-rash cream	☐	☐
extra booties or socks in case baby's go astray	☐	☐
small first-aid kit (painkiller, insect repellent, rashes and stings ointments, prescriptions, doctor's phone number)	☐	☐
favorite comfort toy(s)	☐	☐
pacifiers for your handbag and pocket	☐	☐
individual tape or CD player with tapes or CDs	☐	☐
fave baby book or three	☐	☐
tea towel or bib (old or throwaway)	☐	☐
non-perishable or sealed-jar snacks and strong plastic spoons	☐	☐
spillproof water bottle for older baby	☐	☐
baby sunscreen and sunhat and/or warm hat, mittens, and jacket	☐	☐
extras _____	☐	☐
_____	☐	☐
_____	☐	☐
_____	☐	☐
_____	☐	☐

© *Kidwrangling: The Real Guide to Caring for Babies, Toddlers, and Little Kids*

CARGO TO TAKE FOR A TODDLER WHEN TRAVELING
(and usually bring home)

Item	Packed to go	Packed to come home
packed bag or case of toddler clothes	☐	☐
toddler bag as hand luggage (see next check list)—strong, hands-free backpack is ideal	☐	☐
toddler booster seat	☐	☐
stroller with straps and buckle	☐	☐
black-out fabric for toddler's window (from fabric store), masking tape, or other fastening	☐	☐
travel crib and bedding	☐	☐
night-light	☐	☐
electric outlet safety plugs	☐	☐
highchair	☐	☐
plastic bowls, utensils, and two drink containers	☐	☐
Cooler and ice	☐	☐
disposable diapers or "pull-ons," night diapers or potty	☐	☐
wet wipes	☐	☐
diaper-rash cream	☐	☐
deodorized plastic diaper bags	☐	☐
special toys and books	☐	☐
clothes _____	☐	☐
_____	☐	☐
_____	☐	☐
_____	☐	☐
extras (ask toddler what they'd like to play with)	☐	☐
_____	☐	☐
_____	☐	☐
_____	☐	☐
_____	☐	☐

© *Kidwrangling: The Real Guide to Caring for Babies, Toddlers, and Little Kids*

THINGS TO PACK IN THE TODDLER TRAVEL BAG
(hand luggage)

Item	Packed to go	Packed to come home
bottles	☐	☐
deodorized plastic bags for dirty diapers, sticky clothes, and trash	☐	☐
changes of clothes	☐	☐
disposable diapers	☐	☐
wet wipes	☐	☐
diaper-rash cream	☐	☐
plastic sandals in case shoes go astray	☐	☐
small first-aid kit (painkiller, insect repellent, rashes and stings ointments, prescriptions, doctor's phone number)	☐	☐
pacifiers for your handbag and pocket	☐	☐
individual tape or CD player with tapes or CDs	☐	☐
favorite light toy(s)	☐	☐
fave toddler book or three	☐	☐
activities kit (crayons, paper, small games)	☐	☐
snacks	☐	☐
spillproof toddler's drink	☐	☐
toddler sunscreen and sunhat and/or warm hat, mittens, and jacket	☐	☐
something to suck on when plane taking off and landing	☐	☐
extras _____	☐	☐
_____	☐	☐
_____	☐	☐
_____	☐	☐
_____	☐	☐
_____	☐	☐
_____	☐	☐
_____	☐	☐

© *Kidwrangling: The Real Guide to Caring for Babies, Toddlers, and Little Kids*

Traveling or staying away with a toddler will always be more fun for everyone if there are other toddlers or kids for yours to play with, or devoted relatives or friends of any age who are talented distracters.

The two tick lists for a toddler given on the previous double page, like those for a baby, will help you get away. Some of the items in the Cargo to Take for a Toddler When Traveling check list you could organize in advance to have waiting for you when you arrive. Again you might like to make your own check lists or to photocopy these, adjusting them to suit your trip and your child—the lists could be adapted for a preschooler, for example.

Before you leave, rack your brain for toys and games that absorb your child. Hide them now, then bring them out one by one during the trip. They can include simple things such as a lift-the-flap book, a flashlight for turning on and off, and photos of family and friends to look at and tell stories about. An activities kit is also great value. You can buy one or make your own. A small plastic bucket with a fitted lid and handle (or it could be a yogurt container) is perfect for crayons, paper, games appropriate for limited spaces, and other small things to prevent them from sliding off a tray table or a lap.

A tape of children's songs will also be a help. Otherwise you may have to sing ("And the wheels on the bus go round and round, round and round, round and bloody round, all right already" is not an approved lyric).

Snacks that resist melting, mashing, and other forms of redistribution are essential on journeys. Good bets include no-salt crackers, raisins, chilled cheese sticks, lightly steamed fruit or vegies (or raw fruit or veg if your toddler likes them). If you can stop during a car trip and prepare something out of a cooler, your options are nearly endless. Why not try pheasant under glass, flambéed pomegranate on a bison coulis, and a cheeky little sauterne?

Spillproof cups with straws are good on trips but need their tops loosened frequently in planes and hot weather because otherwise the change in pressure makes the liquid spurt out of the straw. Before you leave, it's handy to teach your toddler to drink from pop-top sports bottles.

Touring vacations will mean a lot more unpacking, packing, and chances to leave behind that adored and indispensable stuffed toy Mr. Fluffypants. Staying in the one spot can be a tad more tranquil. If you're a long way from home and in airports or other transitty places, pin a label on your kid with their name, your cell phone number, flight numbers, airline, train destination, or anything else that will help you reclaim your precious baggage quickly, but watch the kid at all times no matter how distracted you feel.

And listen, I'm serious about banning transit bananas.

accommodation

Most accommodation guide books and local tourist associations will be able to tell you whether a place is happy to have babies and children or bans little ones: it's always best to check with the place itself in case the policy has changed.

Many resorts and hotels have a "children's club"—find out whether it'll be operating when you're there (often it's only for school holidays), what ages are catered for, who staffs it and what qualifications they have, the hours of operation, and any extra costs involved. Remember that a "child-friendly" hotel or resort often has only more independent kids in mind, the sort who can play table tennis for hours.

If you're staying with friends or relatives, try to have your own area, or at least a bedroom you can "childproof." Make sure dogs or other animals can be kept outside, or at least never left unattended with your kid.

Try to re-establish your kid's routine as soon as possible, and don't try to fit it into other people's grown-up schedules such as late dinners and bedtimes. But do remember that babies and toddlers can be exhausting for people who aren't used to them.

TRAVELING WITH SMALL CHILDREN: ACCOMMODATION INTERROGATION PROCEDURE

Any host should be interrogated about the following—before you set out.

* Your ad says "children" welcome but does that mean babies and toddlers as well as teenagers?

* Is the heating or airconditioning in all the rooms? What kind of heating or airconditioning is it?

* Are any of the outlets within a crawler or toddler's reach?

* Is there somewhere I can wash baby bottles and dishes?

* Can I boil water in the room and how can I sterilize bottles?

* Is there a fridge in the room?

* Is there a telephone in the room?

* Are there any stairs? Can they be childproofed before I get there?

* Are appliances out of reach?

* Do domestic or other animals run wild on the property?

* If breakfast is included, what sort of breakfast do you supply for a baby or toddler?

* Can you supply a crib, highchair, or stroller? Do they meet current safety standards? Will they cost extra?

* Why are we doing this? Have I lost my mind?

* Can you turn down the hot-water service temperature to 50 degrees Celsius before we get there?

* Can some Swedish firemen come and give me a free massage?

* Does it look like it does in the brochure or is it a filthy, run-down hovel with rusted-open windows you charge a fortune for at school-holiday times? (Oh, do be tactful.)

If you're paying your way, keep in mind that if both you and your child are crying, service will be quicker, wherever you are. Being stuck in one hotel room with a baby or young child can be blindingly awful whether there's one adult or two. Adjoining hotel rooms can be great but unless someone else is paying or you've accidentally turned into Ivana Trump, it's unlikely you'll have this luxury. Self-sufficient cabins out of town with at least two rooms can be more fun than hotel rooms in town, but are often off limits to people with children because the owners prefer the type of guest who is falling in love rather than falling in the dam.

Bed and breakfast places can be good if the breakfast is early enough for kids. If you are living and sleeping in one room with a toddler, take a flashlight so you can at least read or count your freckles when they are asleep. And earplugs. And an eye mask. Also maybe eight bottles of gin.

Making a child's room dark with black-out fabric can

TOP TEN ACCOMMODATION BROCHURE TRANSLATIONS FOR PARENTS OF LITTLE ONES

1 Deck spa, pool, dam, or delightful koi pond = drowning hazard.

2 Divinely rustic = bloody freezing in winter, suffocating in summer.

3 Romantic open fire or BBQ = burns hazard.

4 Guest lounge = may mean no fridge or TV in your room.

5 Sun drenched = far too light to get the kid to sleep.

6 Private deck, terrace, balcony, verandah, multi-level, mezzanine, open-sided staircase, or staircase of any description = falling hazard.

7 Splendid views = plenty of space to get lost in.

8 Unspoiled land = snakes, wild animals, paranoid city parents.

9 TV, video, or CD player = can be stuffed with mashed avocado and replaced at your expense.

10 Cozy = the toddler will be sleeping up your left nostril.

give you an extra hour or two's sleep in the morning and a better chance of getting the toddler down for morning or afternoon naps. If you've changed time zones, you'll need to get your baby or toddler into a new sleeping rhythm as soon as possible by using familiar routines.

If you can't get hold of a highchair, strap the toddler into a stroller and use a bib or a tea towel as a smock. (Hot-weather holidays are tremendously practical because you can simply hose down offspring after feeding.)

Childproofing a temporary room or house

Put up the travel crib and put your baby or young child in for a sleep or play while you:

- ★ find all the chemicals and dangerous things such as knives in low-down cupboards and drawers—especially under sinks—and move them to higher ground.
- ★ take up any rugs that slide on the floor.
- ★ move any appliances that can be pulled off benches.
- ★ check for other small-child hazards such as bits you can screw off a wall heater.
- ★ turn down the hot-water service temperature to 125 degrees Fahrenheit.
- ★ call room service and ask them to send up smoked salmon, scrambled eggs, and a Swedish masseur, Sven (or Thud). If you do not have room service, go home immediately.

caR TRaveL

Babies, toddlers, and little kids must all be restrained in an approved car seat or booster seat. Kids this young must not use only an adult seatbelt and they must not be in the front of a car where the impact of an airbag would probably kill them.

If you are renting a car, ask the company beforehand:

★ will the rental car have an age-appropriate US–safety standard seat fully installed?

★ does the car have the right attachments for your kid's own safety seat?

Good things to have in a car

★ A shade for the window.

★ A first-aid kit (including acetaminophen, adhesive strips, rashes and stings ointments, tweezers, hydration solutions)—make sure that any medicines won't be affected by a hot car and check use-by dates.

★ Emergency diapers or underpantery.

★ Flattened plastic bags with knots tied in them.

★ Wet wipes.

★ Tissues, old towel, or tea towels for mopping up.

★ A change of kid clothes.

★ A spare top for you.

★ An unopened bottle of commercial water.

★ Non-perishable snacks.

★ Balls and bats in the trunk.

★ Books.

★ Tapes of songs or stories—you can make your own at story time one night.

★ A plastic tray with slightly raised sides that can be balanced on a kid's knee to play games such as Fuzzy Felt, cardboard dominoes, kid's cards, or constructing with click-together blocks. *Martha Stewart Kids* magazine suggests you glue a piece of felt underneath the tray so it doesn't slide about. You can put magnetized letters on a metal cooking tray too.

★ Maps: the kid can learn to read them or pretend they can.

★ A shoe bag or other organizer hanger thing with pockets, for storing soft things, such as furry toys and sticker sheets, and hanging on the back of the seat in front of the kid.

★ Sunscreen and hats for all.

★ Rubber boots or thongs for all.

★ An emergency bribe (stickers or candies for kids old enough for these).

CAR GAMES FOR TINIES

✱ I Spy.

✱ Sing Out if You See a Cow (or horse or sheep or man with green hat).

✱ Count the Red Cars (or yellow).

✱ Count the Trucks.

✱ Name That Tune: make a compilation tape and ask the kid to guess what the song is before the vocal starts.

✱ How Many Times You Can Ask "Are We Almost There?" Before Mom Screams.

Dogs and other identified flying objects

In an accident, an unrestrained dog in a car can be a dangerous, toothy missile that can kill a child. A dog on a short leash can be clipped to the seatbelt with special attachments bought at pet stores. In a station wagon, a dog should be restrained behind an expertly fitted metal cargo barrier, as should any other potential flying objects.

Car sickness

Toddlers and little kids are at the peak age for car sickness. The fluid moving within a kid's ears sloshes about and lets the brain know the body is moving. But when the kid focuses on something inside the car, the eyes tell the brain it's looking at things standing still. Often the result is that the child feels queasy and throws up. The obvious solution is for them to look out a window. Looking out any window is

better than not looking out at all, but the front one seems to be the best. An unusually smooth or bumpy ride could make car sickness worse and windy roads are worst of all. If your kid is a car-sickie:

★ always carry spare clothes, plastic bags, wet wipes, bottled water, hose, a tank of disinfectant, and nose plugs.

★ get the kid to eat a little something—an empty stomach gets squigglier earlier.

★ fresh air and a non-stinky car will help stave off nausea— wind in the windows is better than airconditioning in most cases, except when it's boiling or raining outside. Plan also rest and run-around stops during a long trip.

★ introduce games that focus on spotting things outside the moving car.

★ play songs or stories rather than letting the child read a book.

★ don't give your child over-the-counter motion-sickness drugs meant for adults. These kinds of drugs are usually not the answer for kids, but if you want to explore the option you need to have them prescribed by a doctor.

As for pet car sickness—sedate the little critters because stress is usually the reason rather than motion sickness. A dog throwing up is likely to have everyone else throwing up.

PLANE TRAVEL

Try to travel with a partner or friend who can help you.

Babies on planes
Any long flight is difficult with a baby: try to book a bulkhead seat for yourself. Being confined to your seat with a baby also means it may be harder for you to walk around to keep your blood circulating

properly. Avoid stopovers if possible unless they're for a few days to allow you all to recover, adjust, and then go on.

Change the baby's diaper before each flight to minimize your chances of having to change them in the minuscule plane toilet.

Babies will need to suck on a breast, bottle, finger, or pacifier at take-off and landing to help their ears adjust to the pressure change.

Toddlers and little kids on planes

Children under 2 can sometimes fly free if they sit on your knee (but check first!)—not a great option for a long haul. Very few people can afford to pay for a child under 2 to have their own seat: check with different airlines whether your child is eligible for a discount. Book a child's meal for a toddler or little kid. Domestic airline staff are absolutely charming about little ones (and if an individual employee isn't for any reason, make a complaint politely and promptly). Many overseas carriers, by contrast, just about suggest you pop your tot in cargo. Accept any helpful travel suggestions from these experienced domestic cabin staff.

Shorter flights within the US should be booked for daytime so the little one can look out the window and enjoy themselves. Some people say night travel is good on a long flight because you can sleep, but I think most of the time kids won't sleep unless they're babies. If a stopover is unavoidable, take the lightest, smallest stroller you can to use in transit. As you know, it can be very tiring carrying a child around.

Some planes show PG- or edited R-rated movies so be prepared to distract your child from the images. Don't rely on the plane's activity kit to keep them occupied. It's pot luck whether it's appropriate for their age and it'll almost certainly be the same one on the way back.

Drugs that are often used to sedate children for traveling can unexpectedly knock them out for too long or even sometimes have the opposite effect on them. Some parents have been stuck on a 27-hour flight with kids they can't rouse properly or kids who fling themselves around shrieking. If you're determined to use drugs, discuss dosages with a doctor and test them carefully before you go.

Make sure your child doesn't have an ear infection because the ear could become very painful as cabin pressure changes. A toddler or little kid may need to suck on a pacifier or a sugar-free candy at take-off and landing to help their ears adjust to the pressure change. And they'll need to drink a lot of water to hydrate themselves.

going overseas

Research the places you're going to until you're an expert. Your child will need their own passport. Don't go to a place where the medical system is poor and you feel that if your baby or child was seriously or suddenly ill you couldn't rely on local services. And don't leave the country without massively comprehensive travel and health insurance. Get the kind that covers absolutely everything from prescriptions and dental care to hospital costs and helicopter evacuation home from South Burundi. Before you go, ask your doctor to write prescriptions for things you or your kid might need, get the scripts filled, and take them with you. Also ask your pharmacist for ideas. (And see More Info at the end of this chapter.)

traveling without your children

Some people would never leave their baby for even a night with relatives or friends, whereas members of the jet-set seem to have a tradition of popping off for months on end whether they have a baby under 6 months old or a toddler. Some babies are quite happy with short breaks from parents before they're 6 months old but then get more worried. You may need to travel without your baby or kids for work or personal reasons. Each situation has to be judged individually and you know your kid best, but here are a few thoughts.

Missing you already

Extended or repeated breaks will affect the bond you have with your child. This could be temporary or have long-term repercussions. The most important thing is that the kid is looked after by someone with whom they have a bond. (This is why some parents have holidays or weekends away separately, leaving one at home.)

There's an almost equal pull between wanting a child to miss you and wanting them not to. If they miss you but feel safe and are happily occupied, that's okay. You may find that you seem to miss them more than they miss you, but you can't see inside a kid's head. If they are really distressed or constantly sad during your absence, that's obviously in the not good category.

Don't bang on to your child about missing them and being so sad to be away. Talk about the positive things: "Grandad will come over every afternoon," "Daddy will read you two stories each night."

A kid that has bonded to more than one person will be happier when left by a parent because they'll "transfer" affection to some extent to the onsite parent, other relatives, or caregivers at their child-care center, or preschool. Attachment theorists believe that babies have a hierarchy of people they're bonded to. Usually Mom is at the top, then Dad, and then other friends, family, or caregivers, depending on the family set-up. The absent parent will have to be prepared to possibly be ignored for a while when they get back, but this doesn't happen as often as parents fear.

Set a limit on how long one parent can be absent at any time if possible. Some parents say a week, or three weeks, once a year. In other cases the kid might not see the parent for months on end if the parent is involved with politics or the military, for example.

It is almost always better for the child to stay in their own home while you are away so that their routine and comfort zones are least disrupted. Get someone to stay with your child rather than send the kid to them.

A child may not want you to go away, but if they feel safe and cared for, and are not themselves disrupted or distressed, then you should not feel bad about leaving for short periods. Kids might want chocolate ice-cream for breakfast too, but that doesn't mean you have to give them everything they want.

The child of a sole parent or two parents who need to go away or the child of someone who must leave suddenly may have the most difficult time. The best option is for a familiar and loving person such as an aunt or grandparent to move into your house, and for the parent (or parents) to either build up the absences (a day or two, a weekend) so the kid understands they always come back soon, or keep the time away as short as possible.

Preparing your child

Depending on your child's personality and stage of development, you'll have to gauge whether to give them a long time to consider the departure, or tell them a couple of days before or the day you leave. One day before probably isn't enough time to prepare for an absence of two weeks. Explain why you are going. You might want to start by saying "Mommy will be looking after you for two weeks while I have to go away." Sometimes you might have to hold up fingers to show how many days you'll be away or how many nighttime sleeps. Talk about it on a few different occasions and ask your child to tell other people what's going to happen so you can see if they've fully understood. Emphasize that you'll come back. (See More Info at the end of the Reading chapter for a book on separation anxiety.)

Very young toddlers don't have much idea of time. As long as they are safe, happy, not out of their routine, and have loving people they're used to and their usual environment, they may not notice the difference between two days and a week.

Talk about your plans for the trip and explain what you'll be doing. Show them travel books with pictures of where you are going (this could be a bit hard if it's the inside of a computer room in Siberia).

Give your preschooler a throw-away camera to take photos of what they do while you're away or a binder of plastic sleeves from the office supply store that they can slip their drawings into to save for when you get back.

Write a stack of letters to your child, put them in addressed envelopes with pretend stamps to be given one a day by the other parent or at child care. They will be something special for them to open, with a message that can be read, perhaps some photos of you together, and little drawings (kids don't care if you're not Picasso). Make a tape for them of you reading a story if they're not likely to get upset and look for you when they hear your voice.

While you're away

Call every night or every few days, but don't be annoyed if your child doesn't want to speak to you or breaks off after a quick hello to go and do something else. Kids live in the moment: be happy that they're occupied and fine without you. You can write, phone, email, or send digital photos or postcards.

Put a homemade calendar on the wall that covers the trip away. Your child can place a sticker on the right square as each day passes. Some people put up a map or have a globe, but this is best for sophisticated preschoolers, not toddlers.

Don't resent a nanny or child-care worker whom your child becomes attached to, even if the kid accidentally calls them mommy or daddy sometimes. (Little kids often get the words mommy and daddy mixed up anyway, and in some respects it's not like using your name—it's a way of showing love and trust to a special person.) If you have chosen to raise your child in a way that means they have several special people, you should respect and be thankful for those bonds, not harm them out of jealousy or self-doubt.

Don't say to your child "I'll never go away again."

more info

Travel with Children

by Cathy Lanigan, Lonely Planet, 2002.

A mum, with contributions from other parents who've traveled, writes about planning the trip, gives hints for different types of travel, and shares advice on specific worldwide destinations. The book includes excellent practical and philosophical advice, and it's a must for those going overseas. There are medical and natural health tips, useful websites, and some travel game suggestions. Covers travel with babies to teenagers.

Center for Disease Control

List of immunizations recommended for traveling abroad.
www.cdc.gov/travel/child_travel.htm

www.kidstravelfun.com

Hints for parents traveling to all parts of the world, and with bikes, canoes, and so on. Has stuff you can print out for activity kits and fun questions for the road. If you're lucky enough to have computer access, kids can log on and play games while they're away: some of these are for preschoolers, although a lot are for older kids.

www.thefamilytravelfiles.com

A website with lots of travel advice and info on world destinations, theme vacations, and time zones.

www.roughguides.com

The website of this travel guide and world music company will help you research global destinations.

www.lonelyplanet.com

The travel publisher Lonely Planet has destination reports and lots of parents' questions, with answers from experienced travelers.

US Department of State

Government website for travel abroad with information about passports, visas, traveling tips, country fact sheets, and travel advisories.

202-647-5225

www.travel.state.gov

insidey activities

There are some days when it would be a thrill to be visited by a nomadic troupe of performing kids' entertainers who also clean the bathroom and give you a facial. In lieu of that, here are some ideas for insidey activities on rainy days, very hot days, and middle-of-the-days when the UV rays are beaming down fiercely.

The play ideas are compiled and edited parents' answers to the Kidwrangling Survey. If your kid says "I'm bored," get them to close their eyes and jab a finger onto one of these pages.

You might also like to ask your child-care center staff for their inside-play ideas. And get your kid to brainstorm a list of activities for this kind of day, which stays on the wall so you can refer to it easily. Boredom can be just the lull before another burst of creative energy.

iDeas fRom PaReNts

◎ Bubble spooning for tykes: fill a saucepan with lots of detergent in a bit of water; froth it up with a hand beater; spread towels around your kid, then give them other saucepans, bowls, cups and spoons and they'll sit for hours transferring bubbles from one container to another (you'll have to froth the water up again every so often) ◎ put down big sheets of butcher's paper, ask your kid to lie down, then draw a line around their body and let them put in eyes and mouth and create a full-length self-portrait, using paints, crayons, or pencils (felt-tip pens tend to lose their lids and are harder on clothes) ◎ cut out pictures from magazines and catalogs and have them make scrapbooks ◎ fill in the baby book or memory book together ◎ unroll a ball of string or wool around the house and have a small present at the end ◎ have a puppet show, with bought puppets, your child's stuffed toys, or sock ones with button eyes that you've made ◎ cook a cake or muffins and clean up the mess together ◎ watch a video ◎ sing songs together ◎ go through or compile photo albums and discuss vacations and other family events ◎ make forts with boxes, cushions, and blankets ◎ bake bread and have a nap while it rises ◎ mix food coloring with shaving cream to make pictures in the bath and on the walls around the bath, then splash it off ◎ cut out fish shapes from colored paper and attach a paperclip to each, then tie string with a magnet at one end to a stick (or similar) and let your kid try to pick up all the fish with this "rod" ◎ make a clock from a paper plate and cut out pictures from magazines that resemble things we do at that time of the day ◎ draw roads on a large piece of cardboard (or a flattened cardboard box) and get your kid to place cars, street signs, and stores and houses of blocks around the roads ◎ blend fruit with yogurt to make Popsicles and put them in the freezer ◎ get something out of the "presents cupboard" where you keep bargain toys and games picked up over the year ◎ cover the floor with a few old drop sheets (you can get them from thrift-shops) and do finger and foot painting ◎ have a picnic or tea party on a rug with toys and real cakes ◎ keep cardboard boxes for these times and give your kid the lot, plus sticky tape, colored paper and paints to construct whatever they want to ◎ make up a story that goes around: you say a bit, they add to it, and so it goes on ◎ read books ◎ Kids' videos can really do the trick (if you can put up with the same darn songs over and over and over again) ◎ make pictures, letters, or postcards to send to friends and relatives and end with a trip to the mailbox ◎ blow bubbles in the bathroom ◎ make your own thunder and lightning with pots and pans ◎ do jigsaw puzzles (jigsaws must be for the right age group) ◎ bring out the dress-up box and have everyone in the family join in ◎ clean out your kid's wardrobe, decide which of their clothes is ready to be handed down, talk about growing up, and present the stash of bigger clothes you've been buying at sales for them to try on ◎ dress up in someone else's old gear ◎ put on some music and dance ◎ play musical statues: when the music snaps off everyone has to freeze (best with a remote control) ◎ look through magazines for pictures of animals, cut them out and your child can paste them on cardboard to make up a "zoo" or a wildlife park ◎ make goop (just add water and a few drops of food color to a cup of cornstarch, mix it until it's thick and creamy, pour it onto a tray with sides so that it doesn't run off and they can get their fingers into it); it feels great, is non-toxic and washes out of clothes ◎ cook "speriments" (very popular) ◎ make up and mold papier-mâché over a blown-up balloon to create a mask or round animal ◎ invite a friend over to play ◎ build a world for toy cars to use ◎ go to an indoor-play center ◎ let them help to sort out the little basket of junk (or third drawer down) that accumulates in most homes and is usually out of bounds ◎ give them special permission to kick and throw a blow-up beach ball, play loud music, run, or play hide and seek in the house ◎ supply blocks that stick together ◎ bring out the fabric box that holds materials, ribbons, and some fabric glue and make a fabric poster ◎ pretend to go camping in the house ◎ go shopping together ◎ set up a shop with items from the pantry and some pretend money they draw themselves and play shopping ◎ dress up and act out a play ◎ sing all the rain songs you know ◎ make and decorate gingerbread people ◎ visit friends with larger houses ◎ make a fort with cardboard boxes and decorate it ◎ make up stories for your child to act out as you narrate them—they can be the hero ◎ get them to help chop up veggies with a safe knife for dinner or freezing ◎ collect all the old Christmas and birthday cards and let the child cut and paste them ◎ thread buttons, beads, or cotton spools on string (make sure there are no choking hazards) ◎ help clean the house ◎ they tell you what shapes to cut out of adhesive colored contact paper and then put them on windows (preschoolers can use children's scissors to do the cutting out themselves) ◎ go to the library ◎ sort the laundry into piles and fold it ◎ use playdough or real dough for cutting out shapes with cookie cutters ◎ cut greeting cards with a strong image into simple jigsaws ◎ start a treasure box or dress-up box ◎ play dominoes or cards (surprisingly good fun even if the rules aren't yet grasped—invent or go with the flow) ◎ make your own wrapping paper and cards for birthdays that are coming up ◎ make marshmallow treats—messy, quick, creative, cheap, delicious ◎ make hats (feather ones are fun) ◎ face painting (you'll need the special paints in advance) ◎ make tunnels with sheets and chairs to crawl and walk through ◎ have a bath with bath bubbles and lots of things to pour, squirt, and play with ◎ take blocks into the bath ◎ let a little one cook while sitting in their highchair ◎ visit a free museum (kids of any age love them) or a gallery ◎ run around the house screaming (them not you—they love it too!) ◎ one parent plays the guitar or another musical instrument while the child sings the songs with the other parent ◎ let them tear a newspaper to bits ◎ change the rooms your kid can play in ◎ make a feely box—put a heap of different-textured things in a box and get your child to put their hand in and guess what they are feeling ◎ keep some toys hidden away so when you bring them out they seem like new ones ◎ let them get into the container cupboards ◎ chase Dad or be chased by Dad ◎ play with water at the kitchen sink ◎ paint egg cartons ◎ play computer games ◎ go to the website of a favorite TV show ◎ add blue food coloring to the bath so they think they are at the pool ◎ use an umbrella under the shower ◎ play hopscotch ◎ go to an indoor swimming pool ◎ play Chutes and Ladders ◎ go to a café for a warm drink ◎ make yourselves a morning or afternoon snack and have a grown-up chat ("How are you?" "What's been happening?") ◎ go through recipe books together with bookmarks or tags and mark things that look like they'd be fun to make or eat ◎ go through the toy box to make up a bag for the thrift-store or friends—the kid has the final decision ◎ watch the rain through a window and hunt for a rainbow ◎ blow up balloons and play volleyball with them ◎ test drive the tricycles and fancy cars that live at the big toyshop ◎ place stickers into plain scrapbooks or sticker books ◎ bang anything that makes noise ◎ wrestle ◎ allow them to ride a bike indoors ◎ tie scarves onto bangles and wear them to dance to music ◎ roll on the bed ◎ let them play with that noisy train or car set (if they can't run around the backyard and scream their heads off, you're going to have to be prepared for noise inside) ◎ children love anything that you take time to do with them, especially creating something or cooking ◎ purchase a little table-and-chair set (little ones will spend hours sitting at them with playdough, paper, pencils, and books) ◎ put their favorite CDs on while they are doing activities ◎ dance to *Carmen* or something loud and wild ◎ make a band using the kitchen pots ◎ bake cookies ◎ make a hiding place with a sheet over the table ◎ get your kid to help with vacuuming and folding laundry ◎ lie on the floor and let your baby roll around on top of you ◎ get a little scooter and go for rides in it up and down a hall (you push) ◎ give your child glue, scissors, scrap paper, streamers, and pompoms to decorate tissue boxes, then get them to wear them as slippers ◎ have a teddy bears' picnic using a plastic tea set and a blanket—Barbie can come too if she behaves herself ◎ sail boats in the bath ◎ bring out the trusty shape sorter for a tyke ◎ tidy the bedroom ◎ get them to decorate a pizza base to make it more individual ◎ set up a hospital: use dolls and teddies as patients and tear up old sheets for bandages ◎ supply a bucket of clothes pins and a license to pin up anything ◎ make the room really dark and play with a flashlight ◎ make the whole house a shopping center with different goods available at varying prices (you could use Monopoly money); the kids could even have special offers such as buy this packet of ramen noodles and receive a complimentary glass of lemonade ◎ read a favorite book and get them to act it out ◎ devote a corner in the garage to painting or chalk drawing on the concrete floor ◎ do some potato printing: cut out shapes from a potato, dip the shapes in paint, and stamp them onto paper ◎ blow up balloons and hit them around with fly swatters ◎ finger paint on a window ◎ play indoor bowling ◎ put all the plastic toys and cars in the bath for your child to give them a good scrub ◎ set some special housework activities; for example the kid sprays and you wipe ◎ teach the kid about how things grow by making a terrarium: cut the top off an old soft-drink bottle about a quarter of the way down and make holes in the bottom; "plant" some seeds on damp cotton cloth on a small plate and cover them with the bottle; leave the terrarium in a warm, sunny place—in a couple of days shoots will appear ◎ construct Fuzzy Felt pictures ◎ let your kid dress up in your and your partner's clothes for a good laugh ◎ tape a lot of the PBS children's programs for when you are desperate ◎ make Jell-o and eat it ◎ have toad races (yes, somebody really suggested this)

◎ make a book—they draw the pictures, and tell you the story and you write it down, put their name on it and most importantly KEEP IT ◎ create shadow pictures on the wall ◎ make sandwiches and cut them into shapes with cookie cutters ◎ put on some classical music and make up a story to go with it as it plays ◎ get out your button box so that your child can group the different colors or sizes, then design patterns, make pictures, thread necklaces ◎ together make an absent relative or friend a big book of pictures of what you've been doing ◎ get dressed up in rain- coat and rubber boots and go outside and jump in puddles!

BiRTHDay PaRTies aND PReseNTS

If your kid's only a baby, you won't need to read all this stuff now; plenty of time for operatic, cast-of-thousands, four-weeks-in-the-planning extravaganzas later—but only if that takes your fancy. A bit of color and movement, some streamers and balloons, a cake, and lots of fuss on the morning of the birthday make for a great day. You don't have to get Nanna to do water ballet in the backyard. If you're the sort of insane person who wants a petting zoo, industrial-music circus, and modern mime performance for your baby's first birthday, I suggest you have a good lie down. The kid won't remember any of it. And that old rule about "It's not a great party unless the police arrive" definitely doesn't apply to the under-fives.

If you're not sure what's a good present to take to a party, see the lists provided for kids aged 1 to 5. It's best to steer clear of anything that might create a blood feud between you and other parents—such as a live animal, a toy gun, or "little girl" make-up and high heels. Or a nice bottle of riesling.

PLaNNiNg

Try to start planning early to minimize stress: before you got pregnant would be a good time. And rope in as many people to help as you can—this is a great event for special uncles, aunts, friends, and babysitters, especially ones who don't have their own children, to help with. "Bring a dish" is a good maxim, as is "plan one game,"

TO-DO LIST

Make yourself a list of what you'll need to do. For example:

✱ make or buy and write invitations with your kid.

✱ get decorations.

✱ buy camera film, candles, and matches.

✱ plan and buy the party food and drinks.

✱ organize the birthday cake.

✱ move anything breakable or dangerous.

✱ drain the paddling pool.

✱ stock the first-aid kit with cute adhesive strips.

✱ decorate the party precinct.

✱ find someone to mind the pets.

✱ explain to the birthday kid how to behave at the party.

but coordinate this so nobody doubles up. A party's a dud if the hosts are frazzled out of their minds.

Ask your kid what kind of party they would like and who they'd like to invite, but feel free to use a power of veto. Brief your kid about the behavior expected of them as host (but don't expect them to necessarily get it together).

Sometimes the birthday child behaves very badly at their party or gets hysterical. Time Out may help, but don't treat it as a punishment. The birthday is more likely to be relaxed if you keep your child (and yourself) calm the day before and perhaps only remind your little person it's their birthday on the actual morning rather than creating a "thirty-three more sleeps" anticipation (or not much sleep actually).

Old-fashioned games that involve participation, simple party food, and rituals seem to work best for the under-fives.

Just in case the party falls apart or the entertainment gets eaten by the dog, rained out, or goes missing, have a video ready as a backup. One that will appeal to all ages, has episodic bits, and incorporates music is best, instead of one long narrative story: *Hi-5* or *The*

Wiggles should appeal. The kids will be slack-jawed and zombified in seconds as long as they haven't eaten their body weight in mood-altering additives.

See More Info at the end of this chapter for books and websites with good ideas and hints for parties.

iNvitatioNs

Sorry to be crushingly obvious but when you're busy things do get overlooked. Invitations should go out at least two and preferably three weeks in advance, and should be written, at least to people you don't know well such as the parents of your kid's child-care friends. (And it's always nice to keep an invitation for your baby scrapbook as a souvenir.) They should be mailed or given privately to avoid hurting anyone else's feelings at the child-care center or preschool.

A party invitation should give:

★ the reason for the party ("Francine's third birthday").
★ the day and date.
★ start and finishing times.
★ the address of the venue.
★ the theme of the party and any special instructions, especially if costumes are required ("Please wear old clothes and bring a smock," "Please wear a yellow outfit," "Please come dressed as a jungle animal").
★ an "RSVP," meaning please reply (by a certain date if that's important) and your telephone number.
★ any other relevant details ("Parents welcome to stay," "Brothers and sisters welcome"—unfortunately you can't say "Leave that bossy big brother at home").

venue

The local park always seems like a great idea for the party venue because the squashed cupcakes and sticky drinks go on the grass or in the park trash can, but a park party is difficult to supervise, especially when parents drop their kids off at the start and collect them at the end. Keep this kind of party small and make sure that one of the adults arrives early to "stake out" the area or barbecue and find out if there's a rain shelter nearby. (After three false starts for park parties in summer, I gave up.)

Avoid a pool or beach party if you can't ensure strict supervision. Better not to have to worry about drowning.

Some fast-food chains and other places hold pay-per-head parties. The advantages are obvious—you don't have to prepare the house or clean up afterwards. But the drawbacks are equally clear: a high set fee for each invitee and hell to pay if you lose someone's kid on par 4 of the mini-golf range.

If your party is at home, keep your pets out of the way. You don't want them tortured by strange kids, and some children may be afraid of them. Also put away anything breakable and check for safety risks. Enlist help from the older kids, cousins, or whoever you can for the clean-up afterwards.

Again to save yourself worrying about safety, avoid a party involving anything with wheels or unrestrained animals.

It's not usually a good idea to take children under 5 to a theater production or a film, or even to show them a full-length video or DVD at home. Kids who are the same age will be at different levels of development and concentration. One person's favorite film can  be another's terrifying experience or a dull "been there, done that" time.

THeme

Many parties have a theme: fancy dress, a single color, or a character from a book or TV show. The theme can be carried through a few aspects or everything—from clothes, the color of the streamers, and the pictures on placemats to the design of the cake.

Party shops, organizers, and entertainers (check in the Yellow Pages or free parenting magazines) will supply helium balloons, decorations, hats, tablecloth, napkins, and paper plates to suit a theme, whether it's generic (such as dinosaurs) or specific (TV-show licensed products). Country folk can try ordering by mail or over the Internet, but honestly kids won't notice the difference if it's DIY and will have fun helping to make things and put up the decos.

Decorations

A few balloons and streamers should do the trick. A bunch of balloons tied to the front gate on the day will announce the party venue. If the party is in a park or other outdoorsy place, signs or balloons will help people find you.

Hired entertainment

Please remember that some kids under 5 will scream the house down if they see a giant animal, and it's no use explaining there's a person in it! (You don't ever see this in a magazine article about birthday parties because the party entertainment firms advertising in the magazine wouldn't like it.) Characters such as fairies and magicians are likely to be more successful, at least with older preschoolers. Face painters are always a hit. If you do hire an entertainer, try to get one whose good reputation precedes them, and a written quote beforehand.

LeNgtH of tHe PaRty

Parties for the under-fives are generally an hour and a half or 2 hours maximum (otherwise it's too much for kids and party givers). Mid-morning or early afternoon is a good time, ideally starting at 10:30 a.m. or 2 p.m. This allows for naps and avoids the late afternoon arsenic hour. A morning party avoids hours of anticipation and excitement fatigue. A weekend party is easier for everyone and most people prefer Saturday because Sunday is often a family day—but suit yourself. A sleep-over party at this age is complete insanity and no correspondence will be entered into.

NUMBeRS

One theory for 1- to 3-year-old parties is to keep the number of child guests to the kid's age plus one; in other words, for a 3-year-old's birthday party have four children. Some families have a tradition that the birthday child asks only two or three friends. Others invite ten, fifteen, or more, but it's doubtful whether your child will remember them all the next morning so why put yourself through the chaos? Of course this won't apply if you feel like an extravaganza or have stacks of helpers, or lots of friends and family with young children. (Even so, the kids themselves might find all the color and movement too much.)

Encourage other parents to stay rather than just drop their kids off, and have some adult food and drink for them (but perhaps not whisky sours).

HeLP aND SuPeRVISION

Marshal all the able-bodied friends and rellies you can to help on the day. Some people like to hire a babysitter who is well known to the kids. You might want to assign special tasks, including taking photos or a video, making sure the little ones are being included, and being in charge of hats and sunscreen.

The younger the kids, the more adults you'll need. One adult to four children isn't a bad ratio, but there's nothing wrong with one adult for each kid, especially tinies.

Make sure you make the party area safe for the youngest person there. For example, burst balloons are a choking hazard so need to be carefully cleaned up straight away.

If you are taking your child to someone else's party, you may want to stick around for the whole time. You may feel especially strongly about this if the party involves a park or water or you don't know the parents.

Some people combine adult frolicking with a children's party so several people may need to be Designated Kidwranglers (sober and alert). Even a small amount of alcohol can result in liver and brain damage in a small child: kids this young should never, ever be given even a "sip" of a drink with any alcohol in it. So if you're all having a droi whoite whoine, put it up somewhere hoi.

fooD

Personally, I think only lunatics try to serve tofu cake and bran granola at a kid's party (unless a child has allergies), but you can serve low-calorie lemonade to keep the sugar level down (forget soft drinks with caffeine in them). One mom suggests magic lemonade, using several food colorings. A drop of each color is put at the bottom of an individual clear plastic cup, then low-calorie lemonade is poured into every cup and the different colors appear like magic.

It's probably the excitement of the event that revs kids up the most, but serve protein and carbo things such as little sausages and cheese cubes as well as the sugary stuff with chemical additives. You can get some ideas from your party theme (jungle = tiger = peanut butter and jelly stripes on bread, for example).

Parents should let you know in advance if their child is allergic to common party food ingredients. Try not to use that food if possible and ask the child's parent to come to supervise. (Parents of kids with allergies should have some suggestions of what party foods they can eat and in extreme cases can BYO.)

Individual cupcakes can be easier for littlies to handle than a large slice of birthday cake and easier for you to distribute. The birthday kid's cupcake can be at the top of a stack with a candle in it.

Parties for little ones shouldn't include choking hazards such as marshmallows, whole nuts, popcorn, and corn chips.

Kids under 5 don't always eat a lot of the party food. Kids over 5 generally do. Don't take it personally.

PRESENTS

Often the birthday kid will open the presents as soon as they are offered and they can get over-excited and under-appreciative. You can set aside a special time for opening presents after the party has begun or dispatch an older child or helper to follow the flow of presents and keep a list of givers so that the birthday kid can write thank-you letters later. (You might like to use photos of the party as thank-you postcards.) Some party planners say your child should wait until everyone has gone home before opening their presents. You'll have to judge whether this is acceptable to your kid or whether the very thought would send them into orbit.

Some people will give inappropriate presents, especially well-meaning relatives. If a toy is too fragile for your child or not right for their age group, explain this in a kindly way privately later. Some people give expensive presents, but discourage this because it sets a difficult precedent. A kid will be just as happy with a packet of crayons or some brightly colored discount plastic bath toys as an elaborate toy.

If you're not sure about your idea for a present, check with the birthday kid's parent or caregiver. Always check safety labels on toys—and if an item looks unsafe, it probably is.

party games

Games need to be age specific and are best reserved for older preschoolers if introduced at all before age 6. Group activities are always less likely to cause violence, tantrums, or jealousy because nobody "wins" or "loses." Games that require high levels of dexterity or are set up for the fastest to win are bound to get out of hand and result in disappointment for many under-fives (see the Games and Activities Without Winners list coming up soon).

> *"Don't ask the children what they want to play. Just tell them what the next game is."* KIDS' RETAILING WEBSITE GATEFISH.COM

booty bags

Booty bags, also known as party bags, are a souvenir of the party given to each child guest. They can be as simple as a greaseproof bag with a piece of birthday cake in it or as artful as a party theme bag full of relevant goodies. Parents will appreciate it if the candy quota is low. (Maybe keep a couple of spare bags for potentially tearful unexpected guests such as siblings.)

Party shops have ready-made booty bags, but you can create your own. They can be sewn from felt or calico, or made by decorating ordinary brown-paper bags or takeaway-food boxes. One with handles is good. Buy either random or themed items from a toyshop such as a few pages of stickers, a packet of plastic animals, or something similar from the $1 shop, then throw in some candies from the supermarket. Spread the booty between the bags. Always give the booty bag to the child or their parent as they are walking out the door and not a moment sooner.

Party ideas for 1-year-olds

The consensus of opinion among parents is that a party for a 1-year-old is a ludicrous proposition likely to result in maximum stress for minimum impact on your kid. That doesn't mean you don't take a few nice photos, have a family lunch, or invite some friends over for a barbecue, just that major games, decorations, themes, and berzillions of guests is more about what *you* want than about what the baby will get out of it. The most common suggestion from the Kidwrangling Survey was: keep the first birthday to family only or extended family. But if you're keen, suggestions include ◎ bubble blowing ◎ a picnic ◎ afternoon snack ◎ lots of crunching of wrapping paper ◎ playing with boxes.

Presents for 1-year-olds

◎ A book ◎ a balloon ◎ clothes ◎ something to ride on such as a trike with a pole for the parents to push it with ◎ plastic bath toys ◎ toys that encourage hand-eye coordination such as hammering toys (a plastic hammer on its own will do) ◎ activity toys such as push-down pop-up things ◎ shape sorters ◎ toys that make a noise (but will the adults like the noise quite as much?) ◎ stackable rings, cups, or blocks ◎ soft, squeaky toys ◎ simple, safe musical instruments (clap sticks, not a tuba) ◎ balls with different sounds and textures ◎ mobiles and wind chimes ◎ a baby carriage or mower to push ◎ a tree that you can plant together and then take a photo of with your child in front, every birthday afterwards ◎ touchy-feely textured cloth books ◎ anything bright or musical that the baby can have an effect on (It opens! It squeaks!).

See also the Toys and Games for Babies chapter in *Part 1: Babies*.

> *"Keep it short, otherwise it's too overwhelming for them."*
> TERRESSA

Party ideas for 2-year-olds

Now that their kid is mobile, many parents are keen to introduce races with winners and games that are likely to result in a lot of adults yelling indecipherable encouragement to a bunch of confused, harassed 2-year-olds, but it might be better to wait until after the fifth or even sixth birthday for this. Suggestions included ◎ a family day ◎ a teddy bear's picnic (everyone brings their teddy—don't let them go home without them!) ◎ an indoor picnic (always a good option in winter) ◎ the sandpit ◎ the local playground ◎ playing with special toys from the toy library.

Presents for 2-year-olds

◎ A book ◎ large plastic click-together blocks ◎ simple musical instruments ◎ a *Teletubbies* or *Thomas the Tank Engine* video ◎ a plastic clamshell sandbox ◎ an easel ◎ big crayons ◎ playdough and plastic cookie cutters ◎ a tiny umbrella and rubber boots ◎ a soccer-type ball ◎ a bubble-blowing kit ◎ a dump truck ◎ something that squirts in the bath ◎ a tea set ◎ pull-along toys ◎ a library book with a library card and an explanation of what it's for ◎ toddler dishes and utensils ◎ a plastic tool set ◎ simple large puzzles ◎ a bucket and spade set.

See also the Toys and Games for Toddlers chapter in *Part 2: Toddlers*.

"Don't try to organize them—just let them be together."
LISA

PARTY IDEAS FOR 3-YEAR-OLDS

◎ Themes based on video or TV shows or characters such as Bob the Builder ◎ butterflies ◎ playdough ◎ Winnie-the-Pooh ◎ an indoor playground ◎ fairies and pixies ◎ a single color (for example, purple costumes and decorations) ◎ the local playground ◎ under the sea ◎ a music or dance party ◎ face painting (you'll need the special non-poisonous paints from a craft or toyshop—or you can hire the painter).

PRESENTS FOR 3-YEAR-OLDS

◎ A book ◎ big snap-together blocks ◎ dress-up outfits ◎ crayons ◎ trikes or ride-on wheeled things ◎ an age-specific jigsaw puzzle ◎ a creative kit with crayons, glue, and colored papers, in a bucket with a lid ◎ a plastic tool set ◎ playdough ◎ a rolling pin and plastic cookie cutters ◎ stickers ◎ a personal tape player with earphones and music or story tapes ◎ little cars ◎ a beach ball ◎ character dolls from TV or video shows they already love ◎ a backpack ◎ a tea set ◎ a kite.

See also the Toys and Games chapters in *Part 2: Toddlers* and *Part 3: Little Kids*.

PARTY IDEAS FOR 4-YEAR-OLDS

Rather than traditional only-one-winner games it may be better to have non-specific treasure hunts. Suggestions included ◉ book themes such as Curious George, Bob the Builder, and Madeline ◉ a fish or underwater world ◉ fairies ◉ pink ◉ a beach party in winter (if you have a good heater!) ◉ winter snow party (throw white sheets or tarpaulin over everything and make an "igloo") ◉ disco dancing ◉ dress-ups or come-in-a-costume ◉ dinosaurs ◉ super-heroes or another fad ◉ old-fashioned games ◉ an indoor play center ◉ rockets and space, with themed costumes and food. See also the suggestions for 3- and 5-year-olds.

PRESENTS FOR 4-YEAR-OLDS

◉ A book ◉ a video (try the PBS selections) ◉ toy money and a cash register for playing shops ◉ an age-appropriate jigsaw puzzle ◉ dinosaurs ◉ a train set ◉ a bat and soft ball ◉ puppets ◉ stick-on stars and moons ◉ colored pencils ◉ a drawing-paper book (coloring books are okay but tend to discourage creativity) ◉ a travel pack with interesting activities for the car ◉ stamps and an ink pad ◉ a book about letters or numbers ◉ a first training bike ◉ a doll's house ◉ a hat ◉ children's gardening tools ◉ stickers ◉ a trip to the zoo ◉ children's magnets.

See also the Toys and Games for Preschoolers chapter in *Part 3: Little Kids*.

> *"We didn't try any games with the 4-year-olds. (I've given that up; it's like herding cats.)"* MOM ON A BIRTHDAY-PARTY MARKETING WEBSITE

GAMES AND ACTIVITIES WITHOUT WINNERS

✱ Statues: play bursts of music and each time the music stops everyone has to freeze.

✱ I'm with the band: put on some kid-friendly music, give each child an instrument, and let them march about. Simple dancing to the music is also an option.

✱ Bubble blowing: give everyone a wand to dip into a bowl (or old hub cap) filled with bubble mixture.

✱ A piñata: let everyone have a go at whacking a brightly decorated hollow papier-mâché shape, hung from a tree or a corner of the clothes line, until it breaks and showers down candies and trinkets. Traditionally, long sticks have been used, but a toddler-sized plastic baseball bat is a good whacker. You can make a piñata yourself with a balloon and papier-mâché (although you'll need to get the thickness right otherwise the kids will be whacking all day or it will break at the first hit), or

you can buy a ready-made one at a kids' party shop. This game has to be very closely supervised so no one gets hurt and each child has one go at a time (perhaps with some hefty adult whacks to the piñata every now and again to start it breaking open).

✱ Create a banner or a table-cloth: provide an old sheet or a huge length of paper, some pre-mixed paints, felt-tip pens, crayons, glitter glue, and whatever else takes your fancy and let them at it. Perhaps kids can take their shoes and socks off and make hand- and footprints (make sure an art-party invitation says to wear old clothes and why).

✱ A treasure hunt: hide the treasures—stickers and small but non-hazardous toys and lollipops are good—before the guests arrive and keep a few emergency ones in your pocket to sprinkle near a kid who hasn't had any luck.

✱ Paint your own: buy some cheap white T-shirts, pillowcases, or hankies and let the kids decorate them with fabric paints. This is best done in summer when their creations can dry on the line before the party ends.

✱ Story time: have a good storyteller or actor (every family should have one) read a book to the kids. It could be one that matches the theme of your party.

✱ Pass the Package to music: make a package with many layers of wrapping and put a little novelty gift (one for every child) between each. You'll need someone good on the music control to make sure each child gets a present.

✱ Pass the Treasure Chest (a good alternative to Pass the Package, at the end of the party): when the music stops the kid with the small chest opens the lid, takes a lucky-dip prize, and passes the chest on.

✱ Other old-fashioned games: teach the kids hopscotch, Simon Says, Follow the Leader, or very simple charades ("What's this animal?"). No penalties or prizes for getting it "wrong." Lots of traditional games for kids under 5 and older children can be sourced on the Internet (see More Info at the end of this chapter) or learned from older rellies.

✱ Forts and tunnels: put up a tent for a fort and make tunnels (perhaps from sheets) the kids can crawl through.

Not-so-good games for under-fives' parties include hide and seek ("Oh, there you are, in the poisons cabinet!'"), sack races, any game with more than one or two rules, and anything that requires a helmet or changing clothes quickly.

"Guess what the photos were on the start of that roll we finished at the fourth birthday party? The photos from her third birthday party!"
TIRED-LOOKING GUY IN LOCAL DRUG STORE, LOOKING AT HIS DEVELOPED PHOTOS

PaRTy iDeas foR 5-yeaR-oLDs

◎ A favorite book theme ◎ a builder theme ◎ fairies ◎ a puppet show with lots of audience participation ◎ sing songs ◎ dress as your favorite book character ◎ making mini-pizzas ◎ insects ◎ farm animals ◎ a treasure hunt ◎ craft activities ◎ a barbecue ◎ witches and wizards ◎ spiders ◎ wildlife ◎ a highly supervised piñata ◎ non-score-keeping soccer.

PRESeNTs foR 5-yeaR-oLDs

◎ A book ◎ a disposable camera and a photo album ◎ a kaleidoscope ◎ musical instruments ◎ beach toys and gear ◎ plastic, elasticized jewelery ◎ a game such as dominoes or checkers ◎ a kid's pack of cards ◎ balls of all sizes ◎ art supplies ◎ school equipment such as a backpack, a lunch box, or a pencil case ◎ a video ◎ a soccer ball ◎ a costume or clothing ◎ a flashlight ◎ a board game ◎ a story or music tape ◎ a construction kit ◎ a cookbook ◎ a frisbee.

See also the Toys and Games for Preschoolers chapter in *Part 3: Little Kids*.

"We hatched dinosaurs—a balloon that the kids had to burst so they could eat the dinosaur candies inside; dinosaur egg hunt (mini-Easter eggs), and dinosaur bone search (bone-shaped dog biscuits in the sandbox). The party was a huge success." ANITA

more info

Local parents magazines usually carry pages of party folk for hire. These magazines are usually free at child-centered venues such as day-care centers.

Clever Party Planning: Party Planning Ideas and Themes for Kids, Teens, and Adults
A complete guide of clever party themes for children, teenagers, and adults. Includes ideas for invitations, decorations, games, cakes, food, and more.

The Ultimate Birthday Party Book: 50 Complete and Creative Themes to Make Your Kid's Special Day Fantastic!
by Susan Baltrus, Chariot Victor Pub, 2002.
Focuses on money-saving, creative ways to host parties for your kids. Includes 50 different party theme ideas.

Penny Whistle Birthday Party Book
by Meredith Brokaw, Fireside, 1992.
Features fun suggestions for theme parties including a pig-out party, a secret agent party, or a chocolate factory party.

www.birthdaypartyideas.com
A website with a huge list of ideas for kids parties, complete with suggestions for decorations, games, activities, and invitations, and each party idea is rated by other parents.

www.partykids.com.au
Ideas, games, themes, and merchandise from an Australian site: you don't have to buy; you could just get inspired.

www.birthdayexpress.com
A website full of ideas and inspiration.

www.childrensparties.com.au

A commercial Australian website with good links to kids' games on the web and hints for planning a party.

BIRTHDAY CAKES

Happy Birthday: 22 Spectacularly Easy Birthday Cakes

by Anna Con Marbug, Allen and Unwin, 2003.

The authors offer 22 cakes that are easy and quick to make, but still creative and fun.

extra
Resources

*

CANADIAN CONTACTS

Canada has a very civilized system of nationalized health care and assistance to help working mothers.

Government of Canada

Canada's national website has a downloadable brochure titled *Services for Children: Guide to Government of Canada Services for Children and Their Families,* which provides descriptions of more than 100 programs and services that are offered by the government. These guides are also available in large print, on audio cassette, in Braille, or on computer diskette by calling 1-800-O-Canada.
http://canada.gc.ca/cdns/children_e.html

Caring for Kids

Child health information from the Canadian Pediatric Society. You can locate a doctor or get helpful information on a wide variety of topics.
www.caringforkids.cps.ca

About Kids Health

The website of the Hospital for Sick Children, one of the largest pediatric teaching hospitals in the world. You can access information about medical conditions
www.aboutkidshealth.ca

Canadian Health Network

Their site features extensive information on hundreds of health topics and links to authoritative articles and information.
www.canadian-health-network.ca

Child & Family Canada

Offers articles and resources on child development, child care, family life, health, learning activities, play, safety, social issues, and special needs from 60 Canadian nonprofit organizations.
www.cfc-efc.ca/

National Domestic Violence Hotline

Counselors can provide help and advice covering all provinces. Bilingual (English and French).

1-800-363-9010

Gymboree

For play gyms in your area.

www.gymboree.com

Safe Kids Canada

Safe Kids Canada provides information on how to prevent childhood injuries.

1-888-SAFE TIPS (723-3847)

www.safekidscanada.ca

CHILDREN'S HOSPITALS

National Association of Children's Hospitals (NACHRI)

A searchable database of more than 200 children's hospitals across the country. You can search by name, state, medical specialties, care programs, community outreach programs, camps for children with special needs, or by keyword. You can also locate your local children's hospitals on this site.

www.childrenshospitals.net

Open Directory Project

Alphabetical list and links to 74 major US children's hospitals.

http://dmoz.org/Health/Medicine/Facilities/Children/United_States/

Joint Commission on Accreditation of Healthcare Organizations (JCAHO)

The Joint Commission (JCAHO) is an independent, not-for-profit organization, that sets the standards by which health care quality is measured in America. They visit each hospital and grade them on medication use, anesthesia care, infection control, and more. A list of JCAHO accredited hospitals and organizations and their survey results are posted on the website. You can also call JCAHO's Customer Service Department directly at 630-792-5800 for additional information.

www.jcaho.org

US News and World Reports—Best Hospitals 2004: Pediatrics

The popular news magazine lists the top 29 hospitals ranked by reputation. Hospitals were named by at least 3 percent of the specialists responding to *U.S. News* surveys in 2002, 2003, and 2004.

www.usnews.com/usnews/health/hosptl/rankings/specreppedi.htm

DOWN SYNDROME ASSOCIATIONS

National Down Syndrome Society

Organizers of the "Buddy Walk," an annual walk that takes place in 17 locations across the country to promote acceptance and awareness of people with Down syndrome. The website features an extensive database of services available to parents, listed for each state.

1-800-221-4602

www.ndss.org

National Down Syndrome Congress

An organization that works to influence public policy and research. It also provides education and information on self-advocacy and rights for people with Down syndrome.

1-800-232-NDSC

www.ndsccenter.org

National Parent to Parent Support & Information Systems, Inc. (NPPSIS)

This organization is for parents who want to contact other parents of children with Down syndrome.

1-800-651-1151

National Association for Down Syndrome (NADS)

NADS provides critical counseling and support for parents of babies with Down syndrome as well as advocacy, referral, and information services.

www.nads.org

Club Down Syndrome

A website for kids (and adults) with Down syndrome.

www.clubndss.org

FAMILY VIOLENCE

National Domestic Violence Hotline

Couselors are available to answer calls 24 hours a day, 365 days a year. Provides support and referrals to local services (database of more than 4,000 shelters and service providers across the United States, Puerto Rico, Alaska, Hawaii and the Virgin Islands).

1-800-799-7233

American Domestic Violence Crisis Line

An organization that provides international outreach to Americans overseas. The hotline is open from 10 p.m. to 6 a.m., Pacific Standard Time to allow overseas clients to contact them from various time zones.

3300 N.W. 185th Street, Suite 133

Portland, OR 97229

Toll-free: 1-866-USWOMEN

Child Help USA

The hotline is staffed by counselors who are available 24 hours a day, every day of the year. All calls are anonymous and toll-free. The hotline counselors can help you with your child's problem behaviors and suggest skills and strategies a parent can use to try to change their responses which haven't been working.

1-800-4-A-CHILD (1-800-422-4453)

www.childhelpusa.org

Parents Anonymous

Support groups for parents. You can call their hotline to find a group near you.
1-800-345-5044

www.parentsanonymous.org

Seven-Step Escape Plan

* Have a secret signal arranged with a friend, or more than one friend, for use in an emergency—a special word or sentence that means to come and help or call the police. * Have an excuse ready about why you need to leave quickly and rehearse it so the abusive partner won't be suspicious. * Always carry change or a phone card for phone calls. * Leave a list of emergency numbers with your friend, or somewhere else so that it's hidden but easy to get to. * Organize a safe place to go to in an emergency. Ask your friend to show you where they hide a key to their house. Or it may be safer to use a house that your partner doesn't know about—that of a friend's relative or a friend's friend. * Prepare an escape bag and hide it somewhere safe, or at a friend's house: it could have emergency cash, spare car and house keys, and copies of legal documents and ID. * Call the helplines listed above to find out how the police or a women and children's shelter can offer you protection.

Domestic Violence Services for Abusers

There are many resources available in most communities for helping men and women who want to change their own behavior, but these programs are usually local. Contact your local community health center for resources and counseling that may be available.

GAY FAMILIES

Family Pride Coalition

A national organization that advocates the rights of lesbian, gay, bisexual, and transgendered parents and provides support to local parenting groups.
P.O. Box 50360
Washington, DC 20091
202-583-8029
www.familypride.org

Gay Parent magazine
P.O. Box 750852
Forest Hills, New York 11375-0852
718-997-0392
www.gayparentmag.com

2Moms2Dads
A website with lots of links to articles all over the net about gay families and
gay parenting.
www.2moms2dads.com

GOVERNMENT SERVICES

www.firstgov.gov
The US government's official website lists government services available for
parents. Call the National Contact Center toll-free at 1-800-FED-INFO.

www.GovBenefits.gov
You can find out if you are eligible for any
government benefits at this website. You
can also call 1-800-333-4636.

Administration for Children & Families
The Administration for Children and Families (ACF) is a federal agency funding state, territory, local, and tribal organizations to provide family assistance
(welfare), child support, child care, Head Start, child welfare, and other programs relating to children and families. On their site, you can locate local
contacts for a large variety of parenting issues from child care to child support
to fun stuff for kids. An excellent resource for government programs and help.
www.acf.dhhs.gov

The National Family Support Mapping Project
The Family Support America mapping project locates and collects information
on every family support program in the country and is working to create a
national database of comprehensive information on family support programs.

This is the place to go to find local programs, organizations, and resources. You can search by state, expertise, service, setting, or keyword. Site also has links to articles and essays on a variety of family related topics.
312-338-0900
www.familysupportamerica.org/content/mapping_dir/find.asp

United States Department of Health and Human Services—Families and Children

Has links to everything from child dental health to prenatal care, multiples, head start programs, and child safety.
www.hhs.gov/children/index.shtml

Public Libraries

Your public library is a great resource for finding information about local public services and programs for children.

Insure Kids Now, a program of the US Department of Health and Human Services

If you can't afford health insurance, call to see if your children are eligible for free or low-cost health insurance. Website provides links to each state's Children's Health Insurance Program.
1-877-KIDS-NOW (1-877-543-7669)
www.insurekidsnow.gov/states.htm

LOSS AND GRIEF

When a fetus is lost before it would have been able to survive on its own, this is usually called miscarriage. If a "viable" baby dies before it can be born or is born dead, this is usually called a stillbirth. Other even less thoughtful words may be used by medical professionals.

First Candle organization offers support for parents who are experiencing loss and grief in different circumstances (see the section on Sudden Infant Death syndrome later on).

Miscarriage

Because early miscarriage is so common (believed to be up to one in five pregnancies), many people, including some doctors, suggest you simply try again. But it's important to talk to your obstetrician or another medical specialist in fertility or pregnancy and request any blood tests or surgical procedures that may help determine whether you have a problem (for example, with blood clotting, or your uterus or cervix) that could cause recurrent miscarriage before trying to become pregnant again. You may be able to take preventative steps next time.

The Infertility Survival Handbook: Everything You Never Thought You'd Need to Know
by Elizabeth Swire Falker, Riverhead Books, 2004.
A popular book from a woman who spent seven years trying to get pregnant. She explains all of the tests and options for people dealing with fertility problems.

Websites

Use a search engine such as www.google.com to find websites that are relevant to any diagnosis you may have had of the cause of your miscarriage. For example, if you have been diagnosed with a "factor V Leiden" problem (a blood clotting disorder), you can search variations on the name to find such sites as www.fvleiden.org and www.naturalchildbirth.org/natural/resources/prebirth/prebirth35.htm.

COUNSELING AND HELP
SHARE (National Office)
Offers support to families who have had a miscarriage, stillbirth, or infant death. Provides a newsletter, network of worldwide support groups, literature, and referrals.
St. Joseph's Health Center
300 First Capitol Drive
St. Charles, MO 63301-2893
1-800-821-6819

time to use the phone!

M.I.S.S. (Mothers In Sympathy & Support)

M.I.S.S. provides support to parents confronted with the death of a baby, including babies who have died before being born. They offer grief education for parents and professionals and can direct you to a local chapter.

623-979-1000

www.misschildren.org

Helping After Neonatal Death (HAND)

A volunteer group that provides support and information to bereaved parents, their families and friends following a miscarriage or the death of a baby.

www.handonline.org

The Compassionate Friends

A national parent-to-parent support group. There's lots of valuable information at this site for parents who have lost children of any age under any circumstance. There is information on local chapters.

www.compassionatefriends.org

Still Fathers

Targeted toward the needs of grieving Dads.

www.stillfathers.org

TRYING AGAIN

Trying Again: A Guide to Pregnancy After Miscarriage, Stillbirth, and Infant Loss

by Ann Douglas and John Sussman, Taylor Trade Publishing, 2000.

Selected excerpts can be read on www.having-a-baby.com.

RELATIONSHIPS

The American Psychological Association's Help Center

Free brochures, links to articles, and psychologist referrals.

1-800-964-2000 (for a local APA referral.)

http://helping.apa.org/

American Association for Marriage and Family Therapy
Can help you locate a family therapist near you, links to recommended books or articles on specific family problems.
www.aamft.org/index_nm.asp

The Family & Marriage Counseling Directory
A Nationwide Directory for counselors and therapists in local areas and links to articles about families, relationships, and counseling.
http://family-marriage-counseling.com/index.htm

SINGLE, SOLE, AND SHARED-CUSTODY PARENTS
Parents Without Partners
An international organization devoted to the interests of single parents and their children. Provides help by offering discussions, professional speakers, study groups, publications, and social activities for families and adults. Their website features a search engine to find your local chapter.
561-391-8833
www.parentswithoutpartners.org

National Organization of Single Mothers
Can put you in touch with a group in your area, give practical advice, and inform you of your rights and entitlements.
704-888-5437
www.singlemothers.org

Federal Office of Child Support Enforcement
www.acf.dhhs.gov/programs/cse/

The Single Mother's Survival Guide
by Patrice Karst, Crossing Press, 2000.
Covers the practicalities of being a parent without a partner; child care; dating; rights; and more.

SPINA BIFIDA AND NEURAL TUBE PROBLEMS

Spina Bifida Association of America
Locate local chapters and spina bifida clinics on the website or call for a referral.
1-800-621-3141
www.sbaa.org

SUDDEN INFANT DEATH SYNDROME (SIDS)

First Candle: The SIDS Alliance Support Center
Provides information on ways that may help to prevent SIDS. The organization also has counselors for parents who are grieving.
1-800-221-7437
http://firstcandle.org/

National SIDS Resource Center
The National SIDS/Infant Death Resource Center (NSIDRC) provides information services and technical assistance on sudden infant death syndrome (SIDS) and related topics.
703-821-8955
www.sidscenter.org

Sudden Infant Death Syndrome & Other Infant Death (SIDS/OID) Network
Extremely comprehensive website on all aspects of infant death. Includes searchable database to help find local resources and programs.
www.sids-network.org

TEENAGE MOMS

Community health centers, women's health centers, family planning clinics, your doctor, and religious centers often have young mom groups or can point you in the right direction for career advice, somewhere to live, financial help, and help looking after your baby. Check under community services in the yellow pages.

WOMEN'S HOSPITALS

About one-third of hospitals across the country have a Women's Health Center, and there are hundreds of private practices specializing in women's health. The following Women's Health Centers are designated by the US government as National Centers of Excellence in Women's Health, and are considered some of the best centers in the country that specialize in women's issues, ranging from pregnancy to breast cancer to mental illness.

CALIFORNIA

University of California, Los Angeles National Center of Excellence in Women's Health

100 UCLA Medical Plaza Dr., Suite 290

Los Angeles, CA 90095-7075

Clinical services contact: 1-800-825-2631

University of California, San Francisco National Center of Excellence in Women's Health

2356 Sutter Street, 1st Floor, Box 1694

San Francisco, CA 94143-1694

Clinical services contact: 415-353-2668

ILLINOIS

University of Illinois at Chicago Center of Excellence in Women's Health

1640 West Roosevelt Road, Room 503

Chicago, IL 60608

Clinical services contact: 1-800-UIC-1002

INDIANA

Indiana University School of Medicine National Center of Excellence in Women's Health

535 Barnhill Drive, RT-150

Indianapolis, IN 46202

Clinical services contact: 317-630-2243

LOUISIANA

Tulane Xavier National Center of Excellence in Women's Health

Universities of Louisiana

Tulane University School of Public Health and Tropical Medicine

127 Elks Place, EP-7

New Orleans, LA 70112

Clinical services contact: 1-877-588-5100

MASSACHUSETTS

Boston University Center of Excellence in Women's Health

Boston University Medical Center

720 Harrison Avenue

Doctor's Office Building, Suite 1108

Boston, MA 02118

Clinical services contact: 617-638-7428

Harvard Medical School Women's Hospital

75 Francis Street, Neville 210

Boston, MA 02115

Clinical services contact: 1-800-417-4423

MICHIGAN

University of Michigan Health System Department of Obstetrics, Gynecology

1342 Taubman Center (Level One)

1500 E. Medical Center Dr., Room L-4000

Ann Arbor, MI 48109-0276

Clinical services contact: 734-936-8886

PENNSYLVANIA

Magee-Womens Hospital University of Pittsburgh

Department of Obstetrics, Gynecology, and Reproductive Sciences

300 Halket Street

Pittsburgh, PA 15213-3180

Clinical services contact: 412-647-4747

Drexel University Institute for Women's Health and Leadership

The Gatehouse

3300 Henry Avenue

Philadelphia, PA 19129

Clinical services contact: 215-842-7007

PUERTO RICO

University of Puerto Rico, The Women and Health Center

Medical Sciences Campus

P.O. Box 365067

San Juan, PR 00936-5067

Clinical services contact: 787-764-3707

WASHINGTON

University of Washington, Women's Health Care Center

4245 Roosevelt Way NE , 3rd Floor

Campus Box 354765

Seattle, WA 98105

Clinical services contact: 1-800-826-1121

WISCONSIN

UW Center for Women's Health & Women's Health Research

6W-Meriter, Park

202 South Park Street

Madison, WI 53715

Clinical services contact: 608-267-5566

acknowledgments

This book is dedicated to my mother, for all the kindnesses she showed me as a small girl and for doing the best she could even though when I was four I told the greengrocer she had a beard on her bottom.

Executive Publisher: Julie Gibbs.

Editor and structural engineer: the incomparable Lesley Dunt.

Book designer: the amazing Sandy Cull.

Proofreader and editrixter: Jane Drury.

Editorial assistance: Lindy Leonhardt; Cora Roberts.

Indexer: Fay Donlevy.

Production controllers: Carmen De La Rue; Leah Maarse.

Typesetters (Dog's Breakfast Wranglers): Lisa and Ron Eady, Post Pre-press Group, Brisbane.

Kidwrangling Survey: Danielle Roller (publicity); Sofia Levers (website).

Publicist: Natalie Kaplan.

Bless the wondrous, assiduous and generous consultants (although obviously all the responsibility for what info finally ended up in the book is mine or, in the case of mistakes, my evil twin sister Deirdre's). I would especially like to thank the splendid people who work at the Royal Children's Hospital in Melbourne: many of them helped often and cheerily.

Sleeping, crying, eating, routines, pacifiers, postpartum depression: the indefatigable Gina Ralston, Education Network Manager, Tweddle Child and Family Health Service, Melbourne.

Psychological and emotional development consultant: Frances Thomson-Salo, child psychotherapist, Royal Children's Hospital, Melbourne.

Immunization: Jennifer Irwin, Immunisation Centre co-ordinator and nurse, Dr Jenny Royle, Immunization Centre pediatrician, and Dr Nigel Curtis, infectious diseases and pediatrics specialist, of the Royal Children's Hospital, Melbourne.

General medical consultants: Dr Michael Harari, pediatrician, Royal Children's Hospital, Melbourne; GP Dr David Ungar; paramedic Suzie Spence, Launceston; Prof. David Brewster, head of pediatrics, Royal Darwin Hospital (on babies being too hot); Dr Graham Bury, Medical Director, Women's and Children's Department, Royal Hobart Hospital (on babies being too cold); Dr Michael Rice, AMA council member and pediatric specialist, Adelaide Women's and Children's Hospital (on fever drugs).

Boobs: Margaret Callaghan, lactation consultant.

Newborns, boobs: Melanie Dunlop, midwife.

New mom health: obstetrics specialist Dr Len Kliman.

Exercise: Dr Elizabeth Waters, Director of Research and Public Health, the Centre for Community Child Health, Melbourne.

Cooking for kids: Fiona Wood; Maggie Beer.

Nutrition: Beth Martino, head of dietetics, Princess Margaret Hospital for Children, Perth; Jenny Taylor, acting chief dietician, Royal Women's Hospital, Melbourne; Alexia O'Callaghan, Nutrition and Food Services, Royal Children's Hospital, Melbourne.

Head lice: Susan Anido, Therapeutic Goods Administration.

Child care and development: Susan Deffert; Cornelia Zisu; Caitlin Mason; Kate Hall.

Mental health: Paul Morgan, SANE Australia.

Sun care: Stephanie Harper; Kenton Miller; Cancer Council.

SIDS: Deb Withers; Dorothy Ford; SIDS and Kids.

Safety: Helen Rowan, Child Health Information Centre; Mary Beech, Safety Centre, Royal Children's Hospital, Melbourne.

Helpful suggestions: Jacinta Nancarrow (on breastfeeding); Clare Forster (on twins); Virginia Lumsden, ABC children's television; Ron Saunders, independent producer (children's TV); Kate Mortensen of the Australian Breastfeeding Association's Lactation Resource Centre; and many others.

Research: Sarah Dawson (the groundwork on crying, ear infections, gastro, sleeping, dummies, feeling overwhelmed, newborn worries, autism, routines, circumcision and developmental milestones).

Contacts checking: Nicci Dodanwela; Shannan Harris.

Publishing details research: Chronicles bookshop, St Kilda; Siobhan Jones.

Technical support: MacAdvice, Melbourne; Gail Davidson, Rivet Design.

Travel: an early version of the chapter on travel appeared in the *Sydney Morning Herald* and *The Age* in 2000.

Professional Support Services: the splendid Kevin Whyte and staff of Token Artists.

Personal Support Services: TLG; J. Lucy; Reginaldo.

Stern words at right moment: P. Hawker.

Protype: Ooftus McGooftus.

Thanks to Carrie Rodrigues, Marchelle Brain, and Betsy Stromberg for their work on the US edition.

Kidwrangling Survey respondents (their names appear here as they identified themselves and if anyone has been left out, my sincere apologies): Anne; Anne and Cathy; Annette; Cassie; Hazel; Helen; Hil; J; Jane; Jo; Jacqueline; Jacqueline; Jacqueline; Jill; Karen; Michelle; Petrina; Robyn; Samantha; Kirsty Addison; Heidi Ahrone; Jane Akhurst; Jeanette Albiston; Tracy Allan; Nada Amalfi; Liliane Ammerlaan; Helen Anderson; Leanne Andrews; Cathy Anthofer; Tracey Arnold; Nava Ashurst; Elena Avignone; Jenny Ayliffe; Lara B; Anna Backman; Alice Bailey; Leanne Bailey; Louise Baker; Joelle Ball-Potter; Kellie Ballard; Lydia Banham; Sally Barlee; Wendy Barnes; Elizabeth Barnett; Deanne Baronoff; Jillian Barr; Kris Barrett; Jane Barry; Kerryn Barry; Kate Bartlett; Lynette Bartley; Peg Bartley; Michelle Barton; Tracey Bartz; Marina Bassham; Joanne Basso; Rosie Bates; Deb Batley; Rita Battaglin; Donna Battams; Jodie Baxter; Jeanette Beales; Julie Beauchamp; Mrs Betty Bedford; Mary Bedford; Karen Beggs; Kerry Behrend; Diane Belle; Lisa Bellotti; Prue Beltz;

ACKNOWLEDGMENTS

Luke Bennett; Tes Benton; Kylie Bertram-Bona; Margaret Bester; Catherine Betcher; Simone Bewg; Kierann Bielski; Rebecca Billingham; Dianne Birch; Fleur Bishop; Nancee Biviano; Shiree Bladwell; Fiona Blake; Fiona Bligh; Rob Blum; Wendy Blyth; Mary Bocock; Katie Boney; Hilary Bonney; Linda Boots; Sergeja Bosanac; Pauline Bosnjak; Esther Boucher; Sharon Bouterakos; Michelle Bowker; Box Hill Early Childhood; Julie Boxsell; Brenda Boyd; Kate Boyle; Lisa Bradbury; Nicole Brady; Selina Brendish; Cathy Brennan; Lisa Brennan; Larissa Brenner; Wendy Brereton; Sharynn Britten; Penny Bronar; Lisa Brookman; Louise Brooks; Amanda Brown; Audrey Brown; Fiona Brown; Suzi Brown; Toni Brown; Sue Brunner; Paula Bryant; Mellissa Buchanan; Sarah Buckley; Carolyn Burns; Maureen Burns; Michelle Burpee; Tiffany Burstow; Jennifer Burton; Lisa Byleveld; Karen Cahill; Dianne Cain; Deborah Caldera; Laura Caldwell; Sandra Caligari; Chris Callaghan; Leanne Callaghan; Janice Campbell; Margaret Carew; Kate Carey; Diana Carroll; Robyn Carroll; Sally-Anne Carroll; Kylie Carse; Ann Carstens; Sarah Carter; Caroline Cass; Robyn Causley; Rachel Cavanagh; Ursula Chambel; Carrie-Anne Chandler; Fiona Channon; Caroline Chappell; Jeanette Charman; Mara Chase; Lisa Chawner; Sandra Cheyne; Kerryn Chia; Pat Child; Marj Christion; Joanne Christodoulou; Janice Ciechomski; Sophie Clapperton; Jill Clarke; Julie Clarke; Jeannine Cleeve; Katie Clements; Sharon Coates; Fiona Cochrane; Malira Cocking; Hayley Cole; Leonore Colgan; Susan Collard; Linda Colley; Anne Collins; Fran Collins; Kerry Collins; Claire Collis; Garda Collison; Dominique Comber-Sticca; Julia Comrie; Johanna Connelly; Kate Constable; Verco Cook; Maree Coote; Maria Costello; Samantha Cotton; Jeanette Cowcill; Kaye Cowell; Diane Cowie; Kate Cox; Loyce Cox-Paton; Sue Coyle; Molly Coyne; Rebecca Crabb; Dot Crane; Tracey Crosby; Jude Crossley; Tamsin Crutch; Belinda Cullen; Kellie Cumming; Elise Cummins; Sarah Cunningham; Melinda Dal Bosco; Kris Daly; Jane Darrou; Nicholas Dask; Anna Davidson; Joanne Davies; Tobie-Jane Davies; Emma Davis; John Day; Karen De Bruijn; Hilary Delbridge; Kate Delbridge; Helen Denning; Amanda Dennis-Clarke; Karen Dethomas; Cath Dickens; Megan Dicker; Amanda Diggens; Mira Dixon; Julie Dodd; Dawn Dolinski; Nicole Donovan; Edward Dowling; Ted Dowling; Mary Doyle; Jacqueline Draffan; Dominique Du Cros; Angie Duggan; Mark Duggan; Marie Dunn; Wendy Dunstan; Marie Dyling; Lois Eastley; Dale Eather; Nicky Edwards; Tanya Edwards; Sam Eeles; Linda Egan; Gaye Ellifson-Ryan; Ann Elliott; Terri Ellmer; Fiona Erskine; Stephanie Erwin; Lucinda Esler; Kathy Ettershank; Nola Evangelou; Mary F; Rowena Faenza; Lucy Fahey; Leanne Fallins; Christine Fay; Nadine Fenton; Elizabeth Ferguson; Kajsa Ferguson; Karen Ferguson; Kelly Ferguson; Sue Ferguson; Debbie Fewster; Julie Finemore; Lynda Fitzsimmons; Caren Florance; Mary Flowers; Angela Flux; Robyn Foggo; Kate Fontyn; Donna Ford; Kylie Forno; Shelley Forssman; Lynda Foulis; Tara Fox; Melanie Franklin; Tiffany Fraser-Gillard; Kathryn Freeman; Susan Frowd; Sharon Fry; Lesley Gallimore; Mary Gallop; Kim Galt; Anne Galvin; Jayne Garrod; Jane Gaspar; Kathy Gaudiosi; Kellie Gaukrodger; Karin Gaylard; Emma Gedge; Claire Gee; Patricia George; Kate Giesaitis; Amanda Gilbee; Vanessa Gilbert; Tracey Giles; Kellie Gill; Mary Gilroy; Linda Gittens; Julia Gobbert; Natasha Godfrey; Lennart Goedhart; Sally Goodwin; Julie Gordin; Jan Gosden; Karyn Gottschling; Opal Gough; Heather Gould; Judith Grace; Sue Grant; Carolyn Gray; Penny Grebert; Jenny Green; Sally Green; Chris Greenough; Bill Greenshields; Michelle Griffin; G. Grime; Joanne Groud; Tirzah Grudgfield; Amanda Guest; Melissa Guilmartin; Carolyn Hagl; Meg Haines; Melanie Hall; Kate Hallberg; Cherrie Halliday; Karen Hamilton; Sonja Hamilton; Judith Hansberry; Lorelei Harb; Lisa Harbinson; Tom Harley; Elisha Harris; Nicky Harris; Rebecca Harris; Belinda Hass; Annita Hathaway; Cindy Hattingh; Julie Hawes; Nicole Hayes; Vanessa Hayes;

ACKNOWLEDGMENTS

Jane Healey; Joanne Heffernan; Mandy Henby; April Henderson; Janet Herl; Wilma Herrero; Leanne Heselden; Dani Hewton; Libby Hick; Kylee Hickey; Janet Hoar; Beck Hodge; Jodie Hodge; Sandra Hodgen; Vicki Hodges; Toni Hohn; Emma-Jane Holden; Amanda Hollis; Ricci Holterman; Lesley Honeysett; Nicole Hookey; Gemma Hopetoun-Smith; Melissa Horton; Chris Hortop; Michelle Hose; Simone Hosie; Karan Hudson; Juliette Hughes Norwood; Robyn Humphries; Joanne Hunnisett; Ann Hyde; Anne Hyde; Kelly Hyland; Melanie Ingham; Louise Inglis; Liz Ingram; Caroline Ives; Carol Jack; Mandy Jackson; Tanya Jackson-Vaughan; Kathrine Jacobsen; Ann James; Lisa Jamieson; Merewyn Janson; Lisa Janssen; Carolyn Jensen; Linda Johnson; Tracy Johnston; Anne Jolly; Karen Joncour; Jeannie-Maree Jones; Mary Jones; Samantha Jones; Christine Jordan; Leanne Jordan; Karina Juncal; Allison Kaefer; Fiona Kajewski; Vicki Kakoulis; Merrin Kambouris; Danielle Karis; Shelley Karo; Brenda Katc; Junine Keala; Julia Kearney; Donna Keenan; Melanie Keir; Madelyn Kelly; Sian Kelly; Sue Kemp; Zak Kemp; Zak Kempster; Debbie Kenny; Kathleen Kenny; Jean Kerr; Samantha Killender-Brennan; Michael King; Denise Kirkham; Rebecca Kittel; Alexis Klaebe; Michelle Klass; Amylee Knight; Sophie Knight; Stephanie Knowles; Rachael Kokke; Debbie Kopel; Kylee Kornhaber; Wendy Kosenko; Kylie Kreckler; Nicole L; Vicki Ladson; Anita Landles; Anita Langenberg; Jacqui Lawlis; Kaylene Lawn; Mary Lawson; Kirstin Laxton; Tabitha Lean; Mrs Leah Leckie; Christine Lee; Juliette Lee; Debby Leiper; Carole Lemon; Sue Lennie; Beth Lessells; Jenny Levett; Deborah Lewis; Joanne Lewis; Amy Li; Lisa Liber; Kim Liddell; Amelia Likely; Ann Linzner; Nicole Livaditis; Michelle Loman; Rebecca Lovering; Matt Lowe; Tracey Lowry; Supergin Lucashenko; Louise Luke; Patty Lygris; Joy Lyle; Kristine Lynch; Annette Lynn; Nicole Lyons; Kerry M; Cathy Macdonald; Merrill Mackay; Suzie Mackenzie-Waller; Karen Macolino; Elizabeth Madden; Julie Maddocks; Cathy Madsen; Jenny Magner; Kieley Magri; Melita Maidment; Mel Maliokas; Gillian Mandel; Carrie Manen-Onslow; Jeanelle Manning; Allison March; Anna Marson; Christine Martin; Merona Martin; Tracey Martin; Sylvia Maso; Louise Mason; Sarah Mathews; Adrienne Matthews; Chrissie Matthews; Leanne Matthews; Kempson (Kem) Mayberry; Alison Mayne; Lesley McBurney; Mrs Toni McCrae; Lisa McDonald; Petrina McDonald; Wendy McDonald; Jo-Anne McEwan; Michelle McFadyen; Annette McGill; Stephanie McGovern; Helen McGrath; Lesley McGrath; Natasha McGregor; Erin McKean; Suzy McKenna; Shantelle McKinnon; Melanie McLaren; Michele McLaren; Karel McLaverty; Robyn McLean; Angela McRae; Nicole McVey; Michelle Meaby; Cassandra Meath; Kate Mejaha; Kia Laurae Mellor; Tina Mendicino; Rebbecca Mercier; Melissa Metlitzky; Inger Mewburn; Kim Milde; Jane Miles; Melissa Miller; Elizabeth Milne; Kate Minett; Lisa Minuzzo; Karyn Mitchell; Kerri Mitchell; Alison Mohr; Karen Moloney; Narelle Montauban; Jackie Mooney; Kim Mooney; Julia Morand; Debbie Morrison; Sandra Morrissey; Christine Mortimer; Filiz Mortimer; Helen Moss; Joanne Moynihan; Brenda Munro; Meredith Munro; June Murray; Tracylee Murtagh; Sandra Myerscough; Christine Nangle; Kerri Neef; Melissa Nelson; Rachel Neumann; Julie New; Christine Newell; Kim Newey; Helen Newman; Yvonne Nicholas; Peta Nicholls; Karen Noble; Jenny Noel; Jannette Norman; Ingrid Norris; Natalie Nott; Bernadette Notting; Anitra Nottingham; Cherish Nouata; Mary Nougher; Lesley O'Beirne; Tracey O'Brien; Amy O'Connor; Lisa O'Dwyer; Trish O'Gorman; Denis O'Neill; Matt O'Neill; Jessie O'Rourke; Fiona O'Sullivan; Danielle O'Toole; Jill Odonovan; Megan Ogle-Mannering; Helen Ozols; Leslie Pace; Kim Packham; Angela Palmer; Demmi Paris; Jane Parish; Jane Park; Samantha Parks; Chris Parnham; Amanda Patane; Anne Paul; Robyn Payne; Brooke Pearce; Johanna Peard; Samantha Pearson; Heather Peate; Ann Percival; Kristine Perkin; Sonya

Perks; Pamela Perrett; Diana Perrin; Dianne Perry; Graham Peters; Donna Phillips; Kylie Phillips; Linda Phillips; Julie Pickering; Mark Pickham; Diane Pisegna; Robert Pocock; Sandie Pott; Bronwyn Potter; Sarah Potter; Joanne Potts; Maree Pouloudis; Natalie Poynton; Valerie Price; Pat Pritchard; Ashna Pronk; Greer Pruden; Carrol Quadrio; Trish Radge; Anita Radok; Vicki Rae; Samantha Ratcliffe; Kirsty Rawlinson; Kathleen Rawson; Veronica Ray; Carly Raymond; Bronwen Reed; Helen Reed; Kylie Rees; Marilyn Reid; Tracy Reid; Bec Reiner; Peta Reitsema; Glenn Reynolds; Bianca Ricciardello; Judith Richardson; Scott Riddle; Michelle Rihia; Lauren Rimmington; Mark Rimmington; P. and C. Ritchie; Katharyn Roberts; Marguerite Roberts; Bill Robertson; Geraldine Robertson; Carol Robins; Katrina Robinson; Anne Robson; Kellie Rodgers; Justin Rogan; Ange Rosemann; Clare Ross; Jan Ross; Cherie Rothery; Jean Rouhan; Jane Rowe; Andrea Rowlands; Debbie Rundle; Katrina Russell; Lauren Russell; Judi Rustage; Robyn Ryan; Dianne Sammon; Tracy Sampson; Rachael Sandercock; Sharon Sandilands; Alison Sansom; Kristi Sawka; Susanne Schmidt; Sandy Scholz; Tracey Schriek; Tania Schulte; Patricia Sciberras; Adele Scott; Catherine Scott; Jessica Scrimes; Amy Scurr; Fiona Searls; Paul Segal; Belinda Sell; Corey Sh; Duncan Sharp; Penny Sharpe; Joanna Shearer-Smith; Sarah Sheers; Belinda Shipp; Alannah Shore; Sonia Short; Ninette Shorter; Claire Simmonds; Carrie Simmons; Mariel Simpson; Edwina Sinclair; Tania Skinner; Sharon Slater; Rebecca Slaven; Jayne Smart; Nicole Smedley; Donna Smith; Heather Smith; Janece Smith; Jodi Smith; Libby Smith; Melanie Smith; Sandra Smith; Suzie Smith; Tamika Smith; Tracey Smith; Kim Smooker; Julie Sobolewski; Gaye Somers; Janelle Spear; Kimberly Spencer; Kerry Stane; Kerry Stanek; Nina Stanisheff; Charmaine Statham; Dana Steddy; Kerrie Stimpson; Jodie Stirling; Tricia Stocks; Anne Stokes; Leanne Stones; Sophie Strang; Kim Sutton; John Symes; Gillian Tandy; Susan Tanner; Angela Taylor; Brooke Taylor; Chris Taylor; Jodie Taylor; Kim Taylor; Rebecca Taylor; Tonia Taylor; Mrs Fiona Teudt; Vanessa Thomas; Ian Thompson; Leanne Thompson; Robyn Thompson; Catherine Thompson Fowler; Lesley Tibbak; Wilma Tiley; Matija Tin; Sarah Toaldo; Mari Toffolon; Fiona Toms; Jennifer Tomson; Jenny Tomson; Lisa Tontu; Helen Torrisi; Amber Trench; Zofia Trenfield; Nicki Trenham; Wendy Trethowan; Kathleen Trevena; Alison Trovato; Karen Tuffield; Catherine Turner; Kathy Tynan; Amanda Vadasz; Lina Vallis; Sue Van Bremen; George Van Brugge; Elizabeth Vanderjagt; Brooke Vassallo; Natalie Veitch; Catherine Verschuer; Emilia Verzeletti; Stewart Vidler; Sheryl Vine; Karen Visser; Sharon Vosu; Enza Vujicic; Gail W; Vanessa Wagner; Allyson Waird; Chris Walker; Fiona Walker; Vivian Walker; Joanne Walsh; Anita Warburton; Jessica Ward; Jo-Ann Elizabeth Ward; Melanie Ward; Roslyn Ward; Margie Warrell; Jill Warton; Jo Waterman; Helen Watkin; Heidi Watson; Mel Watson; Michelle Watterston; Whitney Weaver; Kim Webb; Angela Webster; Nicole Webster; Anne Weeks; Karen Wegner; Rachel Weir; Rob Wellington; Kerri Wells; Melinda Wendt; Lisa West; Rachel West; Lisa Westlake; Marianne Whalan; Robyn Whelan; Mrs M Whiffin; Allison White; Caron White; Marianne White; Maggie Whitney; Mrs Deidre Widdison; Corri Wiedemann; Sarah Williams; Sue Williams; Virpi Williams; Les And Mon Williamson; Rosie Willis; Mishelle Wills; Nadine Wilson; Yvonne Wilson; Allison Winchester; Ruth Winchester; Lilian Wings; Kirsten Winkett; Gina Winter; Liz Witherow; Cathy Wood; Nerissa Wood; Sharron Woolley; Maree Worker; Vicky Wynen; Melissa Wyner; Fiona Wysel; Sharon Yogev; Bernadette Young; Rebecca Yourell; Rachel Yule.

iNDeX

Kaz Cooke is the author and illustrator of many books, including *A Bun in the Oven: The Real Guide to Pregnancy* and two children's picture books, *The Terrible Underpants* and *Wanda-Linda Goes Berserk*. She is a Melbourne mummy who has completely let herself go.